AN INTRODUCTION TO WAVELETS AND OTHER FILTERING METHODS IN FINANCE AND ECONOMICS

AN INTRODUCTION TO
WAVELETS AND
OTHER FILTERING METHODS
IN FINANCE AND ECONOMICS

Ramazan Gençay
University of Windsor, Canada

Faruk Selçuk
Bilkent University, Turkey

Brandon Whitcher
National Center for Athmospheric Research, U.S.A.

ACADEMIC PRESS
A Harcourt Science and Technology Company

San Diego   San Francisco   New York   Boston   London   Sydney   Tokyo

This book is printed on acid-free paper. ∞

Copyright 2002, Elsevier (USA)

Academic Press
An imprint of Elsevier
525 B Street, Suite 1900, San Diego, California 92101-4495, USA
http://www.academicpress.com

Academic Press
84 Theobald's Road, London WC1X 8RR, UK
http://www.academicpress.com

Library of Congress Control Number: 2001094298

International Standard Book Number: 0-12-279670-5

PRINTED IN THE UNITED STATES OF AMERICA
04   05   06   9   8   7   6   5   4   3   2

To Carole, Yasemin Selin, and Rana Belle

To Anjariitta

To Floyd and June Whitcher

CONTENTS

I

INTRODUCTION

2

LINEAR FILTERS

3

OPTIMUM LINEAR ESTIMATION

4
DISCRETE WAVELET TRANSFORMS

5
WAVELETS
AND STATIONARY PROCESSES

6

WAVELET DENOISING

7

WAVELETS FOR VARIANCE-COVARIANCE ESTIMATION

8

ARTIFICIAL NEURAL NETWORKS

LIST OF FIGURES

LIST OF TABLES

ACKNOWLEDGMENTS

We are thankful to several colleagues and students who provided comments on the earlier versions of the manuscript. In particular, we thank Buz Brock, Dee Dechert, Yanqin Fan, Tung Liu, Jim Ramsey, Thanasis Stengos, and four anonymous referees who provided valuable comments. Our students Oya Pınar Ardıç, Jian Gao, Haitao Shen, and Abdurrahman Ulugülyağcı provided excellent research assistance and we are grateful to them. Ramo Gençay's research is supported by the Natural Sciences and Engineering Research Council of Canada, the Social Sciences and Humanities Research Council of Canada and the University of Windsor, and he would also like to thank Janice Cahill and Tibor Toronyi for their research support.

We thank Scott Bentley, executive editor of Academic Press, who provided timely feedback and helped to keep the level of motivation high. Amy Hendrickson has been of invaluable assistance in the many LaTeX formatting problems, for a book with many figures. We are thankful to her.

PREFACE

This book presents a unified view of filtering techniques with a special focus on wavelet analysis in finance and economics. It is designed for those who might be starting research in these areas as well as for those who are interested in appreciating some of the statistical theory that underlies parametric and nonparametric filtering methods. The targeted audience includes finance professionals; research professionals in the public and private sector; those taking graduate courses in finance, economics, econometrics, statistics, and time series analysis; advanced MBA students; and students in other applied sciences, such as engineering, physics, medicine, biology and oceanography. Regardless of one's profession, this book assumes a basic understanding of mathematics, including such topics as trigonometry, basic linear algrebra, calculus, and the Fourier transform. A certain level of statistical background is also needed, including a basic understanding of probability theory, statistical inference, and time series analysis.

Many techniques are discussed in the book, including parametric recursive and nonrecursive filters, Kalman filters, Wiener filters, and wavelet and neural network filters. The emphasis is on the methods and the explanation of the theory that underlies them. Our approach concentrates on what exactly wavelet analysis (filtering methods in general) can tell us about a time series. In addition, the presentation contains testing issues that can be performed using wavelets with multiresolution analysis. For neural network methods, there is emphasis on the dynamic architectures (such as recurrent networks) in addition to simple feedforward networks. Recurrent networks together with multistream learning provide a rich filtering framework for long-memory processes.

This book contains numerous empirical applications from economics and finance. These applications illustrate the current use of filter techniques but also provide guidance for potential application areas. Some of the finance applications are presented with high-frequency financial time series. This provides a platform for the usefulness of the wavelet methods in the analysis of intraday seasonality, identification of trader behavior at different trading horizons, and the usefulness of wavelet methods for cross-correlation analysis of two high-frequency series by decomposing the signal into its high- and low-frequency components.

The focus of this book is descriptive and proofs are avoided as much as possible. This focus provides easy access to a wide spectrum of parametric and nonparametric filtering methods. Some of these filtering methods are widely known, whereas others, such as the wavelet methods, are fairly new to economics and finance. Our aim is to provide access to these methods that can be easily followed.

Ramazan Gençay

Faruk Selçuk

Brandon Whitcher

I

INTRODUCTION

The fundamental reason of writing this book is that we believe the basic premise of wavelet filtering provides insight into the dynamics of economic/financial time series beyond that of current methodology. A number of concepts such as non-stationarity, multiresolution and approximate decorrelation emerge from wavelet filters. Wavelet filtering provides a natural platform to deal with the time-varying characteristics found in most real-world time series, and thus the assumption of stationarity may be avoided. Wavelet filters provide an easy vehicle to study the multiresolution properties of a process. It is important to realize that economic/financial time series may not need to follow the same relationship as a function of time horizon (scale). Hence, a transform that decomposes a process into different time horizons is appealing as it differentiates seasonalities, reveals structural breaks and volatility clusters, and identifies local and global dynamic properties of a process at these timescales.[1] Last but not least, wavelet filters provide a convenient way of dissolving the correlation structure of a process across timescales. This would indicate that the wavelet coefficients at one level are not (much) associated with coefficients at different scales or within their

---

[1] Wavelets are in fact related to band-pass filters with properties similar to those used in the business-cycle literature for years.

scale. This is convenient when performing tasks such as simulations, estimation, and testing since it is always easier to deal with an uncorrelated process as opposed to one with unknown correlation structure. These issues are studied in Chapter 5.

1.1 FOURIER VERSUS WAVELET ANALYSIS

At this point, a natural question to ask would be why not use traditional spectral tools such as the Fourier analysis rather than exploring wavelet methods? Fourier series is a linear combination of sines and cosines. Each of these sines and cosines is itself a function of frequency, and therefore the Fourier transform may be seen as a decomposition on a frequency-by-frequency basis. The Fourier basis functions (sines and cosines) are very appealing when working with stationary time series (see Section 4.1.1 for a definition of a stationary time series). However, restricting ourselves to stationary time series is not very appealing since most economic/financial time series exhibit quite complicated patterns over time (e.g., trends, abrupt changes, and volatility clustering). The Fourier transform cannot efficiently capture these events. In fact, if the frequency components are not stationary such that they may appear, disappear, and then reappear over time, traditional spectral tools (such as the Fourier analysis) may miss such frequency components.

The Fourier transform is an alternative representation of the original time series such that it summarizes information in the data as a function of frequency and therefore does not preserve information in time. This is the opposite of how we observe the original time series, where no frequency resolution is provided. The Gabor transform or short-time Fourier transform (STFT) was developed to achieve a balance between time and frequency by *sliding* a window across the time series and taking the Fourier transform of the windowed series. The resulting expansion is a function of two parameters: frequency and time shift. Since the STFT is simply applying the Fourier transform to pieces of the time series of interest, a drawback of the STFT is that it will not be able to resolve events when they happen to fall within the width of the window.

To overcome the fixed time-frequency partitioning, a new set of basis functions are needed. The wavelet transform utilizes a basic function (called the *mother wavelet*), that is stretched and shifted to capture features that are local in time and local in frequency. Figure 1.1a introduces a square-wave function, based on the Haar wavelet filter, and a shifted version of the same function backward in time (Figure 1.1b). The wavelet filter is long in time when capturing low-frequency events (Figure 1.1c), and hence has good frequency resolution. Conversely, the wavelet is short in time when capturing high-frequency events (Figure 1.1d) and therefore has good time resolution for these events. By combining several combinations of shifting and stretching of the mother wavelet, the wavelet transform is able to capture all the information in a time series and associate it with specific time horizons and locations in time.

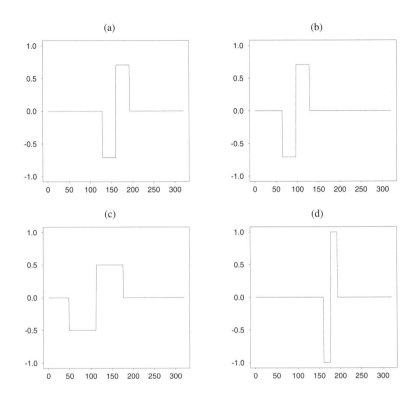

FIGURE 1.1 Application of translation and dilation to the square-wave function. (a) Square-wave function. (b) Square-wave function shifted backward (negatively translated) in time. (c) Square-wave function stretched (positively dilated) to twice its original length in time. (d) Square-wave function compressed (negatively dilated) to half its original length.

The wavelet transform intelligently adapts itself to capture features across a wide range of frequencies and thus has the ability to capture events that are local in time. This makes the wavelet transform an ideal tool for studying nonstationary or transient time series. The following examples demonstrate the convenient usage of wavelet-based methods in seasonality filtering, denoising, identification of structural breaks, scaling, separating observed data into timescales (so-called multiresolution analysis) and comparing multiple time series.

1.2 SEASONALITY FILTERING

The presence of seasonalities (periodicities) in a persistent process may obscure the underlying low-frequency dynamics. Specifically, the periodic component pulls the calculated autocorrelations down, giving the impression that there is

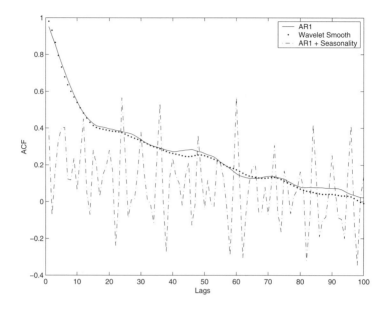

FIGURE   1.2 Sample autocorrelation function for the simulated AR(1) process (straight line), AR(1) plus seasonal process (dashed line), and wavelet smooth of the AR(1) plus seasonal process (dotted line).

no persistence other than particular periodicities. Consider the following AR(1) process with periodic components:

$$y_t = 0.95y_{t-1} + \sum_{s=1}^{4} \left[3\sin\left(\frac{2\pi t}{P_s}\right) + 0.9v_{st} \right] + \epsilon_t \qquad (1.1)$$

for $t = 1, \ldots, N$, $P_1 = 3$, $P_2 = 4$, $P_3 = 5$, and $P_4 = 6$. The process has three, four, five, and six period stochastic seasonalities. The random variables ϵ_t and v_{st} are uncorrelated Gaussian disturbance terms with mean zero and unit variance.

Figure 1.2 presents the autocorrelation functions (ACFs) from a length $N = 1000$ simulated AR(1) process in Equation 1.1 with and without periodic components. The ACF of the AR(1) process without seasonality (excluding $\sum[3\sin(2\pi t/P_s) + 0.9v_{st}]$ from the simulated process) starts from a value of 0.95 and decays geometrically.[2] However, the ACF of the AR(1) process with the seasonality starts from 0.40 and fluctuates between positive and negative values. The seasonality is evident in the peaks at lags that are multiples of 6 (i.e., at lags 12,

---

[2] The autocorrelation coefficient is 0.95^k where k is the number of lags.

24, 36, etc). The underlying persistence of the AR(1) process in the absence of the seasonality component is entirely obscured by these periodic components.

A well-designed seasonal adjustment procedure should therefore separate the data from its seasonal components and leave the underlying inherent nonseasonal structure intact. In Figure 1.2 the solid line is the ACF of the nonseasonal AR(1) dynamics and the dotted lines are the ACF of the seasonally adjusted series using a wavelet multiresolution analysis. As Figure 1.2 displays, using a multiresolution analysis to selectively filter a time series successfully uncovers the nonseasonal dynamics without inducing any spurious persistence into the filtered series. Chapter 4 provides a detailed exposition of the types of wavelet filters used in this example.

1.3 DENOISING

A convenient model for a uniformly sampled process y_t is that of the standard signal plus noise model; that is,

$$y_t = s_t + \epsilon_t, \quad t = 0, 1, \ldots, N - 1. \tag{1.2}$$

For now let us assume s_t is a deterministic function of t and associated with lower frequency oscillations (i.e., it is relatively smooth). Let us also assume that the noise process ϵ_t is a sequence of uncorrelated Gaussian random variables with zero mean and variance σ_ϵ^2. If we want the probability of any noise appearing in our estimate of y_t to be as small as possible, as the number of samples goes to infinity, then applying the wavelet transform to y_t and thresholding the wavelet coefficients with threshold $\sqrt{2\sigma_\epsilon^2 N}$ is a good strategy. Utilizing this threshold one may then remove (hard thresholding) or shrink toward zero (soft thresholding) wavelet coefficients at each level of the decomposition in an attempt to eliminate the noise from the signal. Inverting the wavelet transform yields a nonparametric estimate of the underlying signal s_t. Thresholding wavelet coefficients is appealing, since they capture information at different combinations of time and frequency, thus the wavelet-based estimate is locally adaptive.

Figure 1.3 provides two estimates of an example function

$$s_t = 2 - 5t + 5 \exp\left[-500(t - 0.5)^2\right], \quad t = 0, 1, \ldots, N - 1, \tag{1.3}$$

with additive noise. The true process is in the upper left-hand corner, while the signal plus noise is in the upper right-hand corner. The other panels are wavelet-based estimates using universal and minimax thresholding rules. The "universal estimator" corresponds to the $\sqrt{2\sigma_\epsilon^2 N}$ threshold previously discussed, and the "minimax estimator" is discussed in Section 6.3.2. In each case a soft thresholding rule was utilized; essentially, all wavelet coefficients less than the threshold are set to zero and all remaining coefficients are moved toward zero by the amount of the threshold. Even though the example function varies with time, the wavelet-based estimate is able to resolve both the "bump" and the linear portions simultaneously.

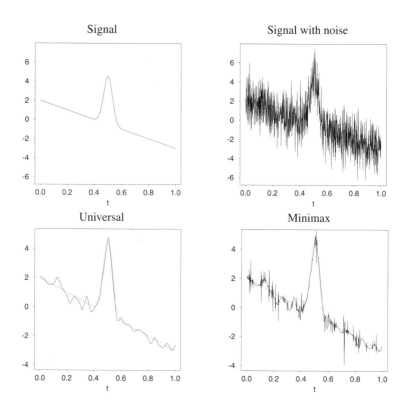

FIGURE 1.3   Universal and minimax estimators for sampled versions of the example function s_t ($N = 1024$) with additive noise. The true function (dotted line) is drawn in the bottom two panels for comparison with the estimate.

1.4   IDENTIFICATION OF STRUCTURAL BREAKS

When developing time series models, a natural assumption is that of (second-order) stationarity. That is, the time series model assumes that the mean and covariance of the process do not vary over time. For quite a few observed time series, this assumption is suspect and statistical hypothesis testing is useful in detecting and locating deviations from stationarity at specific points. This is one example of what is known as a structural break.

Suppose we would like to test for homogeneity of variance for an observed time series. The null hypothesis is that $\sigma_t^2 = \sigma^2$ for all t while the alternative hypothesis is, for example, $\sigma_t^2 = \sigma_1^2$ for $t < k$ and $\sigma_t^2 = \sigma_2^2$ for $t \geq k$. To overcome the restrictive assumption of a white noise process on the observed time series, one common approach is to fit an ARMA time series model and test the residuals. This is adequate only if the true process is in reality an ARMA process. An interesting wavelet-based approach is to test the wavelet coefficients on a level-by-level basis. Two possible scenarios are as follows:

- If the structural break of interest is a sudden change in variance, then the low-level wavelet coefficients (which are associated with high-frequency content of the time series) should retain this sudden shift in variability while the high-level coefficients should be stationary.
- If the structural break of interest is a possible change in the long-range dependence of the series, then all levels of wavelet coefficients should exhibit a structural change since long memory is associated with all scales—especially the low-frequency ones.

We are not proposing the same test for both of these scenarios, but instead argue that the multiscale decomposition of the wavelet transform allows for a straight-forward testing procedure to be applied to each level of the transform instead of developing customized procedures to deal with each type of structural break.

Figure 1.4 shows the results of testing the daily IBM volatility series (absolute returns) for a single change in variance at an unknown time. This volatility series was computed from daily IBM stock prices spanning May 17, 1961, to November 2, 1962 (Box and Jenkins, 1976). We chose the IBM volatility series because it exhibits a slowly decaying ACF and therefore cannot be modeled as a sequence of uncorrelated Gaussian random variables (required by CUSUM procedures), nor can it be effectively modeled by an ARMA process with few parameters. The null hypothesis of constant variance is rejected for the first three scales of the wavelet transform. The normalized cumulative sum of squares is displayed for the first three levels of wavelet coefficients in Figure 1.4. Since the level 1 coefficients (second row from the top in Figure 1.4) are associated with the highest frequencies, we use its maximum as the estimated time of variance change. Here the wavelet transform allowed for a rigorous test for homogeneity of variance, with only mild assumptions on the underlying spectrum of the process.

1.5 SCALING

It is important to understand the limitations of scaling laws because realized volatility plays an essential role in measuring volatility. There are two limi-tations to the precision of the estimation of realized volatility. For long time intervals (a year and more), it becomes difficult to assess the statistical signif-icance of the volatility estimation since there are not more than a handful of independent observations. This number grows and the noise shrinks when the return measurement intervals shrink, but then the measurement bias starts to grow.

Until now, the only choice was a clever trade-off between the noise and the bias, which led to typical return intervals of about an hour. The goal is to define a superior realized volatility, which combines the low noise of short return interval sizes with the low bias of large return intervals.

Instead of calculating realized volatilities at different data frequencies, we proceed with a multiscale approach. The studied data sets are the 20-min Deutsche Mark – U.S. Dollar (DEM-USD) and Japanese Yen – U.S. Dollar

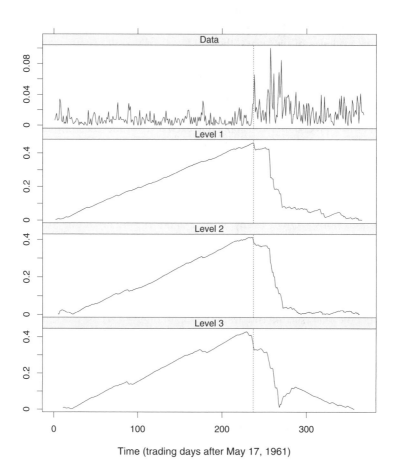

Time (trading days after May 17, 1961)

FIGURE 1.4 The IBM stock price volatility (top panel) along with the normalized cumulative sum of squares for its wavelet decomposition. The top row is the original IBM volatility series, and the following three rows are the normalized cumulative sum of squares (NCSS) of the first three levels of its wavelet decomposition. These three levels are associate with changes in longer and longer timescales; specifically – from top to bottom – changes on the order of one, two, and four days. The dotted vertical line denotes the location of the maximum for the scale one day wavelet coefficients (observation 237).

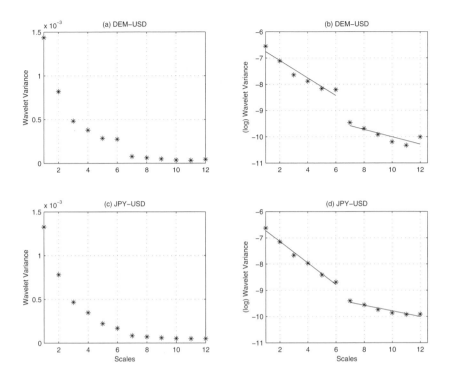

FIGURE 1.5 Multiscale variance for 20-min absolute returns of (a) DEM-USD and (c) JPY-USD. In (a) and (c), the estimated wavelet variances are plotted. In (b) and (d), the results are plotted on a log-log scale. The stars are the estimated variances for each wavelet scale and the straight lines are ordinary least squares (OLS) estimates. Each wavelet scale is associated with a particular time period. For instance, the first wavelet scale is associated with 20-min changes, the second wavelet scale with 40-min changes, the third wavelet scale with 160-min changes, and so on. The seventh wavelet scale is associated with 1280-min changes. Since there are 1440 minutes per day, the seventh scale corresponds to approximately 1 day. Notice that there is a break at 1-day scale. The last wavelet scale is associated with changes of approximately 28 days. The sample period is December 1, 1986, through December 1, 1996. Data source: Olsen & Associates.

(JPY-USD) price series for the period from December 1, 1986, to December 1, 1996. Here the volatility is defined as the absolute value of the returns.

Our results provide evidence that the scaling behavior of volatility breaks at scales higher than one day. Figure 1.5 reports the decomposition of the variance on a scale-by-scale basis through a wavelet multiresolution analysis. For example, the first wavelet scale is associated with changes at 20-min, the second wavelet scale is associated with 40-min changes, and so on. An apparent break in the scaling law is observed in the variance at the seventh wavelet scale for both series. Since there are 1440 minutes in one day, the seventh scale corresponds to 0.89 day. Therefore, the seventh and higher scales are taken to be related with one-day and higher dynamics.

1.6 AGGREGATE HETEROGENEITY AND TIMESCALES

Consider the participants of financial markets who are made of traders with different trading horizons. In the heart of the trading mechanisms are the market makers. The next level up is composed of the intraday traders, who carry out trades only within a given trading day but do not carry overnight positions. Then there are day traders, who may carry positions overnight, short-term traders and long-term traders. Each of these classes of traders may have its own trading tool sets consistent with its trading horizon and may possess a homogeneous appearance within its own class. Overall, it is the sum of the activities of all traders for all horizons that generates the market prices. Therefore, market activity is heterogeneous with each trading horizon (trader class) dynamically providing feedback across all trader classes.

In such a heterogeneous market, a low-frequency shock to the system penetrates through all layers, reaching the market maker by penetrating the entire market. The high-frequency shocks, however, would be short lived and may have no impact outside their boundaries. This apparent aggregate heterogeneity (as a sum of a homogeneous set of trader classes) requires econometric methods that can simultaneously learn and forecast the underlying structure at different timescales (horizons). This involves the separation of the local dynamics from the global one, and the transitory from the permanent dynamics. Wavelet methods provide a natural platform to distinguish these effects from one another by decomposing a time series into different timescales. Furthermore, wavelet methods are localized in time so that they can easily identify nonstationary events, such as sudden regime shifts and transient shocks to a system. Figure 1.6 illustrates such a decomposition by separating the intraday variations of volatility from high-frequency data sampled at 20-min frequency and looking at the volatility at a scale of one day. Here, it is evident that the volatility burst during the first half of the sample is not an intraday phenomena. More applications of multiresolution analysis for separating timescales may be found in Section 4.7.

1.7 MULTISCALE CROSS-CORRELATION

The decomposition of a time series on a scale-by-scale basis has the ability to unveil structure at different time horizons. For example, the wavelet transform produces an alternative, known as the wavelet variance, to the periodogram. This variance decomposition may be easily generalized for multivariate time series. Standard time-domain measures of association for multivariate time series (e.g., cross-covariance and cross-correlation) may be defined using the coefficients from the application of the wavelet transform to each series, thus producing the wavelet cross-covariance and wavelet cross-correlation.

The wavelet cross-covariance decomposes the cross-covariance between two time series on a scale-by-scale basis thereby making it possible to see how the association between two time series changes as a function of time horizon.

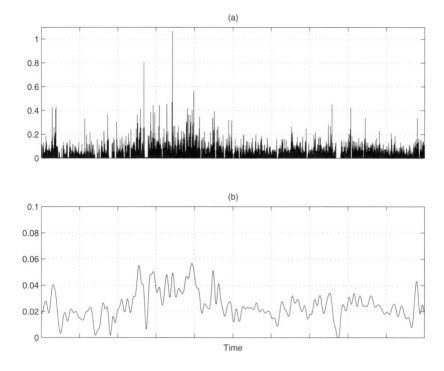

FIGURE 1.6 Multiresolution analysis of foreign exchange volatility. (a) Absolute returns of 20-min for DEM-USD exchange rate. (b) Wavelet smooth corresponding to physical scale of approximately one-day. December 1, 1986, through May 29, 1987. Data source: Olsen & Associates.

Figure 1.7 shows the wavelet cross-correlation for the first six scales between the monthly DEM-USD and JPY-USD exchange rate returns. Approximate 95% confidence intervals are given so that significant cross-correlations may be easily identified. As the wavelet scale increases (from bottom to top in the figure), the variability of the estimated wavelet cross-correlation decreases. This is to be expected since each increase in the scale captures lower and lower frequency content in the series. Not too surprisingly, the maximum wavelet cross-correlation is at lag zero for the first four scales. The fifth wavelet scale exhibits no correlations significantly different from zero, and the sixth scale again exhibits its maximum at lag zero. More interesting features are, for example, the asymmetry in the wavelet cross-correlation sequence for scales 4 and 5. At the fourth scale (associated with oscillations of 16 to 32 months), the DEM-USD exchange rate is negatively correlated with the JPY-USD at a lag of +8 months but not at a lag of −8 months. This feature, which reveals important information about the lead-lag relation in foreign exchange markets, would have remained hidden without the multiscale decomposition of the wavelet transform.

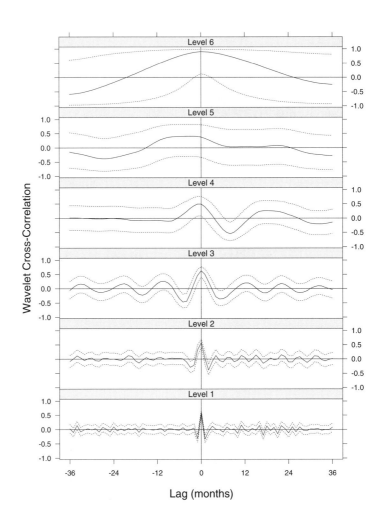

FIGURE 1.7 Wavelet cross-correlation between the DEM-USD and JPY-USD exchange rate returns. The individual cross-correlation functions correspond to – from bottom to top – levels of the wavelet decomposition associated with changes of 1, 2, 4, 8, 16, and 32 months. The dotted lines indicate the approximate 95% confidence interval for the wavelet cross-correlation. At each wavelet scale, there are several lags very close to zero where the confidence interval for the wavelet cross-correlation does not include zero and therefore indicates significant multiscale correlation. For more details, see Chapter 7.

1.8 OUTLINE

We start with a general definition of a linear filter in the time domain in Chapter 2. Finite impulse response (FIR) and infinite impulse response (IIR) filters are introduced with simple examples. Filters in the frequency domain are also reviewed, and some frequency-domain concepts – such as a high-pass filter, low-pass filter, band-pass filter, phase, and gain – are introduced in Chapter 2. Chapter 2 ends with three applications. Chapter 3 views filtering as an optimum linear estimation problem. After reviewing the Wiener filter, the Kalman filter is introduced. The derivation of the Kalman filter is carried out in a single equation framework at several stages so that the reader may gain an intuitive feeling about this approach. The scalar case is extended to a multivariate setting later in this chapter. Chapter 3 ends with four examples of the Kalman filter in practice. Chapter 4 introduces the key concepts of wavelets and wavelet transforms. The history of orthonormal transforms is briefly explored in order to put wavelet transforms in perspective. The continuous wavelet transform (CWT) is introduced, along with its relation to the discrete wavelet transform (DWT). Most of the emphasis in Chapter 4 is placed on discrete wavelet functions (such as those of Daubechies) and implementing the DWT, decomposition of variance and multiresolution analysis (MRA) being two key features. An alternative version of the DWT, the maximal overlap discrete wavelet transform (MODWT), is also introduced. Several examples illustrate the use of the DWT and MODWT with respect to filtering foreign exchange rates, multiscale causality and cointegration, and the multiscale relationship between money growth and inflation. Chapter 5 looks at the DWT applied to two types of stationary time series models: long-memory processes and seasonal long-memory processes. Wavelet-based simulation and estimation (both least squares and maximum likelihood) procedures are provided for these models. A long-memory time series model is fit to IBM volatility. A generalization of the DWT, the discrete wavelet packet transform (DWPT), is introduced in order to deal with seasonal time series models. Seasonal long-memory time series models are fit to Mexican money supply, Japanese gross national product, and several U.S. economic variables. Chapter 6 uses the wavelet transform to recover a "signal" from noisy observations, also known as wavelet denoising or nonparametric regression. Standard methods for deriving the threshold and selecting a thresholding rule are provided to facilitate easy implementation. The IBM stock prices, returns, and volatility are denoised using several combinations of thresholds and rules, along with an application to outlier testing. Chapter 7 looks at decomposing the variance (for a univariate time series) or the covariance (for bivariate time series) using the wavelet transform. The wavelet variance is defined, along with its unbiased estimator and approximate confidence intervals. The wavelet variance decomposes the variance of a time series on a scale-by-scale basis and is related to the spectrum. An application for testing for a change in volatility, using the IBM time series, is presented. The wavelet cross-covariance and cross-correlation are defined for multivariate time series, along with their estimators and approximate confidence intervals. The wavelet cross-covariance decomposes the cross-covariance between two time series on a scale-by-scale basis and is related to the usual cross-covariance. Applications include estimating scaling laws in foreign exchange markets and multiscale beta estimation. Chapter 8 examines neural network filters. The focus in this chapter is confined to the function approximation and nonlinear filtering capabilities of neural network models. It starts with the elements of a typical neural network model and progresses through feedforward and recurrent neural network models. The chapter also provides some examples of neural network applications in financial markets, such as volatility prediction, predictibility in foreign exchange markets, and option pricing.

2

LINEAR FILTERS

2.1 INTRODUCTION

The inherent interaction of a particular variable with the underlying environment may produce complicated features. Filtering methods deal with the identification and extraction of certain features (e.g., trends, seasonalities) from a time series, which are important in terms of modeling and inference. Filtering is a universal research field used in scientific areas such as astronomy, biology, engineering, and physics, as well as in economics and finance. Traditionally, filters in economics and finance are used to extract components of a time series such as trends, seasonalities, business cycles, and noise.[1] Our aim is to provide a unified frame-

---

[1] A commonly used method of decomposition of a macroeconomic time series is known as the *Beveridge-Nelson procedure* (Beveridge and Nelson, 1981). Another well-known method is the *Hodrick-Prescott filter* (Hodrick and Prescott, 1997). Canova (1998a; 1998b) critically evaluated a set of popular filters used in detrending macroeconomic time series and showed that different detrending methods provide different stylized facts of the U.S. business cycle. Burnside (1998) claimed that preferring a commonly used filtering method in macroeconomic analysis does not induce any lack of power. Niemira and Klein (1994) studied forecasting financial and economic cycles in general, and Weigend and Gerschenfeld (1994) investigated time series prediction in natural and physical phenomena. Kaiser and Maraval (2000) and Diebold and Rudebusch (1999) contained a detailed analysis of business cycle measurements and forecasts.

work for filters that will show their applicability in economics and finance. In this chapter, we start with linear filters in the time domain and progress through the introduction of linear filters in the frequency domain.

The standard references in signal processing and filtering are Anderson and Moore (1979), Oppenheim and Schafer (1989), and, more recently, Strang and Nguyen (1996) and Mallat (1998). There are several books in time series analysis of economic and financial data. Introductory-level textbooks are Yaffe (2000), Franses (1998), and Brockwell and Davis (1996). Early classics in the field are Box and Jenkins (1976) and Granger and Newbold (1989). In recent years, Hamilton (1994b) and Campbell *et al.* (1997) have become common references. Campbell *et al.* (1997) covers a broad range of econometric methods as applied to finance, along with some well-known empirical results in the U.S. financial markets. However, it omits some techniques, such as frequency domain methods of time series analysis. Hamilton (1994b) presents several theoretical and empirical issues in time series econometrics in detail. The book covers a wide range of topics including spectral analysis and the Kalman filter. Sargent (1987) offers an advanced treatment of difference equations and filters in a macroeconomics context, and it is a good starting point for economics and finance students. Pollock (1999) presents the formulation and estimation of statistical time series models, including the design of filters and other signal processing devices. An introduction to the techniques and theories of spectral analysis of time series can be found in Koopmans (1974) and Bloomfield (2000). Ramanathan (1993), Ross (2000), and Zaman (1996) provide a necessary background for an advanced study in mathematical statistics and econometrics. Dhrymes (1998) contains a high-level analysis of unit roots and cointegration in time series analysis. Taylor (1986) offers an early study on modeling financial time series. Recent contributions to advanced analysis in financial markets include Hull (2000), Mills (1999), Neftci (2000), Prisman (2000), Holton (2001), and McNelis (2001).

The conventional approach to time series analysis of financial and economic times series considers linear models. However, linearity in financial and economic time series is an exception rather than a rule. The literature on nonlinearity in economics and finance is very rich. See, for example, Gallant (1987), Barnett (1989), Brock *et al.* (1991), Benhabib (1992), Härdle (1990), Dechert (1996), Bierens and Gallant (1997), Pagan and Ullah (1999), Barnett *et al.* (1996, 2000), Franses and Dijk (2000), Härdle (2000), and Urbach (2000).

2.2   FILTERS IN TIME DOMAIN

A discrete time series is a sequence of observations ordered by a time index t, where time spans from minus infinity to plus infinity,

$$\{x_t\}_{t=-\infty}^{\infty} = (\ldots, x_{-2}, x_{-1}, x_0, x_1, x_2, \ldots).$$

An observed time series vector x of finite length may be viewed as one realization of a random process or a segment of an infinite sequence,

$$\overbrace{(\ldots, x_{-2}, x_{-1}, x_0, x_1, x_2, \ldots, x_{N-1}, x_N, x_{N+1}, \ldots)}^{x},$$

observations

where x_0 is the first observation (or realization) and x_{N-1} is the last observation. A linear filter simply converts a time series x_t into another time series y_t by a linear transformation,

$$x_t \longrightarrow \boxed{\text{Filter}} \longrightarrow y_t.$$

The output y_t of a linear filter is the result of the convolution of the input x_t with a coefficient vector w_t.[2] The elements of the vector $w_t = (\ldots w_{-2}, w_{-1}, w_0, w_1, w_2, \ldots)$ are called *filter coefficients*. The convolution of the input vector x_t with the coefficient vector w_t may be expressed via

$$y_t = \sum_{i=-\infty}^{\infty} w_i x_{t-i}, \tag{2.2}$$

where future values of x_t are required to obtain the filter output at time t. This may not be feasible in certain applications. As a result, some restrictions are imposed on a filter such that the output of the filter is not allowed to exist before the realization of the input—that is,

$$y_t = \sum_{i=0}^{\infty} w_i x_{t-i}, \tag{2.3}$$

where only the past and present values of input are utilized. A filter with this property is called a *causal filter* or a *physically realizable filter*. If the filter coefficients are constant over time, the filter is called a *time invariant* filter.[3] Linear filters in the time domain are classified according to their response to a special signal. Consider the following input sequence,

$$x_t = \begin{cases} 1 & \text{if } t = 0 \\ 0 & \text{otherwise,} \end{cases} \tag{2.4}$$

which is known as the *unit impulse* signal. Given a unit impulse signal, the output sequence of a filter is known as the *impulse response* of that filter. If the impulse response of a filter is finite, it is called a *finite impulse response filter*, or an *FIR filter*. On the other hand, if the impulse response of a filter is not finite, the corresponding filter is called an *infinite impulse response filter* or an *IIR filter*.

---

[2] The convolution of two sequences such as x_t and w_t is defined as

$$w * x_t = \sum_{i=-\infty}^{\infty} w_i x_{t-i}. \tag{2.1}$$

[3] If the output of a filter F applied to x_t is y_t, the filter is time invariant if $F(x_{t+h}) = y_{t+h}$ for all integers h (Fuller, 1976, page 151).

2.2.1   Infinite Impulse Response (IIR) Filters

Linear filters may also be viewed as a special case of constant coefficient linear difference equations,

$$y_t = \sum_{i=1}^{L} a_i y_{t-i} + \sum_{i=0}^{M} w_i x_{t-i}, \qquad (2.5)$$

where L lagged values of output y_t and M lagged values of input x_t, as well as the current value of the input, are employed to determine the current value of output. In other words, there is a *feedback* from the past filter outputs to the current filter output. A difference equation in this form can be solved by applying standard techniques.[4] We will present only a simple example of linear difference equations to relate them with filtering.

Consider the following first-order difference equation,

$$y_t = a y_{t-1} + x_t, \qquad (2.6)$$

where the output y_t cannot be determined even if x_t and the coefficient a are available, unless auxiliary information about y_t at some time t_0 for $t_0 \leq t$ is given. Let the process start at time $t = 0$ so that $x_t = 0$ for $t < 0$, and let y_0 be known. A solution to Equation 2.6 may be found by *recursive substitution*; that is,

$$
\begin{aligned}
y_1 &= a y_0 + x_1 \\
y_2 &= a y_1 + x_2 \\
&= a(a y_0 + x_1) + x_2 \\
&= a^2 y_0 + a x_1 + x_2 \\
y_3 &= a y_2 + x_3 \\
&= a^3 y_0 + a^2 x_1 + a x_2 + x_3 \\
&= a^3 y_0 + \sum_{i=0}^{3-1} a^i x_{3-i}.
\end{aligned}
$$

The solution can be generalized for all t as

$$y_t = a^t y_0 + \sum_{i=0}^{t-1} a^i x_{t-i}.$$

---

[4] Linear difference equations in economics and finance context are discussed in detail by Enders (1998), Hamilton (1994b), and Sargent (1987).

Let the initial condition be $y_{-1} = 0$ in Equation 2.6. Given the unit impulse input in Equation 2.4, the impulse response of the filter is

$$
\begin{aligned}
y_0 &= x_0 = 1 \\
y_1 &= ay_0 + 0 = a \\
y_2 &= ay_1 + 0 = a^2 \\
&\vdots \\
y_t &= a^t.
\end{aligned}
$$

The filter has an impulse response with infinite duration. Therefore, it is an infinite impulse response (IIR) filter. In fact, any filter in the form of a difference equation would have an impulse response with infinite duration. If the difference equation is stable as a system, the impulse response will decay asymptotically toward zero. On the other hand, if the system is not stable, the impulse response will diverge. The stability of the difference equations depends on the parameter set a_i in Equation 2.5. For example, the filter in Equation 2.6 is unstable if $|a| > 1$, since the impulse response diverges without limit in this case. On the other hand, if $|a| < 1$, the filter is stable since the impulse response will decay asymptotically toward zero. For the stability condition in higher-order difference equations, the reader may refer to Enders (1998, Ch. 2), Hamilton (1994b, Ch. 1–3), or Sargent (1987, Ch. 9).[5]

2.2.2 Noncausal Finite Impulse Response (FIR) Filters

The general form of an FIR filter is

$$
y_t = \sum_{i=-N}^{M} w_i x_{t-i},
$$

where the filter processes N future and M past values as well as the current value of the input. Therefore, it is a noncausal filter. A common noncausal FIR filter in economics and finance is a simple centered moving average,

$$
y_t = \frac{1}{M+N+1} (x_{t-M} + \ldots + x_{t-1} + x_t + x_{t+1} + \ldots x_{t+N}),
$$

where all filter coefficients are equal. The impulse response of this filter is finite and flat:

$$
w_i = \begin{cases} \frac{1}{M+N+1}, & \text{if } i = -N, \ldots, -1, 0, 1, \ldots, M \\ 0, & \text{otherwise.} \end{cases}
$$

---

[5] For a linear stochastic difference equation, the stability condition is a necessary condition for *stationarity*. See Hamilton (1994b, Ch. 3) for a detailed discussion of stationarity. Clements and Hendry (1999) presented a framework to study non-stationary economic time series.

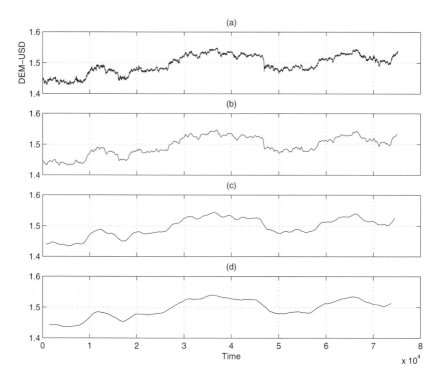

FIGURE 2.1   Five-minute DEM-USD exchange rate and centered moving average filter outputs. (a) The original data. (b) One-day centered moving average with $M = N = 144$ (there are **288** 5-min periods in a given day). (c) One-week centered moving average, $M = N = 720$ (there are 1440 5-min periods in a given business week). (d) Two weeks centered moving average, $M = N = 1440$. Note that M data points at the beginning and N data points at the end of each filter output are missing as a result of the centering. The sample period is January 2, 1996, to December 31, 1996 (weekends excluded). Data source: Olsen & Associates.

Figure 2.1 illustrates three different centered moving averages of 5-min DEM-USD exchange rates for different values of M and N. Since M past values and N future values of the input are required to obtain the filter output at time t, M data points at the beginning and N data points at the end of the output are missing. This feature makes a centered moving average less attractive in practice, in particular when the purpose is to forecast the future values of a signal.

A centered moving average is symmetric with $M = N$ so that $w_i = w_{-i}$. However, the filter coefficients need not be equal to each other. Consider a symmetric centered moving average where w_i is determined according to the successive terms from the expansion in $(0.5+0.5)^{2N}$. For instance, when $N = 1$, the filter is

$$y_t = 0.25x_{t-1} + 0.50x_t + 0.25x_{t+1}.$$

This is known as the *Hanning filter*, after Julius Von Hann, a nineteenth-century Austrian meteorologist (Blackman and Tukey, 1958, page 171). If $M = N = 2$, the filter is

$$y_t = 0.0625x_{t-2} + 0.25x_{t-1} + 0.375x_t + 0.25x_{t+1} + 0.0625x_{t+2}.$$

When N gets large, the shape of the impulse response of this filter approximates a normal curve. A similar technique that sometimes leads to confusion in the literature is called a *Hamming filter*, named after R. W. Hamming (Blackman and Tukey, 1958, page 171). The Hamming filter is

$$y_t = 0.23x_{t-1} + 0.54x_t + 0.23x_{t+1}.$$

Spencer's 15-point moving average, which is used for smoothing mortality statistics, is another example of unequal filter coefficients in a noncausal FIR filter (Chatfield, 1984, page 17). The coefficients of Spencer's filter are

$$\boldsymbol{w} = \frac{1}{320}(-3, -6, -5, 3, 21, 46, 67, 74, 67, 46, 21, 3, -5, -6, -3).$$

If a filtering operation is carried out in several stages, this is known as a *multistage filtering* or a *filter cascade*. In a multistage filtering (a filter cascade), the output of a filter is refiltered with the same or a different filter:

$$x_t \longrightarrow \boxed{\text{Filter I}} \longrightarrow z_t \longrightarrow \boxed{\text{Filter II}} \longrightarrow y_t.$$

Specifically, given the original input x_t, the first step is to filter the input by using the first set of filter coefficients $\boldsymbol{w}_1$:

$$z_t = \sum_{i=-N}^{M} w_{1,i} x_{t-i}.$$

At the second stage, the first stage filter output z_t is filtered once again by using the second set of filter coefficients $\boldsymbol{w}_2$. The final output is

$$y_t = \sum_{j=-N'}^{M'} w_{2,j} z_{t-j}.$$

As an example, set $N = N' = 0$ and $M = M' = 1$ and let the filter coefficients be $w_{1,0} = 0.5$, $w_{1,1} = 0.5$, $w_{2,0} = 0.7$, and $w_{2,1} = 0.3$. The first filter is

$$z_t = 0.5x_t + 0.5x_{t-1}.$$

The output of this filter will be the input to the second filter

$$y_t = 0.7z_t + 0.3z_{t-1}$$

or

$$\begin{aligned} y_t &= 0.7\,(0.5x_t + 0.5x_{t-1}) + 0.30\,(0.5x_{t-1} + 0.5x_{t-2}) \\ &= 0.35x_t + 0.50x_{t-1} + 0.15x_{t-2}. \end{aligned}$$

The coefficients of the final filter can be obtained by the convolution of individual filter coefficient vectors, $\boldsymbol{w}_1 = [0.50, 0.50]$ and $\boldsymbol{w}_2 = [0.70, 0.30]$, as shown:

$$
\begin{aligned}
\boldsymbol{w} &= \boldsymbol{w}_1 * \boldsymbol{w}_2 \\
&= (0.50, 0.50) * (0.70, 0.30) \\
&= (0.35, 0.50, 0.15).
\end{aligned}
$$

It can be shown that Spencer's 15-point centered moving average is actually a convolution of four filters (Chatfield, 1984, page 43):

$$
\begin{aligned}
\boldsymbol{w} &= (0.25, 0.25, 0.25, 0.25) * (0.25, 0.25, 0.25, 0.25) \\
&\quad * (0.20, 0.20, 0.20, 0.20, 0.20) * (-0.75, 0.75, 1, 0.75, -0.75).
\end{aligned}
$$

2.2.3   Causal FIR Filters

A general FIR filter can be reduced to a causal filter by imposing the restriction $N = 0$. As a result, the future values of the input will be ignored in the filtering process:

$$
y_t = \sum_{i=0}^{M} w_i x_{t-i}.
$$

This form of FIR filter is more common in practice, especially in technical analysis of prices in financial markets. An example is the $M + 1$ period simple moving average

$$
y_t = \frac{1}{M+1}(x_t + x_{t-1} + \ldots x_{t-M}).
$$

One advantage of causal FIR filters is that there is no missing output at the end of the data sample. Only the first M output is missing since M past values of the input, in addition to the current value, are required to obtain the filter output at time t. Figure 2.2 provides an illustration with the 5-min DEM-USD exchange rates for different values of M.

In a simple moving average, it may be desirable to give more weight to more recent inputs and less weight to inputs corresponding to the distant past. For example, Fischer (1937) proposed the following linearly declining weights in a simple moving average:

$$
\begin{aligned}
w_0' &= M + 1 \\
w_1' &= M \\
w_2' &= M - 1 \\
&\;\;\vdots \qquad \vdots \\
w_M' &= 1,
\end{aligned}
$$

which has the corresponding moving average representation

$$
y_t = \frac{2}{(M+1)(M+2)} \sum_{i=0}^{M} w_i' x_{t-i}, \quad w_i' = w_{M+1-i}
$$

or

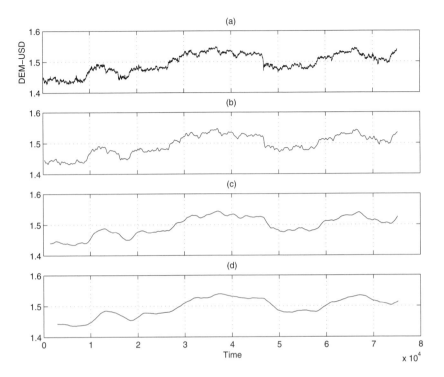

FIGURE 2.2 Five-minute DEM-USD exchange rate and a simple moving average filter outputs. (a) The original data. (b) Simple daily moving average (there are 288 5-min periods in one day so that $M = 288$). (c) Simple one-week moving average, $M = 1440$. (d) Simple two-week moving average, $M = 2880$. Notice that there are no missing outputs at the end of the sample, only at the beginning. Sample period is January 2, 1996, to December 31, 1996 (weekends excluded). Data source: Olsen & Associates.

$$y_t = \sum_{i=0}^{M} w_i x_{t-i}, \quad \text{where} \quad w_i = \frac{2w_i'}{(M+1)(M+2)}.$$

As an example, let $M = 5$ so that

$$y_t = \frac{2}{(6)(7)} (6x_t + 5x_{t-1} + 4x_{t-2} + 3x_{t-3} + 2x_{t-4} + x_{t-5}),$$

which is

$$y_t = 0.29x_t + 0.24x_{t-1} + 0.19x_{t-2} + 0.14x_{t-3} + 0.09x_{t-4} + 0.05x_{t-5}.$$

If the weights in a simple moving average decline exponentially at distant lags, the resulting filter is known as the *exponentially weighted moving average* (EWMA). For example, if $w_i = \phi^i$, where ϕ is an arbitrary constant between 0 and 1, and $i = 0, 1 \ldots M$, the weights obey,

$$w'_0 = \phi^0$$
$$w'_1 = \phi^1$$
$$w'_2 = \phi^2$$
$$\vdots \quad \vdots$$
$$w'_M = \phi^M,$$

which is

$$y_t = \frac{1}{\sum w'_i} \sum_{i=0}^{M} w'_i x_{t-i} = \sum_{i=0}^{M} w_i x_{t-i},$$

where $w_i = w'_i / \sum w'_i$. For $\phi = 0.40$ and $M = 5$, the moving average is

$$
\begin{aligned}
y_t &= \frac{1}{1.66} \Big(x_t + 0.40 x_{t-1} + 0.40^2 x_{t-2} + 0.40^3 x_{t-3} + \\
&\quad 0.40^4 x_{t-4} + 0.40^5 x_{t-5} \Big) \\
&= 0.60 x_t + 0.24 x_{t-1} + 0.10 x_{t-2} + 0.04 x_{t-3} + \\
&\quad 0.01 x_{t-4} + 0.01 x_{t-5}.
\end{aligned}
$$

Coefficients of a simple moving average may increase and then decrease with increasing lags. A special case in economics is known as *Almon lag* (Almon, 1965). In an Almon lag specification, the filter coefficients may be determined according to the following second-order polynomial:

$$w'_i = \phi_0 + \phi_1 i - \phi_2 i^2, \quad i = 0, 1, \ldots M,$$

where ϕ_0, ϕ_1 and ϕ_2 are positive constants between 0 and 1. The filter coefficients in this case are

$$
\begin{aligned}
w'_0 &= \phi_0 \\
w'_1 &= \phi_0 + (1)\phi_1 - (1^2)\phi_2 \\
w'_2 &= \phi_0 + (2)\phi_1 - (2^2)\phi_2 \\
\vdots \quad &\vdots \\
w'_M &= \phi_0 + (M)\phi_1 - (M^2)\phi_2.
\end{aligned}
$$

As an example, let $M = 5$, $\phi_0 = 0.10$, $\phi_1 = 0.03$, and $\phi_2 = 0.005$, the filter coefficients are

$$
\begin{aligned}
w'_0 &= 0.10 \\
w'_1 &= 0.10 + (1)0.03 - (1^2)0.005 = 0.11 \\
w'_2 &= 0.10 + (2)0.03 - (2^2)0.005 = 0.14 \\
w'_3 &= 0.10 + (3)0.03 - (3^2)0.005 = 0.14 \\
w'_4 &= 0.10 + (4)0.03 - (4^2)0.005 = 0.14 \\
w'_5 &= 0.10 + (5)0.03 - (5^2)0.005 = 0.12.
\end{aligned}
$$

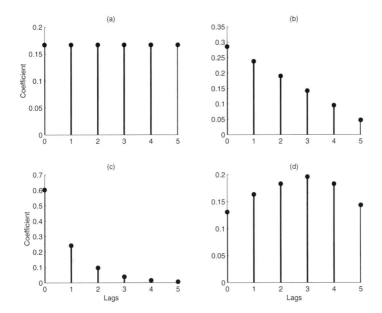

FIGURE 2.3 Filter coefficients in a simple moving average as a function of the lag. (a) Constant coefficients: the coefficients are equal to each other at all lags. (b) Linear decay: the value of the coefficients decays linearly with increasing lags. (c) Geometric decay: the value of the coefficients decays exponentially with increasing lags. (d) The value of the coefficients increases first, then decreases with increasing lags.

Therefore, the corresponding moving average is

$$
\begin{aligned}
y_t &= \frac{1}{0.76}(0.10x_t + 0.11x_{t-1} + 0.14x_{t-2} + 0.14x_{t-3} + \\
&\quad 0.14x_{t-4} + 0.12x_{t-5}) \\
&= 0.13x_t + 0.15x_{t-1} + 0.18x_{t-2} + 0.19x_{t-3} + 0.18x_{t-4} + 0.16x_{t-5}.
\end{aligned}
$$

Different weighting types in a simple moving average are depicted in Figure 2.3.

2.3 FILTERS IN THE FREQUENCY DOMAIN

Consider a circle with a radius of length R centered at O as in Figure 2.4. Let the radius rotate counterclockwise, starting from OA, moving toward OB. When it is back to OA, one cycle is completed. In a specific position such as OP, the radius makes a specific angle θ with OA. The sine, cosine, and tangent functions with angle θ are defined by

$$
\sin \theta = \frac{V}{R}, \qquad \cos \theta = \frac{h}{R}, \qquad \tan \theta = \frac{V}{h}.
$$

Consider the values of $\sin \theta$ at different locations during a complete cycle. It starts from zero at OA ($V = 0$), becomes one at OB ($V = R$), zero at OC

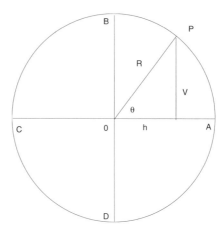

FIGURE 2.4 A circle with radius R. The sine, cosine, and tangent functions with angle θ are defined by $\sin\theta = \frac{V}{R}$, $\cos\theta = \frac{h}{R}$, and $\tan\theta = \frac{V}{h}$. The angle θ is a ratio, and it is measured in degrees or radians. Let the distance between A and P on the arc be equal to the radius R. A *radian* is the size of the angle θ formed by such an R-length arc.

($V = 0$), and minus one at OD ($V = -R$). Hence, a sinusoidal function has a constant range of fluctuation in each cycle: ± 1. Alternatively, the *amplitude* (size) of the fluctuation is one. The cosine function also has a constant range of fluctuations: ± 1. Its value is one at OA, zero at OB, minus one at OC and zero at OD. However, the two functions have different starting values at OA, where the cosine function takes the value of one whereas the sine function has a value of zero.

The angle θ is a ratio and it is measured in degrees, although it may also be measured in *radians*. Consider the distance between A and P on the arc in Figure 2.4 and let this length to be equal to the radius R. A radian is the size of the angle θ formed by such an R-length arc. Since the circumference of a circle is $2\pi R$ and a complete circle is 360°, the following relation holds between degrees and radians:

Degrees	Radians
0	0
90	$\frac{1}{2}\pi$
180	π
360	$2\pi.$

The sine and cosine functions complete a cycle in 2π radians so that their values are repeated for every 2π radian. This implies that adding an integer multiple of

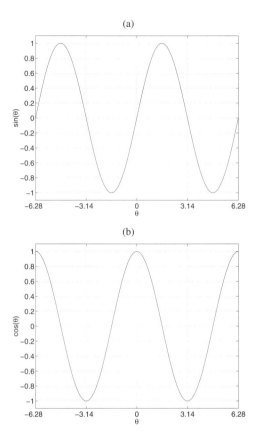

FIGURE 2.5 Cyclical functions. (a) $\sin\theta$. (b) $\cos\theta$ functions during two complete cycles: one counterclockwise (0 to 2π in radians) and one clockwise (0 to -2π in radians). Note that sine and cosine functions have different starting values at $\theta = 0$. If the cosine curve is shifted slightly to the right, an identical curve with the sine function is obtained. The required shift is $\pi/2$. These two curves are said to differ in *phase* (i.e, the location of the peak and the trough of the oscillation in each function is different in each period).

2π to any angle θ would not change the value of $\sin\theta$ or $\cos\theta$. This means that

$$\sin\theta = \sin(\theta + 2\pi n), \qquad \cos\theta = \cos(\theta + 2\pi n),$$

where n is an integer. Figure 2.5 depicts the values of two functions during two complete cycles: one counterclockwise (0 to 2π in radians) and one clockwise (0 to -2π in radians). In Figure 2.5 we notice that the sine and cosine functions both have the same amplitude and the same cycle length. However, as we mentioned earlier, they have different starting values at OA where $\theta = 0$. From Figure 2.5 we see that if the cosine curve is shifted slightly to the right, an identical curve with the sine function is obtained where the required shift is $\pi/2$. These two curves are said to differ in *phase* (i.e., the location of the peak and the trough of the oscillation in each function is different in each period). The relationship between the two functions is given by

$$\cos \theta = \sin \left(\theta + \frac{\pi}{2} \right).$$

A switch from the frequency domain to the time domain may illustrate some other properties of a sinusoidal signal. Consider the following time series:

$$x_t = \sin \left(a + \frac{2\pi t}{p} \right), \quad t = 0, 1, 2, \ldots N - 1, \tag{2.7}$$

where each oscillation completes itself in p time periods so that there are N/p oscillations. When $p = N$, there is only one complete oscillation during the observation period, one peak and one trough, and the number of cycles per unit time is $1/N$. However, if p is different than N, the number of cycles per unit time is $1/p$.[6]

To illustrate, suppose that $N = 12$, $a = 1.57$, and $p = 2$ in Equation 2.7. The successive values of x are

$$(-1, 1, -1, 1, \ldots, -1, 1),$$

so that there are six oscillations ($N/p = 12/2$) and each oscillation (± 1) completes itself in two time periods. The number of cycles per unit time is $1/2$. Suppose now that $p = 4$. The successive values of x are

$$(1, 0, -1, 0, 1, 0, -1, 0, 1, 0, -1, 0).$$

There are three oscillations in this case, and each oscillation $(1, 0, -1, 0)$ completes itself in four time periods. The number of cycles per unit time is $1/4$. Within this context, the *frequency* may be defined by the inverse of the cycle length (period) $f = 1/p$, where f is the number of cycles per unit time. Accordingly, Equation 2.7 may be written by

$$x_t = \sin \left(a + 2\pi f t \right), \quad t = 0, 1, 2, \ldots N - 1.$$

For instance, a monthly macroeconomic time series may have a seasonality—for example, a cycle completing itself in 12 months so that $p = 12$, which indicates that each month has $f = 1/12$ cyclical oscillation. The definition of frequency in terms of the number of cycles per time period is easy to understand and interpret. However, the *angular frequency*, $\omega = 2\pi f$, may also be utilized in certain settings. Within the context of angular frequency, Equation 2.7 is written by

$$x_t = \sin \left(a + \omega t \right), \quad t = 0, 1, 2, \ldots N - 1.$$

---

[6] Notice that if the period length of a cycle is greater than the sample size, $p > N$, only a portion of the cycle is observed.

In discrete time setting, the frequency $f = 1/2$, or the angular frequency $\omega = \pi$, is known as a *Nyquist frequency*, which is the highest possible frequency since the shortest length of a cycle would be two time periods.[7] To illustrate the Nyquist frequency, consider a sample from a continuous signal with a cyclical component with frequency $f = 1/p$, a cycle completing itself in p time periods. If the sampling interval is p, we would have no knowledge about the cyclical component. In order to observe the cyclical component of this continuous signal, the sample must be at a rate of at least twice of p. For example, suppose that a stock market index value is sampled once every day at closing so that the sampling period is one day. Then, there would be no information on the intraday cycle of the index. In order to observe an intraday cycle in the market, at least two measurements (one at mid session and another one at closing) need to be taken per day.

A signal may have several sinusoidal components, possibly with different amplitudes (sizes), different phases, and different frequencies. Figure 2.6 illustrates a mixed signal. Any infinite sequence x_t may also be viewed as a combination of an infinite number of sinusoids with different amplitudes and phases, even if the original sequence is not periodic:[8]

$$x_t = \frac{1}{2\pi} \int_{-\pi}^{\pi} X(f)e^{i2\pi ft}df, \qquad (2.8)$$

where $i = \sqrt{-1}$ is an imaginary number and f is the frequency defined earlier.[9] In Equation 2.8, $X(f)$ is given by

$$X(f) = \sum_{t=-\infty}^{\infty} x_t e^{-i2\pi ft}. \qquad (2.9)$$

Equation 2.8 is referred as the *inverse Fourier transform*, and Equation 2.9 is the *Fourier transform* of x_t. Two equations constitute a *Fourier representation* of the

---

[7] This may be seen from Equation 2.7. In that equation, if $p = 1$,

$$x_t = \sin(a + 2\pi t)$$

and x_t is a constant because adding an integer multiple of 2π to a would not change the value of $\sin a$.

[8] Here it is assumed that the sequence is stationary. If the sequence is not stationary, it can be made stationary by different methods as discussed in Hamilton (1994b, Ch. 3).

[9] A complex number z may be expressed in different forms. The Cartesian or rectangular form for z is

$$z = x + iy,$$

where $i = \sqrt{-1}$ is an *imaginary number* and x and y are real numbers referred to as the *real part* and the *imaginary part*, respectively. The *polar form* for z is

$$z = Ae^{i\theta},$$

where A is the magnitude of z and θ is the angle or phase of z. The relationship between these two representations may be determined from *Euler's relation*,

$$e^{i\theta} = \cos\theta + i\sin\theta.$$

See Chiang (1984, Section 15.2) for a detailed exposition of the complex numbers.

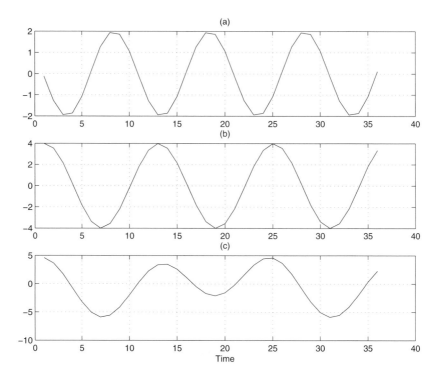

FIGURE 2.6   Time series representation of (a) A cosine function, $2\cos(2\pi t/10 + 1)$. (b) A sine function, $4\sin(2\pi t/12 + 1)$. (c) The sum of the sine and cosine functions in (a) and (b).

sequence x_t, and hence they are called a *Fourier transform pair*. Equation 2.8 is also known as the *synthesis equation* since it represents the original sequence x_t as a linear combination of complex sinusoids infinitesimally close in frequency with $X(f)$ determining the relative weight of each complex sinusoid. Similarly, Equation 2.9 is the *analysis equation*, which analyzes the original sequence x_t to determine how much of each frequency component is required to synthesize it (Bloomfield, 2000). Given x_t and $X(f)$ as a Fourier transform pair,

$$\sum_{t=-\infty}^{\infty} |x_t|^2 = \frac{1}{2\pi} \int_{-\pi}^{\pi} |X(f)|^2 df, \tag{2.10}$$

which is known as *Parseval's theorem*. The left-hand side in Equation 2.10 is the total energy in the signal, which may be obtained by integrating the energy per unit frequency $X|(f)|^2/2\pi$ over 2π interval of discrete-time frequencies. The squared magnitude of the Fourier transform $|X(f)|^2$ is known as the *energy-density spectrum* or the *power spectrum* of the signal x_t (Oppenheim and Schafer, 1989, Chapter 2).

The Fourier representation of a finite sequence is given by

$$x_t = \frac{1}{N} \sum_{k=0}^{N-1} X_k e^{i2\pi f_k t}, \qquad t = 0, 1, \ldots, N-1 \qquad (2.11)$$

and

$$X_k = \sum_{t=0}^{N-1} x_t e^{-i2\pi f_k t}, \qquad k = 0, 1 \ldots, N-1, \qquad (2.12)$$

where $f_k = k/N$. Parseval's relation in this case is (Oppenheim and Schafer, 1989, page 574)

$$\sum_{t=0}^{N-1} |x_t|^2 = \frac{1}{N} \sum_{k=0}^{N-1} |X_k|^2. \qquad (2.13)$$

To illustrate the Fourier transform in a discrete time setting, consider the following time series:

$$x_t = \cos\left(\frac{2\pi t}{12}\right) + \cos\left(\frac{2\pi t}{20}\right) + \epsilon_t \qquad (2.14)$$

$$= \cos\left(2\pi f_1 t\right) + \cos\left(2\pi f_2 t\right) + \epsilon_t, \qquad (2.15)$$

where ϵ_t is a normally distributed random variable with zero mean and unit variance. This time series has two cyclical components with period lengths of 12 and 20 since $f_1 = 1/12$ and $f_2 = 1/20$. Figure 2.7a plots a sample of this time series with $N = 200$. Although there are two periodic components in the signal, the random term ϵ_t makes it difficult to identify them in the time domain representation of the signal. Figure 2.7b plots the magnitude of this Fourier transform as a function of period p.[10] It shows that there are two peaks of the magnitude of the Fourier transform of the original sequence at 12 and 20 periods, which indicates that the relative weights of these periodic components are much higher than any other component of the signal.

2.3.1 Frequency Response

Impulse response function in the time domain is a useful tool for describing and classifying linear filters. An alternative way to classify a filter is to look at the *frequency response function* or the *transfer function*. The frequency response function in discrete time setting is defined by

$$H(f) = \sum_{k=-\infty}^{\infty} w_k e^{-i2\pi f k}, \qquad (2.16)$$

---

[10] We may also plot the squared magnitude of the Fourier transform (spectrum) of the series as a function of the frequency to investigate the energy properties of the signal in frequency domain.

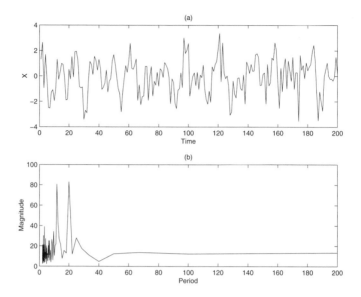

FIGURE 2.7 A signal and its Fourier transform. (a) The original signal defined in Equation 2.14 with two periodic components and an additive random term. (b) The magnitude of the Fourier transform as a function of the period $p = 1/f$. Although it is difficult to identify any periodic component in (a), the Fourier transform in (b) clearly indicates that the relative weights of the components with 12 and 20 period oscillations are much higher than any other component of the signal.

where $i = \sqrt{-1}$, f is the frequency defined earlier and w_k is the impulse response function of a filter. Notice that the frequency response function is the Fourier transform of the impulse response function. In order to analyze filters in the frequency domain, we will consider a signal x_t with a known frequency f,[11]

$$x_t = e^{i2\pi ft}. \tag{2.17}$$

---

[11] An exponential signal $x_t = Ae^{at}$ may have real or complex values depending on A and a. Consider a real exponential signal,

$$x_t = Ae^{rt},$$

where A is the *initial value* and r is the *growth rate* of x_t since

$$\ln\left(\frac{x_t - x_{t-1}}{x_{t-1}} + 1\right) = \ln\left(x_t/x_{t-1}\right)$$
$$= (\ln A + rt) - [\ln A + r(t-1)]$$
$$= r.$$

Therefore, given a positive initial value A, if r is positive (negative), x_t grows (decays) exponentially. For a complex exponential, a is defined to be purely imaginary:

$$x_t = Ae^{i2\pi ft}$$

where $i = \sqrt{-1}$ is an imaginary number. In this case, x_t is periodic with period $p = 1/f$ (Oppenheim and Schafer, 1989, Chapter 2).

An example of this signal is plotted in Figure 2.6. If the filter coefficients are known, the frequency response may easily be calculated. For instance, if the input is the complex exponential in Equation 2.17, a three-period simple moving average

$$y_t = w_0 x_t + w_1 x_{t-1} + w_2 x_{t-2}$$

has

$$y_t = w_0 e^{i2\pi ft} + w_1 e^{i2\pi f(t-1)} + w_2 e^{i2\pi f(t-2)} \tag{2.18}$$

as its output. A close inspection of Equation 2.18 reveals that the filter output is simply a multiplication of the input by the frequency response,

$$
\begin{aligned}
y_t &= \left(w_0 + w_1 e^{-i2\pi f} + w_2 e^{-2i2\pi f} \right) e^{i2\pi ft} \\
&= \left(\sum_{k=0}^{2} w_k e^{-i2\pi fk} \right) e^{i2\pi ft},
\end{aligned}
$$

where the term in parenthesis is the frequency response $H(f)$ defined in Equation 2.16. In general, if the input is complex exponential in Equation 2.17, the general form of a linear filter in Equation 2.2

$$y_t = \sum_{k=-\infty}^{\infty} w_k x_{t-k},$$

becomes

$$
\begin{aligned}
y_t &= \sum_{k=-\infty}^{\infty} w_k e^{i2\pi f(t-k)} \\
&= e^{i2\pi ft} \left(\sum_{k=-\infty}^{\infty} w_k e^{-i2\pi fk} \right), \tag{2.19}
\end{aligned}
$$

where the term in parenthesis is the frequency response defined in Equation 2.16. Therefore, we may write

$$y_t = H(f)e^{i2\pi ft}. \tag{2.20}$$

The frequency response function may be expressed in polar notation as

$$H(f) = G(f)e^{i\theta(f)}.$$

The frequency response in this notation consists of two parts. The first part $G(f)$ is called the *gain* function and it is the magnitude of the frequency response function, $|H(f)|$. The second part is the *phase* function. This decomposition would enable us to obtain the gain function $G(f)$ and the phase angle θ of a filter (Oppenheim and Schafer, 1989, page 39).

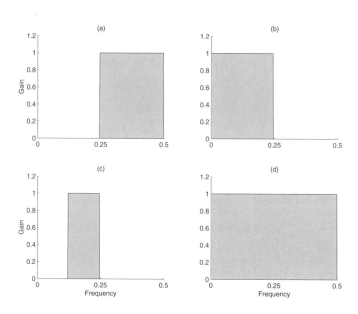

FIGURE 2.8 The magnitude of the gain functions of an ideal filter. (a) A high-pass filter capturing the frequency dynamics between $f = 1/4$ and $f = 1/2$. (b) A low-pass filter capturing the frequency dynamics between 0 and $f = 1/4$. (c) A band-pass filter capturing the frequency dynamics between $f = 1/8$ and $f = 1/4$. (d) An all-pass filter without leaving out any frequency dynamics.

2.3.2 Low-Pass and High-Pass Filters

The plot of the magnitude of the gain as a function of the frequency is known as a *gain diagram*.[12] If the gain is large at low frequencies and small at higher frequencies, the filter is known as a *low-pass filter*. In this case, the low-frequency dynamics of the input are preserved during the filtering, while the high-frequency components are discarded. On the other hand, if the gain is small at low frequencies and large at higher frequencies, the filter is known as a *high-pass filter*. In this case, only the high-frequency characteristics of the input are preserved during the filtering. An *ideal filter* would have a well-defined cutoff frequency with a frequency response

$$H(f) = \begin{cases} 1, & f_l \leq f \leq f_u \\ 0, & \text{otherwise,} \end{cases}$$

where f_l is the lower cutoff frequency and f_u is the upper cutoff frequency of the filter. For an ideal low-pass filter, we would have $f_l = 0$ and $f_u < 1/2$, while an ideal high-pass filter would have $f_l > 0$ and $f_u = 1/2$. Figure 2.8

---

[12] We may also look at the *squared gain function* $\mathcal{H}(f) = |H(f)|^2$ to visualize the frequency domain properties of the filter. The squared gain function of a filter is similar to the spectral density function of stationary time series; only the filter is a deterministic function, while the time series is stochastic.

presents the magnitude of the gain functions of an ideal high-pass filter capturing the frequency dynamics between $f = 1/4$ and $f = 1/2$; an ideal low-pass filter capturing the frequency dynamics between 0 and $f = 1/4$; an ideal band-pass filter capturing the frequency dynamics between $f = 1/8$ and $f = 1/4$; and an all-pass filter, which captures all of the frequency dynamics.

An ideal filter is not computationally realizable as it requires infinitely many coefficients (Oppenheim and Schafer, 1989, page 204). Therefore, the filters in practical applications approximate an ideal filter to a certain extent because they are finite. As an illustration, consider a two-period simple moving average:

$$y_t = 0.50x_t + 0.50x_{t-1}. \tag{2.21}$$

Substituting the complex exponential input in Equation 2.17 into Equation 2.21 results in

$$\begin{aligned} y_t &= 0.50e^{i2\pi ft} + 0.50e^{i2\pi f(t-1)} \\ &= \left(0.50 + 0.50e^{-i2\pi f}\right)e^{i2\pi ft}, \end{aligned}$$

and the frequency response of this moving average is

$$H(f) = 0.50 + 0.50e^{-i2\pi f}.$$

Notice that the frequency response is equal to one when $f = 0$. For small values of f, the frequency response is in the neighborhood of one so that this is a low-pass filter. Figure 2.9 plots the gain functions of different simple moving averages where the filter (a low-pass filter) becomes sharper with increasing averaging periods (i.e., captures a specific frequency band dynamics).

Recall that the frequency response in polar notation is

$$H(f) = G(f)e^{i\theta},$$

and for the two-period simple moving average example it is equal to

$$\begin{aligned} H(f) &= 0.50\left(e^{-i\pi f} + e^{i\pi f}\right)e^{-i\pi f} \\ &= [\cos(\pi f)]e^{-i\pi f}, \tag{2.22} \end{aligned}$$

which shows that the gain function is $\cos(\pi f)$ and the phase is πf. Since the phase of the filter is not zero, there will be a change in the phase of the original time series. This is known as the *phase shift*.

The phase shift has important implications in economics and finance. Since a filter with a nonzero phase shifts the phase of the input, an analysis based on this type of filter would result in misspecification of turning points in the original time series. Figure 2.10 presents an example of the phase shift after filtering. The original time series is the U.S. Industrial Production Index (IPI).[13] The Business

---

[13] Total Production Index, 1992 = 100, Monthly, 1990:01-1993:12, Seasonally Not Adjusted. Source: Datastream.

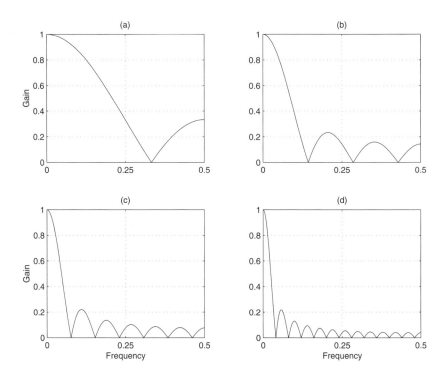

FIGURE 2.9 The magnitude of the gain functions. (a) A simple moving average with a period length of 3. (b) A simple moving average with a period length of 7. (c) A simple moving average with a period length of 13. (d) A simple moving average with a period length of 25.

Cycle Dating Committee of the National Bureau of Economic Research (NBER) maintains a chronology of the U.S. business cycle that is widely used in the analysis of business conditions. The committee announced in October 1991 that the U.S. economy reached a trough of activity in March 1991 and that an expansion began at that time. The committee had announced earlier that the economy reached a peak of activity in July 1990. Therefore, the eight-month period between July 1990 and March 1991 is a recession according to the NBER.

The IPI is one of several monthly indicators analyzed by the Business Cycle Dating Committee to determine the phase of the business cycle. The raw data of the IPI show that the index took the smallest value in March 1991 between January 1990 and December 1993 (see Figure 2.10a). This coincides with the trough date announced by the NBER. However, an eight-period simple moving average of the IPI in Figure 2.10c indicates that the trough was in July 1991. There seems to be a four-period phase shift.

It is desirable to have a *zero phase filter* to preserve the phase properties of the input series. A centered moving average is an example of a zero phase

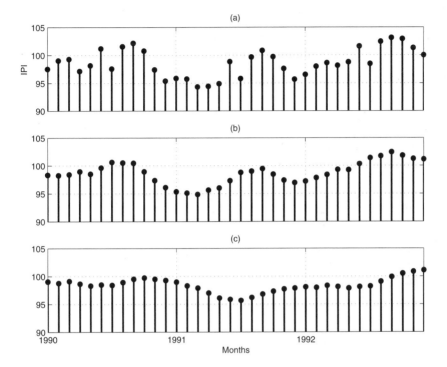

FIGURE 2.10   Phase shift as a result of a simple moving average. (a) The original data: the U.S. Monthly Industrial Production Index (IPI), 1992 = 100. (b) Centered moving average of the IPI, $M = N = 4$. (c) Simple moving average of the IPI, $M = 7$. The raw data in (a) show that the index took the smallest value in March 1991 while an eight-period simple moving average in (c) indicates that the trough was in July 1991. There is a four-period phase shift after filtering with an eight-period simple moving average. Notice that there is no phase shift in centered moving average output in (b). Data source: Datastream.

filter. Consider the following three-period centered moving average with an input sequence $x_t = e^{i2\pi ft}$:

$$
\begin{aligned}
y_t &= \frac{1}{3}\left[e^{i2\pi f(t+1)} + e^{i2\pi ft} + e^{i2\pi f(t-1)} \right] \\
&= \frac{1}{3}\left(1 + e^{-i2\pi f} + e^{i2\pi f} \right) e^{i2\pi ft}.
\end{aligned}
\tag{2.23}
$$

Accordingly, the frequency response is

$$
\begin{aligned}
H(f) &= \frac{1}{3}\left(1 + e^{-i2\pi f} + e^{i2\pi f} \right) \\
&= \frac{1}{3}\left[1 + 2\cos(\pi f) \right],
\end{aligned}
$$

which has a zero phase angle. In fact, the phase angle would be zero for all symmetric centered moving averages, because the frequency response of a moving average with equal weights is given by

$$H(f) = \frac{1}{N + M + 1} e^{i2\pi f[(N-M)/2]} \frac{\sin\left[2\pi f (M + N + 1)/2\right]}{\sin(2\pi f/2)}, \qquad (2.24)$$

where M is the number of lagged values and N is the number of future values of the input (Oppenheim and Schafer, 1989, Ch. 6). Figure 2.10b plots a centered moving average of the IPI with $M = N = 4$, where the trough in the filter output is the same with the original time series indicating that the filter has zero phase.

A causal FIR filter may also be a high-pass filter. For example, the two-period moving *difference*

$$y_t = 0.50x_t - 0.50x_{t-1}$$

has the following frequency response function:

$$
\begin{aligned}
H(f) &= \frac{1}{2}\left(1 - e^{-i2\pi f}\right) \\
&= \frac{1}{2}\left(e^{i\pi f} - e^{-i\pi f}\right)e^{-i\pi f} \\
&= \sin(\pi f)\, i e^{-i\pi f},
\end{aligned}
$$

where the gain is zero at zero frequency ($f = 0$) and increases with increasing f, reaching its maximum at frequency $f = 1/2$. Therefore, it is a high-pass filter. Finally, an IIR filter (a difference equation) may be a high-pass or low-pass filter. Consider the following IIR filter,

$$\sum_{k=0}^{L} a_k y_{t-k} = \sum_{k=0}^{M} w_k x_{t-k},$$

for which the frequency response is

$$H(f) = \frac{Y(f)}{X(f)} = \frac{\sum_{k=0}^{M} w_k e^{-ik2\pi f}}{\sum_{k=0}^{L} a_k e^{-ik2\pi f}},$$

where $Y(f)$ and $X(f)$ are the Fourier transforms of the output y_t and input x_t, respectively (Oppenheim and Schafer, 1989, page 213). As an example, consider the first-order difference equation

$$y_t + a y_{t-1} = x_t, \qquad (2.25)$$

which has the following frequency response:

$$H(f) = \frac{1}{1 - a e^{-i2\pi f}}.$$

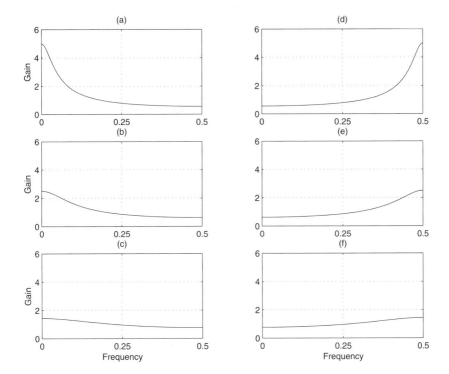

FIGURE 2.11 Gain functions of the first-order difference equation in Equation 2.25 with different parameter settings. The sign of the parameter a determines whether the linear difference equation is a low-pass filter as in the left panel or a high-pass filter as in the right panel. (a) $a = 0.80$. (b) $a = 0.60$. (c) $a = 0.30$. (d) $a = -0.80$. (e) $a = -0.60$. (f) $a = -0.30$. Notice that as the absolute value of the parameter decreases and the gain function becomes flatter around one, approximating an all pass filter.

In Figure 2.11 the frequency response is presented for different values of the parameter a. The sign of the parameter a determines whether the linear difference equation in Equation 2.25 is a low-pass filter as in the left panel or a high-pass filter as in the right panel of Figure 2.11. Also notice that as the absolute value of the parameter decreases, the gain function becomes flatter around one, approximating an all-pass filter.

2.4 FILTERS IN PRACTICE

An ideal band-pass filter removes the frequency components of a time series that lie within a particular range of frequencies. In practice, it is difficult to construct an "ideal" band-pass filter as it requires an infinite number of data points. Therefore, an approximation to an ideal filter is used to extract the components of a time series in a particular frequency range, such as business cycles with known duration. We present four examples of filters in economics and finance in this section. Section 2.4.1 presents an example of an exponentially weighted moving average (EWMA) estimate of volatility in a foreign exchange market. Section 2.4.2 introduces the well-known Hodrick and Prescott (1997) filter in macroeconomics. Section 2.4.3 studies a similar filter proposed by Baxter and King (1999). The chapter ends with some examples of filters used in the technical analysis of prices in financial markets.

2.4.1   The EWMA and Volatility Estimation

The exponentially weighted moving average (EWMA) filter was introduced in Section 2.2.3. This filter plays an important role in the risk management practices used in financial markets. Particularly, the *RiskMetrics* program developed by J. P. Morgan in 1994 relies on the EWMA method to obtain estimates of volatility and correlation of financial instruments for market risk calculations in the Value-at-Risk (VaR) framework. The VaR is a measure of the maximum potential change in the value of a portfolio of financial instruments with a given probability. The following simple example from the RiskMetrics technical document explains the concept (Morgan, 1996).

Suppose that a U.S. based firm holds a DEM 140 million foreign exchange (FX) position. If the foreign exchange rate is 1.40 DEM-USD, the market value of the position is USD 100 million, which is the total exposure of the firm. If the exchange rate declines, the firm would register a loss, whereas an increase in the exchange rate is favorable. The standard deviation of the return on the DEM-USD exchange rate may be taken as an indicator of the potential change in the exchange rate. Standard RiskMetrics assumes that standardized returns on DEM-USD are normally distributed.[14] Therefore, given a value of the daily standard deviation, a potential drop in the exchange rate in one day at a given probability might be calculated from the standard normal distribution. For example, if the daily standard deviation is calculated as 0.5%, VaR at 5% probability is given by 1.65 times 0.5% (1.65σ) (e.g, $0.5 \times 1.65 = 0.825$, since a 5% tail value in the standard normal distribution is 1.65). This means that the exchange rate is not expected to decrease more than 0.825% in one day 95% of the time. Therefore, the VaR of the DEM 140 million position in USD is the total exposure (USD 100 million) times the estimated volatility (0.825), which is USD 825,000.

Even if we accept the assumption of normality, an estimate of the daily standard deviation is required. Simple moving average and EWMA estimators of daily standard deviation are given by

$$\hat{\sigma}_t^s = \sqrt{\frac{1}{N} \sum_{i=0}^{N-1} (r_{t-i} - \bar{r})^2} \tag{2.26}$$

---

[14] Standardized return is defined as r_t/σ_t, where r_t is the log price change and σ_t is the standard deviation.

$$\hat{\sigma}_t^e = \sqrt{\frac{1}{\sum_{i=0}^{N-1} \lambda^i} \sum_{i=0}^{N-1} \lambda^i (r_{t-i} - \bar{r})^2}, \tag{2.27}$$

where $\hat{\sigma}_t$ is an estimate of daily standard deviation, N is filter length (averaging period), r_t is daily log price difference (return), and $\bar{r}$ is period average and λ is the decay factor $(0 < \lambda < 1)$. The decay factor determines the relative importance of recent observations. For large averaging periods, the following approximation to Equation 2.27 might be utilized:

$$\hat{\sigma}_t^e = \sqrt{(1 - \lambda) \sum_{i=0}^{N-1} \lambda^i (r_{t-i} - \bar{r})^2} \tag{2.28}$$

since $\sum_{i=0}^{N-1} \lambda^i = 1/(1 - \lambda)$ as $N \to \infty$.

The RiskMetrics technical document recommends the EWMA method in the standard deviation estimation due to its two advantages. First, an EWMA estimate of volatility reacts to shocks in the market faster than a simple moving average estimate due to the fact that EWMA gives more weight to recent observations. Second, after a shock the EWMA estimate of volatility declines exponentially as time passes. However, a simple moving average estimate of volatility does not change as much and shows abrupt movements in volatility once the large observation falls out of the averaging period.[15]

To illustrate, Figure 2.12 plots the volatility of the daily DEM-USD exchange rate and VaR estimates from June 6, 1997, to December 31, 1997. The upper plot is the absolute value of the daily log price changes (percent) of daily DEM-USD exchange rate. The lower plot is VaR estimates at 5% probability based on a 50-period EWMA and a 50-period simple moving average. The decay factor in the EWMA estimate is 0.94 $(\lambda = 0.94)$ as suggested by RiskMetrics. Since standardized returns are assumed to be normally distributed, the VaR estimate is 1.65 times the estimated standard deviation. Notice that the EWMA estimate of the VaR captures the jump and later fall in volatility around the 110th day much more successfully relative to the simple moving average. The simple moving average is partially successful in capturing the increase in volatility around the 110th day but fails to decline quickly, although there is a noticeable fall in volatility.

---

[15] An extensive usage of exponential moving averages within the context of foreign exchange real-time trading models are studied in Gençay et al. (2001c, 2002), where the authors study the performance of a widely used commercial real-time trading model and compare it with the performance of systematic currency traders. Gençay et al. (2001c) argued that it is not sufficient to develop sophisticated statistical processes and choose an arbitrary data frequency (e.g., one week, one month, annually etc.) claiming afterward that this particular process does a good job of capturing the dynamics of the data-generating process. In financial markets, the data-generating process is a complex network of layers where each layer corresponds to a particular frequency. A successful characterization of such data-generating processes should be estimated with models whose parameters are functions of *intra-* and *inter-frequency* dynamics.

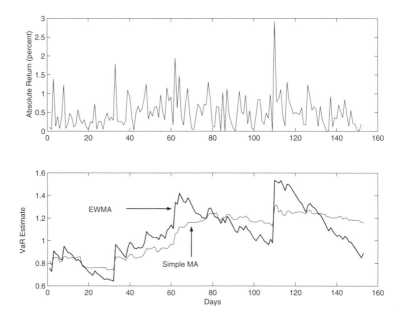

FIGURE 2.12 Volatility of daily DEM-USD exchange rate and Value-at-Risk (VaR) estimates (1.65σ) from June 6, 1997, to December 31, 1997 (weekends excluded). The upper plot is the absolute value of daily DEM-USD log price changes. The lower plot is Value-at-Risk (VaR) estimates at 5% probability based on a 50-period EWMA and a 50-period simple moving average estimates of the daily standard deviation. The decay factor in EWMA estimate is 0.94 ($\lambda = 0.94$) as suggested by RiskMetrics. Notice that the EWMA estimate of volatility captures the sudden jump in volatility around 110th day better relative to the simple moving average.

Figure 2.13 plots the magnitude of the gain function of an EWMA filter versus the magnitude of the gain function of a simple moving average filter. The filter length (averaging period) is 50. The decay factor in the EWMA filter is 0.94 ($\lambda = 0.94$). Notice that the magnitude of the gain function of a simple moving average becomes zero at an integer multiple of frequency $f = 1/N$ for $0 < f < 0.5$, where N is the averaging period (see Equation 2.24). However, we see from Equation 2.16 that this is not the case for an EWMA filter. The magnitude of the gain function of an EWMA filter stays above zero at all frequencies. Therefore, an EWMA filter output contains more high-frequency dynamics than a simple moving average filter output, and hence it provides a better local estimate of volatility than a simple moving average.

An estimate of the daily standard deviation may also be obtained with an infinite lag exponential smoothing as

$$\hat{\sigma}_t^2 = \lambda \sum_{i=0}^{\infty} (1 - \lambda)^i (r_{t-i} - \bar{r})^2, \tag{2.29}$$

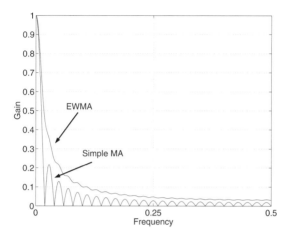

FIGURE 2.13 The magnitude of the gain function of an EWMA versus the magnitude of the gain function of a simple moving average. The averaging period is 50. The decay factor in EWMA filter is 0.94 ($\lambda = 0.94$). Notice that the magnitude of the gain function of an EWMA filter stays above zero at all frequencies. Therefore, an EWMA filter output contains more high-frequency dynamics than a simple moving average filter output and hence it provides a better local estimate of volatility.

which might be written as

$$\hat{\sigma}_t^2 = \lambda(r_t - \bar{r})^2 + \lambda(1 - \lambda)(r_{t-1} - \bar{r})^2 + \lambda(1 - \lambda)^2(r_{t-2} - \bar{r})^2 + \cdots. \tag{2.30}$$

If we shift Equation 2.30 one period back and multiply the resulting equation by $(1 - \lambda)$, we have

$$(1 - \lambda)\hat{\sigma}_{t-1}^2 = \lambda(1 - \lambda)(r_{t-1} - \bar{r})^2 + \lambda(1 - \lambda)^2(r_{t-2} - \bar{r})^2 + \cdots. \tag{2.31}$$

Subtracting Equation 2.31 from Equation 2.30 results in

$$\hat{\sigma}_t^2 = \lambda(r_t - \bar{r})^2 + (1 - \lambda)\hat{\sigma}_{t-1}^2. \tag{2.32}$$

Clearly, the closer λ is to 1, the more weight is given to the current observation. Equation 2.32 may also be modified as

$$\hat{\sigma}_t^2 = \lambda(r_t - \bar{r})^2 + (1 - \lambda)(\hat{\sigma}_{t-1}^2 + s_{t-1}), \tag{2.33}$$

where s_{t-1} is obtained from the following equation:

$$s_t = \gamma(\hat{\sigma}_t^2 - \hat{\sigma}_{t-1}^2) + (1 - \gamma)s_{t-1}, \tag{2.34}$$

and $0 < \gamma < 1$. Equation 2.33 and Equation 2.34 are known as *Holt's exponential smoothing* or the *Holt-Winters smoothing* method (Holt, 1957; Winters, 1960). In Equation 2.34, s_t captures average rate of increase, or trend, of the estimated standard deviation. For applications of the Holt-Winters smoothing method in economics, see Chatfield and Yar (1991) and Grubb and Mason (2001).

2.4.2   The Hodrick-Prescott Filter

The Hodrick and Prescott (HP) filter is widely used to identify business cycle components of a macroeconomic time series (Hodrick and Prescott, 1997). The HP filter aims to decompose a time series into a cyclical y_t^c and a smooth component y_t^s. This filter is obtained by solving the following minimization problem:

$$\min_{y_t^s} \sum_{t=1}^{N} \left\{ (y_t - y_t^s)^2 + \lambda \left[(y_{t+1}^s - y_t^s) - (y_t^s - y_{t-1}^s) \right]^2 \right\},$$

where λ is an arbitrary constant that penalizes variability in the smooth component. The larger the value of λ, the less fluctuations are present in the smooth component. When $\lambda = 0$, the smooth component is the data itself and no smoothing has occured. In the limit when $\lambda \to \infty$, the smooth component is a linear time trend. In many applications, λ is typically set to $\lambda = 1600$ for quarterly data as originally suggested by Hodrick and Prescott (1997).

Once the smooth component is obtained, the residual $y_t^c = y_t - y_t^s$ is taken as the business cycle component of the time series under investigation. King and Rebelo (1993) studied the properties of the HP filter and showed that the cyclical component of the HP filter has the following frequency response function:

$$H(f, \lambda) = \frac{4\lambda \left[1 - \cos(2\pi f) \right]^2}{1 + 4\lambda \left[1 - \cos(2\pi f) \right]^2}. \tag{2.35}$$

King and Rebelo (1993) also showed that the smooth component of the HP filter is given by

$$y_t^s = \frac{\theta_1 \theta_2}{\lambda} \left[\sum_{j=0}^{\infty} \left(A_1 \theta_1^j + A_2 \theta_2^j \right) y_{t-j} + \sum_{j=0}^{\infty} \left(A_1 \theta_1^j + A_2 \theta_2^j \right) y_{t+j} \right], \tag{2.36}$$

where θ_1 and θ_2 are complex conjugates whose values depend on λ, and A_1 and A_2 are the functions of θ_1 and θ_2. Hence, the HP smooth is a centered moving average. As a result, there will be no phase shift in the smooth after filtering. However, the filter in its original form is an infinite order moving average. Therefore, it cannot be implemented without making some restrictive assumptions about the lag length. A practical implementation of the HP filter is studied in Baxter and King (1999).

In Figure 2.14, the magnitude of the HP filter gain function is shown for the cyclical component ($\lambda = 1600$). The cyclical component has no low-frequency dynamics as the magnitude of the frequency response is zero when $f = 0$. The cyclical component starts picking up the frequency components of the original time series at around $f = 0.025$. Notice that $f = 0.025$ corresponds to a period length of 10 years (40 quarters) for a quarterly data set.[16] Therefore, the HP

---

[16] Note that $f = 1/p$, where p is the period length. In this example, $f = 0.025 = 1/40$, which implies a period length of 40 quarters.

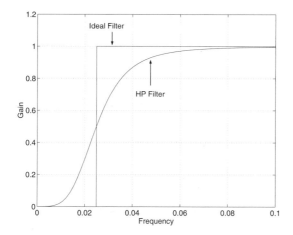

FIGURE 2.14 The magnitude of the gain function of the HP filter cyclical component when $\lambda = 1600$ versus the magnitude of the gain function of an ideal high-pass filter capturing the frequency dynamics greater than $f = 0.025$, which implies a period length of 10 years (40 quarters) for a quarterly data set. Notice that the HP filter only approximates the ideal high-pass filter as its gain function has leakage around $f = 0.025$.

filter with $\lambda = 1600$ and within the context of a quarterly data produces a smooth that contains low-frequency components that extend approximately beyond 10 years. The cyclical component contains the business cycle dynamics (i.e., the variations with a period length of approximately 10 years or less).

Several studies criticize the HP filter on the ground that it distorts the dynamics of the original time series; see, for example, Cogley and Nason (1995) and Cogley (2001). Particularly, Harvey and Jaeger (1993) and Kaiser and Maraval (2000) showed that the HP filter induces spurious cycles if the original time series is difference stationary.[17] Pollock (2000) proposed a rational square-wave filter approach to detrending and points out that the HP filter fails in the task of generating a detrended series by allowing powerful low-frequency components to pass through into the detrended series. As noted by Baxter and King (1999), the HP filter also has some practical problems, such as the unusual behavior of cyclical components near the end of the sample and the choice of the smoothing parameter for data sampled other than quarterly frequency. Finally, McCallum (2000) criticized the HP filter, pointing out that the filter produces a trend so flexible that it follows the time path of the original series rather closely. To illustrate, McCallum (2000) applied the HP filter to the U.S. real gross domestic product

---

[17] Inducing a spurious cycle into a time series through filtering is known as the *Slutsky effect*. Slutsky (1937) showed that it is possible to obtain a filter output with a specific cycle even if the original input is a white noise. See Sargent (1987, page 273) and Pedersen (2001) for more details. Recently, Ghysels *et al.* (1997) investigated the effect of seasonal adjustment filters on volatility estimation and showed that the so-called X-11 seasonal adjustment filter introduces a small seasonal pattern in volatility.

Lead-Lag	BK(6,32)	BK(2,32)	BK(2,8)
0	0.2777	0.9425	0.7741
1	0.2204	-0.0571	-0.2010
2	0.0838	-0.0559	-0.1351
3	-0.0521	-0.0539	-0.0510
4	-0.1184	-0.0513	
5	-0.1012	-0.0479	
6	-0.0422	-0.0440	
7	0.0016	-0.0396	
8	0.0015	-0.0348	
9	-0.0279	-0.0297	
10	-0.0501	-0.0244	
11	-0.0423	-0.0190	
12	-0.0119	-0.0137	

TABLE 2.1 Baxter and King (1999) filter coefficients. BK(6,32), BK(2,32), and BK(2,8) admit approximately the frequency components between 6 to 32 quarters, 2 to 32 quarters, and 2 to 8 years, respectively.

during the 1920s and 1930s. The estimated cyclical component of the HP filter during this period suggests that the Great Depression actually did not occur!

2.4.3 The Baxter-King (BK) Filter

The Baxter and King (1999) filter (BK) is a specific band-pass filter used to capture fluctuations with a period of length 6 to 32 quarters in a given quarterly time series. This is close to the original definition of the longest U.S. business cycle studied in Burns and Mitchell (1946), which defines the duration of a business cycle from more than 1 year to 10 (or 12) years. The BK filter is also a centered moving average with symmetric weights; that is,

$$y_t^f = \sum_{i=-K}^{K} w_i y_{t-i}. \tag{2.37}$$

The coefficients of the BK filter are derived under the constraint that the filter gain should be zero at zero frequency. This constraint leads to the requirement that the sum of the filter coefficients must be zero (see Table 2.1).[18]

In order to capture the major features of business cycles from a quarterly data set, Baxter and King recommended a lead/lag length of $K = 12$. The BK(6,32) filter admits most frequency components between 6 to 32 quarters by removing the low-frequency trend variation and by smoothing high-frequency irregular variation. The BK(2,32) filter admits most frequency components between 2 and

---

[18] In general, if a filter integrates (sums) to one, then it is a low-pass filter (i.e., it has a unit gain at zero frequency). On the other hand, if a filter integrates to zero, it is a high-pass filter (i.e., the gain is one at the highest frequency). The requirement that the sum of the filter coefficients must be zero in the BK filter implies that the filter is a differencing filter and therefore is a high-pass/band-pass filter. This is the same as the idea of the wavelet filter, which will be introduced in Chapter 4.

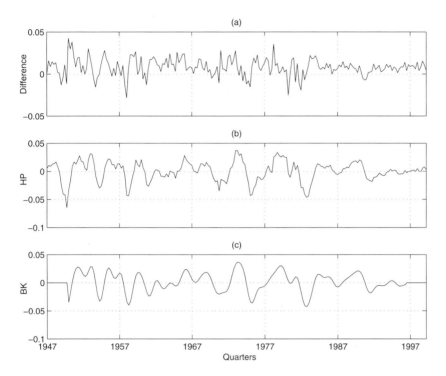

FIGURE 2.15   Filtered log quarterly U.S. real gross national product (seasonally adjusted annual rate, 1992 dollars). (a) First difference of the original time series. (b) HP cycle ($\lambda = 1600$). (c) BK(6,32) cycle. Notice that 12 data points are missing (plotted as zero) at the each end of the BK(6,32) filter output. Source: U.S. Department of Commerce, Bureau of Economic Analysis.

32 quarters by removing the trend variation, but it does not smooth out the high-frequency variations. For annual data, Baxter and King (1999) recommended a single filter with $K = 3$ that admits periodic components between 2 and 8 years.

The BK filter has been criticized on the ground that it may induce spurious dynamic properties and that its cyclical component fails to capture a significant fraction of the variability in business-cycle frequencies (Guay and St-Amant, 1997; Murray, 2001). Nevertheless, both the HP and BK filters have become standard tools in current business cycle studies. Figure 2.15 displays the application of the HP and BK(6,32) filters to the log quarterly U.S. real gross national product (GNP).[19] The first panel is the first difference of the real GNP (quarterly growth rate). In Figure 2.15b, the HP filter output is presented ($\lambda = 1600$). The BK(6,32) output is presented in Figure 2.15c. Notice that the BK output is smoother than the HP output. However, there are 12 missing points (3 years of data) at each end of the BK(6,32) filter output since it is a noncausal filter.

---

[19] Seasonally adjusted annual rate in billions of chained 1992 dollars from 1947:I - 1999:II. Source: U.S. Department of Commerce, Bureau of Economic Analysis.

2.4.4   Filters in Technical Analysis of Financial Markets

Technical analysis in financial markets is the study of market actions such as prices, volumes, and open interests with the aid of charts to forecast the future direction of prices. Most technical analysis tools are filters, such as moving averages. The main premise of technical analysis with moving averages is that prices follow certain trends at certain times. Therefore, the role of a technical analyst (also called a chartist) is to identify different trends (low-frequency components) at their early stages, and take advantage of the trend before other players in the market discover it. The recent research shows that employing simple technical trading rules may improve the forecasting performance of existing models. Also, an optimization of technical trading strategies with neural network models may result in some profitability in security markets; see, for example, Gençay and Stengos (1998) and Gençay (1998a; 1998b; 1999).

The most commonly used tool in technical analysis is a simple moving average. With a simple moving average, a *buy* signal is issued when the last price moves above the simple moving average with a specific length. If the price moves below the simple average, a *sell* signal is generated. A conservative chartist would wait until the moving average itself turns in the direction of the price crossing to conclude that a buy or a sell signal is generated. Figure 2.16a presents an example of simple moving average producing buy and sell signals in a foreign exchange market.

A chartist may place a confidence interval (a band) around a simple moving average. The band might be based on an arbitrary rule, such as "±5%" or some statistical criterion. The ad hoc band construction is known as a *percentage envelope* in technical analysis literature. If the price moves above the upper band, it is taken as a signal of market overreaction (i.e., overbought). If the price falls below the lower band, an oversold signal is produced.

Instead of ad hoc rules to create a band around the simple moving averages, a statistical measure may also be employed. For example, a band with two standard deviations above and two standard deviations below the moving average is known as a *Bollinger band*. Notice that the Bollinger band would expand or contract depending on the price volatility in the market, whereas the percentage envelope would stay constant around the moving average.

Clearly, a short period moving average would give a trend signal earlier than a long period moving average.[20] As a strategy, two moving averages may also be used together to confirm the direction of trend in the market. This technique is called the *double crossing method*. In a double crossing approach, if the short moving average moves above the long moving average, it is accepted as a *buy* signal. If the short moving average crosses below the long moving

---

[20] Technically speaking, the phase shift of a short moving average is smaller than the phase shift of a long moving average. Therefore, a short moving average would indicate a turning point earlier than a long moving average. Nevertheless, both types would indicate the turning point later than the turning actually occurs since their phase shifts are nonzero.

average, a *sell* signal is generated. Figure 2.16b illustrates the double crossing method.

Several moving averages may be combined in technical analysis. For example, a *triple crossover method* (as shown in Figure 2.16c) would employ three different moving averages such as 5, 10, 15 periods. In that case, when a 5-period moving average moves above 10- and 15-period moving averages, an upward trend signal is generated and it is a *buying alert*. In the meantime, if the 10-period moving average also moves above the 15-period average, the upward trend is confirmed and it is a definite *buy* signal. In a downward trend, the shortest period moving average would fall below both medium and long-period moving average first. This is accepted as a *selling alert*. When the medium-term moving average also falls below the long-term moving average, the downward trend is confirmed and it is a definite *sell* signal.

Although there are some conventions in the market regarding the length of moving averages, it is the chartist who decides which moving average works best in a given market for a specific instrument, with a predetermined trading time horizon and cost function.[21] An extensive coverage of technical analysis can be found in Murphy (1999) or Edwards and Magee (1997). The volume by Acar and Satchell (1997) has a collection of more advanced topics in technical trading.

---

[21] Murphy (1999) reported some popular daily moving average combinations in futures markets as 4-9, 9-18, 5-20, and 10-20 days. In stock markets, 50-day moving averages are popular. At longer horizons, 200-day moving averages are commonly employed. Bollinger Bands are usually 20-day and 20-week moving averages. Although these moving averages are not the solutions of some well defined optimization problem, they may indicate some empirical regularities. In other words, they may play an important role in price formation as their usage might be common in the market, causing self-fulfilling price expectations.

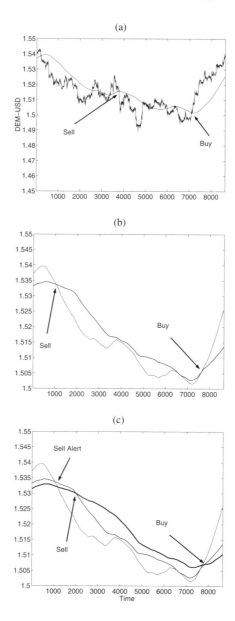

FIGURE 2.16   A technical analysis of 5-min DEM-USD exchange rate from November 26, 1996, to December 31, 1996 (weekends excluded). (a) One-week simple moving average (thin line) versus raw data. (b) Double crossing: one-week simple moving average (thin line) versus two-week moving average (thick line). (c) Triple crossover: one-week simple moving average (thin line), two-week simple moving average (thick line), and three-week simple moving average (darkest line). The original data in panel (a) is not plotted in panels (b) and (c) to make the presentation more visible.

3

OPTIMUM LINEAR ESTIMATION

3.1 INTRODUCTION

In Chapter 2 we classified basic filters in the time domain according to their response functions as either an infinite impulse response (IIR) or a finite impulse response (FIR) filter. We also investigated basic filter properties in the frequency domain and classified them according to their frequency responses as high-pass, low-pass, or band-pass filters. It was assumed that the input to the filter is readily available and the filter coefficients are known. In this chapter, we study the determination of the optimal coefficients of an FIR filter assuming a specific class of observations,

$$y_t = x_t + \epsilon_t, \tag{3.1}$$

where y_t is the observation, ϵ_t is the noise, and x_t is the desired signal from the realization of a random process. In this context, filtering involves the estimation of signal x_t in Equation 3.1. In this section, we limit our attention to a signal x, which is distributed with constant mean μ and variance σ_x^2, denoted by $x \sim (\mu, \sigma_x^2)$.[1] Therefore, the observation of this signal at time t is

$$y_t = x + \epsilon_t, \tag{3.2}$$

---

[1] This assumption will be relaxed in Section 3.2.

51

where observation noise ϵ_t is uncorrelated and distributed with zero mean and constant variance, denoted by $\epsilon_t \sim (0, \sigma_\epsilon^2)$.[2] Filtering in this context can be viewed as extracting (or estimating) x from the noisy observation y_t. Given the observation set,[3]

$$y = (y_1, y_2, y_3, \ldots, y_N),$$

a linear estimate of x at time N may be obtained by assigning a weight w_i to each observation and calculating a weighted average of the observations via

$$
\begin{aligned}
\hat{x}_N &= w_{N-1} y_1 + w_{N-2} y_2 + \ldots + w_0 y_N \\
&= \sum_{i=0}^{N-1} w_i y_{N-i} \\
&= \sum_{i=0}^{N-1} w_i (x + \epsilon_{N-i}) \\
&= x \sum_{i=0}^{N-1} w_i + \sum_{i=0}^{N-1} w_i \epsilon_{N-i}.
\end{aligned}
\tag{3.3}
$$

Recall that this is equivalent to a causal FIR filter (a moving average) introduced in Section 2.2.3. Suppose that the weights in Equation 3.3 are equal to each other as in a simple moving average and each weight is defined to be $w = 1/N$ so that

$$\hat{x}_N = \sum_{i=0}^{N-1} w y_{N-i} = \frac{1}{N} \sum_{i=0}^{N-1} y_{N-i}, \tag{3.4}$$

which is the arithmetic average or mean of the observations. The performance of an estimator such as Equation 3.4 is evaluated using the estimation error defined by the difference between the signal x and the estimate $\hat{x}_N$ via

$$e_N = x - \hat{x}_N.$$

If the expected value of the estimation error is zero, the corresponding estimator is said to be an *unbiased* estimator. In this example,

$$
\begin{aligned}
E(e_N) &= E(x - \hat{x}_N) \\
&= \mu - E\left[\frac{1}{N} \sum_{i=0}^{N-1} (x + \epsilon_{N-i}) \right] \\
&= \mu - \frac{1}{N}(N\mu) = 0.
\end{aligned}
$$

---

[2] A sequence of uncorrelated random variables with zero mean and constant variance is referred to as a *white noise* process. If the elements of this process are also independent across time, then it is called an *independent white noise*. Finally, if an independent white noise process is normally distributed, it is called a *Gaussian white noise*.

[3] In this chapter, we assume that observations start at 1 and end at N in agreement with the generally accepted notation in the Kalman filter literature.

Hence, the sample mean as an estimator of x is an unbiased estimator. In addition to the estimation error, other criteria such as the expected absolute estimation error,

$$E(|e_N|) = E\left(|x - \hat{x}_N|\right),$$

or the expected squared estimation error,

$$E(e_N^2) = E\left[(x - \hat{x}_N)^2\right],$$

may be used to evaluate an estimator. Among these, the expected squared estimation error is known as the *mean square error* (MSE). The mean square error consists of a squared bias term and a variance term,

$$\text{MSE} = \text{Var}(e_N) + [E(e_N)]^2.$$

To illustrate this, consider the variance of the estimation error,

$$
\begin{aligned}
\text{Var}(e_N) &= E\left[e_N - E(e_N)\right]^2 \\
&= E\left[e_N^2 + [E(e_N)]^2 - 2e_N E(e_N)\right] \\
&= E(e_N^2) - [E(e_N)]^2,
\end{aligned}
$$

where the first term on the right-hand side is the MSE and the second term is the squared bias. Therefore, if the expected value of the estimation error is zero (i.e., if the estimator is unbiased) the MSE is the same as the variance of the estimation error. An unbiased estimator is said to be *more efficient* than another unbiased estimator if the variance of the former is less than that of the latter (Griffiths *et al.*, 1993, page 456). In our example, the sample mean as an estimator of x has the following variance:

$$
\begin{aligned}
E(e_N^2) &= E[(x - \hat{x}_N)^2] \\
&= E\left[\left(x - \sum_{i=0}^{N-1} w_i(x + \epsilon_{N-i})\right)^2\right] \\
&= E\left[\left(x - \frac{1}{N}\sum_{i=0}^{N-1}(x + \epsilon_{N-i})\right)^2\right] \\
&= E\left[\left(x - \frac{Nx}{N} - \frac{1}{N}\sum_{i=0}^{N-1}\epsilon_{N-i}\right)^2\right] \\
&= E\left[(-\frac{1}{N}\sum_{i=0}^{N-1}\epsilon_{N-i})^2\right] \\
&= \frac{\sigma_\epsilon^2}{N}.
\end{aligned}
$$

As the sample size increases, the MSE (which is the same with the estimation variance in this case) decreases and converges to zero. An estimator with this property is said to be a *consistent* estimator in mean square.[4]

3.2   THE WIENER FILTER AND ESTIMATION

In this section we utilize the MSE to study the optimal weights of an FIR filter. An early study on determining the weights of a linear filter optimally was carried out by Wiener (1949), and a linear filter based on the minimization of the MSE is known as the *Wiener filter*. In the 1960s, Rudolph E. Kalman made an important contribution to the filtering literature (Kalman, 1960; Kalman and Bucy, 1961). Kalman's approach is based on the use of state-space techniques and recursive algorithms. The filters based on this approach are known as *Kalman filters*. Today, the Kalman filter is used in a wide variety of fields including navigational and guidance systems, radar tracking, satellite orbit determination, as well as in seismic data processing. An early advanced book that exclusively covers the Kalman filter in economics was written by Harvey (1989). Recently, Kim and Nelson (1999) and Durbin and Koopman (2001) covered state-space modeling and the Kalman filter with numerous examples from macroeconomic applications and finance. Bomhoff (1994) wrote an introductory-level book on the subject. Another book by Aoki (1987) covered state-space modeling of time series at an intermediate level. An introductory textbook on Kalman filtering with Matlab[5] exercises and solutions was written by Brown and Hwang (1996). It also provides a background in random process theory and the response of linear systems to random inputs. Sargent (1987) studied several examples of filtering in general and the Kalman filter in particular. Surveys by Engle and Watson (1987) and Hamilton (1994a) provided some examples of applying the Kalman filter in economics.

We will start with the optimum weight determination for an FIR filter.[6] Section 3.2.1 presents an example of an optimum FIR filter in real-wage estimation. Section 3.2.2 introduces the signal-to-noise ratio in a filtering context. The Kalman filter is introduced in Section 3.3. Section 3.6 contains four examples of the Kalman filter in practice.

Consider the noisy observation model introduced in Equation 3.1,[7]

$$y_t = x_t + \epsilon_t,$$

---

[4] Specifically, an estimator $\hat{\mu}$ of a parameter μ is a consistent estimator of μ if and only if

$$\lim_{n \to \infty} P(|\hat{\mu} - \mu| > \epsilon) = 0,$$

where ϵ is an arbitrarily small positive number, n is the sample size, and P denotes probability.

[5] Matlab is a product of the Mathworks Inc., 24 Prime Park Way, Natick, MA 01760-1500.

[6] We will study the optimal coefficients of a filter with known population parameters. The estimation of population parameters is studied in detail in Harvey (1989), Hamilton (1994a; 1994b), Kim and Nelson (1999) and Durbin and Koopman (2001).

[7] In this chapter, it is assumed that the signal and observations are stationary. See Hamilton (1994b, Ch. 3) for a detailed discussion of the stationarity. Clements and Hendry (1999) presented a framework to study nonstationary economic time series.

where we now assume that the signal x_t is a random process with *known* cross-correlation and autocorrelation functions. Our objective is to find the optimum weights w_i^o of the linear estimation equation introduced in Equation 3.3 in the form of an FIR filter,[8]

$$\hat{x}_N = \sum_{i=0}^{N-1} w_i y_{N-i} = \sum_{i=0}^{N-1} w_i (x_{N-i} + \epsilon_{N-i}). \tag{3.5}$$

The criterion for determining the optimum weights is the minimum MSE, which may allow a biased estimator if the variance of the estimator is significantly lower:

$$\min_w E(e_N^2) = \min_w E\left[(x_N - \hat{x}_N)^2\right]$$

$$= \min_w E\left[\left(x_N - \sum_{i=0}^{N-1} w_i(x_{N-i} + \epsilon_{N-i})\right)^2\right]. \tag{3.6}$$

The minimum MSE is obtained by differentiating Equation 3.6 with respect to each w_i and setting the resulting expression equal to zero; that is,

$$\frac{\partial E(e_N^2)}{\partial w_j} = -2E\left[x_N - \sum_{i=0}^{N-1} w_i^o y_{N-i}\right] y_{N-j} = 0, \tag{3.7}$$

for $j = 0, 1, 2 \dots N - 1$, which can be rearranged as

$$\sum_{i=0}^{N-1} w_i^o E(y_{N-i} y_{N-j}) = E(x_N y_{N-j}), \tag{3.8}$$

for $j = 0, 1, 2 \dots N - 1$. The solution of Equation 3.8 gives the optimum filter weights w_i^o for $i = 0, 1, 2, \dots N - 1$. The weights are optimum in the sense that the MSE is minimized. Equation 3.7 can also be written as

$$E(e_N y_{N-j}) = 0, \quad \text{for } j = 0, 1, \dots, N - 1, \tag{3.9}$$

which is known as the *orthogonality condition* in estimation theory.[9] The orthogonality in this context implies that the error e_N in estimating the signal x_N is not correlated with any observation y_t or with any linear combination of observations.

Notice that by expanding Equation 3.8 over i,

$$E(y_N y_{N-j})w_0^o + E(y_{N-1} y_{N-j})w_1^o + \cdots + E(y_1 y_{N-j})w_{N-1}^o = E(x_N y_{N-j}),$$

---

[8] In a similar setup, Hamilton (1994b, Ch. 2) considered a problem of minimum MSE forecasting of a stationary linear process with a Wold representation, which is an IIR filter with white noise inputs.

[9] Two vectors, a and b, are orthogonal if and only if $a^T b = b^T a = 0$. Two random variables x and y are said to be orthogonal if $E(xy) = 0$.

and expanding over j, we have the following matrix representation:

$$
\underbrace{\begin{bmatrix}
E(y_N^2) & E(y_N y_{N-1}) & \cdots & E(y_N y_1) \\
E(y_{N-1} y_N) & E(y_{N-1}^2) & \cdots & E(y_{N-1} y_2) \\
\vdots & \vdots & \ddots & \vdots \\
E(y_1 y_N) & E(y_1 y_{N-1}) & \cdots & E(y_1^2)
\end{bmatrix}}_{\mathcal{A}}
\underbrace{\begin{bmatrix}
w_0^o \\
w_1^o \\
\vdots \\
w_{N-1}^o
\end{bmatrix}}_{\mathbf{W}^o}
=
\underbrace{\begin{bmatrix}
E(x_N y_N) \\
E(x_N y_{N-1}) \\
\vdots \\
E(x_N y_1)
\end{bmatrix}}_{\mathcal{C}} . \quad (3.10)
$$

The matrix $\mathcal{A}$ on the left-hand side contains the second moments of observations while the vector $\mathcal{C}$ on the right-hand side has the cross-covariances between the signal x_N and observations y_t. In order to make this matrix representation operational, consider the following definitions of the autocovariance function (ACV) and the cross-covariance function:[10]

$$
\begin{aligned}
E\left(y_{N-i} y_{N-j}\right) &= \gamma_{yy}(i, j) \\
E\left(x_N y_{N-j}\right) &= \gamma_{xy}(j).
\end{aligned}
$$

Equation 3.8 may then be written in the following form:

$$
\sum_{i=0}^{N-1} w_i^o \gamma_{yy}(i, j) = \gamma_{xy}(j) \quad \text{for } j = 0, 1, 2, \ldots N - 1. \quad (3.11)
$$

Since the autocovariances are symmetric with respect to lag, we may expand Equation 3.11 as

---

[10] The autocovariance function is defined as

$$
\text{Cov}(y_{t-i} y_{t-j}) = E\left[(y_{t-i} - E(y_{t-i}))(y_{t-j} - E(y_{t-j}))\right],
$$

and it becomes $E(y_{t-i} y_{t-j})$ if $E(y_{t-i}) = 0$ or $E(y_{t-j}) = 0$. Similarly, the cross-covariance between x_t and y_{t-j} is given by $E(x_t y_{t-j})$ if $E(x_t) = 0$ or $E(y_{t-j}) = 0$. Notice that we can convert a random variable x into a *centered* random variable $\tilde{x} = x - E(x)$ to make the above autocovariance definition operational as long as we know the first moment of the variable $E(x)$.

$$
\begin{bmatrix}
\gamma_{yy}(0) & \gamma_{yy}(1) & \cdots & \gamma_{yy}(N-1) \\
\gamma_{yy}(1) & \gamma_{yy}(0) & \cdots & \gamma_{yy}(N-2) \\
\vdots & \vdots & \ddots & \vdots \\
\gamma_{yy}(N-1) & \gamma_{yy}(N-2) & \cdots & \gamma_{yy}(0)
\end{bmatrix}
\underbrace{}_{\mathbf{\Gamma}_{yy}}
\begin{bmatrix}
w_0^o \\ w_1^o \\ \vdots \\ w_{N-1}^o
\end{bmatrix}
\underbrace{}_{\mathbf{W}^o}
=
$$

$$
\begin{bmatrix}
\gamma_{xy}(0) \\
\gamma_{xy}(1) \\
\vdots \\
\gamma_{xy}(N-1)
\end{bmatrix}
\underbrace{}_{\mathbf{\Gamma}_{xy}}
, \qquad (3.12)
$$

where $\mathbf{W}^o$ is the vector of optimum weights (coefficients), $\mathbf{\Gamma}_{xy}$ is the cross-covariance vector, and $\mathbf{\Gamma}_{yy}$ is the symmetric autocovariance matrix. Equation 3.11 (or Equation 3.12) is known as the *Wiener-Hopf equation*. If the autocovariance γ_{yy} and the cross-covariance sequence γ_{xy} are known, there are N equations with N unknown optimum filter weights w_i^o and the solution for the optimum weights vector $\mathbf{W}^o$ is straightforward:

$$
\mathbf{W}^o = \mathbf{\Gamma}_{yy}^{-1}\mathbf{\Gamma}_{xy}. \qquad (3.13)
$$

The minimum MSE with the optimal weights in Equation 3.13 may be calculated in the following way. From the definition of the estimation error,

$$
x_N = \sum_{i=0}^{N-1} w_i^o y_{N-i} + e_N,
$$

and since $E[e_N(\sum_{i=0}^{N-1} w_i^o y_{N-i})] = 0$, by virtue of the orthogonality condition in Equation 3.9, it follows that

$$
E(x_N^2) = E(e_N^2) + E\left[\left(\sum_{i=0}^{N-1} w_i^o y_{N-i}\right)^2\right]. \qquad (3.14)
$$

By rearranging the previous equation, we have

$$
\begin{aligned}
E(e_N^2) &= E(x_N^2) - E\left[\left(\sum_{i=0}^{N-1} w_i^o y_{N-i}\right)^2\right] \\
&= E(x_N^2) - E\left[\left(\sum_{i=0}^{N-1} w_i^o y_{N-i}\right)(x_N - e_N)\right], \qquad (3.15)
\end{aligned}
$$

where $\hat{x}_N = x_N - e_N$. Since $E(e_N \hat{x}_N) = 0$ as a result of the orthogonality condition, Equation 3.15 becomes

$$
\begin{aligned}
E(e_N^2) &= E(x_N^2) - E\left[\left(\sum_{i=0}^{N-1} w_i^o y_{N-i}\right) x_N\right] \\
&= p_N^e = \gamma_{xx}(0) - \sum_{i=0}^{N-1} w_i^o \gamma_{xy}(i),
\end{aligned}
\tag{3.16}
$$

where $\gamma_{xx}(0) = E(x_N^2)$ and p_N^e is the minimum MSE. In practice, the minimum MSE may be calculated via

$$
p_N^e = \gamma_{xx}(0) - \Gamma_{xy}^T \mathbf{W}^o.
\tag{3.17}
$$

The complete solution for the linear estimation problem is described by Equations 3.5 (the estimator), 3.13 (the optimum weight calculation), and 3.17 (the minimum mean-square error). We now present an example of a linear estimation problem.

3.2.1   Example: Real Wage Estimation

The decision to work is usually assumed to be a function of the real wage (i.e., the purchasing power of the nominal wage). Suppose that a worker is interested in knowing his or her real wage. Although the worker knows his or her nominal wage, the price level is not evident at the time the worker makes the decision to work. Denote the logarithm of the nominal wage by W and the logarithm of the price level by p. Suppose that wage and prices are governed by the following equations:

$$
W = z + u \quad \text{and} \quad p = z + v,
$$

where z represents the movements in the price level that leave the real wage unchanged so that disturbance terms u and v determine the variations in real wage. Assume that the disturbances are serially uncorrelated processes with $u \sim N(0, \sigma_u^2)$ and $v \sim N(0, \sigma_v^2)$. Furthermore suppose that the disturbances are not correlated with each other or with z. The worker's best estimate of the logarithm of the real wage by observing the nominal wage and *knowing* the first and the second moments of all the variables is given by

$$
(\widehat{W - p}) = w_1 W.
$$

According to the Wiener-Hopf equation (Equations 3.11, 3.12), we have to find the following:

$$
\begin{aligned}
\gamma_{yy} &= E(WW) &&= E(z+u)(z+u) &&= E(u^2) + E(v^2) \\
\gamma_{xy} &= E[W(W-p)] &&= E(z+u)(u-v) &&= E(u^2).
\end{aligned}
$$

Substituting these expressions into the Wiener-Hopf equation (Equation 3.11), the optimum weight w_1 is found to be

$$w_1 = \frac{E(u^2)}{E(u^2) + E(v^2)}.$$

The weight of the nominal wage in making an estimate about the variation in the real wage lies between zero and one. The weight of nominal wage in real-wage estimation becomes zero if all of the variation in the real wage comes from the price level, $E(u^2) = 0$. On the contrary, if $E(u^2)/E(v^2)$ is large (i.e., change in real wage is caused mainly by the nominal wage movements), then the weight of the nominal wage approaches one.[11]

3.2.2 Signal-to-Noise Ratio

The ratio of the standard deviation of the noise to the standard deviation of the signal is called *signal-to-noise* ratio (SNR). Noise with a large standard deviation relative to that of the signal will make it "difficult" to obtain the signal. However, if there is some information about the SNR, the Wiener-Hopf approach implies that the estimator in Equation 3.4 may be improved, especially when the sample size is small (Mallat, 1998, page 426). To illustrate, suppose that the observation y_t is the same noisy observation described in Equation 3.1, which consists of the desired signal x and a noise process

$$y_t = x + \epsilon_t,$$

where the disturbance term is a serially uncorrelated random process with $\epsilon_t \sim N(0, \sigma_\epsilon^2)$. Suppose that the expected value of the signal is zero ($\mu = 0$) so that the second moment of the signal is its variance, $E(x^2) = \sigma_x^2$. The restriction on the first and the second moments of the signal x and the white noise nature of the disturbance term imply the following:

$$\gamma_{yy}(N, i) = E[(x + \epsilon_N)(x + \epsilon_{N-i})] = \begin{cases} \sigma_x^2 + \sigma_\epsilon^2 & \text{if } i = 0 \\ \sigma_x^2 & \text{otherwise,} \end{cases}$$

$$\gamma_{xy}(N, i) = E[x(x + \epsilon_{N-i})] = \sigma_x^2 \quad \text{for all } i.$$

Substituting these two expressions into the Wiener-Hopf equation (Equation 3.11) and solving for the optimum weights w_i^o, we have

$$w_0^o = w_1^o = \ldots = w_{N-1}^o = \frac{1}{N + (\sigma_\epsilon^2/\sigma_x^2)} = \frac{1}{N + \text{SNR}},$$

---

[11] This is an example of a problem in optimal prediction. See Sargent (1987, page 229) for a detailed exposition of this example.

where SNR $= \sigma_\epsilon^2/\sigma_x^2$ is the signal-to-noise ratio. The estimate of x at time N is now given by

$$\hat{x}_N = \frac{1}{N + \text{SNR}} \sum_{i=0}^{N-1} y_{N-i}.$$

As the sample size goes to infinity, this estimator converges to the previously introduced sample mean estimator in Equation 3.4 and therefore is *asymptotically unbiased*. It is worth mentioning that the minimum MSE in this case is given by

$$\text{MSE} = p_N^e = \frac{\sigma_\epsilon^2}{N + \text{SNR}}. \tag{3.18}$$

Note that the MSE in this case is smaller than the MSE of the sample mean estimator, which is a direct consequence of the MSE criterion in finding the optimum weights.

3.2.3   Comments on Wiener Filtering and Estimation

- If the desired signal is Gaussian, then the Wiener filter is an optimal estimator. However, if the variable of interest is non-Gaussian, some other estimators exist that will outperform the Wiener filter (Mallat, 1998, page 430).

- The Wiener filter minimizes the mean-square error. However, the minimum MSE is not a universal criterion and it may lead to undesirable results. For example, suppose that the signal is a technical trading rule with values only +1 (buy signal) and minus 1 (sell signal). Then, the output of the Wiener estimator for this signal in large samples will be zero (i.e., "do not buy or sell"). However, we know that the process *never* takes a zero value.

- The Wiener filter is based on the *true* first and second moments of the processes. This requirement cannot be fulfilled in practical applications of economics and finance as the true moments of the variable of interest are rarely known. An alternative to true moments might be to utilize the full sample autocovariance estimate of the observations and some combination of them. However, as we will show in Section 3.2.4, this approach has severe limitations in practice.

- One disadvantage of Wiener filtering is that each time data is received, the entire data set must be processed again. This requires an ever growing amount of storage space, larger memory in computers, and more computation time. This is a limitation in dealing with large data sets such as high-frequency financial time series.

3.2.4 Pitfalls of the Sample Autocorrelation and Cross-Correlation

In most studies, the discussions of variance, autocorrelation, and cross-correlations are carried out under the assumption that the mean of the underlying process is known. If the mean of the process is unknown, the estimated autocorrelations and cross-correlations (based on the estimated mean) can lead to spurious results (Percival, 1993). Let x_t be a stationary process with mean μ and an autocovariance sequence be given by

$$E\left[(x_t - \mu)(x_{t-i} - \mu)\right] = \gamma_i, \quad i = 0, \pm 1, \pm 2, \ldots ,$$

where the autocovariance sequence (ACVS) is defined for all lags. Given N sample values of x_t, the unbiased estimator of the ACVS is

$$\hat{\gamma}_i^u = \frac{1}{N - |i|} \sum_{t=1}^{N-|i|} (x_t - \bar{x})(x_{t-i} - \bar{x})$$

and the biased estimator is

$$\hat{\gamma}_i^b = \frac{1}{N} \sum_{t=1}^{N-|i|} (x_t - \bar{x})(x_{t-i} - \bar{x}), \tag{3.19}$$

where $\bar{x}$ is the sample mean (Fuller, 1976, page 236). When the population mean is unknown, the biased estimator of the ACVS satisfies the following constraint:

$$\sum_{i=-(N-1)}^{N-1} \hat{\gamma}_i^b = 0, \tag{3.20}$$

where $\hat{\gamma}_i^b$ is the estimated autocovariance at positive lags and $\hat{\gamma}_{-i}^b$ is the estimated autocovariance at negative lags (leads). Since the autocorrelation coefficient is a scaled version of the autocovariance, the sum in Equation 3.20 also holds for the sum of the autocorrelations at all lags, and a contemporaneous correlation (correlation at zero lag) which is 1; that is,

$$\sum_{i=-(N-1)}^{-1} \hat{\rho}_i^b + \sum_{i=1}^{N-1} \hat{\rho}_i^b + \hat{\rho}_0^b = 0, \tag{3.21}$$

where $\hat{\rho}_i$ is the sample autocorrelation coefficient. To demonstrate the zero restriction in Equation 3.21, consider an $N \times N$ matrix whose (t, u) entry is $(x_N - \bar{x})(x_u - \bar{x})$ for $1 \leq t, u \leq N$:

$$\begin{bmatrix} (x_1 - \bar{x})(x_1 - \bar{x}) & (x_1 - \bar{x})(x_2 - \bar{x}) & \cdots & (x_1 - \bar{x})(x_N - \bar{x}) \\ (x_2 - \bar{x})(x_1 - \bar{x}) & (x_2 - \bar{x})(x_2 - \bar{x}) & \cdots & (x_2 - \bar{x})(x_N - \bar{x}) \\ \vdots & \vdots & \ddots & \vdots \\ (x_N - \bar{x})(x_1 - \bar{x}) & (x_N - \bar{x})(x_2 - \bar{x}) & \cdots & (x_N - \bar{x})(x_N - \bar{x}) \end{bmatrix}.$$

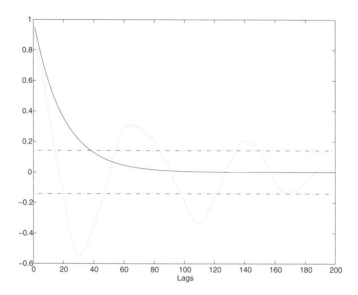

FIGURE 3.1 Sample and population correlograms of the AR(1) process in Equation 3.22. Dotted line represents the sample autocorrelation coefficients while the straight line represents the true autocorrelation coefficients. The dot-dashed line is the approximate 95% confidence interval.

The sum of the elements on the main diagonal is $N\hat{\gamma}_0^b$. The sum of the elements on the ith super diagonal is $N\hat{\gamma}_i^b$, and the same is true for the ith subdiagonal. Since the autocovariances are symmetric, $\hat{\gamma}_i^b = \hat{\gamma}_{-i}^b$, the sum of all the elements in the matrix is $N \sum_{i=-(N-1)}^{N-1} \hat{\gamma}_i^b$. However, the sum of the ith row of the matrix is identically zero for all i, from which the stated result follows immediately (Percival, 1993).

The result has important implications for time series applications. First, note that since $\hat{\gamma}_0^b = \hat{\sigma}^2 > 0$ for any variable x, some of the sample autocovariances *must* be negative, which is not necessarily true for the population ACVS. Second, an important tool of a time series practitioner is the plot of the sample autocorrelation coefficients at certain lags, which is known as a *correlogram*. Equation 3.21 implies that since the sum of the lead-lag autocorrelation coefficients *must* be equal to minus 1, and since $\rho_i^b = \rho_{-i}^b$ for all i, the sum of the autocorrelation coefficients at all lags must be -0.50 regardless of the true ACVS. This result shows that the correlogram as a tool would provide a different picture than the true autocorrelation structure of the time series studied. To illustrate how this may lead to a distorted picture, Figure 3.1 plots the true autocorrelation coefficients and the sample autocorrelation coefficients for the following AR(1) process:

$$x_t = 0.90x_{t-1} + \epsilon_t, \qquad t = 0, 1 \dots, 200, \qquad (3.22)$$

where ϵ_t is a serially uncorrelated random disturbance $\epsilon \sim N(0, \sigma_\epsilon^2)$. This process has an autocorrelation sequence with $\rho_k = 0.90^k$. However, the sample autocorrelation oscillates, giving the impression that the underlying process has some sinusoidal dynamics.

A similar proof may be obtained for the sample cross-correlation sequence for two random processes. Consider the biased estimator of the cross-covariance between two random vectors, x and y:

$$\hat{\gamma}_{i,xy}^b = \frac{1}{N} \sum_{t=1}^{N-|i|} (x_t - \bar{x})(y_{t-i} - \bar{y}),$$

where $\bar{x}$ and $\bar{y}$ are the sample means. The cross-covariance sequence also satisfies the following constraint:

$$\sum_{i=-(N-1)}^{N-1} \hat{\gamma}_{i,xy}^b = 0, \tag{3.23}$$

where $\hat{\gamma}_{i,xy}^b$ is the estimated cross-covariance at positive lags and $\hat{\gamma}_{-i,xy}^b$ is the estimated cross-covariance at negative lags (leads). Since the cross-correlation coefficient is a scaled version of cross-covariance, the sum in Equation 3.23 also holds for the sum of the cross-correlations at all leads and lags, and the contemporaneous correlation

$$\sum_{i=-(N-1)}^{-1} \hat{\rho}_{i,xy}^b + \sum_{i=1}^{N-1} \hat{\rho}_{i,xy}^b + \hat{\rho}_{0,xy}^b = 0, \tag{3.24}$$

where $\hat{\rho}_i$ is the sample cross-correlation coefficient. The estimated cross-correlation sequence is also a common tool of time series practitioner in determining the lead-lag relations between two variables. However, the stated result in Equation 3.24 implies that the sample cross-correlogram also might be very misleading. As an example, consider two time series:

$$y_t = 0.90t + \epsilon_{t,1} \quad \text{and} \quad x_t = 0.80t + \epsilon_{t,2}, \tag{3.25}$$

where $\epsilon_{t,i}$, $i = 1, 2$ are white noise processes. These two time series are highly correlated at all lags. A scatter plot of $x_{t-|i|}$ versus y_t (Figure 3.2) shows a slope close to +1, indicating that the cross-correlation between them at that particular lag (lead) is also positive and close to unity. Equation 3.24 shows that the calculated sample cross-correlation might be zero or even negative.

3.3 RECURSIVE FILTERING AND THE KALMAN FILTER

Consider a sample mean estimate in Equation 3.3 with consecutive observations. Suppose that the observation y_t is received sequentially, which consists of the

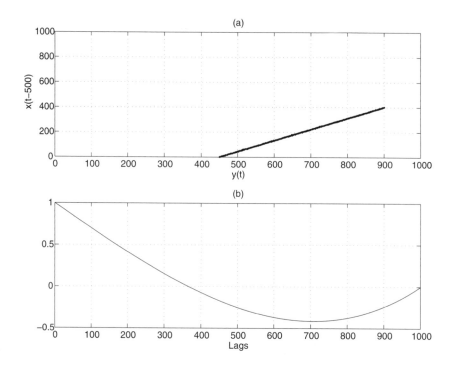

FIGURE 3.2   (a) Scatter plot of simulated x_{t-500} versus y_t from Equation 3.25. The scatter plot indicates that there is a strong positive correlation between the two time series y_t and x_{t-500}. (b) Cross-correlation coefficients between y_t and x_t at all lags. Notice that the correlogram shows that the cross-correlation between the two time series at lag 500 is negative, which is not true.

desired signal x plus noise ϵ_t:

$$y_t = x + \epsilon_t, \tag{3.26}$$

where the disturbance term is serially uncorrelated with $\epsilon \sim N(0, \sigma_\epsilon^2)$. At time $t = 1$, the best guess about the true value of x is the first observation itself:

$$\hat{x}_1 = y_1.$$

At time $t = 2$, the weighted sum of y_1 and y_2 is

$$\hat{x}_2 = \frac{1}{2} y_1 + \frac{1}{2} y_2.$$

The first estimate $\hat{x}_1$ may be substituted for y_1 in this equation and the previous observation discarded:

$$\hat{x}_2 = \frac{1}{2}\hat{x}_1 + \frac{1}{2} y_2.$$

At time $t = 3$,

$$\hat{x}_3 = \frac{2}{3}\hat{x}_2 + \frac{1}{3}y_3.$$

Following this line of reasoning, it can be shown that two things are required at any time $t = N$ to obtain an estimate of the sample mean: the new observation y_N and the previous estimate $\hat{x}_{N-1}$ to yield

$$\hat{x}_N = \frac{N-1}{N}\hat{x}_{N-1} + \frac{1}{N}y_N,$$

or equivalently

$$\hat{x}_N = \hat{x}_{N-1} + \frac{1}{N}(y_N - \hat{x}_{N-1}).$$

This is a simple example of *recursive estimation*. In recursive estimation, a new estimate is obtained by adding a correction term to the previous estimate. In this example, it is implied that "the best guess about x is the previous guess and a correction term after the new information arrives." The correction is such that if the new observation is higher than the previous estimate, the estimate is corrected upward. If the new observation is equal to the previous estimate, there is no reason to change the estimate since there is no new information. If the new observation is less than the previous estimate, the estimation is corrected downward. Notice that the new information has a weight as $1/N$ and it decreases with increasing sample size. This is because the signal x has a constant mean and variance. Therefore, each new piece of information adds very little to our existing knowledge about the signal if a piece of considerable sample has already been processed.

3.3.1 Recursive Mean Estimation

In Section 3.2.2, an estimator of x at time N was derived with the minimum MSE criterion by

$$\hat{x}_N = \frac{1}{N + \text{SNR}} \sum_{i=0}^{N-1} y_{N-i}, \tag{3.27}$$

where $\text{SNR} = \sigma_\epsilon^2/\sigma_x^2$ is the signal-to-noise ratio. Following the reasoning in the previous section, this estimator may also be written recursively as

$$\hat{x}_N = \hat{x}_{N-1} + \alpha_N(y_N - \hat{x}_{N-1}), \tag{3.28}$$

where $\alpha_N = 1/(N + \text{SNR})$. To illustrate this recursive estimation, suppose that the observation starts at time $t = 1$ with an initial estimate of x as $\hat{x}_0 = 0$. If the estimator for x is the sample mean estimator as in the previous section, the first observation y_1 is the best guess of the signal. However, if the SNR is known, the Wiener estimator in Equation 3.28 takes into account the relative variances and discounts the observation accordingly. The minimum MSE in this case was given by (Equation 3.18)

$$p_N^e = \frac{\sigma_\epsilon^2}{N + \text{SNR}} = \frac{\sigma_\epsilon^2 \sigma_x^2}{\sigma_x^2 N + \sigma_\epsilon^2},$$ (3.29)

which may also be written recursively as

$$p_N^e = \frac{\sigma_\epsilon^2 p_{N-1}^e}{p_{N-1}^e + \sigma_\epsilon^2}, \qquad p_0^e = \sigma_x^2.$$ (3.30)

Notice that at time $t = 0$ (before any observation), the MSE is the signal variance, $p_0^e = \sigma_x^2$. After the first observation at time $t = 1$, the MSE is

$$p_1^e = \frac{\sigma_\epsilon^2 \sigma_x^2}{\sigma_x^2 + \sigma_\epsilon^2} = \frac{\sigma_\epsilon^2 p_0^e}{p_0^e + \sigma_\epsilon^2}.$$ (3.31)

At time $t = 2$, it is

$$p_2^e = \frac{\sigma_\epsilon^2 p_0^e}{2 p_0^e + \sigma_\epsilon^2}.$$

From the first period MSE, we already know that

$$\sigma_\epsilon^2 p_0^e = p_1^e (p_0^e + \sigma_\epsilon^2)$$

and

$$p_1^e + \sigma_\epsilon^2 = \sigma_\epsilon^2 + \frac{\sigma_\epsilon^2 p_0^e}{p_0^e + \sigma_\epsilon^2} = \frac{\sigma_\epsilon^2 (2 p_0^e + \sigma_\epsilon^2)}{p_0^e + \sigma_\epsilon^2}.$$

Substituting the last two expressions into p_2^e yields

$$p_2^e = \frac{\sigma_\epsilon^2 p_1^e}{p_1^e + \sigma_\epsilon^2}.$$

By repeated substitution, the recursive form of the MSE in Equation 3.30 may be obtained. There is a direct relationship between the correction coefficient α_N in Equation 3.28 and the MSE p_N^e in Equation 3.30 via

$$p_N^e = \sigma_\epsilon^2 \frac{1}{N + \gamma} = \sigma_\epsilon^2 \alpha_N.$$ (3.32)

After substituting the recursive form of p_N^e in Equation 3.30 into the preceding equation and solving for α_N, the correction coefficient is

$$\alpha_N = \frac{p_{N-1}^e}{p_{N-1}^e + \sigma_\epsilon^2},$$

and the estimator becomes

$$\hat{x}_N = \hat{x}_{N-1} + \frac{p^e_{N-1}}{p^e_{N-1} + \sigma^2_\epsilon}(y_N - \hat{x}_{N-1}).$$

This is a special case of the scalar *Kalman filter*, which will be introduced in the following subsection.

3.3.2 The Kalman Filter and Estimation

So far the unobserved signal x has been assumed to be distributed normally with constant mean μ and variance σ^2_x. Here, let the signal x_t to follow a first-order autoregressive AR(1) process,

$$x_t = \phi x_{t-1} + v_t, \tag{3.33}$$

where the disturbance term $v_t \sim N(0, \sigma^2_v)$ is serially uncorrelated. Let the observation equation be

$$y_t = x_t + \epsilon_t, \tag{3.34}$$

where $\epsilon_t \sim N(0, \sigma^2_\epsilon)$ is also a serially uncorrelated random process. Further assume that the observation noise ϵ_t and signal noise v_t are not correlated

$$E(v_{t-i}\epsilon_{t-j}) = 0, \quad \text{for all } i \text{ and } j.$$

Given N observations, an optimum recursive estimation method for the signal x_N may be obtained through the Kalman filter. Recall that a recursive estimator has the following general form:

$$\hat{x}_N = \alpha_N \hat{x}_{N-1} + \beta_N y_N, \tag{3.35}$$

where $\hat{x}_N$ is the estimate of the desired signal at time N and y_N is the observation made at time N. Two parameters α_N and β_N will be determined optimally from the minimization of the MSE; that is,

$$\min_{\alpha,\beta} E(e^2_N) = \min_{\alpha,\beta} E\left(x_N - \alpha_N \hat{x}_{N-1} - \beta_N y_N\right)^2. \tag{3.36}$$

The optimum weights are found by differentiating the MSE with respect to each parameter α_N and β_N:

$$\frac{\partial p^e_N}{\partial \alpha_N} = -2E\left(x_N - \alpha^o_N \hat{x}_{N-1} - \beta^o_N y_N\right)\hat{x}_{N-1} = 0, \tag{3.37}$$

$$\frac{\partial p^e_N}{\partial \beta_N} = -2E\left(x_N - \alpha^o_N \hat{x}_{N-1} + \beta^o_N y_N\right)y_N = 0. \tag{3.38}$$

Hence, the orthogonality conditions are

$$E(e_N \hat{x}_{N-1}) = 0 \quad \text{and} \quad E(e_N y_N) = 0. \tag{3.39}$$

The orthogonality conditions in this framework imply that the error e_N in estimating x_N is not correlated with the previous estimate $\hat{x}_{N-1}$ or with the current observation y_N. By rearranging Equation 3.37, we have

$$E\alpha_N^o(\hat{x}_{N-1}\hat{x}_{N-1}) = E(x_N - \beta_N^o x_N - \beta_N^o \epsilon_N)\hat{x}_{N-1}.$$

Note that $\hat{x}_{N-1} = x_{N-1} - e_{N-1}$ from the definition of the estimation error. Since the error in estimating the signal and the estimate are not correlated by virtue of the orthogonality condition (Equation 3.39), the preceding equation may be written as

$$E\alpha_N^o(x_{N-1}\hat{x}_{N-1}) = E\left[(1 - \beta_N^o)x_N - \beta_N^o \epsilon_N\right]\hat{x}_{N-1}.$$

After substituting the signal in Equation 3.33 into the above equation, we have

$$E\alpha_N^o(x_{N-1}\hat{x}_{N-1}) = E\left[(1 - \beta_N^o)(\phi x_{N-1} + v_N) - \beta_N^o \epsilon_N\right]\hat{x}_{N-1}.$$

Since the previous period estimate is not correlated with the current observation noise or with the current signal noise $E(\epsilon_N \hat{x}_{N-1}) = E(v_N \hat{x}_{N-1}) = 0$, the solution for α_N is

$$\alpha_N^o = \phi(1 - \beta_N^o). \tag{3.40}$$

After substituting this solution into Equation 3.35, the recursive estimator takes the following form

$$\begin{aligned} \hat{x}_N &= \phi(1 - \beta_N^o)\hat{x}_{N-1} + \beta_N^o y_N \\ &= \phi\hat{x}_{N-1} + \beta_N^o\left(y_N - \phi\hat{x}_{N-1}\right). \end{aligned}$$

The first term on the right-hand side, $\phi\hat{x}_{N-1}$, is the best estimate of $\hat{x}_N$ *before* the observation arrives at time N. The second term represents the correction to this prior estimate after the new observation is obtained. The best estimate of y_N is also given by $\phi\hat{x}_{N-1}$ so that the term in brackets is the error in estimating y_N, which is also called an *innovation*. Each innovation is weighted by β_N^o in the process of updating the previous estimation.

We will now find an optimum solution for β_N in the estimation equation. The MSE p_N^e is given by

$$p_N^e = E\left[e_N(x_N - \hat{x}_N)\right] = E(e_N x_N),$$

where $E(e_N \hat{x}_N) = 0$ as a result of the orthogonality condition. Note that $x_N = y_N - \epsilon_N$ from Equation 3.34, which leads to

$$E(e_N x_N) = E\left[e_N(y_N - \epsilon_N)\right].$$

Since the observation y_N and the estimation error e_N are uncorrelated, it follows that

$$
\begin{aligned}
p_N^e &= -E(e_N \epsilon_N) \\
&= -E\left[x_N - \alpha_N \hat{x}_{N-1} - \beta_N^o y_N\right]\epsilon_N \\
&= -E\left[x_N - \alpha_N \hat{x}_{N-1} - \beta_N^o (x_N + \epsilon_N)\right]\epsilon_N \\
&= \beta_N^o \sigma_\epsilon^2,
\end{aligned}
\tag{3.41}
$$

where $E(x_N \epsilon_N) = E(\hat{x}_{N-1} \epsilon_N) = 0$. The MSE may also be written as

$$
\begin{aligned}
p_N^e &= E(x_N - \hat{x}_N)^2 = E\left[x_N - (\phi \hat{x}_{N-1} + \beta_N^o y_N - \phi \beta_N^o \hat{x}_{N-1})\right]^2 \\
&= E\left(x_N - \phi \hat{x}_{N-1} - \beta_N^o y_N + \phi \beta_N^o \hat{x}_{N-1}\right)^2.
\end{aligned}
$$

Substitution of the signal in Equation 3.33 and the observation in Equation 3.34 into the above expression yields

$$
\begin{aligned}
p_N^e &= E\left[\phi x_{N-1} + v_N - \phi \hat{x}_{N-1} - \beta_N^o (\phi x_{N-1} + v_N + \epsilon_N) + \phi \beta_N^o \hat{x}_{N-1}\right]^2 \\
&= E\left[\phi(x_{N-1} - \hat{x}_{N-1}) - \beta_N^o \phi(x_{N-1} - \hat{x}_{N-1}) + (1 - \beta_N^o)v_N - \beta_N^o \epsilon_N\right]^2 \\
&= E\left[\phi(1 - \beta_N^o)(x_{N-1} - \hat{x}_{N-1}) + (1 - \beta_N^o)v_N - \beta_N \epsilon_N\right]^2.
\end{aligned}
$$

Since the signal noise v_N, previous period MSE p_{N-1}^e, and the observation noise ϵ_N are not correlated with each other, the minimum MSE is

$$
p_N^e = \phi^2 (1 - \beta_N^o)^2 p_{N-1}^e + (1 - \beta_N^o)^2 \sigma_v^2 + (\beta_N^o)^2 \sigma_\epsilon^2.
\tag{3.42}
$$

Using the expression for p_N^e in Equation 3.41,

$$
\begin{aligned}
\beta_N^o \sigma_\epsilon^2 &= \phi^2 (1 - \beta_N^o)^2 p_{N-1}^e + (1 - \beta_N^o)^2 \sigma_v^2 + (\beta_N^o)^2 \sigma_\epsilon^2 \\
\beta_N^o \sigma_\epsilon^2 - (\beta_N^o)^2 \sigma_\epsilon^2 &= \phi^2 (1 - \beta_N^o)^2 p_{N-1}^e + (1 - \beta_N^o)^2 \sigma_v^2 \\
\beta_N^o (1 - \beta_N^o) \sigma_\epsilon^2 &= \phi^2 (1 - \beta_N^o)^2 p_{N-1}^e + (1 - \beta_N^o)^2 \sigma_v^2,
\end{aligned}
$$

and dividing both sides by $(1 - \beta_N^o)^2$ gives us

$$
\frac{\beta_N^o \sigma_\epsilon^2}{(1 - \beta_N^o)} = \phi^2 p_{N-1}^e + \sigma_v^2.
$$

Therefore, the solution for the weight factor β_N is

$$
\beta_N^o = \frac{\phi^2 p_{N-1}^e + \sigma_v^2}{\phi^2 p_{N-1}^e + \sigma_v^2 + \sigma_\epsilon^2} = \frac{s_N}{s_N + \sigma_\epsilon^2}.
\tag{3.43}
$$

This correction coefficient is called the *Kalman gain*. It consists of two terms: the first one $s_N = \phi^2 p_{N-1}^e + \sigma_v^2$ is the variance of *predicting* x_N before observing y_N.

The other term is the variance of the observation noise σ_ϵ^2. Note that if the variance of the observation is very small, the Kalman gain approaches one (i.e., the innovation is fully incorporated into the estimation). On the other hand, if the variance of the observation noise is very high, the Kalman gain approaches zero (i.e., the innovation has no value in the estimation update).

Having found the solution for the Kalman gain, the minimum MSE may be calculated easily. From Equation 3.42,

$$p_N^e = s_N(1 - \beta_N^o)^2 + (\beta_N^o)^2\sigma_\epsilon^2,$$

where s_N is the variance of error in estimating x_N *before* observing y_N. Substitute Equation 3.41 into the above equation to yield

$$
\begin{aligned}
p_N^e &= s_N(1 - \beta_N^o)^2 + \beta_N^o p_N^e \\
&= (1 - \beta_N^o)s_N.
\end{aligned}
$$

So far, it has been assumed that the observation consists of the desired signal and additive noise. However, it is possible that the signal enters into the observation with a constant coefficient as in

$$y_t = \gamma x_t + \epsilon_t \tag{3.44}$$

and the signal follows an AR(1) process,

$$x_t = \phi x_{t-1} + v_t. \tag{3.45}$$

Given N observations, the recursive estimator has the following form:

$$\hat{x}_N = \alpha_N \hat{x}_{N-1} + \beta_N y_N. \tag{3.46}$$

The parameters α_N and β_N may be obtained from the minimization of the MSE again. It can be shown that the solution is given by

$$\alpha_N^o = \phi(1 - \gamma\beta_N^o) \tag{3.47}$$

and

$$\beta_N^o = \frac{\gamma\left(\phi^2 p_{N-1}^e + \sigma_v^2\right)}{\gamma^2\left(\phi^2 p_{N-1}^e + \sigma_v^2\right) + \sigma_\epsilon^2} = \frac{\gamma s_N}{\gamma^2 s_N + \sigma_\epsilon^2}, \tag{3.48}$$

where s_N is the variance of the error in predicting x_N at time $N-1$. The recursive estimator is now

$$\hat{x}_N = \phi\hat{x}_{N-1} + \beta_N^o\left(y_N - \phi\gamma\hat{x}_{N-1}\right). \tag{3.49}$$

After having the solution for the Kalman gain β_N^o, the minimum MSE may be calculated from the following equation:

$$p_N^e = (1 - \beta_N^o)s_N. \tag{3.50}$$

The general framework for scalar Kalman estimation is described in Equations 3.44 (observation), 3.48 (Kalman gain), 3.49 (estimator), and 3.50 (MSE).

3.4 PREDICTION WITH THE KALMAN FILTER

The Kalman filter may also be used to calculate an s-period ahead forecast of the signal, given all the information available at time N. The best predictor for the signal may be obtained by minimizing the mean-square *prediction* error (MSPE). Suppose again that the signal is an AR(1) process,

$$x_t = \phi x_{t-1} + v_t, \tag{3.51}$$

and the observation equation is given by

$$y_t = \gamma x_t + \epsilon_t, \tag{3.52}$$

where both ϕ and γ are assumed to be known. The recursive, one-step ahead prediction equation has the following form:

$$\hat{x}_{N+1} = a_N \hat{x}_N + k_N y_N,$$

where $\hat{x}_{N+1}$ is the one-step ahead predicted value of x conditional on the information set at time N. Before proceeding to find an optimum solution for the coefficients a_N and k_N in the preceding prediction equation, notice that the best estimate of $\hat{x}_{N+1}$ at time N without any other information is given by

$$\hat{x}_{N+1} = \phi \hat{x}_N.$$

By premultiplying Equation 3.49 with ϕ, we have

$$\phi \hat{x}_N = \phi^2 \hat{x}_{N-1} + \phi \beta_N^o \left(y_N - \phi \gamma \hat{x}_{N-1} \right). \tag{3.53}$$

Since $\phi \hat{x}_{N-1} = \hat{x}_N$, the recursive estimator becomes

$$\hat{x}_{N+1} = \phi \hat{x}_N + \phi \beta_N^o \left(y_N - \gamma \hat{x}_N \right). \tag{3.54}$$

It turns out that the solution that may be obtained by minimizing the MSPE gives the same result as in Equation 3.54. The Kalman gain in this case is given by

$$k_N = \phi \beta_N^o = \frac{\phi \gamma s_N}{\gamma^2 s_N + \sigma_\epsilon^2}. \tag{3.55}$$

Hence, the Kalman gain in estimation and the Kalman gain in prediction are related. An expression for the MSPE may be derived as follows:

$$p_{N+1}^p = E(x_{N+1} - \hat{x}_{N+1})^2.$$

Subtracting Equation 3.54 from $x_{N+1} = \phi x_N + v_{N+1}$ results in

$$x_{N+1} - \hat{x}_{N+1} = (\phi - \gamma k_N)(x_N - \hat{x}_N) - k_N \epsilon_N + v_{N+1},$$

which enables us to write

$$p^p_{N+1} = (\phi - \gamma k_N)^2 p^p_N + k^2_N \sigma^2_\epsilon + \sigma^2_v. \tag{3.56}$$

It can be shown that an alternative form for p^p_{N+1} is

$$p^p_{N+1} = (\phi - \gamma k_N)\phi p^p_N + \sigma^2_v. \tag{3.57}$$

Notice the change in notation to differentiate between the *prediction* MSE p^p_N and the *estimation* MSE p^e_N. The previous period prediction error is

$$
\begin{aligned}
p^p_N &= E\left(x_N - \phi \hat{x}_{N-1}\right)^2 \\
&= E\left[(\phi x_{N-1} + v_N - \phi \hat{x}_{N-1})e_N\right] \\
&= \phi^2 p^p_{N-1} + \sigma^2_v = s_N.
\end{aligned}
$$

Therefore, the Kalman gain in Equation 3.55 may also be viewed as

$$k_N = \phi \beta^o_N = \frac{\phi \gamma p^p_N}{\gamma^2 p^p_N + \sigma^2_\epsilon}. \tag{3.58}$$

The complete framework for the scalar Kalman filter prediction problem is given by Equations 3.52 (the observation equation), 3.54 (the prediction equation), 3.58 (the Kalman gain), and 3.57 (the MSPE). A close inspection of these equations shows that given an initial estimation error variance p^e_0, the MSPE p^p_N converges. As a result, the Kalman gain converges.

3.4.1   Convergence of Kalman Gain

Suppose that signal x_t and observation y_t are governed by

$$x_t = x_{t-1} + v_t \quad \text{and} \quad y_t = x_t + \epsilon_t,$$

where v_t and ϵ_t are serially uncorrelated random disturbances with $v_t \sim N(0, 1)$ and $\epsilon_t \sim N(0, 1)$. Assume that the initial prediction error variance is given as $p^p_1 = 5$, so that $s_1 = 5$. We may calculate the first period Kalman gain and the prediction error variance via

$$k_1 = \frac{5}{5+1} = \frac{5}{6} = 0.833, \qquad p^p_2 = \left(1 - \frac{5}{6}\right)5 + 1 = \frac{11}{6} = s_2,$$

at the second period

$$k_2 = \frac{11/6}{11/6 + 1} = \frac{11}{17} = 0.647, \qquad p^p_3 = \left(1 - \frac{11}{17}\right)\frac{11}{6} + 1 = \frac{28}{17} = s_3,$$

and at the third period

$$k_3 = \frac{28/17}{27/17 + 1} = \frac{28}{45} = 0.622, \qquad p^p_4 = \left(1 - \frac{28}{45}\right)\frac{28}{17} + 1 = \frac{73}{45} = s_4.$$

If these recursive calculations are carried out, after a few steps we notice that the Kalman gain and the prediction error variance converge to $k = 0.618$ and $p^p = 1.618$, respectively. This result is not surprising since the steady-state solution of Equation 3.57 in this particular case is given by[12]

$$p = \frac{\sigma_v^2 + \sqrt{(\sigma_v^2)^2 + 4\sigma_v^2\sigma_\epsilon^2}}{2} = \frac{1 + \sqrt{5}}{2} = 1.618,$$

so that the Kalman gain is

$$k = \frac{p}{p + \sigma_\epsilon^2} = \frac{1.618}{1.618 + 1} = 0.618.$$

Notice that the steady state Kalman gain for different values of the noise variances σ_v^2 and σ_ϵ^2 would be different, reflecting the relative importance of observations in estimating the signal.

3.4.2 Example: Adaptive Expectations

Muth (1960) utilized a signal extraction approach to show the rationale behind the formula used by Milton Friedman for permanent income (Friedman, 1956). Suppose that an economic agent observes his or her current income y_t but cannot observe permanent income x_t. Given the past and present values of the current income, the agent's problem is to make an estimate of the permanent income. Suppose that the permanent income follows a random walk:

$$x_t = x_{t-1} + v_t,$$

where $v_t \sim N(0, \sigma_v^2)$. Further suppose that the agent observes this permanent income with noise added via

$$y_t = x_t + \epsilon_t,$$

where $\epsilon_t \sim N(0, \sigma_\epsilon^2)$. Given N observations, Equation 3.54 gives us

$$\hat{x}_{N+1} = \hat{x}_N + \beta_N^o \left(y_N - \hat{x}_N\right), \tag{3.59}$$

where the Kalman gain β_N^o is less than unity. The economic agent has a "perceived permanent income" of $\hat{x}_N$. This perception is updated by looking at the difference between the actual income y_N and the perceived value $\hat{x}_N$. This is a version of a so-called adaptive expectations model, which dominated the economics literature for a considerable period of time.

It may also be shown that the Kalman filter estimation of the permanent income in this particular case is a geometrically weighted average of the past

---

[12] The solution for the steady state value of the prediction mean square error in this particular case is an example of the famous constant $\frac{1+\sqrt{5}}{2}$, known as the *golden ratio*. The golden ratio appears regularly in nature as the ratio of the length to the width.

observed incomes. Assume that the process starts in the distant past so that the Kalman gain β_t^o converges to a constant. By rearranging Equation 3.59,

$$\hat{x}_{N+1} = (1 - \beta)\hat{x}_N + \beta y_N,$$

where the estimate for the current period is

$$\hat{x}_N = (1 - \beta)\hat{x}_{N-1} + \beta y_{N-1}.$$

Substituting the last equation into the previous equation, we have

$$\begin{aligned}
\hat{x}_{N+1} &= (1 - \beta)\left[(1 - \beta)\hat{x}_{N-1} + \beta y_{N-1}\right] + \beta y_N \\
&= (1 - \beta)^2 \hat{x}_{N-1} + (1 - \beta)\beta y_{N-1} + \beta y_N.
\end{aligned}$$

By repeated substitution, the permanent income estimation may be expressed as a geometrically weighted average of the past observed incomes

$$\begin{aligned}
\hat{x}_{N+1} &= \beta y_N + (1 - \beta)\beta y_{N-1} + (1 - \beta)^2 \beta y_{N-2} + (1 - \beta)^3 \beta y_{N-3} + \cdots \\
&= \beta \sum_{i=0}^{\infty} \phi^i y_{N-i},
\end{aligned}$$

where $\phi = (1 - \beta)$ is the decay coefficient

$$\phi = (1 - \beta) = \frac{\sigma_\epsilon^2}{\bar{p} + \sigma_\epsilon^2}.$$

This implies that if the variance of the observation is high, the distant past is discounted less. On the other hand, if the observation is made without noise, the economic agent does not consider the past values of the income at all and accepts the observation as permanent income.

3.5   VECTOR KALMAN FILTER ESTIMATION

The scalar Kalman filter estimator may easily be extended to a multivariate setting. Suppose that we have n different observations at time t containing k different signals with additive noise

$$\mathbf{Y}_t = C\mathbf{X}_t + \boldsymbol{\epsilon}_t, \tag{3.60}$$

where $\mathbf{Y}_t$ is an $(n \times 1)$ observation vector, $\mathbf{X}_t$ is a $(k \times 1)$ signal vector, and C is an $(n \times k)$ coefficient matrix, which describes the relationship between the signals and observations. It is also called the *observation matrix*. The observation noise $\boldsymbol{\epsilon}_t$ is an $(n \times 1)$ vector with

$$E(\boldsymbol{\epsilon}_t) = 0, \qquad E(\boldsymbol{\epsilon}_t \boldsymbol{\epsilon}_t^T) = E \begin{bmatrix} \epsilon_1 \epsilon_1 & \epsilon_1 \epsilon_2 & \cdots & \epsilon_1 \epsilon_n \\ \epsilon_2 \epsilon_1 & \epsilon_2 \epsilon_2 & \cdots & \epsilon_2 \epsilon_n \\ \vdots & & \vdots & \\ \epsilon_n \epsilon_1 & \epsilon_n \epsilon_2 & \cdots & \epsilon_n \epsilon_n \end{bmatrix} = \mathcal{R}_t.$$

The signal vector $\mathbf{X}_t$ is expressed as a first-order vector autoregression (VAR)

$$\mathbf{X}_t = \mathcal{A}\mathbf{X}_{t-1} + \mathbf{v}_t, \tag{3.61}$$

where $\mathbf{X}_t$ is a $(k \times 1)$ signal vector and $\mathcal{A}$ is a $(k \times k)$ coefficient matrix, which describes the dynamics of the system. It is also called the *system matrix*. The system noise $\mathbf{v}_t$ is a $(k \times 1)$ vector with

$$E(\mathbf{v}_t) = 0, \qquad E(\mathbf{v}_t^T \mathbf{v}_t) = E \begin{bmatrix} v_1 v_1 & v_1 v_2 & \cdots & v_1 v_k \\ v_2 v_1 & v_2 v_2 & \cdots & v_2 v_k \\ \vdots & & & \vdots \\ v_k v_1 & v_k v_2 & \cdots & v_k v_k \end{bmatrix} = \mathcal{Q}_t.$$

This representation is known as a *state-space representation*. It is useful to write the system and the observation equations in an explicit form to show their flexibility in modeling. The first-order VAR in Equation 3.61 is given by

$$\underbrace{\begin{bmatrix} x_{1,t} \\ x_{2,t} \\ \vdots \\ x_{k,t} \end{bmatrix}}_{\mathbf{X}_t} = \underbrace{\begin{bmatrix} \theta_{1,1} & \theta_{1,2} & \cdots & \theta_{1,k} \\ \theta_{2,1} & \theta_{2,2} & \cdots & \theta_{2,k} \\ \vdots & \vdots & \vdots & \vdots \\ \theta_{k,1} & \theta_{k,2} & \cdots & \theta_{k,k} \end{bmatrix}}_{\mathcal{A}} \underbrace{\begin{bmatrix} x_{1,t-1} \\ x_{2,t-1} \\ \vdots \\ x_{k,t-1} \end{bmatrix}}_{\mathbf{X}_{t-1}} + \underbrace{\begin{bmatrix} v_{1,t} \\ v_{2,t} \\ \vdots \\ v_{k,t} \end{bmatrix}}_{\mathbf{v}_t},$$

and assuming $n < k$, the observation equation is

$$\underbrace{\begin{bmatrix} y_{1,t} \\ y_{2,t} \\ \vdots \\ y_{n,t} \end{bmatrix}}_{\mathbf{Y}_t} = \underbrace{\begin{bmatrix} \gamma_1 & 0 & \cdots & 0 & \cdots & 0 \\ 0 & \gamma_2 & \cdots & 0 & \cdots & 0 \\ \vdots & & \ddots & & \ddots & \vdots \\ 0 & 0 & \cdots & \gamma_n & \cdots & 0 \end{bmatrix}}_{\mathcal{C}} \underbrace{\begin{bmatrix} x_{1,t} \\ x_{2,t} \\ \vdots \\ x_{k,t} \end{bmatrix}}_{\mathbf{X}_t} + \underbrace{\begin{bmatrix} \epsilon_{1,t} \\ \epsilon_{2,t} \\ \vdots \\ \epsilon_{n,t} \end{bmatrix}}_{\epsilon_t}.$$

Given N observations, the problem of finding an optimum estimator and an optimum predictor is similar to the scalar case. Formally, the solution may be obtained by minimizing the mean variance-covariance matrix of the errors:

$$\mathcal{P}_N^e = E(e_N e_N^T) = E \begin{bmatrix} e_1 e_1 & e_1 e_2 & \cdots & e_1 e_k \\ e_2 e_1 & e_2 e_2 & \cdots & e_2 e_k \\ \vdots & & & \vdots \\ e_k e_1 & e_k e_2 & \cdots & e_k e_k \end{bmatrix}.$$

Instead of deriving a formal solution, the solution found earlier for the scalar case may be converted into a multivariate one. Therefore, the estimator at time N may be written directly via Equation 3.54 as

$$\widehat{\mathbf{X}}_N = \mathcal{A}\widehat{\mathbf{X}}_{N-1} + \mathcal{K}_N \left[\mathbf{Y}_N - \mathcal{C}\mathcal{A}\widehat{\mathbf{X}}_{N-1} \right], \tag{3.62}$$

where $\mathcal{K}_N$ is a $(k \times n)$ Kalman gain matrix given via Equation 3.58

$$\mathcal{K}_N = \mathcal{S}_N \mathcal{C}^T \left[\mathcal{C} \mathcal{S}_N \mathcal{C}^T + \mathcal{R}_N \right]^{-1}. \tag{3.63}$$

Here, $\mathcal{S}_N$ is the $(k \times k)$ error variance-covariance matrix,

$$\mathcal{S}_N = \mathcal{A} \mathcal{P}^e_{N-1} \mathcal{A}^T + \mathcal{Q}_N, \tag{3.64}$$

and the $(k \times k)$ variance-covariance matrix of the estimation error is given by

$$\mathcal{P}^e_N = \mathcal{S}_N - \mathcal{K}_N \mathcal{C} \mathcal{S}_N. \tag{3.65}$$

3.5.1   Time-Varying Coefficients in a Regression

The Kalman filter may be used in a time-varying coefficients regression model. Suppose that the coefficients in a k variable regression vary across time according to the following equation:

$$\boldsymbol{\alpha}_{t+1} = \mathcal{A}_t \boldsymbol{\alpha}_t + \boldsymbol{v}_t,$$

where $\boldsymbol{\alpha}_t$ is the $(k \times 1)$ coefficients vector and the $(k \times k)$ system matrix $\mathcal{A}_t$ is assumed to be known for all t.[13] The disturbance term $\boldsymbol{v}_t$ is a $(k \times 1)$ serially uncorrelated vector with $\boldsymbol{v}_t \sim N(0, \mathcal{Q}_t)$. The regression equation is

$$\mathbf{Y}_t = \mathcal{X}_t \boldsymbol{\alpha}_t + \boldsymbol{\epsilon}_t,$$

where $\mathbf{Y}_t$ is an $(n \times 1)$ observation vector, $\mathcal{X}_t$ is an $(n \times k)$ matrix of independent variables in the regression equation, and the disturbance term $\boldsymbol{\epsilon}_t$ is an $(n \times 1)$ serially uncorrelated vector with $\boldsymbol{\epsilon}_t \sim N(0, \mathcal{R}_t)$. Assume that $\mathcal{Q}_t$, $\mathcal{R}_t$, and an initial estimate $\boldsymbol{\alpha}_0$ with the initial estimation error variance-covariance matrix $\mathcal{P}^e_0$ are given. Suppose we have $N - 1$ observations. According to the estimation and prediction equations, the Kalman filter takes the following form. At time $N - 1$, the best estimate of $\boldsymbol{\alpha}_N$ is given by

$$\hat{\boldsymbol{\alpha}}_N = \mathcal{A}_{N-1} \hat{\boldsymbol{\alpha}}_{N-1}.$$

After the observations $\mathbf{Y}_N$ and $\mathcal{X}_N$ arrive, the estimate of $\boldsymbol{\alpha}_N$ is updated as follows:

$$\hat{\boldsymbol{\alpha}}_N = \mathcal{A}_{N-1} \hat{\boldsymbol{\alpha}}_{N-1} + \mathcal{K}_N (\mathbf{Y}_N - \mathcal{X}_N \mathcal{A}_{N-1} \hat{\boldsymbol{\alpha}}_{N-1}).$$

The $(k \times n)$ Kalman gain matrix $\mathcal{K}_N$ is

$$\mathcal{K}_N = \mathcal{S}_N \mathcal{X}_N^T [\mathcal{X}_N \mathcal{S}_N \mathcal{X}'_N + \mathcal{R}_N]^{-1},$$

---

[13] In practice, this matrix may not be known and it must be estimated. See Harvey (1989), Kim and Nelson (1999), and Durbin and Koopman (2001) for state-space modeling and estimation.

where the $(k \times k)$ previous period prediction error variance-covariance matrix $\mathcal{S}_N$ is given by

$$\mathcal{S}_N = \mathcal{A}_{N-1} \mathcal{P}^e_{N-1} \mathcal{A}^T_{N-1} + \mathcal{Q}_{N-1}.$$

The $(k \times k)$ current period estimation error variance-covariance matrix is

$$\mathcal{P}^e_N = \mathcal{P}^e_{N-1} - \mathcal{K}_N \mathcal{X}_N \mathcal{P}^e_{N-1}.$$

The model as stated is very flexible. For example, if the time variation in coefficients is not allowed, we set $\mathcal{A}_t = I$ (where I is an identity matrix) and $\mathcal{Q}_t = 0$ and this case corresponds to the ordinary least squares (OLS) update of regression coefficients. The system matrix $\mathcal{A}_t$ and the coefficient disturbance covariance matrix may be specified according to some statistical model. A well-known example for the time-varying coefficients is the *random walk* model:

$$\boldsymbol{\alpha}_{t+1} = \mathcal{A}_t \boldsymbol{\alpha}_t + \boldsymbol{v}_t, \qquad \mathcal{A}_t = I.$$

3.5.2 An Autoregressive Model

Given the following observation,

$$y_t = \gamma x_t + \epsilon_t,$$

suppose that the signal follows an AR(2) process:

$$x_t = \phi_1 x_{t-1} + \phi_2 x_{t-2} + v_t.$$

The problem may be formulated in state-space form as follows:

$$\mathbf{X}_t = \begin{bmatrix} x_t \\ x_{t-1} \end{bmatrix}, \qquad \mathbf{X}_{t-1} = \begin{bmatrix} x_{t-1} \\ x_{t-2} \end{bmatrix},$$

$$\mathcal{A} = \begin{bmatrix} \phi_1 & \phi_2 \\ 1 & 0 \end{bmatrix}, \qquad \boldsymbol{v}_t = \begin{bmatrix} v_t \\ 0 \end{bmatrix},$$

and for the observation equation

$$\mathcal{C} = \begin{bmatrix} \gamma & 0 \end{bmatrix} \qquad \text{and} \qquad \epsilon_t = \begin{bmatrix} \epsilon_t \end{bmatrix}.$$

Assuming a constant variance and no serial correlation and cross-correlation among disturbance terms, the variance-covariance matrices have the simple form:

$$\mathcal{Q}_N = \sigma^2_v, \qquad \mathcal{R}_N = \sigma^2_\epsilon.$$

Given this state-space representation, the Kalman filter can be constructed via Equations 3.62 through 3.65.

3.5.3   A Simple Vector Autoregression

Consider the following simple vector autoregression (VAR) model:

$$x_{1,t} = \alpha_{(1,1)}x_{1,t-1} + \alpha_{(1,2)}x_{2,t-1} + v_{1,t}$$
$$x_{2,t} = \alpha_{(2,1)}x_{1,t-1} + \alpha_{(2,2)}x_{2,t-1} + v_{2,t}.$$

The system may be converted into state-space form for the Kalman filter as follows

$$\mathbf{X}_N = \begin{bmatrix} x_{1,t} \\ x_{2,t} \end{bmatrix}, \qquad \mathbf{X}_{N-1} = \begin{bmatrix} x_{1,t-1} \\ x_{2,t-1} \end{bmatrix},$$

$$\mathcal{A} = \begin{bmatrix} \alpha_{(1,1)} & \alpha_{(1,2)} \\ \alpha_{(2,1)} & \alpha_{(2,2)} \end{bmatrix}, \qquad \mathbf{v}_N = \begin{bmatrix} v_{1,t} \\ v_{2,t} \end{bmatrix},$$

and for the observation equation

$$\mathcal{C} = \begin{bmatrix} 1 & 0 \\ 0 & 1 \end{bmatrix}, \qquad \epsilon_N = \begin{bmatrix} 0 \\ 0 \end{bmatrix}.$$

Assuming a constant variance and no cross-correlation between disturbance terms, the variance-covariance matrices are given by

$$\mathcal{Q}_N = \begin{bmatrix} \sigma_{v_1}^2 & 0 \\ 0 & \sigma_{v_2}^2 \end{bmatrix} \quad \text{and} \quad \mathcal{R}_N = 0.$$

3.5.4   Vector Kalman Filter Prediction

The optimum predictor in the multivariate case may be obtained by minimizing the MSPE variance-covariance matrix. However, we will write the solution by extending the scalar case into a multivariate setting as we did previously. The predictor at time $t = N$ may be written directly via

$$\widehat{\mathbf{X}}_{N+1} = \mathcal{A}\widehat{\mathbf{X}}_N + \mathcal{K}_N \left[\mathbf{Y}_N - \mathcal{C}\widehat{\mathbf{X}}_N \right], \tag{3.66}$$

where $\mathbf{Y}_N$ is the $(n \times 1)$ vector of observations, $\widehat{\mathbf{X}}_{N+1}$ is the $(k \times 1)$ vector of predicted signal, $\mathcal{A}$ is the $(k \times k)$ system matrix, $\mathcal{C}$ is the $(n \times k)$ observation matrix, and $\mathcal{K}_N$ is the $(k \times n)$ Kalman gain matrix

$$\mathcal{K}_N = \mathcal{A}\mathcal{P}_N^p \mathcal{C}^T \left[\mathcal{C}\mathcal{P}_N^p \mathcal{C}^T + \mathcal{R}_N \right]^{-1}. \tag{3.67}$$

Here $\mathcal{P}_N^p$ is the $(k \times k)$ current period prediction error variance-covariance matrix, and the prediction error variance-covariance matrix for the next period is given by

$$\mathcal{P}_{N+1}^p = [\mathcal{A} - \mathcal{K}_N\mathcal{C}]\mathcal{P}_N^p \mathcal{A}^T + \mathcal{Q}_N. \tag{3.68}$$

To this point the signal has been modeled as an autoregressive process. However, it may have additional components such as deterministic seasonalities. The Kalman filter may easily be modified, since the existence of additional terms only changes the estimation and prediction equations. The Kalman gain or the prediction-estimation variance-covariance matrices are not affected at all. Suppose the system equation is given by

$$\mathbf{X}_t = \mathcal{A}\mathbf{X}_{t-1} + \mathcal{B}\mathbf{U}_t + \boldsymbol{v}_t,$$

where $\mathbf{X}_t$ is a $(k \times 1)$ signal vector, $\mathcal{A}$ and $\mathcal{B}$ are $(k \times k)$ coefficient matrices. $\mathbf{U}_t$ is a $(k \times 1)$ vector and it is known as a *control variable* in the control theory literature.[14] The $(k \times 1)$ disturbance term $\boldsymbol{v}_t$ is serially uncorrelated with $\boldsymbol{v}_t \sim N(0, \mathcal{Q}_t)$. The observation vector is

$$\mathbf{Y}_t = \mathcal{C}\mathbf{X}_t + \boldsymbol{\epsilon}_t,$$

where $\mathbf{Y}_t$ is the $(n \times 1)$ observation vector, $\mathbf{X}_t$ is the $(k \times 1)$ signal vector, and $\mathcal{C}$ is an $(n \times k)$ observation matrix. The observation noise $\boldsymbol{\epsilon}_t$ is an $(n \times 1)$ vector with $\boldsymbol{\epsilon}_t \sim N(0, \mathcal{R}_t)$. The estimation equation takes the following form:

$$\widehat{\mathbf{X}}_N = \mathcal{A}\widehat{\mathbf{X}}_{N-1} + \mathcal{B}\mathbf{U}_N + \mathcal{K}_N\left[\mathbf{Y}_N - \mathcal{C}\mathcal{A}\widehat{\mathbf{X}}_{N-1} - \mathcal{C}\mathcal{B}\mathbf{U}_N\right]. \qquad (3.69)$$

The $(k \times n)$ Kalman gain matrix is

$$\mathcal{K}_N = \mathcal{S}_N\mathcal{C}^T\left[\mathcal{C}\mathcal{S}_N\mathcal{C}^T - \mathcal{R}_N\right]^{-1}, \qquad (3.70)$$

where $\mathcal{S}_N$ is the $(k \times k)$ current period prediction error variance-covariance matrix. Finally, the estimation error variance-covariance matrix is given by

$$\mathcal{P}_N^e = \mathcal{S}_N - \mathcal{K}_N\mathcal{C}\mathcal{S}_N. \qquad (3.71)$$

3.5.5 Summary: The Kalman Filter

Kalman filtering is a *prediction-correction* procedure. We start with a prediction made earlier, update this prediction with the new information to obtain an estimate for the current period, and predict the one-step-ahead signal. Once the new observation in the next period arrives, the same cycle is repeated.

- At time N, one has a previous estimate of the signal vector $\widehat{\mathbf{X}}_{N-1}$. This previous estimate is used to get a *prediction* of the estimate $\widehat{\mathbf{X}}_N$. This is accomplished by premultiplying it with the system matrix $\mathcal{A}$. The result $\mathcal{A}\widehat{\mathbf{X}}_{N-1}$ is the best estimate of $\mathbf{X}_N$ *before* the observation arrives at time N. This is the *prediction* step.
- The prediction obtained in the first step is premultiplied by the observation matrix $\mathcal{C}$ to find an estimate of the observation $\mathbf{Y}_N$. There are

---

[14] The control vector has a deterministic structure in this framework.

two quantities now: an estimate of the signal $\mathcal{A}\widehat{\mathbf{X}}_{N-1}$ and an estimate of the observation $\mathcal{C}\mathcal{A}\widehat{\mathbf{X}}_{N-1}$. When the actual observation arrives at time $t = N$, the difference between the actual observation $\mathbf{Y}_N$ and its estimate is called an *innovation*. Note that the new information is *not* the observation itself but the difference between the observation and its predicted value. This is the step for *innovation accounting*.

- The innovation in step 2 is weighted by the Kalman gain and added to the predicted estimate $\mathcal{A}\widehat{\mathbf{X}}_{N-1}$ to obtain an updated estimate of $\widehat{\mathbf{X}}_N$. This is the *updating* step.

- In order to obtain a one-step ahead forecast of $\mathbf{X}_t$, the current estimate is premultiplied with the system matrix $\mathcal{A}$. The result is the best estimate of $\mathbf{X}_{N+1}$ given all the information available at time N. The estimate $\widehat{\mathbf{X}}_N$, system and observation coefficient matrices $\mathcal{A}, \mathcal{B}, \mathcal{C}$, and the variance-covariance matrices are stored. When the new observation arrives at time $N + 1$, the same cycle is repeated.

3.6   APPLICATIONS

Four examples of the Kalman filter application are presented here. The first two examples show a step-by-step implementation of the filter. The third example shows how to forecast with a Bayesian Vector Autoregression (BVAR) utilizing the Kalman filter. The fourth example is about the time-varying *beta* estimation in stock markets.

3.6.1   Scalar Kalman Filter Simulation

Suppose that the signal is an AR(1) process,

$$x_t = 1 + 0.80x_{t-1} + v_t, \tag{3.72}$$

where $v_t \sim N(0, 1)$ is a serially uncorrelated disturbance term. The observation equation is given by

$$y_t = 0.90x_t + \epsilon_t, \tag{3.73}$$

where $\epsilon_t \sim N(0, 1)$ is also a serially uncorrelated disturbance term. Furthermore, assume that the observation noise and signal noise are uncorrelated (i.e., $E(\epsilon_{t-i}v_{t-j}) = 0$ for all i and j). Given an initial estimate of the signal and an initial prediction variance, we may simulate the system and calculate the filter output. First note that the Kalman gain and the prediction and estimation variances converge. From Section 2.4.2, the Kalman gain is

$$
\begin{aligned}
k_N &= \frac{\gamma s_N}{\gamma^2 s_N + \sigma_\epsilon^2} \\
&= \frac{(0.90)s_N}{(0.90)^2 s_N + 1},
\end{aligned}
$$

where s_N is the variance of the error in predicting x_N at time $N - 1$, and is given by

$$
\begin{aligned}
s_N &= \phi^2 p_{N-1}^e + \sigma_v^2 \\
&= (0.80)^2 p_{N-1}^e + 1.
\end{aligned}
$$

The estimation variance p_N^e and the prediction variance p_{N+1}^p are

$$
\begin{aligned}
p_N^e &= (1 - \gamma k_N)s_N = (1 - 0.90k_N)s_N, \\
p_{N+1}^p &= p_N^e \phi^2 + \sigma_v^2 = (1 - 0.90k_N)s_N (0.80)^2 + 1.
\end{aligned}
$$

The initial prediction variance is the same as the signal variance so that $p_1^p = 1$. Hence, $s_1 = 1$ and at time $t = 1$, we have

$$
\begin{aligned}
k_1 &= \frac{(0.90)(1)}{(0.90)^2(1)+1} & = 0.497 \\
p_1^e &= [1 - (0.90)(0.497)] \, (1) & = 0.553 \\
p_2^p &= (0.553)(0.80)^2 + 1 & = 1.354.
\end{aligned}
$$

At time $t = 2$, we have

$$
\begin{aligned}
k_2 &= \frac{(0.90)(1.354)}{(0.90)^2(1.354)+1} & = 0.581 \\
p_2^e &= [1 - (0.90)(0.581)] \, (1.354) & = 0.646 \\
p_3^p &= (0.646)(0.80)^2 + 1 & = 1.413.
\end{aligned}
$$

At time $t = 3$, we have

$$
\begin{aligned}
k_3 &= \frac{(0.90)(1.413)}{(0.90)^2(1.413)+1} & = 0.593 \\
p_3^e &= [1 - (0.90)(0.593)] \, (1.413) & = 0.659 \\
p_4^p &= (0.659)(0.80)^2 + 1 & = 1.422.
\end{aligned}
$$

After a few steps, the Kalman gain, prediction variance and estimation variance converge to the following values:

$$
\bar{k} = 0.595, \qquad \bar{p}^p = 1.423 \quad \text{and} \quad \bar{p}^e = 0.661.
$$

We have simulated a set of signals and observations according to Equations 3.72 and 3.73. The estimate of the signal is obtained as follows. Suppose that the initial guess for the signal is zero. Therefore, the predicted value of the observation is zero as well. At time $t = 1$ this initial guess is updated after the observation y_1 arrives as $y_1 = -0.703$ so that

$$
\begin{aligned}
\hat{x}_1^e &= 0 + k_1(y_1 - 0) \\
&= (0.497)(-0.703 - 0) = -0.349.
\end{aligned}
$$

Time	Signal x	Observation y	Estimated $\hat{x}^e$	Predicted $\hat{x}^p$
1	0	-0.703	-0.349	0
2	2.165	2.305	1.683	0.721
3	3.359	3.676	3.274	2.346
4	3.762	3.602	3.824	3.619
5	4.361	3.661	4.064	4.059
.	.	.	.	.
.	.	.	.	.
.	.	.	.	.
.	.	.	.	.

TABLE 3.1   Scalar Kalman filter simulation. The signal and the observation are generated according to Equation 3.72 and 3.73.

The one-step-ahead predicted value of the signal is

$$\begin{aligned}\hat{x}_2^p &= 1 + (0.80)(\hat{x}_1^e) \\ &= 1 + (0.80)(-0.349) = 0.721,\end{aligned}$$

and the one-step-ahead predicted value of the observation is

$$\begin{aligned}\hat{y}_2 &= (0.90)\hat{x}_2^p \\ &= (0.90)(0.721) = 0.649.\end{aligned}$$

At time $t = 2$, the initial guess about the signal is the prediction made at time $t = 1$. This initial guess is updated after the observation y_2 arrives as $y_2 = 2.305$, therefore

$$\begin{aligned}\hat{x}_2^e &= \hat{x}_2^p + k_2(y_2 - \hat{y}_2) \\ &= 0.721 + (0.581)(2.305 - 0.649) = 1.683\end{aligned}$$

and the one-step-ahead prediction of the signal and the observation are obtained via

$$\begin{aligned}\hat{x}_3^p &= 1 + (0.80)\hat{x}_2^e \\ &= 1 + (0.80)(1.683) = 2.346, \\ \hat{y}_3 &= (0.90)\hat{x}_3^p \\ &= (0.90)(2.346) = 2.111.\end{aligned}$$

After the Kalman gain converges, the estimation and prediction equations at time $t = N$ are

$$\hat{x}_N^e = \hat{x}_N^p + 0.595(y_N - \hat{y}_N) \quad \text{and} \quad \hat{x}_{N+1}^p = 1 + 0.80\hat{x}_N^e.$$

Table 3.1 summarizes this procedure. Figure 3.3 plots the true values of the simulated signal and corresponding estimates.

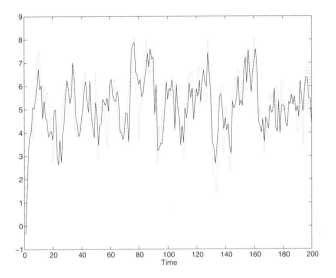

FIGURE 3.3 The signal x_t is generated according to Equation 3.72 (dotted line) and the Kalman filter estimate of it, $\hat{x}_t$, based on observations from Equation 3.73 (solid line).

3.6.2 Vector Kalman Filter Simulation

Suppose that the signal is given by the following equation:

$$x_t = 1 + 0.60x_{t-1} - 0.35x_{t-2} + \sin(t/4) + v_t, \tag{3.74}$$

where $v_t \sim N(0, 1)$ is a serially uncorrelated random disturbance term, and the observation equation is

$$y_t = 0.90x_t + \epsilon_t, \tag{3.75}$$

where $\epsilon_t \sim N(0, 1)$ is also a serially uncorrelated disturbance term. Suppose there is no cross-correlation between disturbance terms, then the system may be put into a state-space form as follows

$$\mathbf{X}_t = \begin{bmatrix} x_t \\ x_{t-1} \end{bmatrix}, \quad \mathbf{X}_{t-1} = \begin{bmatrix} x_{t-1} \\ x_{t-2} \end{bmatrix}, \quad \mathbf{U}_t = \begin{bmatrix} 1 + \sin(t/4) \\ 0 \end{bmatrix},$$

$$\mathcal{A} = \begin{bmatrix} 0.60 & -0.35 \\ 1 & 0 \end{bmatrix}, \quad \mathcal{B} = \begin{bmatrix} 1 & 0 \\ 0 & 0 \end{bmatrix}, \quad \boldsymbol{v}_t = \begin{bmatrix} v_t \\ 0 \end{bmatrix},$$

and for the observation

$$\mathcal{C} = \begin{bmatrix} 0.90 & 0 \end{bmatrix}.$$

Note that the disturbance variances are known (i.e., $\mathcal{Q} = \begin{bmatrix} 1 & 0 \end{bmatrix}^T$ and $\mathcal{R} = 1$). Given an initial estimate of the signal $\widehat{\mathbf{X}}_1$, an initial prediction error variance $\mathcal{P}_1^p$ and a $\mathbf{U}_t$ sequence, the signal and the observation may be simulated. Figure 3.4 presents such a simulation for $t = 1, 2 \ldots 200$. As noted earlier, the scalar Kalman filter estimator and predictor may be extended to the multivariate case. In this example, the Kalman filter is given by

$$\mathcal{K}_t = \mathcal{P}_{t-1}^e \mathcal{C}^T [\mathcal{C}\mathcal{P}_{t-1}^e \mathcal{C}^T + \mathcal{R}]^{-1},$$

which enables us to obtain the estimations recursively from the following formula:

$$\widehat{\mathbf{X}}_t = \mathcal{A}\widehat{\mathbf{X}}_{t-1} + \mathcal{B}\mathbf{U}_t + \mathcal{K}_t \left[\mathbf{Y}_t - \mathcal{C}\mathcal{A}\widehat{\mathbf{X}}_{t-1} - \mathcal{C}\mathcal{B}\mathbf{U}_t \right].$$

The filter output $\widehat{\mathbf{Y}}_t$, estimation variance $\mathcal{P}_t^e$, and prediction variance $\mathcal{P}_{t+1}^p$ are given by

$$
\begin{aligned}
\widehat{\mathbf{Y}}_t &= \mathcal{C}\widehat{\mathbf{X}}_{t-1}, \\
\mathcal{P}_t^e &= \mathcal{P}_{t-1}^e - \mathcal{K}_t \mathcal{C}\mathcal{P}_{t-1}^e, \\
\mathcal{P}_{t+1}^p &= \mathcal{A}\mathcal{P}_t^e \mathcal{A}^T + \mathcal{Q}.
\end{aligned}
$$

Figure 3.5 plots the observations generated according to Equations 3.74, 3.75, and the Kalman filter output.

3.6.3 Bayesian Vector Autoregression

Large-scale simultaneous-equation macroeconometric models, also known as structural models, have long been used for both forecasting and policy-analysis purposes. The way these models are constructed and the use of their outcomes have been criticized by several leading authors. See Lucas and Sargent (1979) and Sims (1980) among others.

Another approach to multivariate time series modeling in economics does not rely on any economic theory and hence is sometimes called *atheoretical modeling* (Cooley and LeRoy, 1985). Granger and Newbold (1989, Ch. 9) reported that this approach has a good record of forecast performance compared to other well-known large-scale models such as Wharton-EFU econometric model. In atheoretical models such as the Box-Jenkins modeling approach (ARIMA), the researcher usually lets the data, rather than a particular economic theory, determine the dynamic structure of the system (Lutkepohl, 1993). Although it is possible to specify a multivariate ARIMA process, the difficulties in the identification and estimation of the system led researchers to estimate VAR models, pioneered by Sims (1980) in macroeconometrics. The main weakness of the traditional VAR modeling is that the number of parameters increases at a rate np where n is the number of variables and p is the number of autoregressive parameters (lags).

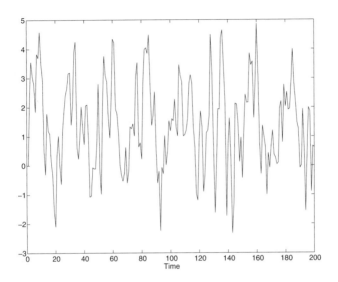

FIGURE 3.4   Simulated AR(2) process with a periodic component in Equation 3.74.

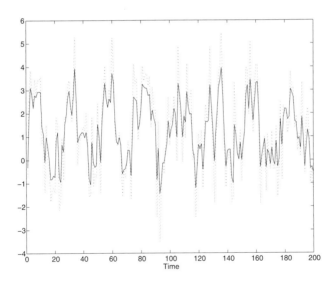

FIGURE 3.5   Observation (dotted line) and the Kalman filter output (straight line) of a simulated AR(2) process with a periodic component.

A Bayesian approach to the overparametrization problem is incorporated into the VAR modeling by Litterman (1979) and later developed by Doan *et al.* (1984). Instead of reducing the number of coefficients in the VAR system by restricting some of them to zero as in traditional VAR modeling, the Bayesian vector autoregression (BVAR) approach assumes that some of the variables have less influence than others. This is achieved by defining a normal prior distribution for the coefficients. The prior distribution, being a probabilistic statement, explicitly shows the modeler's belief about the coefficients and the possible values that they may take. Specification also lets the data override the prior guess. Therefore, the BVAR approach is to guess the influence of each variable, and then revise this guess at each point in time when new information arrives in the form of a new observation. The BVAR approach to modeling and forecasting economic time series has been improved by several researchers since its introduction by Litterman (1979). The methods in Doan *et al.* (1984), LeSage and Magura (1991), Sims (1992), Kadiyala and Karlsson (1993, 1997), and Sims and Zha (1998) show different ways of determining the priors. Litterman (1986), Robertson and Tallman (1999), and Selçuk (1992) demonstrate that the BVAR approach has good forecasting performance.

Let an n variable data vector $\mathbf{x}_t$ be represented as an unrestricted, time-varying, pth order VAR with the following observation equation:

$$\mathbf{x}_t = \mathcal{A}_t(L)\mathbf{x}_{t-1} + \mathcal{C} + \boldsymbol{\epsilon}_t, \tag{3.76}$$

where $\mathcal{A}_t(L)$ is an $(n \times np)$ matrix of polynomials of order p in the lag operator L, and $\mathcal{C}$ stands for the deterministic part. The error process $\boldsymbol{\epsilon}_t$ is a zero mean $(n \times 1)$ vector of disturbances independent of $\mathbf{x}_s$, $s < t$,

$$\boldsymbol{\epsilon}_t \sim N(0, \Gamma_t). \tag{3.77}$$

Let $\boldsymbol{\alpha}_t^i$ be the vector of coefficients (including constants) for the ith equation of this n variable VAR. Then, the ith equation $x_{i,t}$ may be written as[15]

$$x_{i,t} = \alpha_0^i + \sum_{j=1}^{n} \sum_{k=1}^{p} \alpha_{t,j,k}^i x_{j,t-k} + \epsilon_{i,t}. \tag{3.78}$$

If we denote the right-hand side variables and constant term in Equation 3.78 as

$$\mathbf{Z}_t = \begin{bmatrix} 1 & x_{1,t-1} & \cdots & x_{1,t-k} & \cdots & x_{j,t-1} & \cdots & x_{j,t-k} \end{bmatrix}, \tag{3.79}$$

Equation 3.78 may be written as

$$x_{i,t} = \mathbf{Z}_t \boldsymbol{\alpha}_t^i + \epsilon_{i,t}. \tag{3.80}$$

---

[15] The deterministic part is specified as one constant in each equation. Some other deterministic specifications, such as seasonalities, may be implemented in the same framework.

For example, when $n = 2$ and $p = 2$, the system is

$$
\begin{aligned}
x_{1,t} &= \alpha_0^{(1)} + \alpha_{t,1,1}^{(1)} x_{1,t-1} + \alpha_{t,1,2}^{(1)} x_{1,t-2} \\
&\quad + \alpha_{t,2,1}^{(1)} x_{2,t-1} + \alpha_{t,2,2}^{(1)} x_{2,t-2} + \epsilon_{1,t}, \\
x_{2,t} &= \alpha_0^{(2)} + \alpha_{t,1,1}^{(2)} x_{1,t-1} + \alpha_{t,1,2}^{(2)} x_{1,t-2} \\
&\quad + \alpha_{t,2,1}^{(2)} x_{2,t-1} + \alpha_{t,2,2}^{(2)} x_{2,t-2} + \epsilon_{2,t}
\end{aligned}
\tag{3.81}
$$

or

$$
x_{i,t} = \mathbf{Z}_t \boldsymbol{\alpha}_t^i + \epsilon_{i,t}, \quad i = 1, 2, \tag{3.82}
$$

where

$$
\mathbf{Z}_t = \begin{bmatrix} 1 & x_{1,t-1} & x_{1,t-2} & x_{2,t-1} & x_{2,t-2} \end{bmatrix},
$$

and

$$
\boldsymbol{\alpha}_t^i = \begin{bmatrix} \alpha_0^{(i)} & \alpha_{t,1,1}^{(i)} & \alpha_{t,1,2}^{(i)} & \alpha_{t,2,1}^{(i)} & \alpha_{t,2,2}^{(i)} \end{bmatrix}^T.
$$

Suppose that a normal distribution is assumed for the coefficient vector $\boldsymbol{\alpha}_t$ at time t (notice that the superscript is dropped), then the posterior of $\boldsymbol{\alpha}_t$ conditional on the information at time t is

$$
\boldsymbol{\alpha}_t \sim \mathrm{N}\left(\hat{\boldsymbol{\alpha}}_t, \Sigma_t\right). \tag{3.83}
$$

It is assumed that at time $t = 0$,

$$
\boldsymbol{\alpha}_0 \sim \mathrm{N}\left(\bar{\boldsymbol{\alpha}}, \Sigma_0\right). \tag{3.84}
$$

The initial prior vector $\boldsymbol{\alpha}_0$ has the mean $\bar{\boldsymbol{\alpha}}$ and the covariance matrix Σ_0. The covariance matrix Σ_0 is determined as a function of the prior parameter set π, which reflects our prior belief about the dynamics of the system. Any change in the prior parameter set π resulting in smaller (larger) variances of the coefficients is called *tightening (loosening)* the system. The role of the prior parameter set will be explained in detail.

In practice, the best prior guess for the coefficient values comes from the random walk hypothesis. It is well-known that the random walk hypothesis cannot be rejected for most macroeconomic variables. Therefore, the prior mean is assigned to be one for coefficients of the first lagged value of the dependent variables while the mean of the prior distribution for all other coefficients is assumed to be zero in most practical applications. For the deterministic part of each equation (intercepts), noninformative priors can be assumed. In this case, if the variables in the system are in logarithmic form, the constant part in each equation represents the drift (i.e., the percentage increase per period in the variable). If we set the variance for the constant to a very large number, making the prior very diffuse, the data determines the drift. Notice that if the prior is tightened around its mean, the model becomes a random walk with drift. In our previous example, the initial prior vector for each equation is

$$\bar{\alpha} = [\ \bar{\alpha}_0^{(i)} \quad \bar{\alpha}_{t,1,1}^{(i)} \quad \bar{\alpha}_{t,1,2}^{(i)} \quad \bar{\alpha}_{t,2,1}^{(i)} \quad \bar{\alpha}_{t,2,2}^{(i)}]^T$$
$$= [\ 0 \quad 1 \quad 0 \quad 0 \quad 0]^T. \tag{3.85}$$

In general, the number of coefficients including the constant term in each equation is $(np+1)$, where n and p are the number of variables and the number of lags, respectively. Therefore, it would be unrealistic to determine a prior variance for each coefficient in the system. Doan *et al.* (1984) proposes the following procedure, which determines the full set of prior variances once some key assumptions are made.

For any equation in the system, coefficients may be classified as

- coefficients of deterministic part (intercept),
- coefficients of own lags, and
- coefficients of cross lags.

For the intercept in each equation, assume that the variance is given by

$$\sigma_{i,0,0}^2 = \pi_3 \pi_4 f_{i,0}. \tag{3.86}$$

Define the variance for the coefficients of the lagged values of the dependent variable in equation $i = 1, 2, \ldots, n$, as

$$\sigma_{i,i,k}^2 = \frac{\pi_4 \pi_5 f_{ii}}{k \pi_6}, \quad k = 1, 2, \ldots, p. \tag{3.87}$$

For the lags of other variables in equation i, the variance is assumed to be

$$\sigma_{i,j,k}^2 = \frac{\pi_4 \pi_7 f_{ij}}{k \pi_6}, \quad k = 1, 2, \ldots, p. \tag{3.88}$$

For example, in a two-variable VAR system of $p = 2$ mentioned earlier, we have $\sigma_{i,0,0}^2$ for the intercepts and $\sigma_{i,1,1}^2, \sigma_{i,1,2}^2, \sigma_{i,2,1}^2, \sigma_{i,2,2}^2$ for the other coefficients in equation i. Therefore, the prior covariance matrix for equation i is

$$\Sigma_{i,0} = \begin{bmatrix} \sigma_{i,0,0}^2 & 0 & 0 & 0 & 0 \\ 0 & \sigma_{i,1,1}^2 & 0 & 0 & 0 \\ 0 & 0 & \sigma_{i,1,2}^2 & 0 & 0 \\ 0 & 0 & 0 & \sigma_{i,2,1}^2 & 0 \\ 0 & 0 & 0 & 0 & \sigma_{i,2,2}^2 \end{bmatrix}. \tag{3.89}$$

Regardless of the lag structure in the system, setting the variances in Equation 3.88 to a small value through the parameter π_7 implies putting high probability on the existence of small coefficients of the cross lags in all equations.

However, we may have some prior knowledge that some of the variables have relatively more influence in an equation. These prior beliefs can be incorporated into the system through the weight set f_{ij}, which shows the relative weight of variable j in equation i. Similarly, $f_{i,0}$ and $f_{i,i}$ denote the prior belief about the relative importance of the constant and the lagged values of dependent variable in each equation.

The time variation in the coefficient vector is modeled as[16]

$$\alpha_t = \pi_1 \alpha_{t-1} + (1 - \pi_1)\bar{\alpha} + \nu_t, \tag{3.90}$$

where α_t is the $(np \times 1)$ vector of coefficients. The disturbance term ν_t is an $(np \times 1)$ vector and it is normally distributed with zero mean and a covariance matrix proportional to the prior covariance matrix Σ_0,

$$\nu_t \sim N(0, \pi_2 \Sigma_0). \tag{3.91}$$

If π_1 is set to 1, the time variation is modeled as a random walk. If π_2 is set to 0, no time variation is allowed in coefficients.

The parameter set π can be summarized as follows:

- π_1: determines the autoregression structure of the coefficient vector
- π_2: determines the degree of time variation in the coefficient vector
- π_3: relative tightness on constant term
- π_4: overall tightness
- π_5: relative tightness on the lagged values of dependent variable
- π_6: relative tightness on the lag decay
- π_7: relative tightness on cross lags

After these specifications, given an initial covariance matrix $\Sigma_{i,0}$ and the variance of observation equation $\sigma_{\epsilon_i}^2$, the Kalman filter may be applied recursively to obtain an estimate of the coefficients.

From Equation 3.80, the observation equation is

$$x_{i,t} = Z_t \alpha_t^i + \epsilon_{i,t}, \tag{3.92}$$

where $x_{i,t}$ is the observation, $\epsilon_{i,t}$ is the disturbance term, Z_t is the $(1 \times np)$ vector of independent variables and α_t^i is the $(np \times 1)$ vector of coefficients. The estimation equation for the coefficient vector of equation i at time $t = N$ is

$$\hat{\alpha}_N^i = \hat{\alpha}_{N-1}^i + K_{i,N}\left(x_{i,N} - Z_N \hat{\alpha}_{N-1}^i\right). \tag{3.93}$$

The $(np \times 1)$ Kalman gain vector is

$$K_{i,N} = S_{i,N} Z_N^T \left[Z_N S_{i,N} Z_N^T + \sigma_{\epsilon_i}^2\right]^{-1}. \tag{3.94}$$

---

[16] We ignore the deterministic part of each equation.

The $(np \times np)$ previous period variance-covariance matrix $\mathcal{S}_N$ is given by

$$\mathcal{S}_{i,N} = \Sigma_{i,N-1} + \pi_2 \Sigma_{i,0}. \tag{3.95}$$

The current period estimation error variance-covariance matrix is

$$\Sigma_{i,N} = \Sigma_{i,N-1} - \mathcal{K}_{i,N} \mathbf{Z}_N \Sigma_{i,N-1}. \tag{3.96}$$

In most practical applications, it is usually assumed that the coefficients follow a random walk ($\pi_1 = 1$). The time variation is also assumed to be small (e.g., $\pi_2 = 0.00001$), especially in forecasting models, since a large time variation causes large out-of-sample forecast errors. The relative tightness on constant is set to a large number (e.g., $\pi_3 = 10000$) so that the data determine the drift. Other parameters are determined depending on the model in hand. An OLS estimate of the error variance in the observation equation may be substituted for the observation equation variance.

3.6.4   Time-Varying Beta Estimation

In this section, a simple example of time varying systematic risk (beta of the capital-asset pricing model, CAPM) estimation with the Kalman filter is presented. We will start with a derivation of the CAPM of Sharpe (1964) and Lintner (1965) from microeconomic foundations.[17]

Consider the maximization problem of a consumer with a horizon of T periods,

$$\max E_0 \left[\sum_{t=0}^{T-1} \frac{1}{(1+\theta)^t} U(c_t) \right], \tag{3.97}$$

where E_0 denotes expectation conditional on information at time 0, θ is the subjective rate of time preference, $U(\cdot)$ is the utility function and c_t is consumption. According to Equation 3.97, the consumer maximizes the present discounted value of expected utility. At this point, we do not need to introduce a budget constraint. Suppose that the consumer can choose to allocate his wealth among $n-1$ risky assets with a rate of return r_{it} and a riskless asset with a rate of return r_{0t}. This assumption results in n first-order conditions (Blanchard and Fischer, 1989, Chap. 6)

$$U'(c_t) = \frac{E_t \left[U'(c_{t+1})(1 + r_{it}) \right]}{1 + \theta}, \quad i = 0, \ldots, n-1. \tag{3.98}$$

These first-order conditions show that the consumer must choose an optimum consumption path along which the marginal utility of consumption for this period must be equal to the discounted expected marginal utility of the consumption for

---

[17] The derivation of the beta model closely follows Blanchard and Fischer (1989, Ch. 10).

the next period. Notice that these equalities must hold regardless of the nature of the assets. By rearranging the first-order conditions noted earlier,

$$E_t\left[U'(c_{t+1})(r_{it} - r_{0t})\right] = 0, \qquad i = 1, \ldots, n-1, \tag{3.99}$$

which may be rewritten as

$$E\left[U'(c_{t+1})\right] E\left[r_{it} - r_{0t}\right] + \text{Cov}\left[U'(c_{t+1}), r_{it}\right] = 0, \qquad i = 1, \ldots, n-1. \tag{3.100}$$

Given an optimum path for the consumption, Equation 3.100 implies that the return form asset i at the equilibrium should be

$$E(r_{it}) = r_{0t} - \frac{\text{Cov}\left[U'(c_{t+1}), r_{it}\right]}{E\left[U'(c_{t+1})\right]}, \qquad i = 1, \ldots, n-1. \tag{3.101}$$

The interpretation of Equation 3.101 is such that the consumer is willing to accept a lower rate of return (lower than the riskless asset rate of return) if the return from the risky asset has a positive correlation with the marginal utility of consumption. Since low levels of consumption are associated with high marginal utility of consumption, the risky asset provides a hedge against low consumption.

Suppose that there exists an asset (or a portfolio of assets) m such that its return is negatively related with the marginal utility of consumption.[18] Particularly, suppose that $U'(c_{t+1}) = -\gamma r_{mt}$ for some γ. It follows that

$$\text{Cov}[U'(c_{t+1}), r_{it}] = -\gamma \, \text{Cov}(r_{it}, r_{mt}). \tag{3.102}$$

Equation 3.101 must hold for asset m as well so that

$$E(r_{mt}) = r_{0t} - \frac{\text{Cov}\left[U'(c_{t+1}), r_{mt}\right]}{E\left[U'(c_{t+1})\right]} \tag{3.103}$$

or

$$E(r_{mt}) = r_{0t} + \frac{\gamma \sigma_m^2}{E[U'(c_{t+1})]}, \tag{3.104}$$

where σ_m^2 is the return variance for asset m. It follows that

$$E(r_{it}) = r_{0t} + \left[\frac{\text{Cov}(r_{it}, r_{mt})}{\sigma_m^2}\right] [E(r_{mt}) - r_{0t}]. \tag{3.105}$$

If m is the market portfolio (sum of all traded securities in the market), Equation 3.105 is known as the *security market line* in the capital asset-pricing model

---

[18] Because of the diminishing marginal utility of consumption, the assumed portfolio is such that it gives a low rate of return when the level of consumption is low and a high rate of return when the level of consumption is high.

(CAPM), developed by Sharpe (1964) and Lintner (1965). Equation 3.105 implies that the return on an asset in excess of the safe return is proportional to the return in the market in excess of the safe return (market premium). The proportionality factor is known as the *beta* of an asset, β_i. The beta of an asset is also known as *systematic risk*,

$$\beta_i = \frac{\text{Cov}(r_{it}, r_{mt})}{\sigma_m^2}. \tag{3.106}$$

The original work by Markowitz (1959) introduced the concept of a linear relation between the return to a risky asset, r_{it} and the return in the market, r_{mt} as in Equation 3.105. Markowitz argued that investors would hold a mean-variance efficient portfolio (i.e., a portfolio with the highest expected return for a given level of variance). Later, building in Markowitz's work, Sharpe (1964) and Lintner (1965) showed that if individuals with homogeneous expectations optimally hold mean-variance efficient portfolios, the market (sum of all individual portfolios) would also be mean-variance efficient. The Sharpe-Linter version of the CAPM results in Equation 3.105. Notice that Equation 3.105 may also be written in excess return form as

$$E(r_{it}) - r_{0t} = \beta_i [E(r_{mt}) - r_{0t}]. \tag{3.107}$$

In the Sharpe-Lintner version, it has been assumed that a risk-free asset exists in the economy with a sure return of r_{0t}. If there is no risk-free asset, Black (1972) showed that it is still possible to derive the CAPM model. The following market line model is known as Black's version of the CAPM

$$E(r_{it}) = E(z_{mt}) + \left[\frac{\text{Cov}(r_{it}, r_{mt})}{\sigma_m^2}\right] [E(r_{mt}) - E(z_{mt})], \tag{3.108}$$

where z_{mt} is the return on a *zero-beta portfolio*, which is defined as the minimum variance portfolio among all portfolios uncorrelated with m. Also, returns are defined in real terms in Black's version.

In empirical finance, the usual estimator for the beta is the OLS regression coefficient from the following regressions:

$$(r_{it} - r_{0t}) = \beta_i (r_{mt} - r_{0t}) + \epsilon_{it} \tag{3.109}$$

$$r_{it} = \alpha_i + \beta_i r_{mt} + v_{it}, \tag{3.110}$$

where ϵ_{it} and v_{it} are white noise disturbance terms. In the Sharpe and Lintner version of the CAPM (Equation 3.109), the intercept term is restricted to be zero and the beta is estimated with a regression through the origin utilizing excess returns as dependent and independent variables. In the Black's version (Equation 3.110), the intercept α_i is a combination of the expected zero-beta portfolio return and the beta of the asset.

Two of the well-known early studies on beta estimation are Black *et al.* (1972) and Fama and MacBeth (1973). Fama and French (1992) presented evidence that the CAPM does not hold. This study has received a large amount of attention and gave way to other studies that criticize it on several grounds, including the validity of the beta stability assumption. Studies that provide evidence that betas are not stable in different economies include Fabozzi and Francis (1978), Bos and Newbold (1984), Jagannathan and Wang (1996), and Groenewold and Fraser (1999) for the Unites States; Cheng (1997) for Hong-Kong; Brooks *et al.* (1998) for Austria; Wells (1996) for Sweden; Black *et al.* (1992) and Bucland and Fraser (2001) for the United Kingdom.

If the beta stability assumption is rejected, an appropriate modeling and estimation of the beta process is required. A multivariate generalized ARCH (M-GARCH) model as in Braun *et al.* (1995), a rolling regression model as in Groenewold and Fraser (1999), and the Kalman filter as in Wells (1996) or Bucland and Fraser (2001) are some of the most common approaches in the finance literature. The time-varying beta estimation in the Kalman filter framework can be modeled as follows.

Suppose that the beta of asset i follows a random walk

$$\beta_{it} = \beta_{i,t-1} + v_{it}, \tag{3.111}$$

where $v_{it} \sim N(0, \sigma_v^2)$ with no serial correlation. The observation equation is the market line

$$y_{it} = \beta_{it} x_{it} + \epsilon_{it}, \tag{3.112}$$

where $y_{it} = r_{it} - r_{0t}$ is the excess return of asset i, $x_{it} = r_{mt} - r_{0t}$ is the excess return of the market portfolio m, and $\epsilon_{it} \sim N(0, \sigma_{\epsilon i}^2)$ without serial correlation. Given an initial estimate of beta β_0 and an initial prediction error variance p_o^e, the beta in Equation 3.111 can be estimated recursively via the Kalman filter (see Section 3.5.1 for the estimation equation and the Kalman gain). Notice that the disturbance variances $\sigma_{\epsilon i}^2$ and σ_{vi}^2 are assumed to be known.[19]

Figure 3.6 plots the daily absolute return of the S&P 500 and the time-varying daily beta estimation results for three stocks: International Business Machines (IBM), General Motors (GM), and Procter & Gamble (P&G).[20] All beta estimates are filtered with a 20-day (four business weeks) equally weighted zero-phase filter to make the presentation clear.[21] The initial betas are obtained from the

---

[19] In practice, this assumption may not be fulfilled. Therefore, these variances need to be estimated from Equation 3.112 with the full sample.

[20] The sample period is December 31, 1993, to July 28, 2000. The first 200 days are excluded from all plots to eliminate start-off effects. Therefore, the sample period in all plots is October 1994, to July 2000. Source: Datastream.

[21] The filter is such that after filtering in the forward direction of the raw data, the filtered sequence is then reversed and filtered again. The final filtered output is the time reverse of the output of the second-stage filtering operation. Specifically, suppose that $x_1, x_2, \ldots, x_T$ is the sequence to be

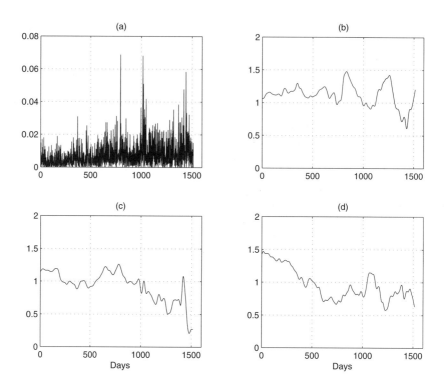

FIGURE 3.6 (a) Absolute daily return of S&P 500. (b) The Kalman filter estimate of daily betas for International Business Machines (IBM) (full sample OLS estimate is 1.07). (c) General Motors (GM) daily betas (full sample OLS estimate is 0.88). (d) Procter & Gamble (P&G) daily betas (full sample OLS estimate is 0.87). All beta estimates are filtered with a zero-phase filter to make the presentation clear. The original sample period in estimations is December 31, 1993, to July 28, 2000. The first 200 days are excluded from all plots to eliminate any start off effects. Therefore, the sample period in all plots is October 1994, to July 2000 (daily). Source: Datastream.

full sample OLS estimation of Equation 3.112. An estimate of the observation equation disturbance variance is also obtained from the OLS estimation. The disturbance variance in the signal equation σ_{vi}^2 is set to 0.05. Risk-free asset return is taken to be the 10-year U.S. Treasury Constant Maturity Rate.[22]

According to the estimation results, the beta of each stock (systematic risk) changes substantially throughout time. The change in beta is most noticeable especially during the last 2 years of the sample period during which there is

---

filtered. The first filter output is $y_1, y_2, \ldots, y_T$. This output is reversed as $y_T, y_{T-1}, \ldots y_1$ and filtered again. The output of this second-stage filtering is $z_T, z_{T-1}, \ldots, z_1$. The final filter output is $z_1, z_2, \ldots, z_T$. See Matlab function `filtfilt` for an application of this zero-phase filter.

[22] The sample period is December 31, 1993, to July 28, 2000. Source: H.15 Release – Federal Reserve Board of Governors. December 2000.

an increase in market volatility as evidenced by the absolute return series in Figure 3.6a.[23]

A time-varying beta has important implications both for investment and research perspectives. Suppose an investor (or a researcher) wants to evaluate the riskiness of the P&G stock. According to the OLS estimation, P&G stock has relatively low risk since the OLS estimate of its beta is 0.87. However, the time-varying beta estimation results in Figure 3.6b indicate that P&G stock had betas ranging from a high level of 1.5 to as low as 0.60 during the sample period. Similarly, the beta of IBM stock reaches 1.5 at certain periods indicating that it was much riskier than what the OLS estimate suggests.

Estimated betas play an important role also in capital budgeting. In order to calculate the cost of capital for a firm, the cost of equity and the cost of debt must be determined. A weighted average of these two costs would give the overall cost of capital for the firm. The cost of equity capital is calculated as

$$C_{it} = r_{0t} + \beta_{it}(r_{mt} - r_{0t}), \qquad (3.113)$$

where C_{it} is the cost of equity for company i, $(r_{mt} - r_{0t})$ is the excess return of the market portfolio m (market premium), and β_{it} is the beta of the company. Clearly, an unstable beta would give a completely different picture about the financial standing of a company or a group of companies in a sector. Several factors such as seasonality in cash flow, change in technology, change in product line, an increase or a decrease in the leverage of a firm can cause a change in the firms's beta. Therefore, an unstable beta for a company should be a concern in practice.[24]

---

[23] The choice of beta equation variance σ_{vi}^2 would alter this result. Increasing the variance σ_{vi}^2 would result in a more time-varying beta and vice versa.

[24] See Ross *et al.* (1999, Ch. 12) for a textbook exposition of capital budgeting.

4

DISCRETE WAVELET TRANSFORMS

4.1 INTRODUCTION

In the second chapter we introduced linear filters and presented examples of commonly used filters in economics and finance. Our toolbox of available filters was expanded in Chapter 3 with the Wiener and Kalman filter. Here we introduce the discrete wavelet transform (DWT). The DWT has several appealing qualities that make it a useful method for time series, exhibiting features that vary in both time and frequency. Although developed originally with geophysical applications in mind (Goupilllaud *et al.*, 1984), the DWT and its variants have found a home in a wide variety of disciplines—geology, atmospheric science, turbulence, and applied mathematics, to name a few. The engineering community quickly realized that common techniques in signal processing were closely related and developed the framework of multiresolution analysis (Mallat, 1989). There are numerous references over the past decade with respect to wavelet analysis. Introductory texts include Ogden (1996), Vidakovic (1999), and Percival and Walden (2000) from a statistical perspective; Vetterli and Kovačević (1995), Burrus *et al.* (1998), and Mallat (1998) from an engineering perspective; and Strang and Nguyen (1996) and Chui (1992, 1997) from a more mathematical perspective.

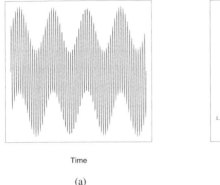
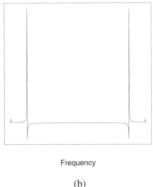

Time   Frequency

(a)   (b)

FIGURE 4.1 Example time series ($N = 512$) composed of a superposition of two sinusoids with differing frequencies $x_t = \sin(8\pi t)/4 + \sin(128\pi t)/2$. (a) Time series. (b) Real portion of its Fourier transform.

This chapter provides a brief discussion of time-frequency representations, such as the classical Fourier transform and short-time Fourier transform, before starting with the wavelet transform. Continuous wavelet functions are introduced and then contrasted to their discrete counterparts. The concept of an ideal bandpass filter (Chapter 3) is reviewed and several wavelet filters are given. The DWT and an alternative transform closely related to it are then outlined. Analysis of variance and multiresolution analysis formulae are provided for both transforms.

4.1.1 Fourier Transform

The discrete Fourier transform (DFT) may be derived from a variety of perspectives (e.g., approximating the Fourier transform of a function, approximating the Fourier coefficients of a function) (Briggs and Henson, 1995). We prefer to take the viewpoint of approximating a discretely sampled process (time series) x_t via a linear combination of sines and cosines. Each of these sines and cosines is itself a function of frequency, and therefore the DFT may be seen as a decomposition on a frequency-by-frequency basis. The Fourier basis functions (sines and cosines) are very appealing when representing a time series that does not vary over time (i.e., a stationary time series).[1]

If we have a time series that is a superposition of two sinusoids which are different size in amplitude and frequency and we look at its Fourier transform (in general this is complex-valued, but here we concern ourselves with the real portion for the moment), the periodic nature of the time series is succinctly captured by only a few Fourier coefficients. Figure 4.1 illustrates this point by

---

[1] A time series x_t is *strictly stationary* if $x_0, x_1, \ldots, x_k$ and $x_l, x_1 + l, \ldots, x_k + l$ have the same joint distribution for all positive integers k and l (Brockwell and Davis, 1991, Ch. 1). A more commonly used definition is *second-order stationarity*, where $E|x_t|^2 < \infty$, $E(x_t) = m$ (a constant) and $\gamma(k, l) = \gamma(k + t, l + t)$ for all positive integers k, l, t. The autocovariance function $\gamma(\cdot)$ is defined in Section 3.2.

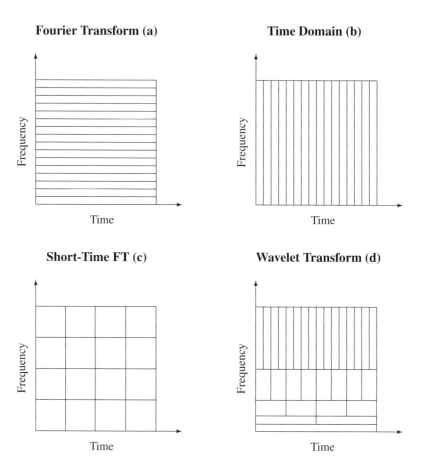

FIGURE 4.2 Partitioning of the time-frequency plane by different techniques. (a) The frequency domain after computing the Fourier transform, representing perfect frequency resolution and no time resolution. (b) The time domain representation of the observed time series, representing perfect time resolution and no frequency resolution. (c) Represents balanced resolution between time and frequency by using the short-time Fourier transform (Gabor transform). (d) The wavelet transform adaptively partitions the time-frequency plane.

plotting $x_t = \sin(8\pi t)/4 + \sin(128\pi t)/2$ in the time domain and the real portion of its Fourier transform (see also Figure 2.7). This time series was constructed via Fourier basis functions to begin with, and is not a realistic example of a real-world time series. In fact, restricting ourselves to stationary time series is not very appealing since most interesting time series exhibit quite complicated patterns over time (trends, abrupt changes, bursts of variability, etc.). The Fourier transform cannot efficiently capture these events.

The Fourier transform is an alternative representation of the original time series such that it summarizes information in the data as a function of frequency and therefore does not preserve information in time. This is the opposite of how we observed the original time series, where no frequency resolution was provided. The two upper panels in Figure 4.2 compare and contrast these two representations of a time series via the time-frequency plane. When observing the time series in the time domain, we have complete time resolution and no frequency resolution, whereas the opposite is true after performing the Fourier transform. This is seen by a fine partitioning in the frequency axis in Figure 4.2a and by a fine partitioning of the time axis in Figure 4.2b.

4.1.2 Short-Time Fourier Transform

Gabor (1946) recognized that the Fourier transform goes too far by eliminating all time resolution in lieu of frequency resolution and attempted to achieve a balance between time and frequency by *sliding* a window across the time series and taking the Fourier transform of the windowed series. This is known as the Gabor transform or Short-Time Fourier Transform (STFT). The resulting expansion is a function of two parameters, frequency and time shift. The key property is that the window size is fixed with respect to frequency. This produces a rectangular partitioning of the time-frequency plane, as shown in Figure 4.2c.

The choice of window is very important with respect to the performance of the STFT in practice. Since the STFT is simply applying the Fourier transform to pieces of the time series of interest, a drawback of the STFT is that it will not be able to resolve events if they happen to appear within the width of the window. In this case, the lack of time resolution of the Fourier transform is present. In general, one cannot achieve simultaneous time and frequency resolution because of the *Heisenberg uncertainty principle*. In the field of particle physics, an elementary particle does not simultaneously have a precise position and momentum. The better one determines the position of the particle, the less precisely the momentum is known at that time, and vice versa. For signal processing, this rule translates into the fact that a signal does not simultaneously have a precise location in time and precise frequency. An interesting discussion of the Heisenberg uncertainty principle in signal processing is found in Hubbard (1996).

4.1.3 Wavelet Transform

What is needed to overcome the fixed time-frequency partitioning is a new set of basis functions. The wavelet transform utilizes a basic function (called the *mother wavelet*), then dilates and translates it to capture features that are local in time and local in frequency. We have not violated the Heisenberg uncertainty principle, just played with it to our advantage. The resulting time-frequency partition corresponding to the wavelet transform is long in time when capturing low-frequency events, thus having good frequency resolution for these events, and long in frequency when capturing high-frequency events, thus having good time resolution for these events. The wavelet transform intelligently adapts itself to capture features across a wide range of frequencies.

While the Fourier transform, and also the STFT, is a function of frequency, the wavelet transform is a function of scale. As we will see in the next section, the scale in a wavelet transform is indeed related to frequency. Loosely speaking, scale is inversely proportional to a frequency interval. If the scale parameter increases, then the wavelet basis is

- stretched in the time domain,
- shrunk in the frequency domain, and
- shifted toward lower frequencies.

Conversely, a decrease in the scale parameter

- reduces the time support,
- increases the number of frequencies captured, and
- shifts toward higher frequencies.

Figure 4.2d shows the partitioning of the time-frequency plane by the discrete wavelet transform. As the frequency increases, time is more heavily partitioned across longer ranges of frequency. This is the balance between time and frequency.

By giving up some frequency resolution, the wavelet transform has the ability to capture events that are local in time. This makes the wavelet transform an ideal tool for studying nonstationary or transient time series. As an example, consider a simple sine wave that has several values removed from it, thus creating a sudden jump discontinuity. Figure 4.3a is just such a function, although the discontinuity is not visible by casual inspection. The Fourier transform of this function (Figure 4.3b) picks up the low-frequency oscillation and lacks strong evidence of the discontinuity. The wavelet transform, as shown in Figure 4.3c, clearly identifies the abrupt change in the function *and* the low-frequency sinusoid.

The ability to analyze economic time series in a flexible manner has been going on for some time. Brock (2000) discussed the need for time-frequency analysis of economic time series when he brought up work on the interface between ecology and economics. The concept of a *Stommel diagram* (Clark, 1985) is very similar to time-frequency analysis in that it looks at time-space relationships. Large amplitudes observed in a Stommel diagram lead the researcher to investigate possible scaling relationships and better capture the evolutionary nature of a process. The effects of periodic market closures (Brock and Kleidon, 1992) also brings up the need for decomposing observed financial time series in order to better observe the range of contributing oscillations. Time-frequency analysis has been used in, for example, Ramsey and Zhang (1997) to better differentiate between short (high-frequency) shocks and longer (low-frequency) movements in a financial time series.

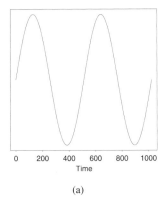

Time

(a)

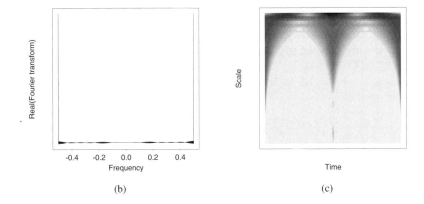

(b)   (c)

FIGURE 4.3 Sine wave with jump discontinuity around its midpoint. It was created by removing five points from the middle of $x_t = \sin(8\pi t)$. (a) Time series coefficients. (b) Real portion of its Fourier transform coefficients. (c) Absolute value of its continuous wavelet transform.

4.2 PROPERTIES OF THE WAVELET TRANSFORM

Although the Fourier transform, STFT, and wavelet transform are all alternative representations, each transform is well suited to certain types of applications. As studied in this book, wavelets, with their ability to quantify events in both time and scale, are well suited to study a wide range of time series. We now introduce some features of wavelets and wavelet transforms before moving to our main point of this chapter—the discrete wavelet transform.

4.2.1 Continuous Wavelet Functions

A wavelet $\psi(t)$ is simply a function of time t that obeys a basic rule, known as the wavelet *admissibility condition*:

$$C_\psi = \int_0^\infty \frac{|\Psi(f)|}{f}\,df < \infty, \tag{4.1}$$

where $\Psi(f)$ is the Fourier transform, a function of frequency f, of $\psi(t)$. This condition ensures that $\Psi(f)$ goes to zero quickly as $f \to 0$ (Grossmann and Morlet, 1984; Mallat, 1998, Sec. 4.3). In fact, to guarantee that $C_\psi < \infty$ we must impose $\Psi(0) = 0$, which is equivalent to

$$\int_{-\infty}^\infty \psi(t)\,dt = 0. \tag{4.2}$$

A secondary condition imposed on a wavelet function is unit energy;[2] that is,

$$\int_{-\infty}^\infty |\psi(t)|^2\,dt = 1. \tag{4.3}$$

By satisfying both Equations 4.2 and 4.3 the wavelet function must have nonzero entries, but all departures from zero must cancel out. The classic example of a continuous-time wavelet function is the *Morlet wavelet* given by

$$\psi^M(t) = \frac{1}{\sqrt{2\pi}} e^{-i\omega_0 t} e^{-\frac{t^2}{2}},$$

where $i = \sqrt{-1}$ is an imaginary number and ω_0 is the central frequency of the wavelet. Figure 4.4 displays two Morlet wavelets, one with center frequency twice that of the other, to illustrate this complex-valued wavelet function. Other examples of continuous-time wavelet functions are those related to derivatives of the Gaussian probability density function (PDF).[3] The renormalized wavelet related to the first derivative of the Gaussian PDF is

$$\psi^{G'}(t) = \frac{\sqrt{2}t}{\sigma^{3/2}\pi^{1/4}} e^{-t^2/2\sigma^2},$$

and the wavelet related to the second derivative is given by

$$\psi^{Mh}(t) = \frac{2}{\pi^{1/4}\sqrt{3\sigma}}\left(1 - \frac{t^2}{\sigma^2}\right) e^{-t^2/2\sigma^2}.$$

---

[2] The *energy* of a function is defined to be the squared function integrated over its domain.

[3] A random variable x is *normally distributed* if the probability density function (PDF) of x is given by

$$f(x) = (2\pi)^{-1/2}\sigma^{-1} \exp\left[-\frac{(x-\mu)^2}{2\sigma^2}\right],$$

where μ is the mean and $\sigma^2 > 0$ is the variance. If the random variable has mean zero, the PDF simplifies to

$$f(x) = (2\pi)^{-1/2}\sigma^{-1} \exp\left[-\frac{x^2}{2\sigma^2}\right].$$

The latter function is also known as the *Mexican hat* wavelet, given its distinctive shape (Figure 4.5). The first derivative wavelet is an example of an asymmetric wavelet function, while the Mexican hat wavelet is an example of a symmetric wavelet function. All three of these wavelet functions are useful for the continuous wavelet transform because they are continuous functions.

4.2.2 Continuous versus Discrete Wavelet Transform

The continuous wavelet transform (CWT) is a function of two variables $W(u, s)$ and is obtained by simply projecting the function of interest $x(t)$ onto a particular wavelet ψ via

$$W(u, s) = \int_{-\infty}^{\infty} x(t)\psi_{u,s}(t) \, dt, \tag{4.4}$$

where

$$\psi_{u,s}(t) = \frac{1}{\sqrt{s}}\psi\left(\frac{t - u}{s}\right)$$

is the translated (by u) and dilated (by s) version of the original wavelet function.[4] The resulting wavelet coefficients are a function of these two parameters, location and scale, even though the original function was only a function of one parameter, say time t. Equation 4.4 is a projection, so that large wavelet coefficients occur when the particular wavelet $\psi_{u,s}(t)$ and function are similar in shape.

By applying shifted and translated versions of the mother wavelet to a function of interest, we are breaking down the complicated structure present in the function into simpler components. This is called *analyzing*, or *decomposing*, the function (see also Section 2.3). If a wavelet satisfies the admissibility condition (Equation 4.1), then an inverse operation may be performed to produce the function from its wavelet coefficients; that is,

$$x(t) = \frac{1}{C_\psi} \int_0^{\infty} \int_{-\infty}^{\infty} W(u, s)\psi_{u,s}(t) \, du \, \frac{ds}{s^2}.$$

This is called *synthesizing*, or *reconstructing*, the function (see also Section 2.3). A key property of wavelet transforms is their ability to decompose and perfectly reconstruct a square-integrable function.[5]

As mentioned previously, the CWT is a function of two parameters and therefore contains a high amount of extra (redundant) information when analyzing a function. As seen in Figure 4.3c, the discontinuity is observed to some degree at every scale. Enough information would be available to easily detect this discontinuity if one were to sample only a portion of the CWT. Thus, we reduce our task

---

[4] The translation of a wavelet function $\psi(t - u)$ simply shifts its range u units to the right, while a dilation of the function $\psi(t/s)$ expands its range by a multiplicative factor.

[5] A function $x(t)$ is square-integrable if it satisfies $\int_{-\infty}^{\infty} x^2(t) \, dt < \infty$.

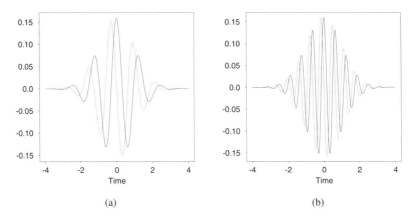

FIGURE 4.4 Morlet wavelet for (a) $\omega_0 = 5$ and (b) $\omega_0 = 10$. The real portion is given by a solid line and the imaginary portion by a dotted line.

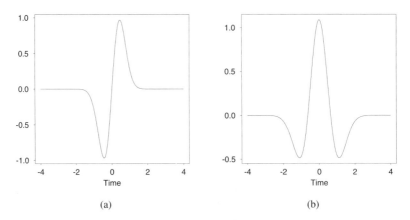

FIGURE 4.5 Wavelets related to the Gaussian probability density function. (a) A wavelet related to the first derivative of the Gaussian PDF. (b) The Mexican hat wavelet, which is related to the second derivative of the Gaussian PDF.

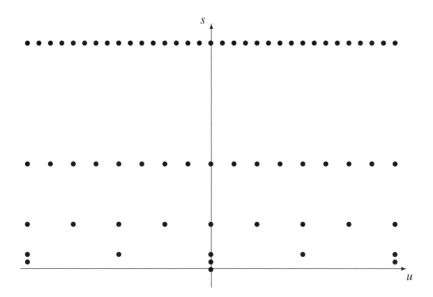

FIGURE 4.6 Critical sampling of the time-frequency plane by discretizing the CWT parameters via $s = 2^{-j}$ and $u = k2^{-j}$. The CWT is defined at all points in the time-frequency plane and corresponds to a redundant representation of the information present in a function. As s increases (by decreasing j) the number of coefficients sampled across time doubles. By using only the points provided, the minimum number of wavelet coefficients are used so that the function may be perfectly reconstructed.

from analyzing an image (the CWT) with continuous parameters u and s to viewing a small number of scales with a varying number of wavelet coefficients at each scale. This is the *discrete wavelet transform* (DWT). Although the DWT may be derived without referring to the CWT, we may view it as a "discretization" of the CWT through sampling specific wavelet coefficients (Vidakovic, 1999, Sec. 3.2). A *critical sampling* of the CWT is obtained via

$$s = 2^{-j} \quad \text{and} \quad u = k2^{-j},$$

where j and k are integers representing the set of discrete translations and discrete dilations. A critical sampling defines the resolution of the DWT in both time and frequency (see Section 4.4). We use the term *critical sampling* to denote the minimum number of coefficients sampled from the CWT to ensure that all information present in the original function is retained by the wavelet coefficients. In Figure 4.6, half of the time-frequency plane is displayed with coordinate axes for the two parameters of the CWT. Concentrating on a continuous process for the moment, the CWT takes on values at every point on the time-frequency plane. The DWT, on the other hand, only takes on values at very few points denoted by the dots and the wavelets that follow these values $\psi_{j,k}(t) = 2^{j/2}\psi(2^j t - k)$, for all integers j, k, produce an orthogonal basis. If we select a sequence of dyadic scales and instead use all integer translations

$$s = 2^{-j} \quad \text{and} \quad u = k,$$

then we arrive at the maximal overlap DWT (see Section 4.5).

Both the DWT and maximal overlap DWT have been utilized in a variety of fields, and under a variety of names, over the past 10 years. With respect to economics and finance, the works of J. B. Ramsey and co-authors first introduced wavelets into the mainstream literature. Ramsey and Zhang (1997) performed a time-frequency analysis of foreign exchange rates (Deutsche Mark versus U.S. Dollar and Japanese Yen versus U.S. Dollar) using wavelets. They found that wavelet analysis succinctly captured a variety of nonstationary events in the series. Ramsey and Lampart (1998a; 1998b) decomposed economic variables across several wavelet scales in order to identify different relationships between money and income, and between consumption and income. See Ramsey (1999) for a recent review article on wavelets in economics and finance. Recently, Stengos and Sun (2001) designed a consistent specification test for a regression model based on wavelet estimation, and Fan (2000) proposed a wavelet estimator of a partial linear model by regressing boundary independent DWT coefficients of the dependent variable on the corresponding DWT coefficients of the regressors in the linear part of the model across several scales.

We propose to introduce wavelet transforms in this chapter and offer a variety of situations where they provide insight into problems relevant to practitioners in economics and finance. More information concerning the CWT and its uses may be found in, for example, Mallat (1998) and Carmona *et al.* (1998).

4.3 DISCRETE WAVELET FILTERS

Before formulating the DWT or maximal overlap DWT, we must consider what discrete wavelet filters are available to us. Fundamental properties of the continuous wavelet functions (filters), such as integration to zero and unit energy (Equations 4.2 and 4.3), have discrete counterparts. Let $h_l = (h_0, \ldots, h_{L-1})$ be a finite length discrete wavelet filter such that it integrates (sums) to zero

$$\sum_{l=0}^{L-1} h_l = 0 \tag{4.5}$$

and has unit energy

$$\sum_{l=0}^{L-1} h_l^2 = 1. \tag{4.6}$$

In addition to Equations 4.5 and 4.6, the wavelet (or high-pass) filter h_l is orthogonal to its even shifts; that is,

$$\sum_{l=0}^{L-1} h_l h_{l+2n} = 0, \quad \text{for all nonzero integers } n. \tag{4.7}$$

This comes from the relationship between the DWT and CWT via a critical sampling (Section 4.2.2). To construct the orthonormal matrix that defines the DWT, wavelet coefficients cannot interact with one another. Equations 4.6 and 4.7 may be succinctly expressed in the frequency domain via the squared gain function (Section 2.3.2)

$$\mathcal{H}(f) + \mathcal{H}(f + \tfrac{1}{2}) = 2 \quad \text{for all } f. \tag{4.8}$$

To better explain this result, consider Equation 4.7. The DFT of the left-hand side of Equation 4.7 is given by $[\mathcal{H}(f/2) + \mathcal{H}(f/2 + 1/2)]/2$. Hence, we may re-express Equation 4.7 via its inverse DFT

$$\sum_{l=0}^{L-1} h_l h_{l+2n} = \int_{-\infty}^{\infty} \frac{1}{2} \left[\mathcal{H}(\tfrac{f}{2}) + \mathcal{H}(\tfrac{f}{2} + \tfrac{1}{2}) \right] e^{i2\pi f n} \, df.$$

By plugging in Equation 4.8 into the above equation, we show that

$$\sum_{l=0}^{L-1} h_l h_{l+2n} = \int_{-\infty}^{\infty} e^{i2\pi f n} \, df = \begin{cases} 1 & n = 0 \\ 0 & \text{otherwise} \end{cases}$$

and, thus, Equations 4.6 and 4.7 are both satisfied. Figure 4.7a shows an ideal high-pass filter for $f \in [0, 1/4]$ and an approximation to this ideal filter by the Daubechies extremal phase wavelet filter of length 4.

The natural object to complement a high-pass filter is a low-pass (scaling) filter whose squared gain function monotonically increases as $f \to 0$. By applying both h_l and g_l to an observed time series, we have separated high-frequency oscillations from low-frequency ones. We will denote a low-pass filter as $g_l = (g_0, \ldots, g_{L-1})$ in this chapter, and its transfer and squared gain function are given by $G(f)$ and $\mathcal{G}(f)$, respectively. Figure 4.7b shows an ideal low-pass filter for $f \in [0, 1/4]$ and an approximation to this ideal filter by the Daubechies extremal phase scaling filter of length 4. For all the wavelets considered here, the low-pass filter coefficients are determined by the *quadrature mirror relationship*[6]

$$g_l = (-1)^{l+1} h_{L-1-l} \quad \text{for} \quad l = 0, \ldots, L - 1. \tag{4.9}$$

---

[6] Quadrature mirror filters (QMFs) are often used in the engineering literature because of their ability for perfect reconstruction of a signal without aliasing effects (Vetterli and Kovačević, 1995). Aliasing occurs when a continuous signal is sampled to obtain a discrete time series. All frequencies $f - 1, f + 1, f - 2, f + 2, f - 3, f + 3, \ldots$ will appear to have frequency f. The frequency f is said to be the "alias" of all its integer translates.

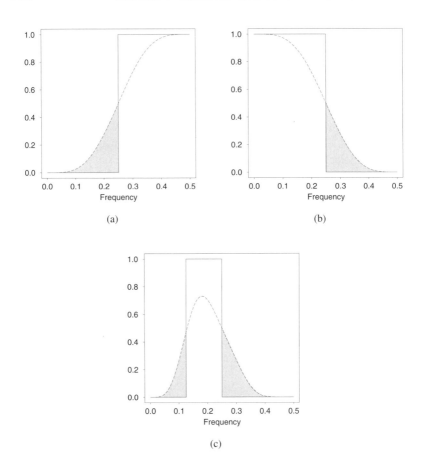

FIGURE 4.7   Squared gain functions for ideal filters (solid line) and their wavelet approximations (dotted line). The shaded regions represent *leakage* , meaning frequencies outside the nominal pass-band persist in the filtered output. (a) An ideal high-pass filter (solid line) over the frequency interval $f \in [1/4, 1/2]$ and its approximation via the D(4) wavelet filter (dotted line). (b) An ideal low-pass filter over $f \in [0, 1/4]$ and its approximation via the D(4) scaling filter. (c) An ideal band-pass filter over $f \in [1/8, 1/4]$ and its approximation via the second scale D(4) wavelet filter.

The inverse relationship is given by $h_l = (-1)^l g_{L-1-l}$. Using Equation 4.9 allows us to relate the transfer function for g_l and h_l via

$$G(f) = \sum_{l=0}^{L-1} g_l e^{-i2\pi f} = e^{-i2\pi f(L-1)} H(f - \tfrac{1}{2}),$$

and, thus, the squared gain functions follow

$$G(f) = \left|e^{-i2\pi f(L-1)}H(f - \tfrac{1}{2})\right|^2 = \left|H(\tfrac{1}{2} - f)\right|^2 = \mathcal{H}(\tfrac{1}{2} - f). \qquad (4.10)$$

Finally, a band-pass filter has a squared gain function that covers an interval of frequencies and then decays to zero as $f \to 0$ and $f \to 1/2$. We may construct a band-pass filter by recursively applying a combination of low-pass and high-pass filters. Let $h_{J,l}$ be a band-pass filter produced by a combination of J filters.[7] Starting with $h_{1,l}$, we obtain the filtered output $u_{J,t}$ via

$$
\begin{aligned}
u_{1,t} &= h_{1,l} * x_t \\
u_{2,t} &= h_{2,l} * u_{1,t} \\
&\vdots \quad \vdots \quad \vdots \\
u_{J,t} &= h_{J,l} * u_{J-1,t}
\end{aligned}
\qquad (4.11)
$$

for $t = 0, \pm 1, \pm 2, \ldots$ The *equivalent filter* h_l for the "cascade" of filters in Equation 4.11 has the transfer function

$$H(f) = \prod_{j=1}^{J} H_j(f). \qquad (4.12)$$

This may be seen by viewing Equation 4.11 in the frequency domain via Fourier transforms; that is,

$$
\begin{aligned}
U_1(f) &= H_1(f)X(f) \\
U_2(f) &= H_2(f)U_1(f) = H_2(f)H_1(f)X(f) \\
&\vdots \quad \vdots \quad \vdots \\
U_J(f) &= H_J(f)U_{J-1}(f) = H_J(f)H_{J-1}(f) \cdots H_1(f)X(f),
\end{aligned}
$$

where $X(f)$ is the DFT of x_t. After applying a series of J filters, the DFT of the output series $u_{J,t}$ is given by the product of all previous Fourier transforms and may be depicted graphically through the following flowchart:

$$x_t \longrightarrow \boxed{H_1(f)} \longrightarrow \boxed{H_2(f)} \longrightarrow \cdots \longrightarrow \boxed{H_J(f)} \longrightarrow u_{J,t}.$$

Using Equation 4.12 and the convolution property of the Fourier transform, $U_J(f) = H(f)X(f)$ and, therefore, $u_{J,t}$ is simply the convolution of x_t with h_l; that is,

$$x_t \longrightarrow \boxed{H(f)} \longrightarrow u_{J,t}.$$

Figure 4.7c shows an ideal band-pass filter for $f \in [1/8, 1/4]$ and an approximation to this ideal filter by a filter cascade of the Daubechies extremal phase scaling and wavelet filters of length 4.

---

[7] This is referred to in the engineering literature as a *cascade of filters*. It is the same idea as multistage filtering introduced in Chapter 2.

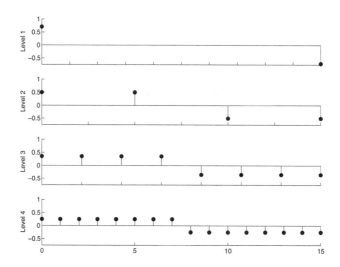

FIGURE 4.8   Haar wavelet filter coefficients for the first four scales. The nonzero coefficients indicated by vertical lines attached to the solid circles—from top to bottom—are given by $h_{1,l} = (1, -1)/\sqrt{2}$, $h_{2,l} = (1, 1, -1, -1)/2$, $h_{3,l} = (-1/\sqrt{8} \cdot \mathbf{1}_4, 1/\sqrt{8} \cdot \mathbf{1}_4)$, and $h_{4,l} = (-1/16 \cdot \mathbf{1}_8, 1/16 \cdot \mathbf{1}_8)$, where $\mathbf{1}_N$ is a length N vector of ones.

4.3.1   Haar Wavelets

The first wavelet filter, the Haar wavelet (Haar, 1910), remained in relative obscurity until the convergence of several disciplines to form what we now know in a broad sense as wavelet methodology. It is a filter of length $L = 2$ that can be succinctly defined by its scaling (low-pass) filter coefficients

$$g_0 = g_1 = \frac{1}{\sqrt{2}},$$

or equivalently by its wavelet (high-pass) filter coefficients $h_0 = 1/\sqrt{2}$ and $h_1 = -1/\sqrt{2}$ through the inverse quadrature mirror relationship.

The Haar wavelet is special since it is the only symmetric compactly supported orthonormal wavelet (Daubechies, 1992, Ch. 8). It is also useful for presenting the basic properties shared by all wavelet filters we consider here (Equations 4.5–4.7). Figure 4.8 shows the unit scale wavelet filter coefficients $h_{1,l} = (1/\sqrt{2}, -1/\sqrt{2})$, where the first subscript denotes the scale of the filter, along with higher scale wavelet filter coefficients. The first row of filter coefficients illustrate a simple difference operation, where projecting $h_{1,l}$ onto a vector produces a difference between two adjacent observations. The next set of filter coefficients $h_{2,l}$ is a simple difference also, but two pairs of observations are averaged and those averages differenced. This theme is repeated in $h_{3,l}$ and $h_{4,l}$, where the averages are growing in length before being differenced.

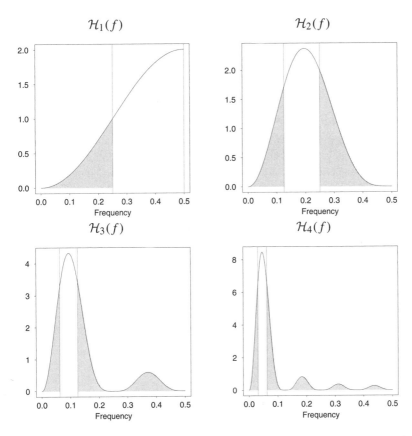

FIGURE 4.9 Frequency-domain representations of the Haar wavelet filter. Each plot shows the squared gain function corresponding to the wavelet coefficient vectors in Figure 4.8. An ideal band-pass filter would only exhibit positive values on the frequencies between the dotted lines. Frequencies with positive weight $\mathcal{H}(f) > 0$ outside of the dotted lines (shaded regions) indicate poor approximation of the Haar wavelet filter to an ideal band-pass filter. This is known in the engineering literature as *leakage*.

Although the Haar wavelet filter is easy to visualize and implement, it is inadequate for most real-world applications in that it is a poor approximation to an ideal band-pass filter. Figure 4.9 shows the squared gain functions for the scale 1–4 wavelet filter coefficients. An ideal band-pass filter is proportional to one inside the desired frequency interval and zero at all other frequencies (see Figure 2.8 and discussion in Section 2.3.2). The dotted lines in each panel of Figure 4.9 indicate the frequency interval for the ideal (nominal) band-pass filter. The squared gain functions associated with the level j Haar wavelet filter do not decay rapidly outside this nominal frequency range, indicating the filter is a poor approximation to the ideal band-pass filter. Orthonormal wavelets of even lengths $L \geq 4$ were developed in the late 1980s that yield much better approximations.

Looking at the first line of Figure 4.8, the unit scale Haar wavelet filter is proportional to the first difference operator $Bx_t = x_t - x_{t-1}$. Thus, its squared gain function $\mathcal{H}(f) = 4\sin^2(\pi f)$ is identical to the first difference operator. This indicates that the wavelet filter is a simple "difference" filter. We will explore this connection between wavelet filters and differencing in future sections.

4.3.2   Daubechies Wavelets

The Daubechies wavelet filters represent a collection of wavelets that improve on the frequency-domain characteristics of the Haar wavelet and may still be interpreted as generalized differences of adjacent averages (Daubechies, 1992). Daubechies derived these wavelets from the criterion of a compactly supported function with the maximum number of vanishing moments.[8] In general, there are no explicit time-domain formulae for this class of wavelet filters (when possible, filter coefficients will be provided). The simplest way to define the class of Daubechies wavelet filters is through the squared gain function of their scaling (low-pass) filter,

$$G(f) = 2\cos^L(\pi f) \sum_{l=0}^{L/2-1} \binom{L/2 - 1 + l}{l} \sin^{2l}(\pi f), \qquad (4.13)$$

where the length L of the filter is a positive even integer and

$$\binom{a}{b} = \frac{a!}{b!(a-b)!} = \frac{\Gamma(a+1)}{\Gamma(b+1)\Gamma(a-b+1)}. \qquad (4.14)$$

Two remarks may be made with respect to Equation 4.13. If we let $L = 2$ and perform the inverse DFT on $G(f)$, the resulting scaling filter coefficients are identical to those of the Haar wavelet. Hence, the Haar wavelet may be seen as a length 2 Daubechies wavelet. Second, the squared gain function of the scaling filter is related to the squared gain function of the wavelet filter via Equation 4.10 and from basic trigonometric relations between the sine and cosine we have

$$\mathcal{H}(f) = 2\sin^L(\pi f) \sum_{l=0}^{L/2-1} \binom{L/2 - 1 + l}{l} \cos^{2l}(\pi f).$$

The squared gain function does not uniquely characterize a sequence of Daubechies wavelet filters. If we think of a sequence of wavelet filter coefficients h_l, it may be represented using the DFT yielding its transfer function $H(f)$. In polar notation the complex-valued transfer function may be written as

$$H(f) = |H(f)| \exp[i\theta(f)] = [\mathcal{H}(f)]^{1/2} \exp[i\theta(f)],$$

so that although two filters share the same squared gain function, they may differ in phase. The process of *spectral factorization* (Oppenheim and Schafer, 1989) may be used to obtain the different filters via finding the roots of $|H(f)|$.

---

[8] A function $\psi(t)$ with P vanishing moments satisfies $\int t^P \psi(t)dt = 0$, where $p = 0, 1, \ldots$, $P - 1$.

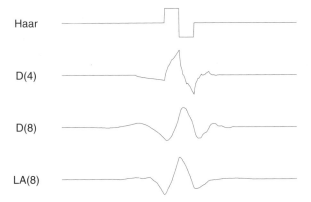

Haar

D(4)

D(8)

LA(8)

FIGURE 4.10 Daubechies wavelet filters of lengths $L \in \{2, 4, 8\}$ for level $j = 6$. From top to bottom, the first three rows are extremal phase Daubechies compactly supported wavelets (the Haar wavelet is equivalent to the D(2)), while the last row is a least asymmetric Daubechies compactly supported wavelet.

The number of possible factorizations increases as the length of the filter L increases. Daubechies first choose an *extremal phase* factorization,[9] whose resulting wavelets we denote by D(L) where L is the length of the filter. An alternative factorization leads to the *least asymmetric* class of wavelets, which we denote by LA(L).[10] The D(4) wavelets have a simple expression in the time domain via

$$h_0 = \frac{1 - \sqrt{3}}{4\sqrt{2}}, \ h_1 = \frac{-3 + \sqrt{3}}{4\sqrt{2}}, \ h_2 = \frac{3 + \sqrt{3}}{4\sqrt{2}} \quad \text{and} \quad h_3 = \frac{-1 - \sqrt{3}}{4\sqrt{2}}.$$

A recent article by Shann and Yen (1999) provided exact values for both the extremal phase and least asymmetric wavelets of length $L \in \{8, 10\}$. Longer extremal phase wavelet and least asymmetric filters do not have a closed form and have been tabulated by, for example, Daubechies (1992, Sec. 6.2) and Percival and Walden (2000, Sec 4.8). Tables 4.1 and 4.2 provide selected Daubechies wavelet filters. Figure 4.10 shows wavelet filter coefficients associated with Daubechies families of wavelets with lengths $L \in \{2, 4, 8\}$. All sets of filter coefficients are associated with the sixth level of the DWT and, although they are not continuous functions, they well approximate the underlying basis function as $j \to \infty$.

---

[9] The term *extremal* (or minimum) *phase spectral factorization* is associated with a solution to the roots of $|H(f)|$ that are all inside the unit circle (Daubechies, 1992, Ch. 6). Filters with this property are also known as minimum-delay sequences (Oppenheim and Schafer, 1989).

[10] Symmetric filters are known as *linear phase* filters in the engineering literature. The degree of asymmetry for a filter may therefore be measured by the deviation from linearity of its phase. Least asymmetric filters are associated with a phase that is as close to linear as possible (Daubechies, 1992, Ch. 8).

l	D(4)	D(6)	D(8)
0	0.4829629131445341	0.3326705529500827	0.2303778133074431
1	0.8365163037378077	0.8068915093110928	0.7148465705484058
2	0.2241438680420134	0.4598775021184915	0.6308807679358788
3	−0.1294095225512603	−0.1350110200102546	−0.0279837694166834
4		−0.0854412738820267	−0.1870348117179132
5		0.0352262918857096	0.0308413818353661
6			0.0328830116666778
7			−0.0105974017850021

l	D(12)	D(16)	D(20)
0	0.1115407433501094	0.0544158422431049	0.0266700579005546
1	0.4946238903984530	0.3128715909143031	0.1881768000776863
2	0.7511339080210954	0.6756307362972904	0.5272011889317202
3	0.3152503517091980	0.5853546836541907	0.6884590394536250
4	−0.2262646939654399	−0.0158291052563816	0.2811723436606485
5	−0.1297668675672624	−0.2840155429615702	−0.2498464243272283
6	0.0975016055873224	0.0004724845739124	−0.1959462743773399
7	0.0275228655303053	0.1287474266204837	0.1273693403357890
8	−0.0315820393174862	−0.0173693010018083	0.0930573646035802
9	0.0005538422011614	−0.0440882539307952	−0.0713941471663697
10	0.0047772575109455	0.0139810279173995	−0.0294575368218480
11	−0.0010773010853085	0.0087460940474061	0.0332126740593703
12		−0.0048703529934518	0.0036065535669880
13		−0.0003917403733770	−0.0107331754833036
14		0.0006754494064506	0.0013953517470692
15		−0.0001174767841248	0.0019924052951930
16			−0.0006858566949566
17			−0.0001164668551285
18			0.0000935886703202
19			−0.0000132642028945

TABLE 4.1   Scaling filter coefficients g_l for selected Daubechies extremal phase wavelets.

For Daubechies wavelets, the number of vanishing moments[11] is half the filter length, thus the Haar has a single vanishing moment, the D(4) wavelet has two vanishing moments, and the D(8) and LA(8) wavelets both have four vanishing moments. One implication of this property is that longer wavelet filters may produce stationary wavelet coefficient vectors from "higher degree" nonstationary stochastic processes.

---

[11] In fact, all wavelets proposed here have at least one vanishing moment given by Equation 4.2.

l	LA(8)	LA(16)	LA(20)
0	−0.0757657147893407	−0.0033824159513594	0.0007701598091030
1	−0.0296355276459541	−0.0005421323316355	0.0000956326707837
2	0.4976186676324578	0.0316950878103452	−0.0086412992759401
3	0.8037387518052163	0.0076074873252848	−0.0014653825833465
4	0.2978577956055422	−0.1432942383510542	0.0459272392237649
5	−0.0992195435769354	−0.0612733590679088	0.0116098939129724
6	−0.0126039672622612	0.4813596512592012	−0.1594942788575307
7	0.0322231006040713	0.7771857516997478	−0.0708805358108615
8		0.3644418948359564	0.4716906668426588
9		−0.0519458381078751	0.7695100370143388
10		−0.0272190299168137	0.3838267612253823
11		0.0491371796734768	−0.0355367403054689
12		0.0038087520140601	−0.0319900568281631
13		−0.0149522583367926	0.0499949720791560
14		−0.0003029205145516	0.0057649120455518
15		0.0018899503329007	−0.0203549398039460
16			−0.0008043589345370
17			0.0045931735836703
18			0.0000570360843390
19			−0.0004593294205481

TABLE 4.2 Scaling filter coefficients g_l for selected Daubechies least asymmetric wavelets.

We mentioned in the previous section that the Haar wavelet filter is a poor approximation to an ideal band-pass filter and that the level of approximation improves as L increases. Figure 4.11 provides the filter coefficients, while Figure 4.12 shows the squared gain functions for the LA(8) wavelet. Note, the D(8) will have an identical squared gain function since it only differs from the LA(8) with respect to its phase function. Contrasting the squared gain functions between Figures 4.9 and 4.12, we see that the LA(8) is a much better approximation to an ideal band-pass filter than the Haar (less leakage).

4.3.3 Minimum Bandwidth Discrete-Time Wavelets

The minimum-bandwidth discrete-time (MBDT) wavelets are a new class of orthonormal wavelet filters that were developed by Morris and Peravali (1999). They are generated via an iterative optimization of the spectral factorization procedure. This results in a family of filters that have similar values to those of the Daubechies wavelets, but were obtained through a completely iterative procedure. Hence, although Daubechies wavelets have closed form expressions for their squared gain functions, the MBDT wavelets do not.

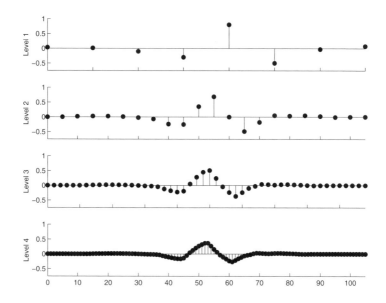

FIGURE 4.11   LA(8) wavelet filter coefficients for the first four scales $h_{1,l}, \ldots, h_{4,l}$. Starting with eight nonzero coefficients at the first scale, the LA(8) wavelet filter is smoother than the Haar and is nearly symmetric with a positive peak and a negative dip on either side. Unlike the Haar wavelet filter, the LA(8) coefficients do not have a convenient closed-form expression.

What MBDT wavelets offer is an improved approximation to an ideal band-pass filter for lengths $L \geq 8$. This can be seen in Figure 4.13, which displays the squared gain functions for both the level 1 and 2 wavelet filters associated with an MB(8) wavelet and Daubechies wavelets of length $L \in \{4, 8, 16\}$. Comparing $\mathcal{H}_1(f)$ between these wavelet filters, we see a steady improvement in the Daubechies wavelets as L increases as to be expected. The surprising fact is that the squared gain function of the MB(8) wavelet is nearly identical to that of the D(16), even though its length is half that of the Daubechies wavelet filter. Thus, the MBDT wavelets offer superior frequency-domain properties to Daubechies wavelets given a filter of the same length. Band-pass filtering a time series is important, from a statistical point of view, in order to produce approximately uncorrelated wavelet coefficients for processes with quite general spectra. This will be investigated more in Chapter 5.

The MBDT wavelets offer improved frequency resolution to that of the Daubechies family of wavelets, but what do they look like? Figure 4.14 shows the MBDT wavelet basis functions for lengths $L \in \{4, 8, 16\}$. They are most similar to the Daubechies extremal phase family of wavelets, which are also plotted for comparison. In fact, the MB(4) wavelet basis function is essentially identical to the D(4) wavelet filter. For longer filters, the MBDT wavelet basis

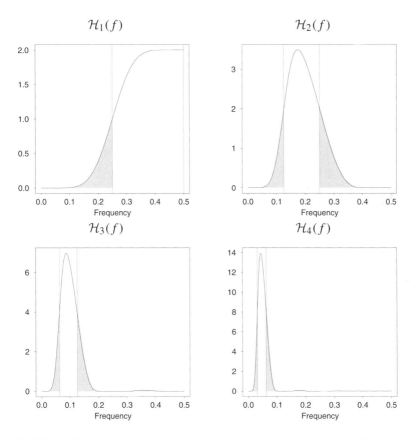

FIGURE 4.12 Frequency-domain representations of the LA(8) wavelet filter. Each plot shows the squared gain function corresponding to the wavelet coefficient vectors in Figure 4.11. Frequencies with positive weight $\mathcal{H}(f) > 0$ outside of the dotted lines (shaded regions) correspond to the leakage associated with this approximation to an ideal band-pass filter. The filters associated with these squared gain functions suffer from much less leakage than the Haar wavelet filters.

functions are not as smooth as their Daubechies extremal phase counterparts but quite similar in shape. Table 4.3 presents selected MBDT scaling coefficients.

4.4 THE DISCRETE WAVELET TRANSFORM

These days, data availability is becoming less and less of a problem. For instance, most of the exchanges and especially those that trade electronically would gladly provide tick-by-tick data to interested parties. Data vendors have themselves improved their data structures and provide their users with tools to collect data from over-the-counter (OTC) markets. Data vendors like Reuters, for instance, transmit more than 275,000 prices per day for foreign exchange spot rates alone.

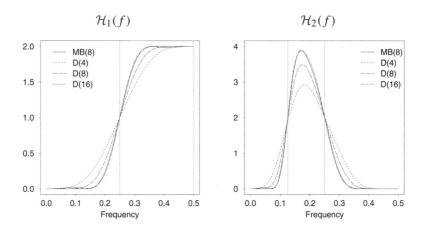

FIGURE 4.13   Squared gain functions for the MB(8) and Daubechies wavelet filters of length $L \in \{4, 8, 16\}$. As L increases, we see a gradual improvement in the approximation of the Daubechies wavelet filter to an ideal band-pass filter. The MB(8) appears to perform as well as a Daubechies wavelet filter of length $L = 16$.

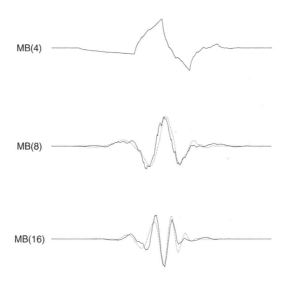

FIGURE 4.14   Minimum-bandwidth discrete-time wavelet basis functions (solid line) for lengths $L \in \{4, 8, 16\}$. The dotted lines are the Daubechies extremal phase wavelet basis functions $D(L)$. The sign of the MB(8) wavelet filter was reversed for better comparison.

l	MB(8)	MB(16)	MB(24)
0	0.064363450	0.005765899	$5.361301e-05$
1	0.007106015	0.009620427	$1.193006e-03$
2	−0.110867300	−0.049846980	$-2.062335e-03$
3	0.294785500	−0.024838760	$-1.644859e-02$
4	0.735133100	0.054746280	$1.027154e-02$
5	0.572577100	−0.019879860	$1.479342e-01$
6	0.018477510	−0.056566570	$-4.575448e-03$
7	−0.167361900	0.234534200	$-3.622424e-01$
8		0.670164600	$-3.091111e-01$
9		0.634922800	$2.556731e-01$
10		0.118872500	$6.176385e-01$
11		−0.227835900	$4.581101e-01$
12		−0.057765700	$1.949147e-01$
13		0.113611600	$1.243531e-01$
14		0.021736770	$1.689456e-01$
15		−0.013027700	$1.019512e-01$
16			$-6.559513e-03$
17			$-2.658282e-03$
18			$4.199576e-02$
19			$-1.482995e-03$
20			$-4.879053e-03$
21			$7.456041e-04$
22			$4.745736e-04$
23			$-2.132706e-05$

TABLE 4.3 Scaling filter coefficients g_l for selected minimum-bandwidth discrete time wavelets. The notation $2.0e-04$ is equivalent to $2 \times 10^{-4} = 0.0002$.

With such massive amounts of financial data being collected at any given time, the discrete wavelet transform is computationally cheaper relative to the continuous wavelet transform. Furthermore, economic and financial data are inherently discrete, and thus we consider discrete transformations here.

In this section we introduce notation and concepts in order to compute the DWT of a finite-length vector of observations. There are a variety of ways to express the basic DWT. As we have seen from the definition of the CWT (Equation 4.4), wavelet coefficients were obtained from projecting (or correlating) portions of a time series with translated and dilated versions of the wavelet function. We also noted that projection is closely related to convolution and we have introduced filtering concepts for discrete series. Here it is most straightforward to introduce the DWT through a simple matrix operation.

Let x be a dyadic length vector ($N = 2^J$) of observations. The length N vector of discrete wavelet coefficients w is obtained via

$$w = \mathcal{W}x,$$

where $\mathcal{W}$ is an $N \times N$ orthonormal matrix defining the DWT. The vector of wavelet coefficients may be organized into $J + 1$ vectors,

$$w = [w_1, w_2, \dots, w_J, v_J]^T, \tag{4.15}$$

where w_j is a length $N/2^j$ vector of wavelet coefficients associated with changes on a scale of length[12] $\lambda_j = 2^{j-1}$ and v_J is a length $N/2^J$ vector of scaling coefficients associated with averages on a scale of length $2^J = 2\lambda_J$.

The matrix $\mathcal{W}$ is composed of the wavelet and scaling filter coefficients arranged on a row-by-row basis. Let

$$h_1 = [h_{1,N-1}, h_{1,N-2}, \dots, h_{1,1}, h_{1,0}]^T \tag{4.16}$$

be the vector of zero-padded unit scale wavelet filter coefficients in reverse order. That is, the coefficients $h_{1,0}, \dots, h_{1,L-1}$ are taken from an appropriate orthonormal wavelet family of length L, and all values such that $L < t < N$ are defined to be zero. Now circularly shift h_1 by factors of two so that

$$h_1^{(2)} = [h_{1,1}, h_{1,0}, h_{1,N-1}, h_{1,N-2}, \dots, h_{1,3}, h_{1,2}]^T,$$

$$h_1^{(4)} = [h_{1,3}, \dots, h_{1,0}, h_{1,N-1}, h_{1,N-2}, \dots, h_{1,5}, h_{1,4}]^T,$$

and so on. Define the $N/2 \times N$ dimensional matrix $\mathcal{W}_1$ to be the collection of $N/2$ circularly shifted versions of h_1; that is,

$$\mathcal{W}_1 = \left[h_1^{(2)}, h_1^{(4)}, \dots, h_1^{(N/2-1)}, h_1 \right]^T.$$

Let h_2 be the vector of zero-padded scale 2 wavelet filter coefficients defined similarly to Equation 4.16. Now construct the matrix $\mathcal{W}_2$ by circularly shifting the vector h_2 by factors of four. Repeat this to construct the matrices $\mathcal{W}_j$ by circularly shifting the vector h_j (the vector of zero-padded scale j wavelet filter coefficients) by factors of 2^j. The matrix $\mathcal{V}_J$ is simply a column vector whose elements are all equal to $1/\sqrt{N}$ (McCoy and Walden, 1996). The structure of the $N \times N$ dimensional matrix $\mathcal{W}$ is seen through the submatrices $\mathcal{W}_1, \dots, \mathcal{W}_J$

---

[12] Wavelet coefficients are obtained by projecting the wavelet filter onto a vector of observations. Since Daubechies wavelets may be considered as generalized differences (Section 4.3.1), we prefer to characterize the wavelet coefficients this way. For example, a unit scale Daubechies wavelet filter is a generalized difference of length one—that is, the wavelet filter is essentially taking the difference between two adjacent observations. We call this a wavelet scale of length $\lambda_1 = 2^0 = 1$. A scale two Daubechies wavelet filter is a generalized difference of length two—that is, the wavelet filter first averages adjacent pairs of observations and then takes the difference of these averages. We call this a wavelet scale of length $\lambda_2 = 2^1 = 2$. The scale length increases by powers of two as a function of scale.

and $\mathcal{V}_J$ via

$$\mathcal{W} = \begin{bmatrix} \mathcal{W}_1 \\ \mathcal{W}_2 \\ \vdots \\ \mathcal{W}_J \\ \mathcal{V}_J \end{bmatrix}. \tag{4.17}$$

To complete our construction of the orthonormal matrix $\mathcal{W}$, we must be able to explicitly compute the wavelet filter coefficients for scales $1, \ldots, J$. The wavelet filter h_l is associated with unit scale and we assume it satisfies Equations 4.6 and 4.7. Given the transfer functions of the unit scale wavelet and scaling filters, define the wavelet filter $h_{j,l}$ for scale $\lambda_j = 2^{j-1}$ as the inverse DFT of

$$H_{j,k} = H_{1,2^{j-1}k \bmod N} \prod_{l=0}^{j-2} G_{1,2^l k \bmod N}, \quad k = 0, \ldots, N-1.$$

The modulus operator is required in order to deal with the boundary of a finite length vector of observations. Thus, we are implicitly assuming that x may be regarded as periodic (this issue is explored further in Section 4.6.3). The resulting wavelet filter associated with scale λ_j has length

$$L_j = (2^j - 1)(L - 1) + 1. \tag{4.18}$$

Also, let us define the scaling filter g_J for scale λ_J as the inverse DFT of

$$G_{J,k} = \prod_{l=0}^{J-1} G_{1,2^l k \bmod N}, \quad k = 0, \ldots, N-1.$$

4.4.1   Implementation of the DWT: Pyramid Algorithm

In practice the DWT is implemented via a pyramid algorithm (Mallat, 1989) that, starting with the data x_t, filters a series using h_1 and g_1, subsamples both filter outputs to half their original lengths, keeps the subsampled output from the h_1 filter as wavelet coefficients, and then repeats the above filtering operations on the subsampled output from the g_1 filter. Figure 4.15 gives a flow diagram for the first stage of the pyramid algorithm. The symbol $\downarrow 2$ means that every other value of the input vector is removed (downsampling by 2).

Let us go through the pyramid algorithm step by step with the intention of writing a short program to automate this process. For each iteration of the pyramid algorithm, we require three objects: the data vector x, the wavelet filter h_l, and the scaling filter g_l. Assuming those quantities are passed into the program, the first iteration of the pyramid algorithm begins by filtering (convolving) the data

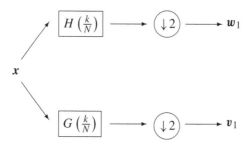

FIGURE 4.15 Flow diagram illustrating the decomposition of x into the unit scale wavelet coefficients w_1 and the unit scale scaling coefficients v_1. The time series x is filtered using the wavelet filter $H(f)$ and every other value removed (downsampled by 2) to produce the length $N/2$ wavelet coefficient vector w_1. Similarly, x is filtered using the scaling filter $G(f)$ and downsampled to produce the length $N/2$ vector of scaling coefficients v_1.

with each filter to obtain the following wavelet and scaling coefficients:

$$w_{1,t} = \sum_{l=0}^{L-1} h_l x_{2t+1-l \bmod N} \quad \text{and} \quad v_{1,t} = \sum_{l=0}^{L-1} g_l x_{2t+1-l \bmod N},$$

where $t = 0, 1, \ldots, N/2 - 1$ (this may be combined into the same loop for computational efficiency). Note that the downsampling operation has been included in the filtering step through the subscript of x_t. The N length vector of observations has been high- and low-pass filtered to obtain $N/2$ coefficients associated with this information. The second step of the pyramid algorithm starts by defining the "data" to be the scaling coefficients v_1 from the first iteration and apply the filtering operations as above to obtain the second level of wavelet and scaling coefficients:

$$w_{2,t} = \sum_{l=0}^{L-1} h_l v_{1,2t+1-l \bmod N} \quad \text{and} \quad v_{2,t} = \sum_{l=0}^{L-1} g_l v_{1,2t+1-l \bmod N},$$

$t = 0, 1, \ldots, N/4 - 1$. Keeping all vectors of wavelet coefficients, and the final level of scaling coefficients, we have the following length N decomposition $w = [w_1 \ w_2 \ v_2]^T$. After the third iteration of the pyramid algorithm, where we apply filtering operations to v_2, the decomposition now looks like $w = [w_1 \ w_2 \ w_3 \ v_3]^T$. This procedure may be repeated up to J times where $J = \log_2(N)$ and gives the vector of wavelet coefficients in Equation 4.15.

Inverting the DWT is achieved through upsampling the final level of wavelet and scaling coefficients, convolving them with their respective filters (wavelet for wavelet and scaling for scaling) and adding up the two filtered vectors. Figure 4.16 gives a flow diagram for the reconstruction of x from the first levels

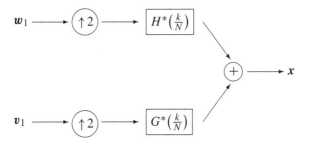

FIGURE 4.16 Flow diagram illustrating the reconstruction of x from the unit scale wavelet coefficients w_1 and the unit scale scaling coefficients v_1. Both w_1 and v_1 have zeros inserted in front of every observation (upsampling by 2). The upsampled wavelet coefficients are then filtered using the filter $H^*(f)$ and added to the upsampled scaling coefficients filtered by $G^*(f)$ to form x.

wavelet and scaling coefficient vectors. The symbol $\uparrow 2$ means that a zero is inserted before each observation in w_1 and v_1 (upsampling by 2). Starting with the final level of the DWT, upsampling the vectors w_J and v_J will result in to new vectors:

$$w_J^0 = [0 \ w_{J,0}]^T \quad \text{and} \quad v_J^0 = [0 \ v_{J,0}]^T.$$

The level $J - 1$ vector of scaling coefficients v_{J-1} is given by

$$v_{J-1,t} = \sum_{l=0}^{L-1} h_l w_{J,t+l \bmod 2}^0 + \sum_{l=0}^{L-1} g_l v_{J,t+l \bmod 2}^0,$$

$t = 0, 1$. Notice that the length of v_{J-1} is twice that of v_J, as to be expected. The next step of reconstruction involves upsampling to produce

$$w_{J-1}^0 = [0 \ w_{J-1,0} \ 0 \ w_{J-1,1}]^T \quad \text{and} \quad v_{J-1}^0 = [0 \ v_{J-1,0} \ 0 \ v_{J-1,1}]^T,$$

and the level $J - 2$ vector of scaling coefficients v_{J-2} is given by

$$v_{J-2,t} = \sum_{l=0}^{L-1} h_l w_{J-1,t+l \bmod 4}^0 + \sum_{l=0}^{L-1} g_l v_{J-1,t+l \bmod 4}^0,$$

$t = 0, 1, 2, 3$. This procedure may be repeated until the first level of wavelet and scaling coefficients have been upsampled and combined to produce the original vector of observations; that is,

$$x_t = \sum_{l=0}^{L-1} h_l w_{1,t+l \bmod N}^0 + \sum_{l=0}^{L-1} g_l v_{1,t+l \bmod N}^0,$$

$t = 0, 1, \ldots, N - 1$. This is exactly what is displayed in Figure 4.16.

4.4.2   Partial Discrete Wavelet Transform

When we are provided with a dyadic length time series, it is not necessary to implement the DWT down to level $J = \log_2(N)$. A *partial* DWT may be performed instead that terminates at a level $J_p < J$. The structure of the orthonormal matrix $\mathcal{W}$ is similar to Equation 4.17,

$$
\mathcal{W} = \begin{bmatrix} \mathcal{W}_1 \\ \mathcal{W}_2 \\ \vdots \\ \mathcal{W}_{J_p} \\ \mathcal{V}_{J_p} \end{bmatrix},
$$

except that the matrix of scaling filter coefficients will be a $N/2^{J_p} \times N$ matrix of circularly shifted scaling coefficient vectors. Let

$$
\boldsymbol{g}_{J_p} = [g_{J_p,N-1}, g_{J_p,N-2}, \dots, g_{J_p,1}, g_{J_p,0}]^T
$$

be the vector of zero-padded scale λ_{J_p} scaling filter coefficients in reverse order. The matrix $\mathcal{V}_{J_p}$ is defined to be the collection of $N/2$ circularly shifted versions of $\boldsymbol{g}_{J_p}$; that is,

$$
\mathcal{V}_{J_p} = \left[\boldsymbol{g}_{J_p}^{(2)}, \boldsymbol{g}_{J_p}^{(4)}, \dots, \boldsymbol{g}_{J_p}^{(N/2^{J_p}-1)}, \boldsymbol{g}_{J_p} \right]^T.
$$

The resulting vector of wavelet coefficients will now contain $N - N/2^{J_p}$ wavelet coefficients and $N/2^{J_p}$ scaling coefficients.

4.4.3   Multiresolution Analysis

Using the DWT, we may formulate an additive decomposition of a series of observations. Let $\boldsymbol{d}_j = \mathcal{W}_j^T \boldsymbol{w}_j$ for $j = 1, \dots, J$, define the jth level *wavelet detail* associated with changes in $\boldsymbol{x}$ at scale λ_j. The wavelet coefficients $\boldsymbol{w}_j = \mathcal{W}_j \boldsymbol{x}$ represent the portion of the wavelet analysis attributable to scale λ_j, while $\mathcal{W}_j^T \boldsymbol{w}_j$ is the portion of the wavelet synthesis attributable to scale λ_j. For a length $N = 2^J$ vector of observations, the final wavelet detail $\boldsymbol{d}_{J+1} = \mathcal{V}_J^T \mathbf{V}_J$ is equal to the sample mean of the observations.

A multiresolution analysis (MRA) may now be defined via

$$
x_t = \sum_{j=1}^{J+1} d_{j,t} \quad t = 0, \dots, N-1. \tag{4.19}
$$

That is, each observation x_t is a linear combination of wavelet detail coefficients. Let $\boldsymbol{s}_j = \sum_{k=j+1}^{J+1} \boldsymbol{d}_k$ define the jth level *wavelet smooth* for $0 \le j \le J$, where $\boldsymbol{s}_{J+1}$ is defined to be a vector of zeros. Whereas the wavelet detail $\boldsymbol{d}_j$ is associated with variations at a particular scale, s_j is a cumulative sum of these variations and will be smoother and smoother as j increases. In fact, $x - s_j = \sum_{k=1}^{j} d_j$ so that only lower-scale details (high-frequency features) will be apparent. The jth level *wavelet rough* characterizes the remaining lower-scale details through $r_j = \sum_{k=1}^{j} d_k$ for $1 \leq j \leq J + 1$, where r_0 is defined to be a vector of zeros. A vector of observations may thus be decomposed through a wavelet smooth and rough via

$$x = s_j + r_j,$$

for all j. The terminology "detail" and "smooth" were used by Percival and Walden (2000) to describe additive decompositions from Fourier and wavelet transforms.

4.4.4 Analysis of Variance

Like the DFT, orthonormality of the matrix $\mathcal{W}$ implies that the DWT is an energy (variance) preserving transform; that is,

$$\|w\|^2 = \sum_{j=1}^{J} \sum_{t=0}^{N/2^j - 1} w_{j,t}^2 + v_{J,0}^2 = \sum_{t=0}^{N-1} x_t^2 = \|x\|^2$$

(we use the term "energy" to mean the sum of squared coefficients of a vector). This can be easily proven through basic matrix manipulation via

$$
\begin{aligned}
\|x\|^2 = x^T x &= (\mathcal{W}w)^T \mathcal{W}w \\
&= w^T \mathcal{W}^T \mathcal{W}w = w^T w = \|w\|^2.
\end{aligned}
$$

Given the structure of the wavelet coefficients, $\|x\|^2$ is decomposed on a scale-by-scale basis via

$$\|x\|^2 = \sum_{j=1}^{J} \|w_j\|^2 + \|v_J\|^2, \tag{4.20}$$

where $\|w_j\|^2$ is the energy (proportional to variance) of x due to changes at scale λ_j and $\|v_J\|^2$ is the information due to changes at scales λ_J and higher. The orthonormality of $\mathcal{W}$ and $\mathcal{V}$ provides us with the following relationships: $d_j^T d_j = w_j^T w_j$ for $1 \leq j \leq J$ and $s_J^T s_J = v_J^T v_J$, respectively. Combining these produces an alternative decomposition of $\|x\|^2$ to Equation 4.20 via

$$\|x\|^2 = \sum_{j=1}^{J} \|d_j\|^2 + \|s_J\|^2.$$

4.4.5 Example: IBM Returns

In Section 4.4, we have studied the DWT. In this example, we apply the DWT to the daily IBM stock prices from May 17, 1961, to November 2, 1962. This is the classic data set studied in Box and Jenkins (1976). A return series was computed via the first difference of the log-transformed prices—that is, $r_t = \log(p_{t+1}) - \log(p_t)$. This series has been analyzed for changes in variance by Inclán (1993) and de Alba and Boue (2000). The returns series is plotted in the upper row of Figure 4.17a. There is an obvious increase in variance in the returns toward the latter third of the series. The length of the returns series is $N = 368$, which is divisible by $2^4 = 16$, and therefore we may perform an order $J_p = 4$ partial DWT on it.

The wavelet coefficient vectors $w_1, \ldots, w_4$ and scaling coefficient vector v_4 using the Haar wavelet are shown in the lower part of Figure 4.17a. The first scale of wavelet coefficients w_1 are filtering out the high-frequency fluctuations by essentially looking at adjacent differences in the data. There is a large group of rapidly fluctuating returns between observations 250 and 300. A small increase in the magnitude w_2 is also observed between observations 250 and 300, but smaller than the unit scale coefficients. This vector of wavelet coefficients is associated with changes of scale λ_2. Since the IBM return series does not exhibit low-frequency oscillations, the higher scale (low-frequency) vectors of wavelet coefficients w_3 and w_4 do not indicate large variations from zero. The same is true for the scaling coefficients, which are associated with averages of scale $2\lambda_4$ or greater.

The same decomposition was performed using the LA(8) wavelet filter and provided in Figure 4.17b. The interpretations for each of the vectors of coefficients is the same as in the case of the Haar wavelet filter. The wavelet coefficients will be different given the length of the filter is now eight versus two, and should isolate features in a specific frequency interval better since the LA(8) is a better approximation to an ideal band-pass filter over the Haar wavelet. Note, the LA(8) wavelet coefficient vectors have been circularly shifted in order to better align features in the wavelet coefficients with the original time series. To be precise, the first vector of coefficients has been shifted to the left by two time units $w_1^{(-2)}$ due to the specific phase properties of the LA(8) wavelet filter. See Section 4.6.3 for a simple heuristic on how much to shift vectors of DWT coefficients.

Figure 4.18 displays the sum of squared DWT coefficients for the IBM return series, normalized by N^{-1}. The decomposition of variance is governed by Equation 4.20, but the distribution of variance will vary depending on the wavelet filter. As the length of the wavelet filter increases, the approximation to an ideal band-pass filter improves and therefore the wavelet filter will better capture the variability in the frequency intervals associated with the DWT wavelet coefficients. The sum of squared wavelet coefficients for the Haar wavelet filter decreases for the first three scales and then peaks for the vector w_4, whereas

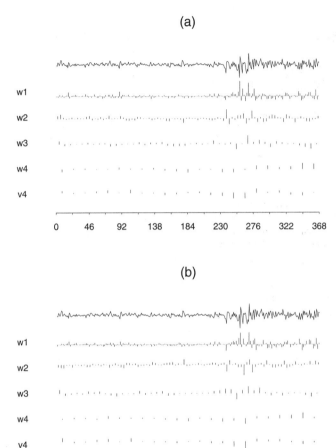

FIGURE 4.17   Wavelet decompositions of the IBM return series ($N = 368$). In each plot, the upper row is the original time series. (a) Haar DWT coefficient vectors – from top to bottom – $w_1, \ldots, w_4$ and scaling coefficient vector v_4. (b) Circularly shifted LA(8) DWT coefficient vectors – from top to bottom – $w_1^{(-2)}$, $w_2^{(-2)}$, $w_3^{(-3)}$, $w_4^{(-3)}$ and $v_4^{(-2)}$—to better align them with the original series (see text for details).

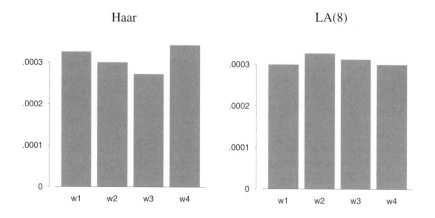

FIGURE 4.18 Sum of squared wavelet coefficient vectors $\left\| \boldsymbol{w}_j \right\|^2$, $j = 1, \ldots, 4$, for the IBM return series using the Haar and LA(8) wavelet filters. Although both transforms will capture the variance of the series, they distribute it differently because of their approximate band-pass properties.

$\left\| \boldsymbol{w}_j \right\|^2$ varies only slightly between all scales $j = 1, \ldots, 4$ when using the LA(8) wavelet filter (Figure 4.18).

Let us now look at the volatility $v_t = |r_t|$ of the IBM stock price series through a DWT multiresolution analysis. The volatility series is provided in the top row of Figure 4.19a and exhibits the increase in volatility we observed in the return series. A DWT multiresolution analysis (MRA) using the Haar wavelet filter is given below the volatility series in Figure 4.19a. The five rows below the data display the first four wavelet details and wavelet smooth that form an additive decomposition via Equation 4.19. That is, at each time point t adding up the wavelet detail coefficients $d_{j,t}$, $j = 1, \ldots, 4$, and the wavelet smooth $s_{4,t}$ will produce the coefficient v_t from the volatility series. All the information contained in the volatility series is perfectly captured in the MRA. No anomalies have been introduced by this procedure.

Figure 4.19b shows a similar MRA of the IBM volatility series, but instead of the Haar wavelet we utilize the LA(8) wavelet filter. As in the case of the Haar MRA, Equation 4.19 holds regardless of the wavelet filter chosen. How do we explain the differences between the wavelet details and smooth? This follows from the definitions of $\boldsymbol{d}_j$ and $\boldsymbol{s}_J$ via projection. From Section 4.4.3, we know that $\boldsymbol{d}_j = \mathcal{W}_j^T \boldsymbol{w}_j$, so the jth level wavelet detail is a projection of the jth level wavelet basis vectors onto the level j wavelet coefficients. If $\boldsymbol{w}_j$ contains a large coefficient (in magnitude), then the wavelet detail will contain a large copy of the basis function at that location. This is clearly seen in Figure 4.19a where each of the wavelet details and smooth are composed of piecewise constant functions (i.e., Haar wavelet basis functions). Given the choice of wavelet filter, the MRA will mimic its aesthetic characteristics. The LA(8) wavelet is relatively smooth,

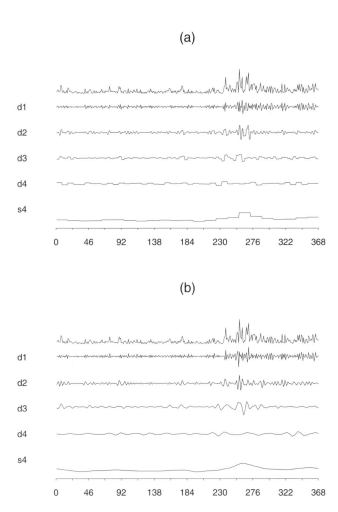

FIGURE 4.19 DWT multiresolution analysis of the IBM volatility series using the (a) Haar and (b) LA(8) wavelet filters. The volatility series is plotted in the top row of each plot. Below it – from top to bottom – are the wavelet details $d_1, \ldots, d_4$ and wavelet smooth s_4. All rows are plotted on the same vertical scale.

when compared with the Haar wavelet filters, and therefore produces a smoothly varying MRA. According to the LA(8) MRA, the large fluctuations in volatility occur across the first three scales across trading days 230 to 299. There is a lack of volatility activity at the fourth scale, but an increase during those days in the low-frequency content (wavelet smooth).

4.4.6   Example: An Overlapping Generations Model

In this section we provide an example from an overlapping generation (OLG) framework with multiple nonstationary equilibria (McCandless and Wallace, 1991). The utility function of the individual h of generation k is written by

$$u_t^h = -\left(c_t^{h,k} - b^y\right)^2 - \beta \left(c_{t+1}^{h,k} - b^0\right)^2, \tag{4.21}$$

where

$$b = \begin{bmatrix} b^y \\ b^o \end{bmatrix} = \begin{bmatrix} 2 \\ 2 \end{bmatrix}$$

is the bliss point, and $c_t^{h,k}$ and $c_{t+1}^{h,k}$ are the consumption levels of individual h, when young (time t) and old (time $t+1$), respectively. The number of individuals in a given generation is assumed to be $N_t = 100$ and the amount of land $A = 100$ for all t. The land is assumed to provide no crop. The endowments of person h are

$$\begin{bmatrix} w_t^{h,k} \\ w_{t+1}^{h,k} \end{bmatrix} = \begin{bmatrix} 2 \\ 1 \end{bmatrix}$$

for young and old, respectively.

The equilibrium conditions that satisfy the utility maximization and market clearing in the markets for land, private borrowing, and the consumption good yield the following pricing function:

$$p_t = f(p_{t+1}) = \left(\beta p_{t+1} - \beta p_{t+1}^2\right)^{1/2}. \tag{4.22}$$

Equation 4.22 is plotted for two different values, $\beta = 3.1$ and $\beta = 4$, in Figure 4.20. The function is bell shaped and means that there are two values of p_{t+1} that will produce the same value of p_t—except for the p_{t+1} value where the function f takes the largest p_t value. The stationary equilibrium price sequences satisfy the equality $p_{t+1} = p_t = p^* = f(p^*)$ so that the two stationary equilibria are the origin $p^* = 0$ and

$$p^* = \frac{\beta}{1+\beta}, \quad \beta > 1. \tag{4.23}$$

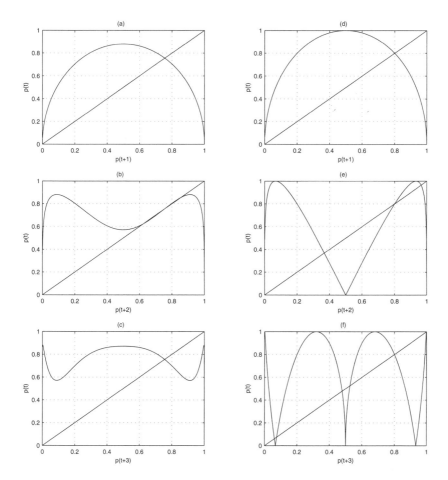

FIGURE 4.20 Phase diagram for the OLG pricing function in Equation 4.22. The left and the right panels refer to $\beta = 3.1$ and $\beta = 4$ values, respectively. The rows are the phase diagrams for the price function in the $(t, t+1)$, $(t, t+2)$, and $(t, t+3)$ space, respectively. (a) Two stationary equilibria at 0 and 0.7561. (b) The system exhibits a stable two-period cycle and (c) there is no three-period cycle. (d) There are two stationary equilibria at 0 and 0.80, (e) a two-period cycle, and (f) two different three-period cycles.

The stationary equilibrium values are the points at which the 45° line crosses the function $f(p_{t+1})$. When $\beta = 3.1$, there are two stationary equilibria at 0 and 0.7561. Similarly, there are two stationary equilibria for $\beta = 4$ at 0 and 0.80. If the economy starts at one of these stationary equilibria, prices will stay at these equilibrium values at every time period.

The stationary equilibrium $p^*(\beta) > 0$ is stable as long as the slope of $f(p^*)$ is absolutely smaller than one—that is, $|df(p^*)/dp^*| < 1$. As the slope of the function increases everywhere when β is increased, there will be a value of β such that the stationary equilibrium p^* becomes unstable. The slope of function

f when evaluated at $p = p^*$ is given by

$$\frac{df(p_{t+1})}{dp_{t+1}} = \frac{1 - \beta}{2},$$
(4.24)

so that the stationary equilibria when $\beta < 3$ are stable.[13] In our example, the stationary equilibrium of 0.7561 for $\beta = 3.1$ and 0.80 for $\beta = 4$ are not stable. In addition to these stationary equilibria, the function f also exhibits infinitely many nonstationary equilibria.

The two and three-period cycles in prices occur at $p_{t+2} = p_t$ and $p_{t+3} = p_t$. These cycles are obtained from the composite functions

$$p_t = f(f(p_{t+2})) = g^2(p_{t+2})$$
(4.25)

and

$$p_t = f(f(f(p_{t+3}))) = g^3(p_{t+3}).$$
(4.26)

The composite function g^2 is illustrated in Figure 4.20b. At $\beta = 3.1$ the system exhibits a stable two-period cycle. Figure 4.20c illustrates the composite function g^3 for $\beta = 3.1$, where there is only one equilibrium at which $p_{t+3} = p_t$. This is the stationary equilibrium $p^* = 0.7561$ we found earlier. Therefore, there is no three-period cycle when $\beta = 3.1$.

For $\beta = 4$ (see Figure 4.20d), there is a two-period cycle (see Figure 4.20e) other than the stationary equilibria at 0 and 0.8. The two-period cycle occurs at 0.368 and 0.965. If the economy starts at one of these prices, the price path follows: 0.368, 0.965, 0.368, 0.965, 0.368, 0.965, and so on. Figure 4.20f presents the composite function g^3 for $\beta = 4$ such that two different three-period cycles emerge.

From Sarkovskii's theorem,[14] a system contains some starting value that will give rise to a cycle of any chosen periodicity, if that system has a three-period cycle. Therefore, Equation 4.22 contains cycles of any order for $\beta = 4$ and exhibits chaotic dynamics.

We constructed two different price series from Equation 4.22. The first price series is 5000 observations that are generated by setting $\beta = 3.1$. The first and last 1000 points of the resulting series are excluded in order to eliminate any start-off effects and the remaining points are plotted[15] in Figure 4.21a. The price series has a constant oscillation around the average value of 0.738. The price series in Figure 4.21a is decomposed into a wavelet detail and a smooth ($J = 1$) through DWT multiresolution analysis (MRA) using the LA(8) wavelet filter. The results are presented in Figure 4.21b-c. The wavelet detail and wavelet

---

[13] When $\beta = 3$, the stationary equilibrium value 0.75 is said to be *marginally stable* (i.e., the system makes a slow gradual oscillatory converge to the stationary equilibrium).

[14] For a proof, see Devaney (1986).

[15] Only the first 50 from the 3000 observations are plotted so that the figure is not cluttered.

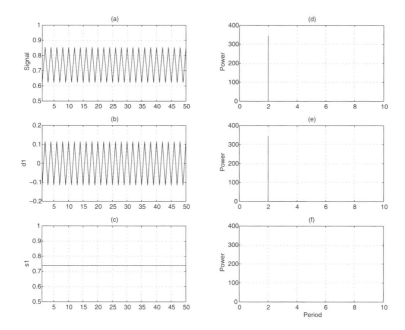

FIGURE 4.21 LA(8) DWT multiresolution analysis (MRA) of the OLG price series of Equation 4.22 for $\beta = 3.1$ (left panel). The price series is plotted in the top row and below it – from top to bottom – is the wavelet detail d_1 and wavelet smooth s_1. In the right panel are the power spectra of the series in the left panel. The power spectra in (d) and (e) indicate a unique peak at period 2 in the price series and wavelet detail d_1, whereas (f) confirms the absence of any periodicities in the wavelet smooth s_1.

smooth form an additive decomposition via Equation 4.19. As indicated earlier in Section 4.4.5, adding up the wavelet detail coefficients $d_{1,t}$ and the wavelet smooth $s_{1,t}$ at each time t will produce the price series coefficient p_t.

It is expected that a two-period cyclical component will be captured by the wavelet detail d_1. Since there is no other periodicity, the wavelet smooth (s_1) should represent the average value around which the price series oscillates. Figure 4.21b indicates that the oscillations are precisely captured by the wavelet detail. In Figure 4.21e, the power spectrum indicates that there is a unique peak at period 2. The wavelet smooth in Figure 4.21c is flat at 0.738 indicating the average value of the price series and the power spectrum in Figure 4.21f confirms the absence of any periodicities.

For $\beta = 4$, the price series is plotted[16] in Figure 4.22a. The price series is decomposed into three wavelet details and a wavelet smooth ($J = 3$) through a DWT MRA by using the LA(8) wavelet filter. The results are presented in Figure 4.22b-e. Note that for a level j MRA, the wavelet decomposition of the original time series consists of j wavelet details and a single wavelet smooth. At each

---

[16] As before, the first 300 from the 3000 observations are plotted.

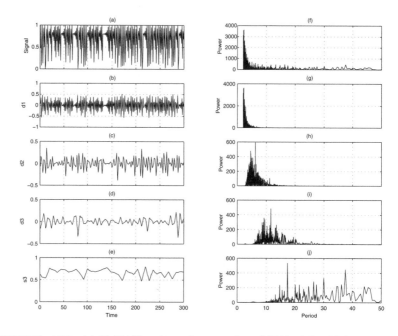

FIGURE 4.22 LA(8) DWT multiresolution analysis (MRA) of the OLG price series of Equation 4.22 for $\beta = 4$ (left panel). The price series is plotted in the top row while below it – from top to bottom – are the wavelet details d_1, d_2, d_3, and wavelet smooth s_3. In the right panel are the power spectra of the original series in the left panel. The power spectra in (g)–(j) indicate the corresponding periodic components in the wavelet details and wavelet smooth.

increasing level j, the new wavelet smooth represents the low-frequency characteristics of the previous approximation while the wavelet details at each level represent the higher-frequency dynamics. The power spectra in Figure 4.22f-j indicate the corresponding periodic components in the wavelet details d_1, d_2, d_3, and wavelet smooth s_3. If there were infinitely many data points available, we could have decomposed the data (signal) into an infinite number of wavelet details with each detail capturing certain periodicities in the data.

4.5 THE MAXIMAL OVERLAP DISCRETE WAVELET TRANSFORM

We have introduced the DWT as an alternative to the Fourier transform for a time series. It provides wavelet coefficients that are local in both time and frequency. The DWT may be thought of as a critical sampling of the CWT—that is, it uses the least number of coefficients possible. As we will explore in future chapters, the DWT possesses key attributes such as approximately decorrelating certain processes and efficiently captures important features of a process in a limited number of coefficients. An alternative wavelet transform—the maximal overlap[17] discrete wavelet transform (MODWT)—is computed by *not* subsampling the filtered output (Figure 4.15). The MODWT gives up orthogonality in order to gain features the DWT does not possess. A consequence of this is the wavelet and scaling coefficients must be rescaled in order to retain the variance preserving property of the DWT.

The following properties are important in distinguishing the MODWT from the DWT (Percival and Mofjeld, 1997):

1. The MODWT can handle any sample size N, while the J_pth order partial DWT (Section 4.4.2) restricts the sample size to a multiple of 2^{J_p}.

2. The detail and smooth coefficients of a MODWT multiresolution analysis (Section 4.5.2) are associated with zero phase filters. This means events that feature in the original time series may be properly aligned with features in the multiresolution analysis.

3. The MODWT is invariant to circularly shifting the original time series. Hence, shifting the time series by an integer unit will shift the MODWT wavelet and scaling coefficients the same amount. This property does not hold for the DWT.

4. While both the DWT and MODWT can perform an analysis of variance on a time series, the MODWT wavelet variance estimator is asymptotically more efficient than the same estimator based on the DWT (Percival, 1995).

The MODWT goes by several names in the statistical and engineering literature, such as, the "stationary DWT" (Nason and Silverman, 1995), "translation-invariant DWT" (Coifman and Donoho, 1995; Liang and Parks, 1996), and "time-invariant DWT" (Pesquet *et al.*, 1996).

4.5.1 Definition

Let x be an arbitrary length N vector of observations. The length $(J + 1)N$ vector of MODWT coefficients $\widetilde{w}$ is obtained via

$$\widetilde{w} = \widetilde{\mathcal{W}}x,$$

where $\widetilde{\mathcal{W}}$ is a $(J+1)N \times N$ matrix defining the MODWT. The vector of MODWT coefficients may be organized into $J + 1$ vectors via

$$\widetilde{w} = [\widetilde{w}_1, \widetilde{w}_2, \dots, \widetilde{w}_J, \widetilde{v}_J]^T, \tag{4.27}$$

where $\widetilde{w}_j$ is a length $N/2^j$ vector of wavelet coefficients associated with changes on a scale of length $\lambda_j = 2^{j-1}$ and $\widetilde{v}_J$ is a length $N/2^J$ vector of scaling coefficients associated with averages on a scale of length $2^J = 2\lambda_J$, just as with

---

[17] The term *maximal overlap* comes from the relationship of the MODWT with estimators of the Allan variance (Allan, 1966; Greenhall, 1991; Percival and Guttorp, 1994).

the DWT. For time series of dyadic length ($N = 2^J$), the MODWT may be subsampled and rescaled to obtain DWT wavelet coefficients via

$$w_{j,t} = 2^{j/2} \widetilde{w}_{j,2^j(t+1)-1}, \quad t = 0, \dots, N/2^j - 1,$$

and DWT scaling coefficients via

$$v_{J,t} = 2^{J/2} \widetilde{v}_{J,2^J(t+1)-1}, \quad t = 0, \dots, N/2^J - 1.$$

Similar to the orthonormal matrix defining the DWT, the matrix $\widetilde{\mathcal{W}}$ is also made up of $J + 1$ submatrices, each of them $N \times N$, and may be expressed as

$$\widetilde{\mathcal{W}} = \begin{bmatrix} \widetilde{\mathcal{W}}_1 \\ \widetilde{\mathcal{W}}_2 \\ \vdots \\ \widetilde{\mathcal{W}}_J \\ \widetilde{\mathcal{V}}_J \end{bmatrix}.$$

Instead of using the wavelet and scaling filters from Section 4.4, the MODWT utilizes the rescaled filters ($j = 1, \dots, J$)

$$\tilde{\boldsymbol{h}}_j = \boldsymbol{h}_j / 2^j \quad \text{and} \quad \tilde{\boldsymbol{g}}_J = \boldsymbol{g}_J / 2^J.$$

To construct the $N \times N$ dimensional submatrix $\widetilde{\mathcal{W}}_1$, we circularly shift the rescaled wavelet filter vector $\tilde{\boldsymbol{h}}_1$ by integer units to the right so that

$$\widetilde{\mathcal{W}}_1 = \left[\tilde{\boldsymbol{h}}_1^{(1)}, \tilde{\boldsymbol{h}}_1^{(2)}, \tilde{\boldsymbol{h}}_1^{(3)}, \dots, \tilde{\boldsymbol{h}}_1^{(N-2)}, \tilde{\boldsymbol{h}}_1^{(N-1)}, \tilde{\boldsymbol{h}}_1 \right]^T. \tag{4.28}$$

This matrix may be interpreted as the interweaving of the DWT submatrix $\mathcal{W}_1$ with a circularly shifted (to the right by one unit) version of itself. The remaining submatrices $\widetilde{\mathcal{W}}_2, \dots, \widetilde{\mathcal{W}}_J$ are formed similarly to Equation 4.28, only replace $\tilde{\boldsymbol{h}}_1$ by $\tilde{\boldsymbol{h}}_j$.

In practice, a pyramid algorithm is utilized similar to that of the DWT to compute the MODWT. Starting with the data x_t (no longer restricted to be a dyadic length), filter it using $\tilde{\boldsymbol{h}}_1$ and $\tilde{\boldsymbol{g}}_1$ to obtain the length N vectors of wavelet and scaling coefficients $\widetilde{\boldsymbol{w}}_1$ and $\widetilde{\boldsymbol{v}}_1$, respectively. This is similar to the operation in Figure 4.15 except that no downsampling is performed.

For each iteration of the MODWT pyramid algorithm, we require three objects: the data vector $\boldsymbol{x}$, the wavelet filter $\tilde{\boldsymbol{h}}_l$ and the scaling filter $\tilde{\boldsymbol{g}}_l$. The first iteration of the pyramid algorithm begins by filtering (convolving) the data with each filter to obtain the following wavelet and scaling coefficients:

$$\widetilde{w}_{1,t} = \sum_{l=0}^{L-1} \tilde{h}_l x_{t-l \bmod N} \quad \text{and} \quad \widetilde{v}_{1,t} = \sum_{l=0}^{L-1} \tilde{g}_l x_{t-l \bmod N},$$

where $t = 0, 1, \ldots, N - 1$. The length N vector of observations has been high- and low-pass filtered to obtain N (redundant) coefficients associated with this information. The second step of the MODWT pyramid algorithm starts by defining the data to be the scaling coefficients $\tilde{v}_1$ from the first iteration and apply the filtering operations as above to obtain the second level of wavelet and scaling coefficients

$$\tilde{w}_{2,t} = \sum_{l=0}^{L-1} \tilde{h}_l \tilde{v}_{1,t-l \bmod N} \quad \text{and} \quad \tilde{v}_{2,t} = \sum_{l=0}^{L-1} \tilde{g}_l \tilde{v}_{1,t-l \bmod N},$$

$t = 0, 1, \ldots, N - 1$. Keeping all vectors of wavelet coefficients, and the final level of scaling coefficients, we have the following length N decomposition: $\tilde{w} = [\tilde{w}_1 \; \tilde{w}_2 \; \tilde{v}_2]^T$. After the third iteration of the pyramid algorithm, where we apply filtering operations to v_2, the decomposition now looks like $\tilde{w} = [\tilde{w}_1 \; \tilde{w}_2 \; \tilde{w}_3 \; \tilde{v}_3]^T$. This procedure may be repeated up to J times where $J = \log_2(N)$ and gives the vector of MODWT coefficients in Equation 4.27.

Inverting the MODWT is achieved through convolving the final level of wavelet and scaling coefficients with their respective filters (wavelet for wavelet and scaling for scaling) and adding up the two filtered vectors. Starting with the final level of the DWT, the vectors $\tilde{w}_J$ and $\tilde{v}_J$ are filtered and combined to produce level $J - 1$ vector of scaling coefficients $\tilde{v}_{J-1}$ given by

$$\tilde{v}_{J-1,t} = \sum_{l=0}^{L-1} \tilde{h}_l \tilde{w}_{J,t+l \bmod N} + \sum_{l=0}^{L-1} \tilde{g}_l \tilde{v}_{J,t+l \bmod N},$$

$t = 0, 1, \ldots, N - 1$. Notice that the length of $\tilde{v}_{J-1}$ is the same as $\tilde{v}_J$. The level $J - 2$ vector of scaling coefficients $\tilde{v}_{J-2}$ is given by

$$\tilde{v}_{J-2,t} = \sum_{l=0}^{L-1} \tilde{h}_l \tilde{w}_{J-1,t+l \bmod N} + \sum_{l=0}^{L-1} \tilde{g}_l \tilde{v}_{J-1,t+l \bmod N},$$

$t = 0, 1, \ldots, N - 1$. This procedure may be repeated until the first level of wavelet and scaling coefficients have been combined to produce the original vector of observations; that is,

$$x_t = \sum_{l=0}^{L-1} \tilde{h}_l \tilde{w}_{1,t+l \bmod N} + \sum_{l=0}^{L-1} \tilde{g}_l \tilde{v}_{1,t+l \bmod N},$$

$t = 0, 1, \ldots, N - 1$.

4.5.2   Multiresolution Analysis

An analogous MRA to that of the DWT may be performed utilizing the MODWT via

$$x_t = \sum_{j=1}^{J+1} \tilde{d}_{j,t}, \quad t = 0, \ldots, N - 1,$$

where $\widetilde{d}_{j,t}$ is the tth element of $\widetilde{\boldsymbol{d}}_j = \widetilde{\mathcal{W}}_j^T \widetilde{\boldsymbol{w}}_j$ for $j = 1, \ldots, J$. We may also define the MODWT-based wavelet smooths and roughs to be

$$\widetilde{s}_{J,t} = \sum_{k=j+1}^{J+1} \widetilde{d}_{k,t} \quad \text{and} \quad \widetilde{r}_{j,t} = \sum_{k=1}^{j} \widetilde{d}_{k,t}, \quad t = 0, \ldots, N - 1,$$

respectively. A key feature to an MRA using the MODWT is that the wavelet details and smooth are associated with zero-phase filters (Section 2.3.2). Thus, interesting features in the wavelet details and smooth may be perfectly aligned with the original time series. This attribute is not available through the DWT since it subsamples the output of its filtering operations (Figure 4.15).

4.5.3   Analysis of Variance

Percival and Mofjeld (1997) proved that the MODWT is an energy (variance) preserving transform—that is, the variance of the original time series is perfectly captured by the variance of the coefficients from the MODWT. Specifically, the total variance of a time series can be partitioned using the MODWT wavelet and scaling coefficient vectors; that is,

$$\|\boldsymbol{x}\|^2 = \sum_{j=1}^{J} \|\widetilde{\boldsymbol{w}}_j\|^2 + \|\widetilde{\boldsymbol{v}}_J\|^2. \tag{4.29}$$

This will allow us to construct MODWT versions of the wavelet variance (Section 7.2) and the wavelet covariance (Section 7.4).

Whereas a variance decomposition using the wavelet details and smooth is valid for the DWT, it is not valid for the MODWT in general. To see this, consider the squared coefficients from the unit scale detail:

$$\|\widetilde{\boldsymbol{d}}_1\|^2 = \|\widetilde{\mathcal{W}}_1^T \widetilde{\boldsymbol{w}}_1\|^2 = \widetilde{\boldsymbol{w}}_1^T \widetilde{\mathcal{W}}_1 \widetilde{\mathcal{W}}_1^T \widetilde{\boldsymbol{w}}_1.$$

The $N \times N$ matrix $\widetilde{\mathcal{W}}_1$ is not orthonormal and therefore $\|\widetilde{\boldsymbol{d}}_1\|^2 \neq \|\widetilde{\boldsymbol{w}}_1\|^2$. Percival and Walden (2000, Sec. 5.3) shows that, in fact, $\|\widetilde{\boldsymbol{d}}_1\|^2 \leq \|\widetilde{\boldsymbol{w}}_1\|^2$. Hence, when analyzing the variance of a time series we are restricted to using the MODWT coefficients – not the wavelet details!

4.5.4   Example: IBM Stock Prices

To provide an example wavelet analysis using the MODWT, we consider the IBM returns r_t and volatility series v_t. The both have length $N = 368$, but with the MODWT we are no longer limited to decomposing a sample size of dyadic length. The only limiting factor is the overall depth of the transform given by $J = \lfloor \log_2(N) \rfloor = 8$. For display purposes, we choose to perform a level $J = 4$ MODWT on the return series again using the Haar and LA(8) wavelet filters. Figure 4.23a shows the MODWT coefficient vectors of r_t using the Haar

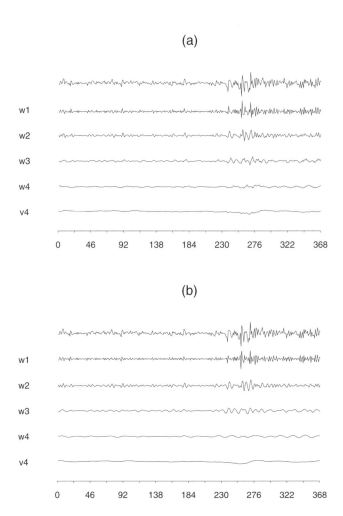

FIGURE 4.23 MODWT decompositions of the IBM return series ($N = 368$). In each plot, the upper row is the original time series. (a) Haar MODWT coefficient vectors – from top to bottom – $\widetilde{w}_1, \ldots, \widetilde{w}_4$ and scaling coefficient vector $\widetilde{v}_4$. (b) Circularly shifted LA(8) MODWT coefficient vectors – displayed vectors are actually $\widetilde{w}_1^{(-4)}$, $\widetilde{w}_2^{(-10)}$, $\widetilde{w}_3^{(-25)}$, $\widetilde{w}_4^{(-53)}$ and $\widetilde{v}_4^{(-45)}$ – to better align them with the original series (see text for details).

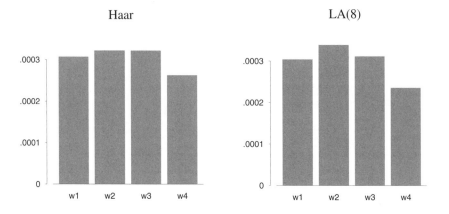

FIGURE 4.24 Sum of squared MODWT coefficient vectors $\left\| \widetilde{\boldsymbol{w}}_j \right\|^2$, $j = 1, \ldots, 4$, for the IBM return series using the Haar and LA(8) wavelet filters.

wavelet. Note that there are N wavelet coefficients at each scale because the MODWT does not subsample after filtering. The first scale of wavelet coefficients $\widetilde{\boldsymbol{w}}_1$ contain the DWT coefficients in Figure 4.17a, scaled by $1/\sqrt{2}$, and also the DWT coefficients applied to $\boldsymbol{x}$ circularly shifted by one. This means the MODWT coefficients are correlated and will appear smoother than the DWT coefficients. This is more noticeable when we move to higher scales (lower frequencies). This smoothness is even more apparent when we look at the LA(8) MODWT coefficients in Figure 4.23b. The longer wavelet filter has induced significant amounts of correlation between adjacent coefficients, thus producing even smoother vectors of wavelet and scaling coefficients. The LA(8) wavelet coefficient vectors have been circularly shifted in order to better align features in the wavelet coefficients with the original time series. To be precise, the first vector of coefficients has been shifted to the left by four time units $\boldsymbol{w}_1^{(-4)}$ due to the specific phase properties of the LA(8) wavelet filter. See Section 4.6.3 for a simple heuristic on how much to shift vectors of MODWT coefficients.

The sum of squared MODWT coefficients, normalized appropriately for comparison with Figure 4.18, for the IBM return series is displayed in Figure 4.24. The decomposition of variance by the MODWT is governed by Equation 4.29, and the distribution of variance will appear similar – but not identical – to that of the DWT because more information is being used to estimate this unknown amount of variability on a scale-by-scale basis.

Figure 4.25 displays the MODWT multiresolution analysis using the LA(8) wavelet filter. When contrasted against Figure 4.19b, there does not appear to be any obvious "contamination" by the wavelet basis function. The correlation between coefficients is effectively smoothing over features specific to the wavelet filter. Hence, even when using nonsmooth wavelet filters, such as the Haar

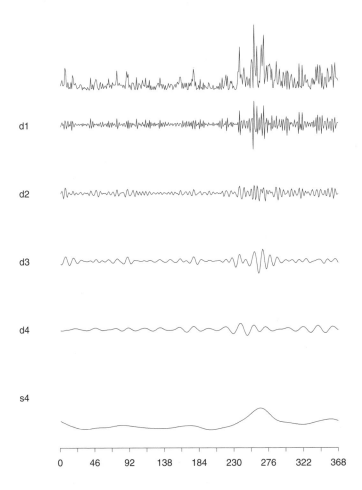

FIGURE 4.25 LA(8) MODWT multiresolution analysis of the IBM volatility series. The volatility series is plotted in the top row. Below it – from top to bottom – are the wavelet details $\widetilde{d}_1, \ldots, \widetilde{d}_4$, and wavelet smooth $\widetilde{s}_4$. All rows are plotted on the same vertical scale.

or D(4), we may observe reasonably smooth wavelet details and smooth. As noted in the beginning of Section 4.5, $\tilde{d}_j$ and $\tilde{s}_J$ are associated with zero-phase filters, and therefore features in the original time series line up perfectly with the MRA. Thus, we may observe the flow of increased volatility in the wavelet details between observations 250 and 300 as a function of scale. The wavelet smooth, corresponding to low-frequency trends and the sample mean, shows a significant bump in this same region indicating that this change in volatility is a very broadband feature in the volatility series.

4.5.5 Example: AR(1) with Seasonalities

The presence of seasonalities (periodicities) in a persistent process may obscure the underlying low frequency dynamics. Specifically, the periodic component pulls the calculated autocorrelations down, giving the impression that there is no persistence other than particular periodicities. Consider the following AR(1) process with a periodic component

$$y_t = 0.95 y_{t-1} + \sum_{s=1}^{4} \left[3 \sin\left(\frac{2\pi t}{P_s} \right) + 0.9 v_{st} \right] + \epsilon_t \qquad (4.30)$$

for $t = 1, \ldots, N$. The process has three, four, five, and six period stochastic seasonalities with periodic components, $P_1 = 3$, $P_2 = 4$, $P_3 = 5$, and $P_4 = 6$. The random variables ϵ_t and v_{st} are identically and independently distributed $N(0, 1)$ disturbance terms.

Figure 4.26 presents the autocorrelation functions (ACFs) from a length $N = 1000$ simulated AR(1) process with and without periodic components. The ACF of the AR(1) process without seasonality (excluding $\sum [3 \sin(2\pi t / P_s) + 0.9 v_{st}]$ from the simulated process) starts from a value of 0.95 and decays hyperbolically.[18] However, the ACF of the AR(1) process with the seasonality starts from 0.40 and fluctuates between positive and negative values. The seasonality is evident in the peaks at lags that are multiples of 6 (at lags 12, 24, 36, etc.). The underlying persistence of the AR(1) process in the absence of the seasonality component is entirely obscured by these periodic components.

A well-designed seasonal adjustment procedure should therefore separate the data from its seasonal components and leave the underlying inherent nonseasonal structure intact. In Figure 4.26 the solid line is the ACF of the nonseasonal AR(1) dynamics and the dotted lines are the ACF of the de-seasonalized series using a MODWT multiresolution analysis (MRA). We perform a level $J = 2$ MODWT on the simulated AR(1) series in Equation 4.30 using LA(8) wavelet filters.[19]

The wavelet detail d_1 (associated with changes on the unit scale) captures frequencies $1/4 \leq f \leq 1/2$ (i.e., any oscillation with a period length of 2 to 4

---

[18] The autocorrelation coefficient is 0.95^k, where k is the number of lags.

[19] The results are not very sensitive to the choice of the wavelet family as long as the underlying process is stationary or an integer difference of the process is stationary.

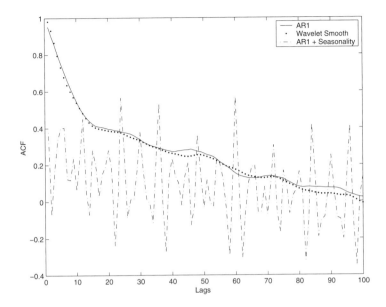

FIGURE 4.26 Sample ACF for a simulated AR(1) process (straight line), AR(1) plus seasonal process (dashed line), and MODWT smooth of the AR(1) plus seasonal process (dotted line).

time units). Similarly, d_2 contains frequencies $1/8 \leq f \leq 1/4$, any oscillation with a period length of 4 to 8 units of time. We expect the wavelet smooth s_2 only contains the long-memory dynamics and is free of seasonalities. As Figure 4.26 displays, using an MRA to selectively filter a time series successfully uncovers the true ACF without inducing any spurious persistence into the filtered series.

4.6 PRACTICAL ISSUES IN IMPLEMENTATION

We have provided a basic introduction to wavelets and two discrete wavelet transforms. From this foundation there are a variety of choices to make when performing a wavelet analysis in practice. We have brought up some of these points when analyzing the IBM return and volatility series, and we revisit them now.

4.6.1 Selecting a Wavelet Basis

The choice of wavelet basis function is important when analyzing a given time series for two reasons. First, as we noted in Section 4.3, the length of a discrete wavelet function determines how well it approximates an ideal band-pass filter, which dictates how well the filter is able to isolate features to specific frequency intervals. Second, as illustrated in the DWT MRAs shown in Figures 4.19a and 4.19b the wavelet basis function is being used to represent the information contained in the time series of interest and, hence, should mimic its underlying features. If the data appear to be constructed of piecewise constant functions, then the Haar wavelet would be the most appropriate wavelet function, or if it is fairly smooth, then a longer wavelet filter such as the LA(8) may be desired. Because of its added correlation between adjacent wavelet coefficients, the choice of wavelet function is not as vital when using the MODWT to decompose a given time series.

4.6.2   Nondyadic Length Time Series

The assumption of a dyadic length time series ($N = 2^J$), made for convenience in Section 4.4, is not always available to us in practice. Although when computing a partial DWT we may relax the requirement for a dyadic-length vector and instead only require $N = 2^{J_p}$, we must consider methods for computing the DWT on nondyadic sample sizes. Recall that the MODWT is valid for any length time series and does not require any augmentation of the data.

One obvious remedy is to "pad" the time series with values and increase its length to the next power of two. There are several choices for the value of these padded coefficients, such as zeros or the sample mean or the last value in the series. Repeating the last value of the series can be viewed as using a polynomial of order zero. Higher-order polynomials may also be used to pad the series; see, for example, Bruce and Gao (1996, Ch. 15) and Oh *et al.* (2001). Ogden (1997) compared four methods: padding with zeros, repeating the last observation, interpolation, and numerical integration. He found that, although no method proved to be clearly superior, the numeric integration method may be superior in terms of second-order properties of the wavelet coefficients, but more computationally intense than the alternatives.

4.6.3   Boundary Conditions

Application of the DWT and MODWT to finite-length time series brings up the crucial issue of wavelets affected by the boundary. That is, the wavelet transform is based on filtering a time series, and when one end of the vector is encountered there must be an established method for computing the remaining wavelet coefficients. The most natural method for dealing with the boundary is to assume the length N series is periodic and grab observations from the other end to finish the computations. This is reasonable for some time series where strong seasonal effects are observed but cannot be applied universally in practice.

A common technique in Fourier analysis is to "reflect" the time series about its last observation, thus producing a time series of length $2N$. We then apply the wavelet transform using the assumption of periodic boundary conditions to this reflected series; that is,

$$x_0, x_1, \ldots, x_{N-2}, x_{N-1}, x_{N-1}, x_{N-2}, \ldots, x_1, x_0.$$

Reflecting the series does not alter the sample mean nor the sample variance, since all coefficients have been duplicated once.

Cohen *et al.* (1993) constructed special wavelet basis functions at the boundaries that are zero outside the range of the data. Using these boundary wavelets, the DWT retains orthogonality and is numerically stable. Discrete-time implementation has been investigated by Herley and Vetterli (1994) and Herley (1995).

To keep track of boundary effects, it is important to know which wavelet coefficients have been computed using observations across the boundary. Percival and Walden (2000, Sec. 4.11) show that the number of DWT coefficients L'_j affected by the boundary depends on the level j of the transform and length L of the wavelet filter via

$$L'_j = \lceil (L - 2)(1 - 2^{-j}) \rceil,$$

where $\lceil x \rceil$ is the smallest integer greater than or equal to x. For display purposes, circularly shifting the level j vector of DWT coefficients by a given amount, depending on the filter used, approximately lines up the DWT coefficient vectors with the original time series. A precise table of integer shifts for the least asymmetric wavelet filter is given in Percival and Walden (2000, Sec. 4.11), but a simple heuristic to follow is to place half the boundary coefficients at each end of the series. If the number of coefficients affected by the boundary is odd, then place the "extra" coefficient at the beginning of the series. Shifting coefficients from the extremal phase wavelet filter is not as straightforward given its poor phase properties.

The MODWT uses integer translates of the wavelet and scaling filters, both of length $L_j = (2^j - 1)(L - 1) + 1$ (Equation 4.18), and therefore contains L_j wavelet coefficients affected by the boundary. McCoy *et al.* (1995) determined that circularly shifting each vector of MODWT coefficients aligns features in the wavelet coefficients with those in the data. Precise integer shifts are given by

$$\xi_j^G = \begin{cases} -\frac{(L_j-1)(L-2)}{2(L-1)} & \text{if } \frac{L}{2} \text{ is even} \\ -\frac{(L_j-1)L}{2(L-1)} & \text{if } L = 10 \text{ or } 18 \\ -\frac{(L_j-1)(L-4)}{2(L-1)} & \text{if } L = 14, \end{cases}$$

for the least asymmetric low-pass filter $g_{j,l}$ and

$$\xi_j^H = \begin{cases} -\frac{L_j}{2} & \text{if } \frac{L}{2} \text{ is even} \\ -\frac{L_j}{2} + 1 & \text{if } L = 10 \text{ or } 18 \\ -\frac{L_j}{2} - 1 & \text{if } L = 14, \end{cases}$$

for the least asymmetric high-pass filter $h_{j,l}$. An alternative definition of shifts for both extremal phase and least asymmetric wavelet filters was provided by Hess-Nielsen and Wickerhauser (1996). Only minor differences exist between these alternative shifts and the ones explicitly given here.

4.7   APPLICATIONS

4.7.1   Filtering FX Intraday Seasonalities

Strong intraday seasonalities may induce distortions in the estimation of volatility models. These periodicities are also the dominant source for misspecifications present in various volatility models. Therefore, an obvious route is to filter out the intraday seasonalities from the high-frequency data. The literature has demonstrated that practical estimation and extraction of the intraday periodic component of the return volatility are both feasible and indispensable for meaningful intraday studies. Earlier studies of modeling intraday seasonalities are provided by Müller *et al.* (1990), Dacorogna *et al.* (1993) and Andersen and Bollerslev (1997). Dacorogna *et al.* (1993) utilize a time-invariant polynomial approximation to the daily activity in the distinct geographical regions of the foreign exchange market.[20] This type of seasonal trend removal is appropriate for foreign exchange markets but may not be directly applicable to other financial markets.

Andersen and Bollerslev (1997) model intraday periodicities with the so-called flexible Fourier form (FFF) as a nonlinear regression model. This approach is not market specific so that it is easily applicable to any high-frequency data such as stock or foreign exchange series. The results in Andersen and Bollerslev (1997) indicate that the FFF is successful in extracting most of the intraday seasonalities, but short-term intraday periodicities remain in the filtered returns. The estimation of the FFF regression involves selecting the interaction terms, truncation lag for the Fourier expansion, and dummy variables to minimize distortions. The model selections are based on choosing models that best match the basic shapes of the periodic pattern with a minimal number of parameters. In particular, the position of the dummy variables that are included to minimize the distortions are based on the researcher's view of the data and are therefore model specific.

Gençay *et al.* (2001b) proposed a simple method for extracting intraday seasonality, which is simple to calculate and easily implemented as it does not depend on a particular model selection criterion or parameter choices. The proposed method is based on an MRA using the MODWT (Section 4.5).

There are two important results from Gençay *et al.* (2001b). First, a model-free estimate of the foreign exchange rate volatility is entirely disentangled from intraday seasonalities. One way of eliminating intraday seasonalities is to work with daily and weekly aggregate data. This is contrasted by a recent study from Andersen *et al.* (2001), where daily volatility estimates are constructed from high-frequency data. The drawback of Andersen *et al.* (2001) is that the theoretical underpinnings are based on diffusion-theoretic motivations, which are highly parametric. Andersen *et al.* (2001) eliminated various features from the data such as weekends, several fixed holidays, moving holidays, and days with 15 longest zero returns. In the Gençay *et al.* (2001b) approach, there is no data elimination except the weekends. The filtering method is robust to misspecifications as it is fully nonparametric.

---

[20] The details of this method is presented in Dacorogna *et al.* (2001).

The studied data sets are the 5-min Deutsche Mark – U.S. Dollar (DEM-USD) and Japanese Yen – U.S. Dollar (JPY-USD) price series for the period from October 1, 1992, to September 29, 1993.[21] Bid and ask prices at each 5-min interval are obtained by linear interpolation over time, as in Müller *et al.* (1990) and Dacorogna *et al.* (1993). Prices are computed as the average of the logarithm of the bid and ask prices via

$$P_t = \frac{1}{2} \left[\log P_t(\text{bid}) + \log P_t(\text{ask}) \right] \quad t = 1, \ldots, 74,800. \qquad (4.31)$$

Olsen & Associates applied data cleaning filters to the price series (as received from Reuters) in order to correct for data errors and remove suspected outliers. We also removed the weekend quotes from Friday 21:05 GMT to Sunday 21:00 GMT. Apart from this no further filtering was applied to the data, nor were any data points excluded.[22]

Continuously compounded 5-min returns are calculated by

$$r_t = 100 \cdot (P_t - P_{t-1}). \qquad (4.32)$$

Figures 4.27a and 4.27b show that the sample autocorrelation functions (ACFs) of the 5-min DEM-USD and JPY-USD absolute return series exhibit strong intraday seasonalities. This phenomenon is well known and has been reported extensively in the literature; see, for example, Dacorogna *et al.* (1993) and Andersen and Bollerslev (1997).

Our model of intraday returns is similar to that in Andersen and Bollerslev (1997), which is given by

$$r_t = v_t s_t \epsilon_t, \qquad (4.33)$$

where r_t is the raw returns, v_t is the long-term volatility, s_t is the seasonal volatility, and ϵ_t is the identically and independently distributed innovations. Squaring both sides of Equation 4.33, taking in natural logarithm, and dividing both sides by two leads to

$$\log |r_t| = \log |v_t| + \log |s_t| + \log |\epsilon_t|. \qquad (4.34)$$

Equation 4.34 provides an additive separation of the long-term volatility from the seasonal volatility. We use $\log |r_t|$ to obtain the MODWT decomposition of the DEM-USD and the JPY-USD series. A MODWT MRA ($J = 8$) is used to form an additive decomposition of $\log |r_t|$ at the 5-min frequency by using the

---

[21] The data set is provided by Olsen & Associates in Zurich, Switzerland, and is known as the HFDF-I data set.

[22] Andersen *et al.* (2001) utilized a longer (10 years) sample of DEM-USD and JPY-USD series. They removed weekends and several (mostly North American) holidays from the sample. They have also excluded the days containing "fifteen longest zero and constant runs." Andersen and Bollerslev (1997) and Andersen and Bollerslev (1998) analyzed the same data set. They also removed the weekend quotes from their sample.

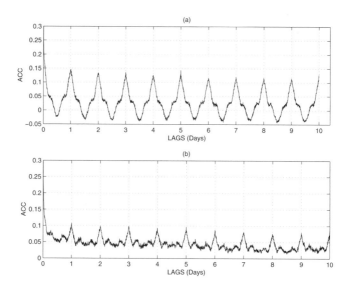

FIGURE 4.27 Sample ACF for the 5-min absolute returns of (a) Deutsche Mark-U.S. Dollar spot exchange rate and (b) Japanese Yen-U.S. Dollar spot exchange rate from October 1, 1992, through September 29, 1993.

LA(8) wavelet filter. The highest-level wavelet detail d_8 captures frequencies $1/512 \le f \le 1/256$ (i.e., any oscillation with a period length of 256 to 512). Since there are 288 5-min returns per day, wavelet details from $j = 1, \dots, 8$ will capture the intraday periodicities. The filtered returns are defined as

$$r_t(f) = \frac{r_t}{\hat{s}_t}, \qquad (4.35)$$

where $\hat{s}_t$ is the estimated seasonal volatility obtained through summing the wavelet details. The filtered absolute returns are therefore free from any intraday periodicities.

For a long-memory process, the autocovariance sequence (ACVS) at lag k satisfies $\gamma_k \sim Ck^{-\alpha}$, where C is the scaling parameter and $\alpha \in [0, 1]$ (Beran, 1994; Granger and Joyeux, 1980; Hosking, 1981). A common model is the fractional difference process (Section 5.2.1) for which $\alpha = 1 - 2d$ and d is the fractional difference parameter. In Andersen and Bollerslev (1997), the fractional difference parameter is estimated to be $\hat{d} = 0.36$ for the same DEM-USD series used here. Andersen *et al.* (2001) calculated six estimates of d from various volatility measures for the DEM-USD and JPY-USD series. These six estimates of d vary from 0.346 to 0.448. In our comparisons, we therefore set $d = 0.4$ to represent the average of these six estimates. Figure 4.28 presents the sample ACF of the filtered 5-min absolute returns along with the theoretical ACF of an FDP with $d = 0.4$.

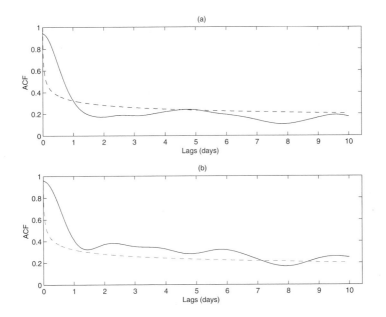

FIGURE 4.28 Sample ACF for the MODWT filtered 5-min absolute returns of (a) Deutsche Mark-U.S. Dollar spot exchange rate and (b) Japanese Yen-U.S. Dollar spot exchange rate from October 1, 1992, through September 29, 1993. The dotted line is the theoretical ACF for a fractional difference process (FDP) with $d = 0.40$. In the calculation of the filtered absolute returns, a MODWT MRA ($J = 8$) is used to form an additive decomposition of $\log |r_t|$ at the 5-min frequency from the LA(8) wavelet filter. The highest level wavelet detail d_8 captures frequencies $1/512 \leq f \leq 1/256$ (i.e., any oscillation with a period length of 256 to 512). Since there are 288 5-min returns per day, the details from $j = 1, \ldots, 8$, will capture the intraday periodicities. The filtered returns are defined as $r_t(f) = r_t/\hat{s}_t$ where $\hat{s}_t$ is the estimated seasonal volatility obtained through the sum of the wavelet details.

The ACFs for the filtered absolute returns exhibit hyperbolic decay. The rate of this decay mimics the hyperbolic decay observed in a fractionally integrated process with the fractional difference parameter $d = 0.4$. This decay rate is similar across both DEM-USD and JPY-USD series.

4.7.2 Causality and Cointegration in Economics

One of the central issues in macroeconomics is the causality between two macroeconomic variables, such as the money supply and the real (or nominal) output. The question of whether money causes a change in output is investigated empirically using different methods. One approach is to employ the Granger causality test, proposed by Granger (1969) and Sims (1972). The idea behind the Granger causality test is the following: If money causes output, the change in money should come before the change in output. This is equivalent to saying that the lagged values of money should help predict the current values of output. In addition, the past values of output should not have any significant power in explaining the current variations in money. Formally,

$$m_t = \alpha_0 + \sum_{i=1}^{k} \alpha_{m,i} m_{t-i} + \sum_{i=1}^{k} \alpha_{y,i} y_{t-i} + \epsilon_{m,t}, \qquad (4.36)$$

$$y_t = \beta_0 + \sum_{i=1}^{k} \beta_{m,i} m_{t-i} + \sum_{i=1}^{k} \beta_{y,i} y_{t-i} + \epsilon_{y,t}, \qquad (4.37)$$

where m_t is money, y_t is output, and $\epsilon_{m,t}$ and $\epsilon_{y,t}$ are independent white noise processes. In regression equations 4.36 and 4.37, failing to reject the null hypothesis

$$H_0 : \alpha_{y,1} = \alpha_{y,2} = \cdots = \alpha_k = 0$$

implies that output does not Granger cause money. Similarly, failing to reject the null hypothesis

$$H_0 : \beta_{m,1} = \beta_{m,2} = \cdots = \beta_{m,k} = 0$$

indicates that money does not Granger cause the output. In order to conclude that money does Granger cause output, two conditions should be met. First, the null hypothesis of "money does not Granger cause output" should be rejected. Second, the null hypothesis of "income does not Granger cause money" should *not* be rejected. If the two null hypotheses are rejected simultaneously, there is said to be a feedback relation between money and income. On the other hand, if the two null hypotheses are *not* rejected, the results are inconclusive.

In macroeconomic applications it is widely accepted that the majority of macroeconomic time series contain a unit root. The implementation of the Granger causality and unit-root tests require certain transformations of the original variables of interest, and the regression equations need to be adapted accordingly. A well-known unit root test is the augmented Dickey-Fuller (ADF) test (Dickey and Fuller, 1981). This test is calculated via

$$\Delta y_t = \alpha + \beta t + (\rho - 1) y_{t-1} + \sum_{i=1}^{k} \theta_i \Delta y_{t-i} + e_t, \qquad (4.38)$$

where Δ is the difference operator such that $\Delta y_t = y_t - y_{t-1}$. The linear time trend is denoted by t, and e_t is a white noise process. If the null hypothesis that $\rho = 1$ is not rejected, the time series y_t is said to follow a random walk. The critical values of the test are provided by Dickey and Fuller (1979) and MacKinnon (1991).

It is possible that two time series may follow a random walk but a linear combination of them may be stationary. In that case, two variables are said to be *cointegrated*. If two variables such as money and output are cointegrated, Engle and Granger (1987) showed that an error correction term is required in testing for Granger causality; that is,

$$\Delta m_t = \alpha_0 + \gamma_1(m_{t-1} - y_{t-1})$$
$$+ \sum_{i=1}^{k} (\alpha_{m,i} \Delta m_{t-i} + \alpha_{y,i} \Delta y_{t-i}) + \epsilon_{m,t}, \qquad (4.39)$$
$$\Delta y_t = \beta_0 + \gamma_2(m_{t-1} - y_{t-1})$$
$$+ \sum_{i=1}^{k} (\beta_{m,i} \Delta m_{t-i} + \beta_{y,i} \Delta y_{t-i}) + \epsilon_{y,t}, \qquad (4.40)$$

where γ_1 and γ_2 represent the *speed of adjustment*. Failing to reject the null hypothesis

$$H_0 : \alpha_{y,1} = \alpha_{y,2} = \cdots = \alpha_{y,k} = 0 \quad \text{and} \quad \gamma_1 = 0$$

implies that output does not Granger cause money. Similarly, failing to reject the null hypothesis

$$H_0 : \beta_{m,1} = \beta_{m,2} = \cdots = \beta_{m,k} = 0 \quad \text{and} \quad \gamma_2 = 0$$

indicates that money does not Granger cause output.

In his original paper using U.S. data, Sims (1972) found that money Granger causes real output (measured as the industrial production index). Subsequent studies on the subject have provided mixed conclusions. The results are sensitive to the sample period, the sampling frequency, the monetary aggregate employed, and the inclusion of other variables in the regression equation.

Ramsey and Lampart (1998a) utilized the DWT of Section 4.3 to analyze the causality between money and output at different timescales in the United States. Using the Daubechies LA(12) wavelet filter, Ramsey and Lampart (1998a) showed that the direction of causality between the national personal income (as a proxy to the output) and the money supply in the United States reverses with changing timescales.[23] Particularly, they presented statistical evidence that at the very finest scale (highest frequencies) national income Granger causes money supply, whereas at intermediate scales money supply Granger causes national income. At the highest scale, there is feedback between the money supply and the output. Their interpretation is such that at the finest timescale λ_1, the economic activity initiates corresponding changes in money supply. Therefore, the causality runs from output to money at this level. At higher scales, the monetary authorities try to control the money supply so that money Granger causes output. At the very highest scale (lower frequencies), there is feedback between two variables.

---

[23] They reported that the qualitative results did not change significantly under alternative wavelet filters.

Series	1%	5%	10%	ADF t-stat	Result
USIP	−2.584	−1.957	−1.631	2.777	I(1)
ΔUSIP	−2.584	−1.957	−1.631	−21.095	
USM	−2.584	−1.957	−1.631	6.445	I(1)
ΔUSM	−2.584	−1.957	−1.631	−21.856	
UKIP	−2.607	−1.964	−1.635	0.128	I(1)
ΔUKIP	−2.607	−1.964	−1.635	−21.398	
UKM	−2.607	−1.964	−1.635	5.236	I(1)
ΔUKM	−2.607	−1.964	−1.635	−20.609	
JPIP	−2.584	−1.957	−1.631	1.603	I(1)
ΔJPIP	−2.584	−1.957	−1.631	−35.776	
JPM	−2.584	−1.957	−1.631	5.734	I(1)
ΔJPM	−2.584	−1.957	−1.631	−27.062	
AUSIP	−2.584	−1.957	−1.631	0.922	I(1)
ΔAUSIP	−2.584	−1.957	−1.631	−23.340	
AUSM	−2.584	−1.957	−1.631	5.903	I(1)
ΔAUSM	−2.584	−1.957	−1.631	−19.996	

TABLE 4.4 Unit-root test results for raw and first differenced (Δ) series. USM, UKM, JPM, and AUSM denote the M_1 definition of money supply in the United States, United Kingdom, Japan, and Austria, respectively. USIP, UKIP, JPIP and AUSIP denote industrial production in their corresponding countries. Augmented Dickey-Fuller (ADF) t-statistics were obtained from Equation 4.38 under the null hypothesis of a unit root. Critical values were obtained by simulation (MacKinnon, 1991).

We extend the wavelet analysis of money-income causality to investigate whether the causality reversal exists in other developed economies as it does in the United States. In our application, we use seasonally unadjusted monthly data for the United States, the United Kingdom, Japan, and Austria.[24] The industrial production index is taken as a proxy to the real output since monthly GDP is not available. The money supply is taken as narrow definition of money supply (M_1). Both variables are in natural logarithms. For the original data set, which averages all the timescales, we conducted unit-root tests. According to the test results presented in Table 4.4, all of the variables are difference stationary. Further tests of cointegration between the industrial production index and the money supply revealed that two variables are cointegrated in all countries except Japan. Therefore, Equations 4.39 and 4.40 are used in testing the Granger causality between real output and money supply in the United States, the United Kingdom,

---

[24] Source: Datastream. The sample periods are January 1959 to December 1999 for the United States, January 1970 to December 1999 for the United Kingdom, January 1960 to December 1999 for Japan, and January 1960 to December 1998 for Austria.

	US	UK	Japan	Austria
Raw Data	?	?	?	?
λ_1	$y \xrightarrow{1\%} m$	$m \xrightarrow{5\%} y$	$y \xrightarrow{5\%} m$	$m \xrightarrow{5\%} y$
λ_2	$m \xrightarrow{1\%} y$	$m \xrightarrow{5\%} y$	$m \xrightarrow{5\%} y$	$m \xrightarrow{5\%} y$
λ_3	$m \xrightarrow{1\%} y$	$m \xleftrightarrow{1\%} y$	$m \xleftrightarrow{1\%} y$	$m \xrightarrow{1\%} y$
λ_4	$m \xleftrightarrow{1\%} y$	$m \xleftrightarrow{1\%} y$	$m \xleftrightarrow{1\%} y$	$m \xleftrightarrow{1\%} y$

TABLE 4.5 Granger causality tests at different scales. Raw data are the monthly observations of money supply (M_1) and industrial output index in corresponding countries. A MODWT multiresolution analysis was performed using the Daubechies LA(8) wavelet filter. The wavelet scales λ_1, λ_2, λ_3, and λ_4, are associated with oscillations of periods 2–4, 4–8, 8–16, and 16–32 months, respectively. The notation $y \longrightarrow m$ means that output y Granger causes the money supply m, while $m \longrightarrow y$ means that money m Granger causes the output y, and "?" means the test was inconclusive. The significance level is provided above each causal relation.

and Austria. Since two variables are not cointegrated in Japan, Equations 4.36 and 4.37 are used for this country.

The first row of Table 4.5 presents the probabilities of rejecting the null hypothesis of no Granger causality between money and income with the raw data. With these findings, we conclude that the results are inconclusive at the 1% significance level; that is, there is no clear evidence of Granger causality from money to output or from output to money in the raw data. At weaker significance levels, output Granger (weakly) causes the money supply in the United States, the United Kingdom and Japan. In Austria, the money supply (weakly) Granger causes the real output.

In order to test for Granger causality between money and output at different timescales, a level $J = 4$ MODWT multiresolution analysis (MRA) is applied to the money supply and industrial production series using the Daubechies LA(8) wavelet filter. Table 4.5 presents the Granger causality results for each country at different timescales. At the finest wavelet scale λ_1, the real output Granger causes money supply in the United States, United Kingdom, and Japan. At the second wavelet scale λ_2, the causality reverses and the money supply Granger causes real output in all three countries. The causality from money to real output remains at the third wavelet scale λ_3 for the United States, but disappears for the United Kingdom, and Japan. We observe a feedback between the money supply and output in all three countries at higher wavelet scales. The Austrian case stands as a counter-example of causality reversal. The money supply Granger causes real output in Austria at the first three wavelet scales. The feedback between two variables is observed at the fourth wavelet scale λ_4 for this country.

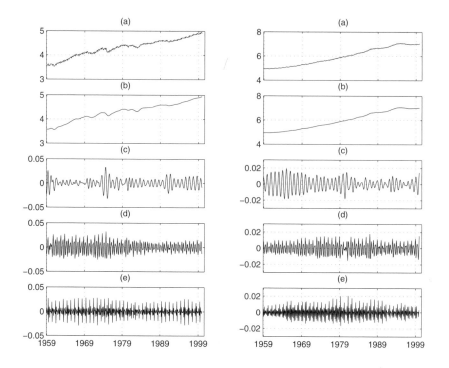

FIGURE 4.29 MODWT multiresolution analysis of the (log) industrial production index (left panel) and the (log) nominal money supply M_1 (right panel) in the United States using the Daubechies LA(8) wavelet filter. (a) Original time series (b) Wavelet smooth $\tilde{s}_3$. (c) Wavelet detail $\tilde{d}_3$ (8- to 16-month periods). (d) Wavelet detail $\tilde{d}_2$ (4- to 8-month periods). (e) Wavelet detail $\tilde{d}_1$ (2- to 4-month periods).

Figures 4.29 to 4.32 provide the wavelet details, the wavelet smooth and the original time series for each country. It should be noted that the MODWT MRA representation contains no phase shifts in wavelet smooths and details. This enables a point-to-point comparison between all scales. There is a noticeable decrease in the variability of U.S. industrial output in the first and, in particular, at the second wavelet detail, whereas the output variability slightly increases at the third wavelet detail after 1979. The money supply variability sharply decreases at the third wavelet detail after 1979. However, only a slight drop in variability at the first and the second wavelet details is observed much later, around 1989. An MRA provides some insight on U.S. monetary policy. In October 1979, the U.S. Federal Reserve Bank (Fed) announced a major change in its policy to contain the growth in monetary aggregates. The policy change implied that the volatility of monetary aggregates would fall since the Fed would stay close to its monetary target path and let the interest rate fluctuate. Friedman (1984) criticized the Fed policy during this period pointing out that the volatility of the monetary growth, measured as a standard deviation of the quarterly growth rate of monetary

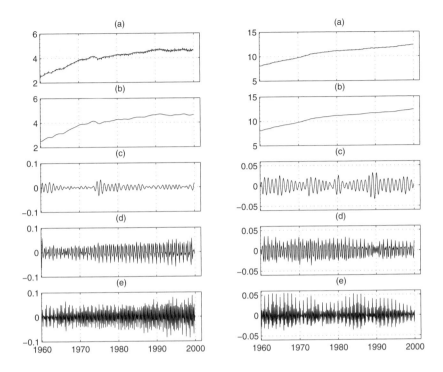

FIGURE 4.30 MODWT multiresolution analysis of the (log) industrial production index (left panel) and the (log) nominal money supply M_1 (right panel) in Japan using the Daubechies LA(8) wavelet filter. (a) Original time series. (b) Wavelet smooth $\tilde{s}_3$. (c) Wavelet detail $\tilde{d}_3$ (8- to 16-month periods). (d) Wavelet detail $\tilde{d}_2$ (4- to 8-month periods). (e) Wavelet detail $\tilde{d}_1$ (2- to 4-month periods).

aggregates, did not decrease but increased. This policy was abandoned in 1982. The wavelet details in Figure 4.29 suggest that the policy horizon for the Fed was not a month or a quarter, but around a year since there is a significant drop in monetary volatility in the third wavelet detail d_3 corresponding to cyclical variations with a period of 8 to 16 months.

The Japanese industrial output has almost no high-scale dynamics. However, the variability of the industrial output at the first and second wavelet details (oscillations with a period length of 2 to 8 months) has been increasing since 1970. There is also a noticeable break in the industrial output wavelet smooth $\tilde{s}_3$ at around 1974. A similar break in the wavelet smooth is observed in other countries as well. The money supply has an interesting pattern at all wavelet details in Japan. The amplitude of the wavelet details gives the impression that they have some cyclical pattern.

In Austria, the industrial output variability has the same pattern at the first two wavelet details starting at 1960. The variability of the output at the third wavelet

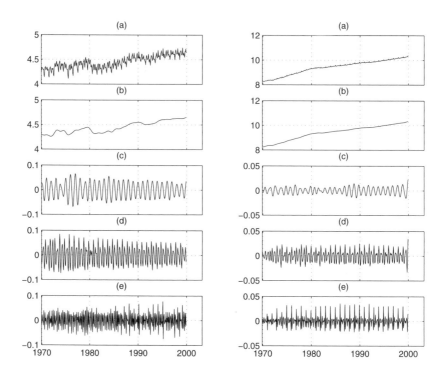

FIGURE 4.31 MODWT multiresolution analysis of the (log) industrial production index (left panel) and the (log) nominal money supply M_1 (right panel) in the United Kingdom using the Daubechies LA(8) wavelet filter. (a) Original time series. (b) Wavelet smooth $\tilde{s}_3$. (c) Wavelet detail $\tilde{d}_3$ (8- to 16-month periods). (d) Wavelet detail $\tilde{d}_2$ (4- to 8-month periods). (e) Wavelet detail $\tilde{d}_1$ (2- to 4-month periods).

detail increases after 1974. The third wavelet detail shows that the variability of money supply in Austria has decreased significantly after 1980. However, it has increased during the same period at the first and second wavelet details. This might be interpreted as a change in horizon of the monetary authorities in conducting the monetary policy.

The evidence provided here corroborates with Ramsey and Lampart (1998a) and leads to the conclusion that interactions between macroeconomic variables have different characteristics at different timescales. There is no one global causality behavior that prevails at all scales (or time horizons).

4.7.3 Money Growth and Inflation

The economics literature has documented a substantial amount of evidence that persistent changes in money supply eventually lead to persistent changes in price level by showing that the nominal quantity of money and the price level are

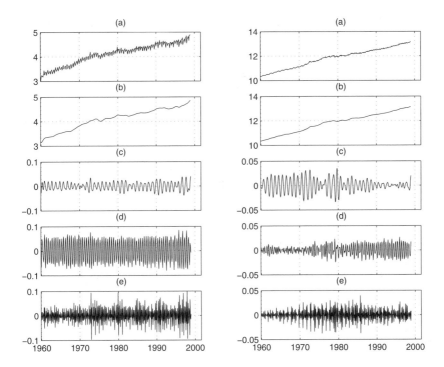

FIGURE 4.32 MODWT multiresolution analysis of the (log) industrial production index (left panel) and the (log) nominal money supply M_1 (right panel) in Austria using the Daubechies LA(8) wavelet filter. (a) Original time series. (b) Wavelet smooth $\tilde{s}_3$. (c) Wavelet detail $\tilde{d}_3$ (8- to 16-month periods). (d) Wavelet detail $\tilde{d}_2$ (4- to 8-month periods). (e) Wavelet detail $\tilde{d}_1$ (2- to 4-month periods).

strongly related.[25] Yet the level of association between money supply and price level in empirical studies changes according to the sampling period, the level of monetary aggregation, and the methodology employed to filter the price level and money before conducting the research. Two of the key stylized facts about money and inflation are as follows:

- There is an underlying rate of inflation in an economy, which is the driving force of actual, observed inflation. This "core" inflation is basically determined by the fundamentals of the economy, such as the aggregate supply and the aggregate demand imbalances, the exchange rate regime, the level of indexing in the economy, and so on. There are several approaches to measure the core inflation. The proposals range from a value-free *trimmed mean* approach to some macrotheoretic measurements such as the difference between the rate of change of wages

---

[25] See, for example, Lucas (1980), Friedman (1992), Barro (1993), and Rolnick and Weber (1997), among others.

and the trend rate of change of productivity. If the idea of core inflation is accepted, the actual rate of inflation is viewed as deviations around the core inflation. The deviations are caused by seasonal factors, temporary aggregate supply or aggregate demand shocks, measurement errors, cycles in commodity prices, and so on.[26]

- The effect of money on inflation strongly manifests itself in the long run. Some authors define the core inflation as a "long-run, or persistent component of the measured price index, which is tied in some way to money growth" (Bryan and Cechetti, 1993). This definition of the core inflation is built on Friedman's proposition that "inflation is always and everywhere a monetary phenomenon." However, the definition of long-run differs in different economies.

Although the majority of studies on money and inflation are carried out in a time domain, some authors have used frequency domain techniques to analyze the interaction between money and inflation; see, for example, Lucas (1980), Geweke (1984), Cochrane (1989) and Thoma (1994), among others. Geweke (1984) employed Granger causality tests within a specific frequency band to analyze the long-run and short-run relationships between money and inflation. Thoma (1994) adopted band spectrum regression techniques to remove particular frequency dynamics from money growth and inflation to obtain long-term components. He later conducted Granger causality tests by studying different smooth components.

The proposition that the observed data is an average of different time-scale components may lead to further understanding of the association between money growth and inflation. Particularly, wavelet multiresolution analysis (MRA) of inflation and growth rate of the money stock enables us to determine the degree of interaction and direction of causation between two variables at different time horizons (or scales). The study here focuses on monthly money stock and price-level data from six different high-inflation economies.[27] We want to analyze the money growth and inflation dynamics using wavelet techniques.

Augmented Dickey Fuller (ADF) tests (Dickey and Fuller, 1981) were conducted on all series. The test results showed that the monthly growth rate of money m and monthly inflation π in all countries were stationary. The first row of Table 4.6 summarizes the Granger causality tests between money growth and inflation for the raw data. The results are inconclusive for Chile and Mexico.

---

[26] See Wynne (1999) for a review of the core inflation literature.

[27] Source: Datastream. All series are seasonally unadjusted. Sample periods and time series are Argentina, Consumer Price Index, 1995=100 and M_1, 1973:1-1999:12; Brazil, Wholesale Price Index, 1995=100 and M_1, 1961:1-1999:12; Chile, Consumer Price Index, 1995=100 and M_1, 1979:1-1999:12; Israel, Industrial Products Prices, 1995=100 and M_1, 1968:1-1999:12; Mexico, Consumer Price Index, 1995=100 and M_1, 1957:1-1999:12; Turkey, Consumer Price Index, 1995=100 and M_1, 1969:1-1999:12.

Series	Argentina	Brazil	Chile	Israel	Mexico	Turkey
Raw Data	$m \to \pi$	$m \leftrightarrow \pi$	?	$m \to \pi$	?	$m \to \pi$
λ_1	$m \to \pi$	$m \leftrightarrow \pi$	?	$\pi \to m$	$\pi \to m$	$m \to \pi$
λ_2	$m \to \pi$	$m \leftrightarrow \pi$	?	$m \leftrightarrow \pi$	$m \leftrightarrow \pi$	$m \to \pi$
λ_3	$m \leftrightarrow \pi$	$m \leftrightarrow \pi$	$\pi \to m$	$m \to \pi$	$m \leftrightarrow \pi$	$m \to \pi$
λ_4	$m \leftrightarrow \pi$	$m \leftrightarrow \pi$	$m \to \pi$	$m \leftrightarrow \pi$	$m \to \pi$	$m \leftrightarrow \pi$

TABLE 4.6   Granger causality F-tests. Raw data are the seasonally unadjusted monthly percentage changes in money supply (m) and percentage changes in price level (π). A MODWT MRA was performed using the Daubechies LA(8) wavelet filter. The wavelet scales $\lambda_1, \lambda_2, \lambda_3, \lambda_4$ are associated with oscillations of periods 2–4, 4–8, 8–16, and 16–32 months, respectively. The notation $m \to \pi$ indicates that money supply growth Granger causes inflation, $\pi \to m$ indicates that inflation Granger causes money supply growth, $m \leftrightarrow \pi$ indicates that there is feedback between money, and price level, and "?" means the test was inconclusive.

Money growth Granger causes inflation in Argentina, Israel, and Turkey, while there is feedback between two variables in Brazil.

A MODWT MRA ($J = 5$) was performed on each time series in order to test the Granger causality between money growth and inflation at different timescales. The Daubechies LA(8) wavelet filter was used in computing the MODWT. The decomposition was stopped at the fifth level since there was feedback at higher details for all countries. The wavelet scale λ_5 is associated with periods of 32 to 64 months (approximately 5 years). Table 4.6 summarizes the Granger causality test results for each country at different timescales. In Argentina, the causality runs from money growth to inflation at the first two wavelet scales. Starting at the third wavelet scale, we observe feedback between the two variables. Similarly, money growth Granger causes inflation in Turkey in the first three wavelet scales. The feedback is observed at the fourth scale. In Chile, Israel, and Mexico, there is a causality reversal between money growth and inflation. Inflation Granger causes money growth in the first wavelet scale, then at higher scales it is the money growth that Granger causes inflation. As with other countries, we observe feedback between money and inflation in these countries. Interestingly, there is feedback between money and inflation in all wavelet scales in Brazil.

Since the oscillations with a period of 2 to 64 months in inflation are removed, the wavelet smooth $\tilde{s}_5$ may be viewed as a measure of the core inflation for each country. Figure 4.33 depicts the core inflation measured by the wavelet smooth in each of the countries presented here.

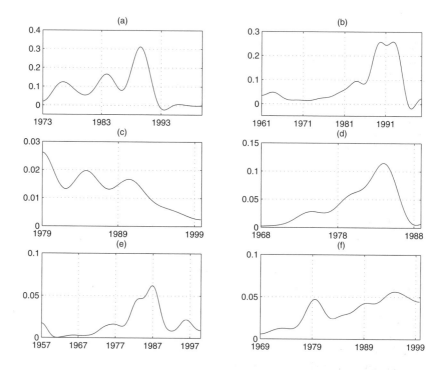

FIGURE 4.33 Monthly core inflation in some high-inflation economies. The core inflation is calculated as the wavelet smooth $\widetilde{s}_5$ from an LA(8) MODWT multiresolution analysis of the inflation rates in corresponding countries. (a) Argentina. (b) Brazil. (c) Chile. (d) Israel. (e) Mexico. (f) Turkey.

5

WAVELETS AND STATIONARY PROCESSES

5.1 INTRODUCTION

In the latter part of the twentieth century, several disciplines came to the realization that naturally occurring phenomena (river flow, atmospheric patterns, telecommunications, astronomy, financial markets, etc.) exhibit correlations that do *not* decay at a sufficiently fast rate. This means that observations separated by great periods of time still exhibit significant correlation. These time series are known as *long-memory* or *long-range dependent* processes and require different approaches to modeling than the so-called short-memory time series. At first, Fourier-based methods dominated the literature in terms of identifying and fitting models to long-memory processes. Wavelets have shown great promise in handling long memory and a combination of short-memory and long-memory processes. Both least squares and maximum likelihood procedures have been established for estimating the model parameters in the case of long-range dependence. By generalizing the concept of a long-memory process to a seasonally persistent process, one may apply these estimation procedures to a much broader class of time series models.

By performing a wavelet decomposition to an observed time series, one makes an implicit assumption about the underlying nature of the process.

Specifically, there is a hierarchical structure present in the data so that information in the time series is evolving at different time horizons (scales) and different magnitudes. When decomposed appropriately, one may more easily view the individual factors that make up the (potentially) complicated process. More precisely, the correlation matrix of the decomposition is essentially block diagonal. Large values on the diagonal represent the information at a particular level of the decomposition and near zero values on the off-diagonal denote little interaction between elements. This concept was recently discussed in Brock (2000).

This chapter begins with an introduction to a particular class of stationary long-memory processes known as fractional difference processes (Section 5.2.1) and then illustrates how the discrete wavelet transform (DWT) approximately decorrelates such time series (Section 5.2.2). A simple method for generating fractional difference processes is introduced along with two methods, least squares and maximum likelihood, for fitting such a time series model to observed data. Finally, a fractional difference process is fit to the IBM volatility series (Section 5.2.6). In Section 5.3, generalizations to the DWT and MODWT are introduced in order to extend the procedures in Section 5.2 to a broader class of stochastic processes – those exhibiting seasonal long memory. A wavelet decomposition of monthly changes in Mexico's money supply (Section 5.3.3) illustrates the application of these new transforms. The class of seasonal persistent processes is introduced in Section 5.4.1, and a wavelet-based simulation procedure is outlined in Section 5.4.2. Before investigating wavelet-based estimation procedures (Sections 5.4.4 and 5.4.5), methods for selecting an orthonormal basis in more general wavelet transforms is discussed in Section 5.4.3. Finally, applications are presented where seasonal persistent processes are fit to observed economic time series.

5.2 WAVELETS AND LONG-MEMORY PROCESSES

One of the earliest studies that observed time series may exhibit long-range dependence is due to the pioneering work of Hurst (1951). While looking at time series from the physical sciences (rainfall, tree rings, river levels, etc.) he noticed that his R/S-statistic,[1] on a logarithmic scale, was randomly scattered around a line with slope $H > 1/2$ for large sample sizes. For a stationary process with short-term dependence, $\log R/S$ should be proportional to $k^{1/2}$, for k large. Hurst's discovery of slopes proportional to k^H, with $H > 1/2$, was in direct contradiction to the theory of such processes at the time. This discovery is known as the *Hurst effect* and H is the *Hurst parameter*.

Mandelbrot and coworkers (Mandelbrot and van Ness, 1968; Mandelbrot and Wallis, 1969) showed that the Hurst effect may be modeled by fractional Gaussian

---

[1] The R/S-statistic is the *rescaled adjusted range* and was used to calculate the ideal capacity of a water reservoir from time t to time $t + k$. Loosely, the numerator R (or *adjusted range*) measures the cumulative inflow to the reservoir and the denominator S is proportional to the standard deviation of all measured inflows.

noise with self-similarity parameter $0 < H < 1$. This process exhibits stationary long-memory dynamics when $1/2 < H < 1$ and reduces to white noise when $H = 1/2$. The spectrum of fractional Gaussian noise may be derived from an appropriately filtered spectral density function of fractional Brownian motion and evaluated via numeric integration, although finite-term approximations may be used in practice. We will instead focus our attention on a convenient class of time series models known as fractional difference processes.

5.2.1 Fractional Difference Processes

In the early 1980s, a family of models were developed to help analyze long-memory processes. Granger and Joyeux (1980) and Hosking (1981) introduced fractional ARIMA models, which are a generalization of the standard ARIMA(p, d, q) models defined by Box and Jenkins (1976).

Let x_t be a stochastic process whose dth order backward difference

$$(1 - B)^d x_t = \sum_{k=0}^{\infty} \binom{d}{k} (-1)^k x_{t-k} = \epsilon_t \tag{5.1}$$

is a stationary process, where d is a real number and $\binom{a}{b}$ is defined in Equation 4.14. For example, the first-order difference is $(1 - B)x_t = x_t - x_{t-1}$ when $d = 1$. If ϵ_t is a white noise process with variance σ_ϵ^2, then x_t is the simplest case of a fractional ARIMA process, a fractional ARIMA($0, d, 0$) or fractional difference process (FDP).

Now let x_t be a zero mean FDP(d) with $-1/2 < d < 1/2$. This process is stationary and invertible (Hosking, 1981). The autocovariance sequence (ACVS) of x_t is defined to be

$$\gamma_\tau = E(x_t, x_{t-\tau}) = \frac{\sigma_\epsilon^2 (-1)^\tau \Gamma(1 - 2d)}{\Gamma(1 + \tau - d)\,\Gamma(1 - \tau - d)},$$

which means the variance is given by

$$\mathrm{Var}(x_t) = \gamma_0 = \frac{\sigma_\epsilon^2 \Gamma(1 - 2d)}{[\Gamma(1 - d)]^2}. \tag{5.2}$$

The spectral density function (SDF) of x_t is

$$S_x(f) = \frac{\sigma_\epsilon^2}{|2 \sin(\pi f)|^{2d}} \quad \text{for} \quad -\frac{1}{2} < f < \frac{1}{2}, \tag{5.3}$$

so that $S_x(f) \propto f^{-2d}$ approximately as $f \to 0$ and, thus, the SDF is approximately linear on the log scale. This property can be seen in Figure 5.1 for various FDPs. The spectra, plotted on a log-log scale, are approximately linear with slope

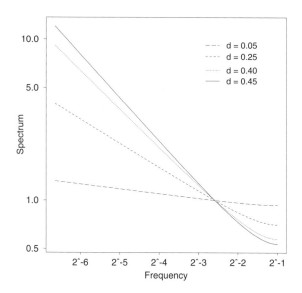

FIGURE   5.1 Spectral densities for fractional difference processes with $d \in \{0.05, 0.25, 0.40, 0.45\}$. Notice that the slope of the SDF, on a log-log scale, increases as d increases. This feature is present when $0 < d < 1/2$.

varying with the fractional difference parameter d. When $0 < d < 1/2$, this SDF has an asymptote at frequency zero,[2] in which case the process exhibits slowly decaying autocovariances and provides a simple example of a long-memory process.

5.2.2   The DWT of Fractional Difference Processes

The ability of the DWT to decorrelate time series, such as FDPs, producing wavelet coefficients for a given scale, which are approximately uncorrelated, is well known; see, for example, Tewfik and Kim (1992), McCoy and Walden (1996) and Wornell (1996). Ramsey (1998) showed this fact empirically in order to validate previous results with respect to performing regressions at different timescales. Here, we explore the output of the DWT when applied to an FDP. Emphasis will be on the spectral properties of the DWT coefficients, instead of looking at the rate of decay of the ACVS between wavelet coefficients as in the references given above.

   Let x_t be a FDP(d) with spectrum given by Equation 5.3. We restrict our attention to processes with fractional difference parameters $0 < d < 1/2$ (i.e., stationary long-memory processes). We know the vector of unit scale DWT coefficients $\boldsymbol{w}_1$ is simply the original time series convolved with the wavelet filter $\boldsymbol{h}_1$ and subsampled by two (Figure 4.15). Now, the spectrum of a subsampled

---

[2] An asymptote in the spectrum at frequency zero is such that as $f \to 0$, $S(f) \to \infty$.

process, say $u_t = x_{2t}$, is given by

$$S_u(f) = \frac{S_x(\frac{f}{2}) + S_x(\frac{f+1}{2})}{2}, \tag{5.4}$$

and from basic Fourier analysis, we know that filtering a time series corresponds to a multiplication of its spectrum with the squared gain function of the filter. Hence, the filtered coefficients have spectrum $\mathcal{H}(f)S_x(f)$, and

$$S_{w_1}(f) = \frac{\mathcal{H}(\frac{f}{2})S_x(\frac{f}{2})}{2} + \frac{\mathcal{H}(\frac{f+1}{2})S_x(\frac{f+1}{2})}{2} \tag{5.5}$$

is the SDF of the unit scale DWT coefficients (Figure 4.15).

Let us look into the characteristics of the spectrum of unit scale DWT coefficients for the Haar wavelet. It is relatively simple to calculate, since $\mathcal{H}^{\text{Haar}}(f) = 2\sin^2(\pi f)$. The spectrum of the filtered FDP, $v_t = h_1 * x_t$, (where '$*$' denotes the convolution operator) is therefore

$$\mathcal{H}^{\text{Haar}}(f)S_x(f) = \frac{1}{2}|2\sin(\pi f)|^{-2(d-1)}.$$

That is, the SDF of the filtered process is proportional to an FDP with parameter $d' = d - 1$. Since we were looking at so-called red processes with $0 < d < 1/2$, this means $-1 < d' < -1/2$ and hence the filtered process is "blue."[3] The spectrum of the DWT coefficients using the Haar wavelet is thus

$$S_{w_1}^{\text{Haar}}(f) = \frac{1}{4}\left[\left|2\sin\left(\frac{\pi f}{2}\right)\right|^{-2(d-1)} + \left|2\cos\left(\frac{\pi f}{2}\right)\right|^{-2(d-1)}\right].$$

When $d = 0$, $S_{w_1}^{\text{Haar}}(f) = \sin^2(\pi f/2) + \cos^2(\pi f/2f) = 1$, and therefore the spectrum of the unit scale DWT coefficients is constant. Whitcher (1998) investigated the SDFs for the unit scale DWT coefficients of FDPs with $-1/2 \leq d \leq 1/2$. As d approaches its boundary (1/2 or $-1/2$), the wavelet coefficients have a greater amount of correlation. However, the vertical range between the minimum and maximum of the spectrum in each plot is around 3 decibels or less.[4] The SDF for any choice of fractional difference parameter does not have much structure beyond that of white noise.

The formula given in Equation 5.5 can be extended to an arbitrary scale λ_j using the notion of a filter cascade (Section 4.3). Since we are downsampling by 2 at each level of the transform, the SDF for a vector of DWT wavelet coefficients

---

[3] The colorful terminology comes from optics, where low frequencies of light are seen as red and high frequencies seen as blue.

[4] A decibel (dB) is a logarithmic transformation defined to be $10\log_{10}(x)$ and commonly used in the engineering literature to express the spectrum of a process.

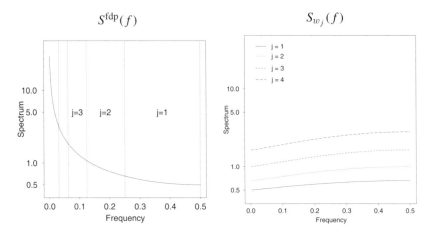

FIGURE 5.2   Spectra for an FDP(0.4) and Haar wavelet coefficient vectors w_1, w_2, w_3, and w_4. Although the spectrum for the FDP is rapidly changing between the frequency intervals denoted by the vertical dotted lines, the combination of filtering and subsampling produces relatively flat spectra for the DWT coefficients. Since a constant spectrum corresponds to an uncorrelated (white noise) process, the DWT approximately decorrelates FDPs.

w_j associated with scale λ_j is

$$S_{w_j}(f) = \frac{1}{2^j} \sum_{k=0}^{2^j-1} \mathcal{H}_j\left(\frac{f+k}{2^j}\right) S\left(\frac{f+k}{2^j}\right), \tag{5.6}$$

where $\mathcal{H}_j(f)$ is computed via

$$\mathcal{H}_j(f) = \mathcal{H}(2^{j-1}f) \prod_{l=0}^{j-2} \mathcal{G}(2^l f).$$

Recall that $\mathcal{H}(f)$ is the squared gain function of the wavelet (high-pass) filter h_l and $\mathcal{G}(f)$ is the squared gain function of the scaling (low-pass) filter g_l. Equation 5.6 reveals that the spectrum of a DWT coefficient vector w_j is stretched by 2^j, and then $2^j - 1$ aliased versions of it are averaged together. This can be seen intuitively through successive applications of Equation 5.4 to the filtered spectrum. Figure 5.2 shows the SDFs for the first four levels of the Haar DWT applied to an FDP with $d = 0.4$. The spectrum of the FDP is rapidly increasing as $f \to 0$, but the spectra of the Haar wavelet coefficients exhibit limited variation at all four scales. The ability to produce flat spectra is the key property we will use when simulating and fitting models to FDPs in this section.

Level	Haar $[-\frac{1}{2}, 0]$	Haar $[0, \frac{1}{2}]$	D(4) $[-\frac{1}{2}, 0]$	D(4) $[0, \frac{1}{2}]$	LA(8) $[-\frac{1}{2}, 0]$	LA(8) $[0, \frac{1}{2}]$
1	1.43	1.48	1.40	1.56	1.36	1.59
2	1.83	2.26	2.28	2.56	2.51	2.71
3	2.07	2.71	2.64	2.93	2.81	3.00
4	2.21	2.87	2.76	3.07	2.80	3.14
5	2.33	2.93	2.84	3.10	2.82	3.16
6	2.42	2.95	2.88	3.10	2.83	3.16

TABLE 5.1 Maximum dynamic range for the spectra of DWT wavelet coefficients, in decibels (dB), when applied to an FDP(d). FDPs with $d \in [-\frac{1}{2}, 0]$ are known as antipersistent with $\mathcal{H}(0) = 0$, while stationary long-memory processes may be modeled by $d \in [0, \frac{1}{2}]$ with $\mathcal{H}(0) = \infty$.

To summarize the information contained in the spectra of DWT coefficient vectors, a useful measure to introduce is the *dynamic range* of a spectrum, defined to be

$$10 \cdot \log_{10} \left[\frac{\max_f S(f)}{\min_f S(f)} \right].$$

Table 5.1 gives the maximum dynamic ranges, in dB, for the spectra of DWT coefficients applied to FDPs with fractional difference parameter $-1/2 \le d \le 1/2$. As the level of the DWT increases, more and more energy is present for red processes; the dynamic range of the spectra is negligible and appears to level off around 3 dB regardless of the chosen wavelet filter. This lack of dynamic range, which corresponds to almost uncorrelated observations in the original process, is utilized in upcoming sections to simulate FDPs and also estimate d in practice.

5.2.3 Simulation of Fractional Difference Processes

A popular time-domain technique for simulating time series is based on the Levinson-Durbin recursions (Hosking, 1984). This time-domain method is exact, but the Levinson-Durbin recursions require $O(N^2)$ operations and become unwieldy for larger sample sizes. Davies and Harte (1987) described a method for simulating certain stationary Gaussian time series of length N with known autocovariances $\gamma_0, \gamma_1, \ldots, \gamma_{N-1}$. The method is based on the Fourier transform and is provided in Wood and Chan (1994) and Beran (1994, pp. 216–217). This method is exact for short-memory processes, like the typical ARMA time series models, but is approximate when used to generate FDPs (Percival, 1992). Even so, the Fourier-based method is very efficient and produces realizations of FDPs with good statistical properties. Recently, Parke (1999) proposed a simulation procedure through representing the FDP via an error duration model.

A DWT-based method for generating realizations of FDPs was proposed by McCoy and Walden (1996). We give a brief outline here and provide a

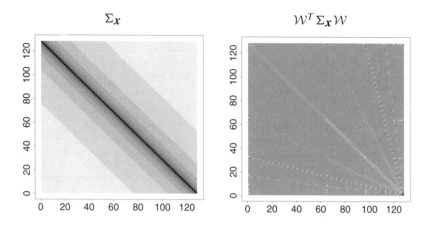

FIGURE 5.3   Covariance matrices for an FDP(0.4) and the DWT coefficients using the D(4) wavelet filter. The covariance matrix for the FDP slowly decays for positive lags (i.e., away from the diagonal). On the other hand, the covariance matrix for the DWT coefficients are zero except on the diagonal and very few off-diagonal elements.

generalization of this method to processes with arbitrarily unbounded spectra in Section 5.4.2. As pointed out in the previous section, the DWT produces wavelet coefficients with flat spectra and therefore exhibit little correlation within scales. In fact, there is very little cross-correlation between scales too. Figure 5.3 shows the covariance matrix Σ_x for an FDP with $d = 0.4$ and $\mathcal{W}^T \Sigma_x \mathcal{W}$, which is the covariance matrix corresponding to the vector of DWT coefficients computed using the D(4) wavelet filter. Whereas Σ_x exhibits slowly decaying autocovariances as the lag moves away from the diagonal, the covariance matrix for the DWT coefficients is nearly zero for all nondiagonal elements. This leads to the idea that the covariance matrix of x may be well approximated by treating $\mathcal{W}^T \Sigma_x \mathcal{W}$ as if it were a diagonal matrix (McCoy and Walden, 1996; Jensen, 2000).

The band-pass variance B_j for an FDP, with spectrum given in Equation 5.3, in the frequency interval $[-2^{-j}, -2^{-j-1}) \cup (2^{-j-1}, 2^{-j}]$ is

$$B_j = 2 \cdot 4^{-d} \int_{1/2^{j+1}}^{1/2^j} \frac{\sigma_\epsilon^2}{|\sin(\pi f)|^{2d}} \, df. \qquad (5.7)$$

Replace the true SDF at each frequency interval with a constant $S_j = S_j(f)$, for all f, such that the band-pass variances are equal. This step assumes the SDF is slowly varying across the frequency interval. Integrating the constant spectrum over $[-2^{-j}, -2^{-j-1}) \cup (2^{-j-1}, 2^{-j}]$ gives

$$\int_{1/2^{j+1}}^{1/2^j} S_{j,n} \, df = S_j 2^{-j-1}.$$

Equating this to the band-pass variance gives

$$2S_j 2^{-j-1} = B_j \implies S_j = 2^j B_j. \tag{5.8}$$

The variance of $w_{j,t}$ is therefore given by S_j through the band-pass nature of the DWT.

Let us consider simulating a length $M = 2^{J_M}$ FDP with known fractional difference parameter d. It is common when using Fourier-based methods to simulate a series several times longer than required and then use a segment of the appropriate length. We recommend using simulation lengths of $M = 2N$ or $M = 4N$, where $N = 2^J$ is the desired length of the simulated series. For nondyadic sample sizes, one can simply increase the length of the simulation to the minimum dyadic length that exceeds the desired sample size and then subsample it appropriately. The DWT-based simulation procedure can be implemented as follows:

1. Calculate the band-pass variances B_j, $j = 1, \ldots, J$. They are defined in Equation 5.7 and may be calculated via numeric integration. We use Equation 5.8 to obtain S_j. Each DWT coefficient $w_{j,t}$, $j = 1, \ldots, J$, $t = 1, \ldots, 2^{J_M - j}$ is an independent Gaussian random variable with zero mean and variance S_j.

2. Compute the variance of the scaling coefficient $v_{J,0}$ using the variances of the wavelet coefficients S_j, $j = 1, \ldots, J$. Since FDPs have a closed form expression for their variance (Equation 5.2), the variance of $v_{J,0}$ may be found by first computing the band-pass variance

$$B_{J+1} = \frac{\sigma_\epsilon^2 \Gamma(1 - 2d)}{[\Gamma(1 - d)]^2} - \sum_{j=1}^{J} B_j,$$

and then rescaling it to produce $S_{J+1} = 2^j B_{J+1}$. Hence, $v_{J,0}$ is a Gaussian random variable with zero mean and variance S_{J+1}.

3. Organize the simulated wavelet coefficients and scaling coefficient into the vector w and apply the inverse DWT via $\hat{x} = W^T w$ to produce a length M portion of the desired FDP. By generating a uniform random integer ξ on the interval $[1, M - N + 1]$, we may obtain a length N segment $\hat{x}_\xi, \ldots, \hat{x}_{\xi+N-1}$.

The numeric integration for the band-pass variances required in Step 1 is easily computed using the routine QAGS from QUADPACK (Piessons *et al.*, 1983), since the SDF is finite for all frequency intervals $\lambda_{j,n}$, for $j = 1, \ldots, J; n = 1, \ldots, 2^j - 1$. McCoy and Walden (1996) provided simulation results that show the DWT-based simulation method performs comparably to the exact time-domain method of Hosking (1984).

5.2.4   Ordinary Least-Squares Estimation of Fractional Difference Processes

The approximate linear relationship between the periodogram and Fourier frequencies (on a log-log scale) has been known for a long time now. Geweke and Porter-Hudak (1983) first proposed regressing the log values of the periodogram on the log SDF to estimate the fractional differencing parameter d (we refer to this as the GPH estimator). Although very popular, the GPH estimator suffers from the poor asymptotic properties of the periodogram. Improvements to the GPH estimator have been suggested, such as restricting the number of frequencies used in the regression or using an alternative spectral estimator (smoothed or multitaper). Here we introduce a wavelet-based estimator of d also using ordinary least-squares (OLS) regression (Jensen, 1999b). Tkacz (2000) has applied this technique to nominal interest rates in the United States and Canada.

For a vector of observations y, the OLS model is formulated via

$$y = X\beta + e,$$

where

$$
y = \begin{bmatrix} y_1 \\ y_2 \\ \vdots \\ y_J \end{bmatrix}
\quad
X = \begin{bmatrix} 1 & x_{1,1} \\ 1 & x_{2,1} \\ \vdots & \vdots \\ 1 & x_{J,1} \end{bmatrix}
\quad
\beta = \begin{bmatrix} \beta_0 \\ \beta_1 \end{bmatrix}
$$

are the length J vector of dependent observations, the $J \times 2$ dimensional model matrix and the length 2 parameter vector, respectively. The final vector

$$e = [e_1, e_2, \ldots, e_J]^T$$

is the column of model errors with $E(e) = 0$ and $\mathrm{Var}(e) = \sigma_e^2 I_J$. The OLS estimator $\hat{\beta}$ of β is

$$\hat{\beta} = (X^T X)^{-1} X^T y, \tag{5.9}$$

and the covariance matrix of $\hat{\beta}$ is given by

$$\Sigma_{\hat{\beta}} = \sigma_e^2 (X^T X)^{-1}. \tag{5.10}$$

For the remainder of this section, we are interested in estimating the slope parameter β_1 when the dependent observations are $y_j = \log(\hat{\sigma}_x^2(\lambda_j))$ and the independent observations are $x_{j,1} = \log(\lambda_j)$ for $j = 1, \ldots, J$.

There is a clear linear relationship between the wavelet variance $\sigma_x^2(\lambda_j)$ and scale λ_j (on a log-log scale) for FDPs, as Figure 5.4 shows. Jensen (1999b) proved that $\sigma_x^2(\lambda_j) \to C\lambda_j^{2d-1}$ as $j \to \infty$ for FDPs with $-1/2 \le d \le 1/2$. A reasonable regression model is therefore

$$\log(\hat{\sigma}_x^2(\lambda_j)) = \beta_0 + \beta_1 \log(\lambda_j) + e_j,$$

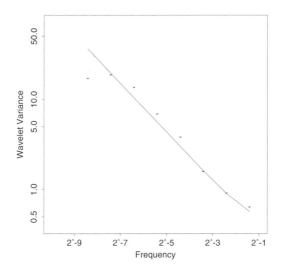

FIGURE 5.4 Sample variances for the LA(8) DWT coefficients (dots) of a length 1024 realization of an FDP(0.45). The true spectrum for this process is given by the solid curve. The variance of the wavelet coefficients appear to track the linear portion of the curve.

where $\beta_1 = 2d - 1$. Defining $y_j = \log(\hat{\sigma}_x^2(\lambda_j))$ and $x_{j,1} = \log(\lambda_j)$ for $j = 1, \ldots, J$, the OLS estimator of β_1 is given by the second element of $\hat{\boldsymbol{\beta}}$ in Equation 5.9, or explicitly,

$$\hat{\beta}_1 = \frac{\sum_{j=1}^{J} \left[\log(\lambda_j) - \overline{\log(\lambda_j)}\right] \log(\hat{\sigma}_x^2(\lambda_j))}{\sum_{j=1}^{J} \left[\log(\lambda_j) - \overline{\log(\lambda_j)}\right]^2},$$

where $\overline{\log(\lambda_j)}$ is the sample mean of $\log(\lambda_j)$. Hence, the OLS estimator of the fractional difference parameter is $\hat{d} = (\hat{\beta}_1 + 1)/2$. To determine the variance of our OLS estimator, we take the lower-right corner of $\Sigma_{\hat{\beta}}$ in Equation 5.10; that is,

$$\mathrm{Var}(\hat{\beta}_1) = \frac{\hat{\sigma}_e^2}{\sum_{j=1}^{J} \left[\log(\lambda_j) - \overline{\log(\lambda_j)}\right]^2},$$

where the estimated variance of the model errors is given by (most easily expressed in matrix notation)

$$\hat{\sigma}_e^2 = \frac{(\boldsymbol{y} - \boldsymbol{X}\hat{\boldsymbol{\beta}})^T (\boldsymbol{y} - \boldsymbol{X}\hat{\boldsymbol{\beta}})}{J - 2}.$$

Basic properties of the variance tell us that $\mathrm{Var}(\hat{d}) = \frac{1}{4}\mathrm{Var}(\hat{\beta}_1)$.

To reduce the mean squared error (MSE) of $\hat{d}$, several authors have proposed a weighted least squares (WLS) estimator of d instead of the OLS estimator (Abry *et al.*, 1995; Abry and Veitch, 1998). The WLS procedure allows the model errors to have different variances, but they must still be uncorrelated. The estimation of $\hat{d}_{\mathrm{wls}}$ follows from the OLS procedure by simply introducing a diagonal matrix $(J \times J)$ of weights $\mathcal{C}$ such that

$$\mathcal{C} = \mathrm{diag}(\sigma_1^2, \sigma_2^2, \ldots, \sigma_J^2).$$

The WLS estimator of $\boldsymbol{\beta}$ is given by

$$\hat{\boldsymbol{\beta}}_{\mathrm{wls}} = (X^T \mathcal{C}^{-1} X)^{-1} X^T \mathcal{C}^{-1} y,$$

and the covariance matrix of $\hat{\boldsymbol{\beta}}_{\mathrm{wls}}$ is given by $\Sigma_{\hat{\boldsymbol{\beta}}_{\mathrm{wls}}} = (X^T \mathcal{C}^{-1} X)^{-1}$. As before the WLS estimator of the fractional difference parameter is $\hat{d}_{\mathrm{wls}} = (\hat{\beta}_{1,\mathrm{wls}} + 1)/2$ and $\mathrm{Var}(\hat{d}_{\mathrm{wls}}) = \frac{1}{4}\mathrm{Var}(\hat{\beta}_{1,\mathrm{wls}})$. Percival and Walden (2000, Sec. 9.5) showed that the WLS estimator reduces the MSE by a factor of two in comparison to the OLS estimator in simulation studies.

The possibility that the long-memory parameter d is not constant over time is an interesting generalization of the usual FDP. Veitch and Abry (1999) developed a testing procedure for the time constancy of d while Whitcher and Jensen (2000) proposed an OLS estimator for a nonstationary FDP,[5] and Jensen and Whitcher (2000) applied the OLS-based estimator to a year of high-frequency foreign exchange rates. Parameter estimation for a nonstationary long memory time series model, through OLS or maximum likelihood, is in its infancy and should benefit greatly from wavelet-based methods.

5.2.5   Approximate Maximum Likelihood Estimation of Fractional Difference Processes

Wavelet-based maximum likelihood estimation procedures have been investigated by McCoy and Walden (1996) and Jensen (1999a, 2000). Although least-squares estimation is popular because of its simplicity to program and compute, it produces much larger mean square errors when compared to maximum likelihood methods. The methodology presented here overcomes the difficulty of computing the exact likelihood by replacing the covariance matrix of the process with an approximation using the DWT. This is possible through the ability of the DWT to decorrelate long-memory processes (Section 5.2.2).

If x is a length $N = 2^J$ FDP with mean zero and covariance matrix given by Σ_x, then we may write its likelihood as

$$L(d, \sigma_\epsilon^2 \mid x) = (2\pi)^{-N/2} |\Sigma_x|^{-1/2} \exp\left[-\tfrac{1}{2} x^T \Sigma_x^{-1} x\right] \qquad (5.11)$$

---

[5] In Whitcher and Jensen (2000) the nonstationarity is caused by a time-varying autocovariance function induced through a time-varying fractional difference parameter d_t in an FDP.

(Brockwell and Davis, 1991, Sec. 8.6). The quantity $|\Sigma_x|$ is the determinant of Σ_x. The maximum likelihood estimators (MLEs) of the parameters (d and σ_ϵ^2) are those quantities that maximize Equation 5.11. We now avoid the difficulties in computing the exact MLEs by using the approximate decorrelation of the DWT as applied to FDPs; that is,

$$\Sigma_x \approx \widehat{\Sigma}_x = W^T \Omega_N W,$$

where W is the orthonormal matrix defining the DWT (Section 4.4) and Ω_N is a diagonal matrix containing the variances of DWT coefficients computed from FDPs; that is,

$$\Omega_N = \text{diag}(\underbrace{S_1, \ldots, S_1}_{N/2}, \underbrace{S_2, \ldots, S_2}_{N/4}, \ldots, \underbrace{S_j, \ldots, S_j}_{N/2^j}, \ldots, S_J, S_{J+1}).$$

The approximate likelihood function is now

$$\widehat{L}(d, \sigma_\epsilon^2 \,|\, x) = (2\pi)^{-N/2} |\widehat{\Sigma}_x|^{-1/2} \exp\left[-\tfrac{1}{2} x^T \widehat{\Sigma}_x^{-1} x\right].$$

Hence, we want to find values of d and σ_ϵ^2 that minimize the log-likelihood function

$$
\begin{aligned}
\widehat{\mathcal{L}}(d, \sigma_\epsilon^2 \,|\, x) &= -2\log\left(\widehat{L}(d, \sigma_\epsilon^2 \,|\, x)\right) - N\log(2\pi) \\
&= \log\left(|\widehat{\Sigma}_x|\right) + x^T \widehat{\Sigma}_x^{-1} x.
\end{aligned}
$$

From Section 5.2.3 we know that the variance for scale λ_j DWT coefficients is given by S_j. We note that S_j depends on two parameters related to the FDP, the fractional difference parameter d and variance σ_ϵ^2. Let $S_j(d, \sigma_\epsilon^2) = \sigma_\epsilon^2 S_j'(d)$. Through properties of diagonal and orthonormal matrices, the approximate log-likelihood function may be rewritten as

$$
\begin{aligned}
\widehat{\mathcal{L}}(d, \sigma_\epsilon^2 \,|\, x) = {}& N\log\left(\sigma_\epsilon^2\right) + \log\left(S_{J+1}'(d)\right) + \sum_{j=1}^{J} N_j \log\left(S_j'(d)\right) \\
&+ \frac{1}{\sigma_\epsilon^2}\left[\frac{v_J^T v_J}{S_{J+1}'(d)} + \sum_{j=1}^{J} \frac{w_j^T w_j}{S_j'(d)}\right].
\end{aligned}
\tag{5.12}
$$

Differentiating Equation 5.12 with respect to σ_ϵ^2 and setting the result to zero, the MLE of σ_ϵ^2 is found to be

$$\hat{\sigma}_\epsilon^2 = \frac{1}{N}\left[\frac{v_J^T v_J}{S_{J+1}'(d)} + \sum_{j=1}^{J} \frac{w_j^T w_j}{S_j'(d)}\right].$$

Substituting $\hat{\sigma}_\epsilon^2$ into Equation 5.12 we obtain the reduced log-likelihood

$$\widehat{\mathcal{L}}(d \mid \boldsymbol{x}) = N \log \left(\hat{\sigma}_\epsilon^2 \right) + \log \left(S'_{J+1}(d) \right) + \sum_{j=1}^{J} N_j \log \left(S'_j(d) \right).$$

The reduced log-likelihood is now a function of only the fractional difference parameter $d \in (-1/2, 1/2)$. In most practical situations, we will be interested in fractional difference parameters that are strictly positive. An exact maximum likelihood method for ARMA and fractional ARIMA processes may be found in Brockwell and Davis (1991).

This maximum likelihood (ML) procedure may be extended to allow for short-memory (ARMA) components in the time series model – producing a fractional ARIMA(p, d, q) given by

$$\Phi(B)(1 - B)^d x_t = \Theta(B)\epsilon_t,$$

where $\Phi(B)$ and $\Theta(B)$ are p and q degree polynomials in the backshift operator with autoregressive (AR) parameters $\boldsymbol{\phi} = (\phi_1, \phi_2, \dots, \phi_p)$ and moving-average (MA) parameters $\boldsymbol{\theta} = (\theta_1, \theta_2, \dots, \theta_q)$, respectively. The SDF for this process is simply

$$S_{p,d,q}(f) = \frac{|\Theta(e^{-i2\pi f})|^2}{|\Phi(e^{-i2\pi f})|^2} \frac{\sigma_\epsilon^2}{|2\sin(\pi f)|^{2d}}.$$

Constructing the approximate log-likelihood $\widehat{\mathcal{L}}(d, \boldsymbol{\phi}, \boldsymbol{\theta}, \sigma_\epsilon^2 \mid \boldsymbol{x})$ only differs through substituting $S_{p,d,q}(f)$ for $S_x(f)$ in Equation 5.3. This has been investigated by Jensen (1999a), who compared an approximate wavelet-based ML procedure to the approximate frequency-domain ML procedure in Fox and Taqqu (1986).

5.2.6   Example: IBM Stock Prices

We return to the IBM stock price series analyzed in Sections 4.4.5 and 4.5.4. It has been hypothesized that long memory is present in daily stock price volatility; see, for example, Lobato and Savin (1998) and the subsequent discussion. Ramsey *et al.* (1995) used wavelet analysis to detect self-similarity (i.e., long memory) in the Standard and Poor's 500 stock market index and found evidence of quasi-periodicity in the occurrence of large amplitude shocks to the system. If we define volatility as the absolute value of the returns $v_t = |r_t|$ for the IBM series, then we have an appropriate time series with which to estimate the long-memory parameter d. Applying the methodology from Section 5.2.5 to a partial DWT ($J_p = 4$) using the D(4) wavelet filter of the volatility series, we obtain the MLEs $\hat{d} = 0.405$ and $\hat{\sigma}_\epsilon^2(\hat{d}) = 6.832 \times 10^{-5}$. This yields the following time series model:

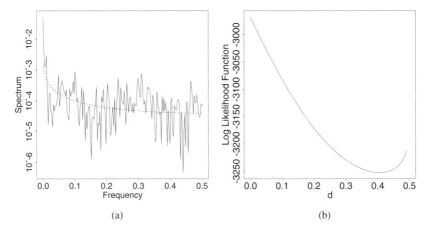

(a)   (b)

FIGURE 5.5 Long memory estimation for IBM volatility. (a) Estimated spectrum (periodogram) of the IBM volatility series given by the solid line, with the model-based spectrum using the MLEs $\hat{d}$ and $\hat{\sigma}_\epsilon^2(\hat{d})$ (dashed line). The model appears to capture the dominant features of the volatility series spectral estimate with some random variation between the two. (b) Reduced log-likelihood function $\widehat{\mathcal{L}}(d \mid \boldsymbol{v})$ of the long memory parameter d for the IBM volatility series. With only $N = 368$ observations, a partial DWT ($J_p = 4$) was applied to the series using the D(4) wavelet filter.

$$(1 - B)^{0.405} v_t = \epsilon_t.$$

To see how the model compares with the observed volatility series in Figure 5.5a, we plot an estimate of the spectrum from the data (periodogram) and also generate the theoretical model-based spectrum using the MLEs already computed. We observe good agreement between the two spectra with some random variation. When examining the residuals, no further evidence of correlation was found and hence no additional parameters (AR or MA) were fit.

Figure 5.5b shows the reduced log-likelihood function for the IBM stock volatility series. We observe a relatively sharp minimum in $\widehat{\mathcal{L}}(d \mid \boldsymbol{v})$ around 0.4. The asymptotic Cramér–Rao lower bound for the MSE of unbiased estimators of d is $6/(N\pi^2)$ (Kashyap and Eom, 1988). Hence, the asymptotic root MSE for d is 0.0406 ($N = 368$) and allows us to construct an approximate 95% confidence interval by adding and subtracting 0.0812 from our estimator $\hat{d}$. This confidence interval does not include either zero nor 1/2, allowing us to conclude that this IBM volatility series may be adequately modeled via a stationary long-memory time series.

With various methods for computing the long-memory parameter of a stationary time series, the DWT allows fast and efficient maximum likelihood estimation of both d and the innovations variance $\sigma_\epsilon^2(d)$. In addition, an approximate confidence interval is available to perform a statistical hypothesis test for the presence of long-range dependence.

5.3 GENERALIZATIONS OF THE DWT AND MODWT

5.3.1   The Discrete Wavelet Packet Transform

The DWT has a very specific band-pass filtering structure that partitions the spectrum of a long-memory process finer and finer as $f \to 0$ (i.e., where the spectrum is unbounded). This is done through a succession of filtering and downsampling operations (Section 4.4). In order to exploit the approximate decorrelation property for seasonal long-memory and other processes, we need to generalize the partitioning scheme of the DWT. This is easily obtained by performing the discrete wavelet packet transform (DWPT) on the process; see, for example, Wickerhauser (1994, Ch. 7) and Percival and Walden (2000, Ch. 6). Instead of one particular filtering sequence, the DWPT executes all possible filtering combinations to obtain a wavelet packet tree, denoted by $\mathcal{T}$ (Figure 5.6). Let $\mathcal{T} = \{(j, n) \mid j = 0, \ldots, J; n = 0, \ldots, 2^j - 1\}$ be the collection of all doublets (j, n) that form the indices of the nodes of a wavelet packet tree. An orthonormal basis $\mathcal{B} \subset \mathcal{T}$ is obtained when a collection of DWPT coefficients is chosen, whose ideal band-pass frequencies are disjoint and cover $[0, 1/2]$. The set $\mathcal{B}$ is simply a collection of doublets (j, n) that correspond to an orthonormal basis. Ramsey and Zhang (1996) used a similar, but more extensive, wave-form dictionary to analyze the Standard and Poor's 500 stock index. They found that this decomposition brought out the intermittent nature of the stock market index, that of intense bursts of activity across a wide frequency range followed by periods of relative quiet.

Let x be a dyadic length vector ($N = 2^J$) of observations, then the length N vector of DWPT coefficients $w_\mathcal{B}$ is obtained via

$$w_\mathcal{B} = \mathcal{W}_\mathcal{B} x,$$

where $\mathcal{W}_\mathcal{B}$ is an $N \times N$ orthonormal matrix defined by the orthonormal basis $\mathcal{B}$. All $(J + 1)N$ wavelet packet coefficients may be computed by constructing an overcomplete matrix $\mathcal{W}_\mathcal{T}$ and applying it to the vector of observations; that is, $w_\mathcal{T} = \mathcal{W}_\mathcal{T} x$, where $\mathcal{W}_\mathcal{T}$ is an $(J + 1)N \times N$ matrix.

There is no longer a convenient interpretation of wavelet packet coefficient vectors with differences at various scales. Instead, the vector $w_{j,n}$ is associated with the frequency interval $\lambda_{j,n} = [\frac{n}{2^{j+1}}, \frac{n+1}{2^{j+1}}]$. From Figure 5.6 the sequence of filtering steps at the left of the wavelet packet table involve strictly low-pass filters, and therefore, the scaling (low-frequency) coefficient vectors are denoted by $w_{j,0}$ at each scale. The DWPT coefficient vectors corresponding with the DWT coefficients are given by $w_{j,1}$ at each scale.

Construction of the matrices $\mathcal{W}_\mathcal{B}$ or $\mathcal{W}_\mathcal{T}$ involves a minor amount of book-keeping in order to retain the sequency ordering of the wavelet packet filters. Let $h_0, \ldots, h_{L-1}$ be the unit scale wavelet (high-pass) filter coefficients from a Daubechies compactly supported wavelet family of even length L, with scaling (low-pass) coefficients computed via the quadrature mirror relationship

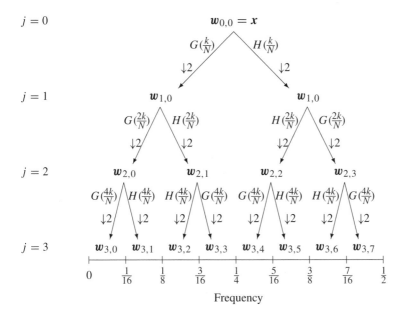

FIGURE 5.6   Flow diagram illustrating the decomposition of x into DWPT coefficients $w_{j,n}$ for levels $j = 1, 2$, and 3. The time series x is first filtered using the wavelet filter $H(f)$ and scaling filter $G(f)$ then subsampled by two, just like the DWT. The output is then filtered again and again to complete the wavelet packet table $\mathcal{T}$. The execution of the filtering is done in *sequency* order to preserve the natural frequency ordering. For levels $j = 0$, 1 and 2 the wavelet coefficient vectors cover all frequencies spanned by their children.

(Equation 4.9). Now define

$$u_{n,l} = \begin{cases} g_l, & \text{if } n \bmod 4 = 0 \text{ or } 3; \\ h_l, & \text{if } n \bmod 4 = 1 \text{ or } 2, \end{cases}$$

to be the appropriate filter at a given node of the wavelet packet tree. The wavelet packet filters $u_{n,l}$ preserve the ordering of the DWPT by increasing frequency.

Let x be a length N vector of observations and $w_{j,n}$ denote the vector of wavelet packet coefficients associated with the frequency interval $\lambda_{j,n}$. Let $w_{j,n,t}$ denote the tth element of the length $N_j = N/2^j$ vector $w_{j,n}$. Given the vector of DWPT coefficients $w_{j-1,\lfloor \frac{n}{2} \rfloor}$, we may compute $w_{j,n,t}$ directly via

$$w_{j,n,t} = \sum_{l=0}^{L-1} u_{n,l} w_{j-1,\lfloor \frac{n}{2} \rfloor, 2t+1-l \bmod N_{j-1}}, \quad t = 0, 1, \ldots, N_j - 1,$$

where $L_j = (2^j - 1)(L - 1) + 1$ is the length of a level j wavelet filter. To start the recursion set $w_{0,0} = x$. As with the DWT, the DWPT is most efficiently

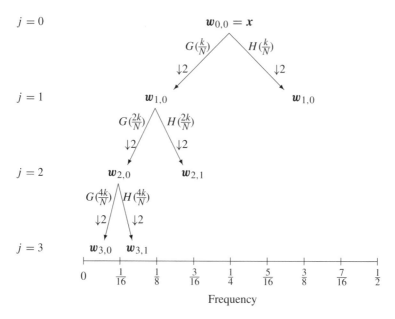

FIGURE 5.7 Flow diagram illustrating the decomposition of x into DWT coefficients $w_{1,1}$, $w_{2,1}$, $w_{3,1}$, and $w_{3,0}$.

computed using a pyramid algorithm (Wickerhauser, 1994, Ch. 7). The algorithm has $O(N \log N)$ operations, like the fast Fourier transform.

For every orthonormal basis $\mathcal{B}$, an analysis of variance may be performed. With respect to the orthonormal basis in Figure 5.6, we have the following decomposition

$$\|x\|^2 = \sum_{n=0}^{7} \|w_{3,n}\|^2,$$

and the usual DWT basis (Figure 5.7) gives us

$$\|x\|^2 = \|w_{1,1}\|^2 + \|w_{2,1}\|^2 + \|w_{3,1}\|^2 + \|w_{3,0}\|^2. \qquad (5.13)$$

Equation 5.13 duplicates the analysis of variance provided by the DWT with $w_{3,0} = v_3$ (Equation 4.20). For an arbitrary orthonormal basis $\mathcal{B}$, the decomposition is given by

$$\|x\|^2 = \sum_{(j,n)\in\mathcal{B}} \|w_{j,n}\|^2.$$

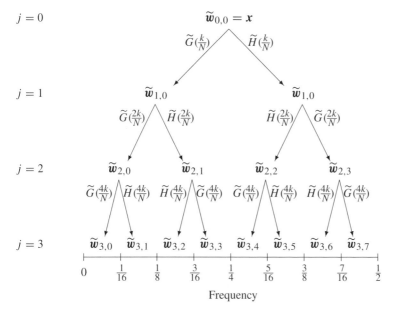

FIGURE 5.8 Flow diagram illustrating the decomposition of x into MODWPT coefficients $\widetilde{w}_{j,n}$ for levels $j = 1$, 2, and 3. The time series x is filtered using the filters $\widetilde{H}(f)$ and $\widetilde{G}(f)$ but *not* subsampled, just like the MODWT. The output is then filtered again and again to complete the wavelet packet table $\mathcal{T}$. The execution of the filtering is done in *sequence* order to preserve the natural frequency ordering. For levels $j = 0$, 1, and 2, the wavelet coefficient vectors cover all frequencies spanned by their children.

5.3.2   The Maximal Overlap Discrete Wavelet Packet Transform

Definition of the maximal overlap DWPT (MODWPT) is straightforward and follows directly from the DWPT. The rescaled wavelet packet filter is defined to be $\tilde{u}_{n,l} = u_{n,l}/2^{1/2}$. Using $\tilde{u}_{n,l}$ instead of the filter $u_{n,l}$ and *not* subsampling the filtered output produces MODWPT coefficients (Figure 5.8). Hence, the vector of MODWPT coefficients $\widetilde{w}_{j,n}$ is computed recursively given $\widetilde{w}_{j-1,\lfloor \frac{n}{2} \rfloor}$ via

$$\widetilde{w}_{j,n,t} = \sum_{l=0}^{L-1} \tilde{u}_{n,l}\widetilde{w}_{j-1,\lfloor \frac{n}{2} \rfloor,t-2^{j-1}l \bmod N}, \quad t = 0, 1, \ldots, N-1.$$

Each vector of MODWPT coefficients has length N (to begin the recursion simply define $\widetilde{w}_{0,0} = x$). This formulation leads to efficient computation using a pyramid-type algorithm (Percival and Walden, 2000, Ch. 6). As with the DWPT, the MODWPT is an energy preserving transform and we may define the decomposition of energy at each level of the transform via

$$\|x\|^2 = \sum_{n=0}^{2^j-1} \left\| \widetilde{w}_{j,n} \right\|^2, \quad \text{for} \quad j = 1, \dots, J.$$

This corresponds to the basis $\mathcal{B}_j = \{(j,n) \mid n = 0, \dots, 2^j - 1\}$. Given a particular level j of the transform, we may also reconstruct x by projecting the MODWPT coefficients back onto their rescaled filter coefficients via

$$x_t = \sum_{n=0}^{2^j-1} \sum_{l=0}^{L_j-1} \tilde{u}_{j,n,l} \widetilde{w}_{j,n,t+l \bmod N}, \quad t = 0, \dots, N-1. \tag{5.14}$$

Let $\widetilde{d}_{j,n} = (\widetilde{d}_{j,n,0}, \widetilde{d}_{j,n,1}, \dots, \widetilde{d}_{j,n,N-1})$ be the MODWPT detail associated with the frequency interval $\lambda_{j,n}$, then the tth element of $\widetilde{d}_{j,n}$ is given by

$$\widetilde{d}_{j,n,t} = \sum_{l=0}^{L_j-1} \tilde{u}_{j,n,l} \widetilde{w}_{j,n,t+l \bmod N}, \quad t = 0, \dots, N-1,$$

and an additive decomposition in Equation 5.14 may be rewritten as

$$x = \sum_{(j,n) \in \mathcal{B}} \widetilde{d}_{j,n}$$

for any orthonormal basis $\mathcal{B}$. These details are associated with zero-phase filters, just like the MODWT, and therefore line up perfectly with features in the original time series x at the same time.

5.3.3 Example: Mexican Money Supply

Money growth was investigated using a multiresolution analysis (MRA) approach in Section 4.7.3 using seasonally unadjusted time series. We take the monthly percentage changes in money supply from Mexico m_t to illustrate the DWPT and MODWPT here. Figure 5.9a shows the original series, which spans 1957:1 to 1999:12 ($N = 516$) with an obvious trend in the mean over time. We removed the trend by defining the series $\widetilde{m}_t = m_t - \widetilde{s}_{4,t}$ for all t. The new series is shown in Figure 5.9b and is guaranteed to have mean zero. The series $\widetilde{m}_t$ displays an obvious seasonal pattern that is suppressed before 1970, but appears to be relatively stationary after 1970.

When viewing the MODWT MRA (not shown), the wavelet details displayed a complicated structure not easily attributable to an oscillation at a single frequency. This is due to the fact that the underlying spectrum of this process is rapidly changing within the frequency intervals induced by the wavelet transform. We may investigate the time-frequency nature of $\widetilde{m}_t$ by performing the

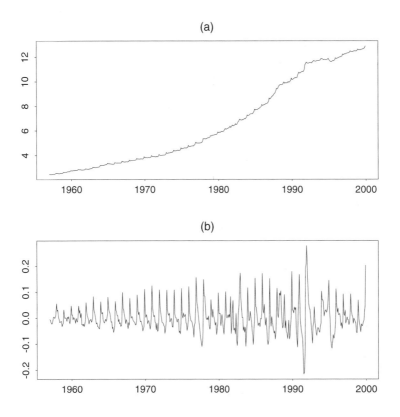

FIGURE 5.9 Monthly percentage changes in money supply for Mexico. (a) Log trans-formation of the original time series (1957:1–1999:12). (b) De-trended series via a MODWT MRA where the wavelet smooth $\widetilde{s}_4$ was removed from the data. This corresponds to eliminating all information associated with the frequencies $f \in [0, 1/32]$.

DWPT.[6] Figure 5.10 displays a level $J = 7$ DWPT using the MB(8) wavelet filter (Section 4.3.3). The structure of the wavelet packet table is identical to the flowchart in Figure 5.6. That is, the two blocks in the top row of Figure 5.10 represent the low-pass and high-pass filtered output from the original series. The second row is the low-pass and high-pass output from the two blocks in the first row, and so on. The horizontal axis is a function of frequency and has been multiplied by the change in time between observations (1 month) to produce cycles per year.

To distill information from the wavelet packet table in Figure 5.10, recall that nonzero wavelet coefficients correspond to activity in a particular range of

---

[6] The first four observations of $\widetilde{m}_t$ were discarded in order to analyze a dyadic-length ($N = 512$) series.

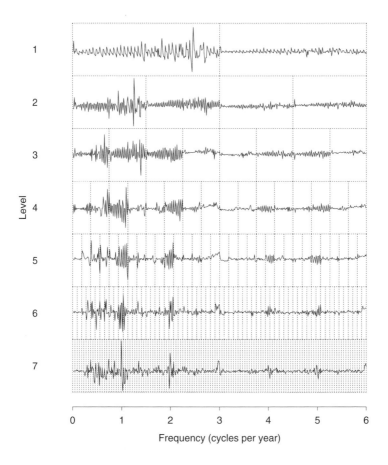

FIGURE 5.10   Wavelet packet table of monthly percentage changes in money supply for Mexico. A level $J = 7$ DWPT was performed on these data using the MB(8) wavelet filter. Since the time series contains monthly values, the x-axis is expressed in cycles per year. Each "block" in the wavelet packet table represents the vector $\boldsymbol{w}_{j,n}$ obtained using the filter $u_{j,n}$.

frequencies over time. Hence, when a vector of wavelet coefficients $\boldsymbol{w}_{j,n}$ is rapidly changing, this implies that its corresponding frequency interval contains information about the original process. Looking at Figure 5.10, it is quite clear that persistent oscillations are present at each integer number of cycles per year. The most activity is seen at one cycle per year (annual trend), then two cycles per year (6-month trend or the *first harmonic*), then three cycles per year (4-month trend), and to a lesser degree, four and five cycles per year. Since we observe the data monthly, no cycles higher than six per year are available to us. Notice that there is no activity in the lower frequencies at levels five and higher. This is a direct result of our trend-removal procedure.

5.4 WAVELETS AND SEASONAL LONG MEMORY

5.4.1 Seasonal Persistent Processes

Let y_t be a stochastic process such that

$$\left(1 - 2\phi B + B^2\right)^{\delta} y_t = \epsilon_t \tag{5.15}$$

is a stationary process, then y_t is a seasonal persistent process (SPP); a simple example of a seasonal long-memory process. Gray *et al.* (1989) showed that y_t is stationary and invertible for $|\phi| = 1$ and $-1/4 < \delta < 1/4$ or $|\phi| < 1$ and $-1/2 < \delta < 1/2$. Clearly, the definition of an SPP also includes a fractional difference process (FDP), a simple example of a long-memory process. When $\phi = 1$, we know that y_t is an FDP with parameter $d = 2\delta$. If ϵ_t is a Gaussian white noise process, then y_t is also called a Gegenbauer process since Equation 5.15 may be written as an infinite moving-average process via

$$y_t = \sum_{k=0}^{\infty} C_{k,\phi}^{(\delta)} \epsilon_{t-k},$$

where $C_{k,\phi}^{(\delta)}$ is a Gegenbauer polynomial (Rainville, 1960, Ch. 17). The SDF of y_t is given by

$$S_y(f) = \frac{\sigma_\epsilon^2}{\{2|\cos(2\pi f) - \phi|\}^{2\delta}}, \quad \text{for} \quad -\frac{1}{2} < f < \frac{1}{2}, \tag{5.16}$$

so that $S_y(f)$ becomes unbounded at frequency $f_G = (\cos^{-1}\phi)/(2\pi)$, sometimes called the Gegenbauer frequency. Figure 5.11 shows spectra from several SPPs plotted in decibels (dB) and was taken from Anděl (1986). The top two plots have the same Gegenbauer frequency f_G but differ in the magnitude of their fractional difference parameter. Notice that the closer δ approaches $1/2$, the steeper the SDF is around its asymptote. The bottom two plots have the same fractional difference parameter, but they have different Gegenbauer frequencies. The SPP with $f_G = 0.352$ will exhibit persistent high-frequency oscillations, while an SPP with $f_G = 0.016$ will contain a long-period oscillation.

The autocovariance sequence (ACVS) of an SPP may be expressed via the Fourier transform of its SDF; that is,

$$\gamma_\tau = \int_{-1/2}^{1/2} S_y(f) \cos(2\pi f \tau) \, df.$$

An explicit solution is known only for special cases. Gray *et al.* (1994) showed that the autocorrelation sequence of an SPP is given by[7]

$$\rho_\tau \sim \tau^{2\delta-1} \cos(2\pi f_G \tau) \quad \text{as} \quad \tau \to \infty. \tag{5.17}$$

---

[7] Two sequences are related via $a_\tau \sim b_\tau$ as $\tau \to \infty$ if $\lim_{\tau\to\infty}\{a_\tau/b_\tau\} = c$, where c is a finite nonzero constant.

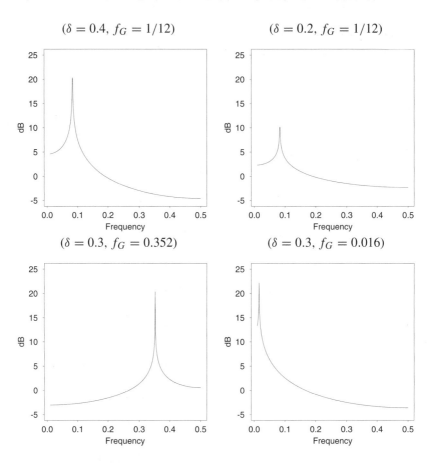

FIGURE 5.11   Spectral density functions (in decibels) for SPPs taken from Anděl (1986) (Figures 8-11). The first parameter δ indicates the rate of growth around the singularity in the spectrum - while the second parameter f_G provides the location (frequency) of the singularity.

An obvious extension of the single factor SPP would be to allow multiple singularities to appear in the SDF of the process. Consider the zero mean k-factor SPP given by

$$\prod_{i=1}^{k} \left(1 - 2\phi_i B + B^2 \right)^{\delta_i} y_t = \epsilon_t,$$

exhibiting k asymptotes located at the frequencies $f_i = (\cos^{-1} \phi_i)/(2\pi)$, $i = 1, \dots, k$, in its spectrum

$$S_y^{(k)}(f) = \sigma_\epsilon^2 \prod_{i=1}^{k} \{2|\cos(2\pi f) - \phi_i|\}^{-2\delta_i}, \qquad (5.18)$$

$|f| < 1/2$. This process was introduced by Woodward *et al.* (1998) under the name "k-factor Gegenbauer process." Using this model allows one to incorporate several observed oscillations, such as an annual frequency and its harmonics.

5.4.2 Simulation of Seasonal Persistent Processes

Both time- and frequency-domain techniques have been established for the simulation of FDPs (Section 5.2.3). The partitioning of the time-frequency plane by the DWT makes it a natural alternative to the discrete Fourier transform for decomposing long-memory processes. However, the DWT cannot adapt to a general SDF, instead we may make use of the DWPT. To determine an appropriate orthonormal basis, we propose a method based on achieving the most shallow spectrum for each level of the DWPT, thus producing the least correlated wavelet coefficients. Simulation may be performed through a method similar to the one outlined in Section 5.2.3. The technique proposed by McCoy and Walden (1996) may be considered a special case of the method given here.

An extra complication involved in simulating an SPP is that the orthonormal basis $\mathcal{B}$ is not explicitly defined. Whitcher (2001) investigated simulating SPPs using an "ideal" basis based on perfect frequency resolution of the wavelet filter. This was found to produce correlated wavelet packet coefficients in most circumstances. One way to overcome the poor approximation of the wavelet filters to that of ideal band-pass filters is to adaptively select an orthonormal basis $\mathcal{B}$ where the squared gain function of the wavelet filter associated with $w_{j,n}$ is sufficiently small at the Gegenbauer frequency. Let us define $\mathcal{U}_{j,n}(f) = |U_{j,n}(f)|^2$ to be the squared gain function for the wavelet packet filter $u_{j,n,l}$, where $U_{j,n}(f)$ is the DFT of

$$u_{j,n,l} = \sum_{k=0}^{L-1} u_{n,k} u_{j-1,\lfloor \frac{n}{2} \rfloor, l-2^{j-1}k}, \quad l = 0, \ldots, L_j - 1, \qquad (5.19)$$

with $u_{1,0,l} = g_l$, $u_{1,1,l} = h_l$ and $L_j = (2^j - 1)(L - 1) + 1$. The partition of the time-frequency plane would therefore depend on the choice of wavelet filter, overall depth of the partition being inversely proportional to the length of the wavelet filter. Hence, the basis selection procedure involves selecting the combination of wavelet basis functions that will achieve $\mathcal{U}_{j,n}(f_G) < \varepsilon$, for some $\varepsilon > 0$ at the minimum level j.

Figure 5.12 gives an orthonormal basis, according to the criterion $\mathcal{U}_{j,n}(f_G) < 0.01$, for Daubechies wavelet filters (extremal phase or least asymmetric) of various lengths $L \in \{2, 4, 8, 16\}$ applied to the SPP($\delta = 0.4$, $f_G = 1/12$) shown in Figure 5.11. The black rectangles indicate filter combinations to be included in the orthonormal basis $\mathcal{B}$. As to be expected, the shorter wavelet filters $L \in \{2, 4\}$ are poor approximations to an ideal band-pass filter and produce an orthonormal basis that must finely partition the lower frequencies $0 \leq f \leq 1/4$ with only some coarse partitioning of the higher frequencies $1/4 \leq f \leq 1/2$. As the length of the wavelet filter increases, the frequencies captured outside the nomi-

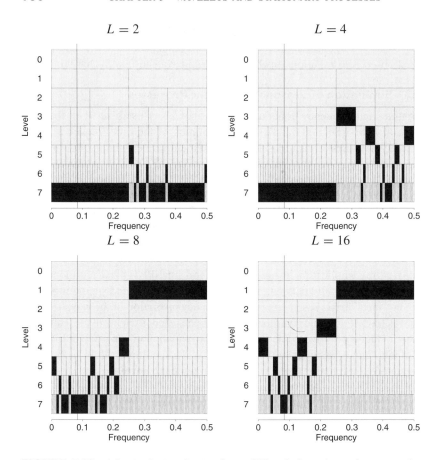

FIGURE 5.12   Adaptive basis selection for an SPP with Gegenbauer frequency $f_G = 1/12$ (indicated by the solid vertical line). These wavelet packet tables are based on the Daubechies extremal phase $D(L)$ or least asymmetric $LA(L)$ family of wavelet filters with lengths $L \in \{2, 4, 8, 16\}$. The black rectangles indicate filter combinations to be included in the orthonormal basis $\mathcal{B}$. The y-axis is in units of $1/f$, so it is in the opposite direction of the time-frequency partitions given in Figure 4.2.

nal pass-band are reduced, and thus it better mimics an ideal band-pass filter. The Daubechies wavelet filter with $L = 8$ produces a basis that adaptively partitions the entire frequency interval, but suffers from poor frequency resolution around the Gegenbauer frequency. The longest wavelet filter used here ($L = 16$), and therefore the best approximation to an ideal band-pass filter, generates an orthonormal basis that closely follows the underlying spectrum with only a few anomalies. Figure 5.13 provides the SDFs for the wavelet coefficient vectors $w_{1,1}$, $w_{3,3}$, $w_{4,0}$, and $w_{4,4}$, elements in the adaptive orthonormal basis in Figure 5.12, from an MB(16) DWPT applied to an SPP(0.4, 1/12). The spectrum of the SPP is rapidly increasing as $f \to 1/12$, but the spectra of the MB(16)

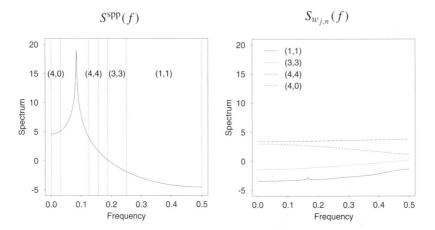

FIGURE 5.13 Spectra for an SPP(0.4, 1/12) and MB(16) wavelet coefficient vectors $w_{1,1}$, $w_{3,3}$, $w_{4,0}$, and $w_{4,4}$. Although the spectrum for the SPP is rapidly changing between the frequency intervals denoted by the vertical dotted lines, the combination of filtering and subsampling produces relatively flat spectra for the DWPT coefficients. As seen in Figure 5.2, flat spectra indicate that the filter combinations are producing approximately uncorrelated wavelet coefficient vectors.

wavelet coefficients exhibit limited variation. The ability to produce flat spectra is the key to simulating and fitting time series models to SPPs.

The band-pass variance $B_{j,n}$ for an SPP, with spectrum given in Equation 5.16, in the frequency interval $\lambda_{j,n}$ is

$$B_{j,n} = 2 \cdot 4^{-\delta} \int_{\frac{n}{2^{j+1}}}^{\frac{n+1}{2^{j+1}}} \frac{\sigma_\epsilon^2}{|\cos(2\pi f) - \phi|^{2\delta}} \, df. \qquad (5.20)$$

As in Section 5.2.3, we replace the true SDF at each frequency band with a constant $S_{j,n} = S_{j,n}(f)$, for all f, such that the band-pass variances are equal. This step assumes the SDF is slowly varying across the frequency interval $\lambda_{j,n}$. Integrating the constant spectrum over $\lambda_{j,n}$ gives

$$\int_{\frac{n}{2^{j+1}}}^{\frac{n+1}{2^{j+1}}} S_{j,n} \, df = S_{j,n} 2^{-j-1}.$$

Equating this to the band-pass variance gives

$$2S_{j,n} 2^{-j-1} = B_{j,n} \quad \Longrightarrow \quad S_{j,n} = 2^j B_{j,n}. \qquad (5.21)$$

The variance of $W_{j,n,t}$ is therefore given by $S_{j,n}$ because of the band-pass nature of the DWPT.

Let us consider simulating a length $M = 2^{J_M}$ SPP with known parameters f_G and δ. Simulation lengths of $M = 2N$ or $M = 4N$ where $N = 2^J$ are recommended. For nondyadic sample sizes, one can simply increase the length of the simulation to the minimum dyadic length that exceeds the desired sample size and then subsample. The DWPT-based simulation procedure can be implemented as follows:

1. Determine the appropriate orthonormal basis $\mathcal{B}$ from the wavelet packet tree $\mathcal{T}$. This is done by computing, for levels $j = 1, \ldots, J_M - 1$, the squared gain function of the desired wavelet filter at the Gegenbauer frequency (Equation 5.19). Applying the criterion

$$\mathcal{U}_{j,n}(f_G) < \varepsilon, \quad (j, n) \in \mathcal{T}$$

and orthogonalizing yields the doublets to be included in $\mathcal{B}$. At the final level J_M, all remaining doublets corresponding to uncovered frequency intervals must be included in order to complete the orthonormal basis.

2. Calculate the band-pass variances $B_{j,n}$, $(j, n) \in \mathcal{B}$. They are defined in Equation 5.20 and may be calculated via numeric integration. We use Equation 5.21 to obtain $S_{j,n}$. Each DWPT coefficient $w_{j,n,t}$, $(j, n) \in \mathcal{B}$, $t = 1, \ldots, 2^{J_M - j}$ is an independent Gaussian random variable with zero mean and variance $S_{j,n}$.

3. Organize the DWPT coefficients into the vector $\mathbf{w}_{\mathcal{B}}$ and apply the inverse DWPT via $\widehat{\mathbf{x}} = \mathcal{W}_{\mathcal{B}}^T \mathbf{w}_{\mathcal{B}}$ to produce a length M portion of the desired SPP. By generating a uniform random integer ξ on the interval $[1, M - N + 1]$, we may obtain a length N segment $\hat{x}_{\xi}, \ldots, \hat{x}_{\xi+N-1}$.

The numeric integration for all band-pass variances (except the one such that $f_G \in \lambda_{j,n}$ for $(j, n) \in \mathcal{B}$) required in Step 2 is easily computed using the routine QAGS from QUADPACK (Piessons *et al.*, 1983), since the SDF is bounded on all frequency intervals. The final band-pass variance will capture the unbounded portion of the spectrum, where numeric integration using QAGS may still be performed by splitting the integral at the Gegenbauer frequency.

Through simulation studies Whitcher (2001) found that the DWPT-based method adequately captures the second-order characteristics of SPPs, when compared to the Hosking method, and at greatly reduced computational cost. For example, a length $N = 2^{20} > 1,000,000$ SPP may be generated in less than 30 seconds.

5.4.3   Basis Selection Procedures

Since we are working with processes that may exhibit a wide range of characteristics, selecting the orthonormal basis for the DWPT is important. We want to adapt as best as possible to the underlying SDF, but we only have the observations for direction. For long-memory processes, the DWT works extremely well at approximately decorrelating the process. In Section 5.2.2, we related this ability to the fact that the SDFs of the wavelet coefficient vectors are essentially flat – that is, only varying by 3 dB (decibels) for the unit scale DWT coefficients when the fractional difference parameter is associated with FDPs where $-1/2 < d < 1/2$ (Table 5.1). The criterion of "approximately flat" SDFs was used to simulate

SPPs in Section 5.4.2, but there we had the luxury of knowing the parameter values of the process.

A constant spectrum is associated with a white noise process, where $\int S(f)$ $df = \sigma^2$. Several methods have been proposed in order to test for white noise in time series, such as the cumulative periodogram and portmanteau tests (Box–Pierce and Ljung–Box); see, for example, Brockwell and Davis (1991). Percival *et al.* (2001) used these two white noise tests to determine an appropriate orthonormal basis for the DWPT in order to construct a bootstrap distribution for the lag-one sample autocorrelation. A cumulative sum of squares (CSS) test statistic was proposed by Brown *et al.* (1975) for testing the constancy of regression relationships over time and was successfully applied to Nile River annual minimum water levels by Whitcher *et al.* (1998) (Section 7.3).

One disadvantage of the cumulative periodogram test is that, by applying the discrete Fourier transform (DFT) to each vector of DWPT coefficients, the number of values used in the test is halved. Given the inherent downsampling of the DWPT, each level j of the DWPT has only $N/2^j$ coefficients, and hence the cumulative periodogram test will only contain $N/2^{j+1}$ periodogram ordinates. This may be alleviated by using reflection boundary conditions when computing the DWPT, thus "doubling" the number of DWPT coefficients at each level.

In the following two sections, these white noise tests are used to determine an orthonormal basis that adequately decorrelates observed time series. More research is needed in this area to develop a better methodology. One possibility is to use best-basis algorithms with additive cost functions (Coifman and Wickerhauser, 1992) or nonadditive cost functions (Taswell, 1996). The choice of wavelet filter, with respect to selecting an orthonormal basis, is crucial. The MBDT wavelets in Section 4.3.3 were particularly useful for SPPs. Families of wavelets, such as the Jackson or Fejér-Korovkin wavelets (Nielsen, 2001), may also prove useful.

5.4.4 Ordinary Least-Squares Estimation of Seasonal Persistent Processes

The observed linear relationship (on a log-log scale) between the wavelet variance $\sigma_x^2(\lambda_j)$ and scale λ_j provided the impetus to use OLS estimation for the fractional difference parameter d of FDPs (Section 5.2.4). A natural question is, does such a linear relationship exist for SPPs? To investigate this question, apply the logarithmic transform to both sides of Equation 5.16 yielding

$$\log S_y(f) = -2\delta \log 2 |\cos(2\pi f) - \phi|. \qquad (5.22)$$

This suggests a simple linear regression of $\log \widehat{S}_y(f)$ on $\log 2|\cos(2\pi f) - \phi|$ in order to estimate the fractional difference parameter δ, where $\widehat{S}_y(f)$ is an estimate of the true spectrum at each frequency (e.g., the periodogram or multitaper spectrum estimator). Arteche and Robinson (2000) suggested a simple modification to Equation 5.22, which consists of replacing the explicit parametric form

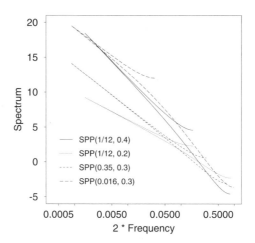

FIGURE 5.14   Approximate log-linear relationship between the spectra of SPPs, given in Figure 5.11, and frequency. Due to reflection, there are two curves for each process. The longer is $\log S(f)$ versus $\log 2|f - f_G|$ for frequencies $f_G < f < 1/2$, while the shorter curve is $\log S(f)$ versus $\log 2|f - f_G|$ for frequencies $0 < f < f_G$. Unlike the spectra for FDPs, there is *not* a simple linear relationship between the SDF and frequency. This complicates estimation of the fractional difference parameter for SPPs.

of the SDF with just the frequency, yielding

$$\log S_y(f) \approx -2\delta \log 2|f - f_G|. \tag{5.23}$$

Using the notation conventions in Section 5.2.4, our variables for the OLS regression $y = X\beta + e$ based on Equation 5.22 are

$$
y = \begin{bmatrix} \log \widehat{S}_y(f_1) \\ \log \widehat{S}_y(f_2) \\ \vdots \\ \log \widehat{S}_y(f_k) \end{bmatrix}
\quad
X = \begin{bmatrix} 1 & \log 2|\cos(2\pi f_1) - \phi| \\ 1 & \log 2|\cos(2\pi f_2) - \phi| \\ \vdots & \vdots \\ 1 & \log 2|\cos(2\pi f_k) - \phi| \end{bmatrix}
\quad
\beta = \begin{bmatrix} \beta_0 \\ \beta_1 \end{bmatrix}
$$

and model errors $e = [e_1, e_2, \ldots, e_J]^T$. Hence, the OLS estimator of β_1 is the second element of $\hat{\beta} = (X^T X)^{-1} X^T y$, and using the transformation $\hat{\delta}_{\text{ols}} = -\hat{\beta}_1/2$ gives the estimated fractional difference parameter. To utilize the regression based on Equation 5.23, simply construct the model matrix X using $\log 2|f - f_G|$ instead of $\log 2|\cos(2\pi f) - \phi|$. Additional modifications to this log-periodogram regression scheme may be found in Arteche and Robinson (2000).

Robinson (1995) replaced the parametric form of the SDF with frequency in Equation 5.23 and found to it work quite well for long-memory processes. Figure 5.14 plots the logarithm of the SDF for various SPPs against the logarithm of frequencies centered at the Gegenbauer frequency. While the approximation for FDPs is quite good for frequencies $0 < f < 1/4$ (Figure 5.1), the relationship for SPPs depends heavily on the location of the Gegenbauer frequency and is not linear for most frequencies! Looking at the first two curves, corresponding to processes with the same Gegenbauer frequency $f_G = 1/12$ but different fractional difference parameters, we see that the slope of the curves are linear for a range of frequencies and differ dramatically in slope. When looking at the last two curves, corresponding to processes with the same fractional difference parameter $\delta = 0.3$ but different Gegenbauer frequencies, the two curves start out with similar slopes but the one with $f_G = 0.352$ bends downward and parallels the first curve with fractional difference parameter $\delta = 0.4$. Obviously the range of frequencies included in the regression will seriously affect the estimation of δ in practice.

We extend the results from Section 5.2.4 to formulate a wavelet packet variance estimator for the fractional difference parameter of SPPs. The basic equation is

$$\log \sigma^2(\lambda_{j,n}) = -2\delta \log 2|\cos(2\pi\mu_{j,n}) - \phi|, \tag{5.24}$$

where $\mu_{j,n}$ is the midpoint of the frequency interval $\lambda_{j,n}$. In strict terms, the (j, n)th wavelet packet variance covers the entire interval of frequencies $\lambda_{j,n}$ but it suffices to represent this interval by its midpoint here. As in Equation 5.22, the slope from a simple linear regression of $\log \tilde{\sigma}^2(\lambda_{j,n})$ on $\log 2|\cos(2\pi\mu_{j,n}) - \phi|$, appropriately normalized, provides an estimate of the fractional difference parameter. Simplifying Equation 5.24 to just the frequencies, and not the full SDF, yields

$$\log \sigma^2(\lambda_{j,n}) \approx -2\delta \log 2|\mu_{j,n} - f_G|. \tag{5.25}$$

For the wavelet packet variance, the variables for the OLS regression $y = X\beta + e$ based on Equation 5.24 are

$$
y = \begin{bmatrix} \log \hat{\sigma}_y(\lambda_{j,n}) \\ \log \hat{\sigma}_y(\lambda_{j,n}) \\ \vdots \\ \log \hat{\sigma}_y(\lambda_{j,n}) \end{bmatrix}
\qquad
X = \begin{bmatrix} 1 & \log 2|\cos(2\pi\mu_{j,n}) - \phi| \\ 1 & \log 2|\cos(2\pi\mu_{j,n}) - \phi| \\ \vdots & \vdots \\ 1 & \log 2|\cos(2\pi\mu_{j,n}) - \phi| \end{bmatrix}
$$

with model parameters $\beta = [\beta_0, \beta_1]^T$ and model errors $e = [e_1, e_2, \ldots, e_J]^T$. As with the log-periodogram estimator, the OLS estimator of β_1 is the second element of $\hat{\beta} = (X^T X)^{-1} X^T y$ and using the transformation $\hat{\delta}_{ols} = -\hat{\beta}_1/2$ gives the estimated fractional difference parameter with $\mathrm{Var}(\hat{\delta}_{ols}) = \frac{1}{4}\mathrm{Var}(\hat{\beta}_1)$. To utilize the regression based on Equation 5.25, simply construct the model matrix X using $\log 2|\mu_{j,n} - f_G|$ instead of $\log 2|\cos(2\pi\mu_{j,n}) - \phi|$.

Whereas the OLS estimate of the fractional difference parameter for long memory processes (Section 5.2.4) has been shown to exhibit reasonable bias and MSE characteristics in simulation studies, Whitcher (2000) showed that the log-periodogram estimator using Equation 5.23 is heavily biased and the wavelet packet OLS estimate also performs poorly when using a nonadaptive orthonormal basis. This basis mimics frequency-domain estimators of the SDF. When utilizing an adaptive orthonormal basis (Section 5.4.3), the wavelet packet OLS estimate of the fractional difference parameter outperforms both the log-periodogram and nonadaptive wavelet packet estimates. In practice, the OLS estimator $\hat{\delta}_{ols}$ for SPPs should be restricted in its use to input into a maximum likelihood procedure (Section 5.4.5) and not be seen as a viable estimator on its own.

5.4.5 Approximate Maximum Likelihood Estimation of Seasonal Persistent Processes

We have provided an approximate maximum likelihood estimator for the fractional difference parameter of a long-memory process. The DWT provides a simple and effective method for approximately diagonalizing the covariance matrix of the original process (Figure 5.3). We extend these results to the case of SPPs, where two parameters δ and ϕ define the SDF (Section 5.4.1). The key point is to utilize the DWPT under a particular choice of orthonormal basis $\mathcal{B}$ to approximately diagonalize the covariance matrix of an SPP.

Let x be a realization of a zero mean stationary SPP with unknown parameters δ, ϕ, and $\sigma_\epsilon^2 > 0$. Recall that the likelihood function for x, under the assumption of multivariate Gaussianity, is given by

$$L(\delta, \phi, \sigma_\epsilon^2 \mid x) = (2\pi)^{-N/2} |\Sigma_x|^{-1/2} \exp\left[-\tfrac{1}{2} x^T \Sigma_x^{-1} x\right]. \tag{5.26}$$

The MLEs of the parameters (δ, ϕ, and σ_ϵ^2) are those quantities that maximize Equation 5.26. We now avoid the difficulties in computing the exact MLEs by using the approximate decorrelation of the DWPT as applied to SPPs; that is,

$$\Sigma_x \approx \widehat{\Sigma}_x = \mathcal{W}_\mathcal{B}^T \Omega_N \mathcal{W}_\mathcal{B},$$

where $\mathcal{W}_\mathcal{B}$ is an $N \times N$ orthonormal matrix defining the DWPT through the basis $\mathcal{B}$ and Ω_N is a diagonal matrix containing the band-pass variances associated with $(j, n) \in \mathcal{B}$. The approximate likelihood function is now

$$\widehat{L}(\delta, \phi, \sigma_\epsilon^2 \mid x) = (2\pi)^{-N/2} |\widehat{\Sigma}_x|^{-1/2} \exp\left[-\tfrac{1}{2} x^T \widehat{\Sigma}_x^{-1} x\right].$$

Hence, we want to find values of δ, ϕ, and σ_ϵ^2 that minimize the log-likelihood function

$$\begin{aligned} \widehat{\mathcal{L}}(\delta, \phi, \sigma_\epsilon^2 \mid x) &= -2\log\left(\widehat{L}(\delta, \phi, \sigma_\epsilon^2 \mid x)\right) - N\log(2\pi) \\ &= \log\left(|\widehat{\Sigma}_x|\right) + x^T \widehat{\Sigma}_x^{-1} x. \end{aligned}$$

From Section 5.4.2 we know that the variance for DWPT coefficients associated with the frequency interval $\lambda_{j,n}$ is given by $S_{j,n}$. We note that $S_{j,n}$ depends on three parameters related to the SPP: the fractional difference parameter δ, the Gegenbauer frequency ϕ, and variance σ_ϵ^2. Let $S_{j,n}(\delta, \phi, \sigma_\epsilon^2) = \sigma_\epsilon^2 S'_{j,n}(\delta, \phi)$. Through properties of diagonal and orthonormal matrices, the approximate log-likelihood function may be rewritten as

$$\widehat{\mathcal{L}}(\delta, \phi, \sigma_\epsilon^2 \mid x) = N \log\left(\sigma_\epsilon^2\right) + \sum_{(j,n)\in\mathcal{B}} N_j \log\left(S'_{j,n}(\delta, \phi)\right)$$

$$+ \frac{1}{\sigma_\epsilon^2}\left[\sum_{(j,n)\in\mathcal{B}} \frac{w_{j,n}^T w_{j,n}}{S'_{j,n}(\delta, \phi)}\right]. \qquad (5.27)$$

Differentiating Equation 5.27 with respect to σ_ϵ^2 and setting the result to zero, the MLE of σ_ϵ^2 is found to be

$$\hat{\sigma}_\epsilon^2 = \frac{1}{N}\left[\sum_{(j,n)\in\mathcal{B}} \frac{w_{j,n}^T w_{j,n}}{S'_{j,n}(\delta, \phi)}\right].$$

Substituting $\hat{\sigma}_\epsilon^2$ into Equation 5.27, we obtain the reduced log-likelihood

$$\widehat{\mathcal{L}}(\delta, \phi \mid x) = N \log\left(\hat{\sigma}_\epsilon^2\right) + \sum_{(j,n)\in\mathcal{B}} N_j \log\left(S'_{j,n}(\delta, \phi)\right).$$

The reduced log-likelihood above is now a function of only the fractional difference parameter δ and Gegenbauer frequency through

$$f_G = (\cos^{-1}\phi)/(2\pi),$$

whose space of possible solutions is $(-1/2, 1/2) \times (0, 1/2)$. In most practical situations, we will be interested in fractional difference parameters that are strictly positive, thus reducing the solution space even more. This estimation procedure differs from the frequency-based semiparametric estimator of Arteche and Robinson (2000) by simultaneously determining MLEs for both the fractional difference parameter and Gegenbauer frequency, whereas their procedure requires user-specified frequencies for the asymptotes in the SDF of the model.

The estimation procedure outlined here has assumed only one singularity in the spectrum of x. In practice it is common to observe a fundamental frequency, say the annual cycle, and several harmonics, such as cycles of two per year, and so on. These may be included in the ML procedure by using the spectrum of a k-factor SPP (Equation 5.18). The likelihood function would then be a function of $\delta = (\delta_1, \delta_2, ..., \delta_k)$, $\phi = (\phi_1, \phi_2, ..., \phi_k)$ and σ_ϵ^2. Long memory may also be incorporated into the modeling by allowing one of the Gegenbauer frequencies to be zero. The fractional difference parameter associated with this zero frequency would be constrained via $|\delta| \leq 1/4$, but the relation to a fractional difference parameter of an FDP is $d = 2\delta$. Finally, short-memory may also be included through adding AR or MA terms to the spectrum of the model as in Section 5.2.5. Thus, we allow ML estimation for parameters covering a wide variety of time series models involving seasonal long memory.

5.5 APPLICATIONS

5.5.1 Mexican Money Supply

The exploratory data analysis performed in Section 5.3.3 provided insight into an appropriate time series model for the monthly percentage changes in money supply from Mexico. The DWPT indicated that strong seasonal components are present in the series, the strongest being the annual cycle, then a six-month cycle (first harmonic) and to a lesser degree higher-order harmonics. Using the procedure outlined in Section 5.4.5 we may fit a variety of seasonal long-memory time series models to this observed series. The simplest one is an SPP with only one singularity in its spectrum, corresponding to one persistent oscillation. If we let $\tilde{m}_t = m_t - \tilde{s}_{4,t}$ denote the monthly percentage change in the money supply with trend removed and utilize the methodology in Section 5.4.5, then our time series model is

$$\left(1 - 1.74B + B^2\right)^{0.3} \tilde{m}_t = \epsilon_t,$$

where the Gegenbauer frequency is approximately 0.082 cycles per year and $\hat{\sigma}^2 = 0.00089$. Thus, f_G corresponds to the annual frequency and the fractional difference parameter $\hat{\delta} = 0.3$ is quite strong. The log-likelihood for this particular model is -3234.16.

  Without performing any statistical tests, a visual diagnostic may be performed by viewing the sample ACF of $\tilde{m}_t$ (not shown). There is an asymmetry in the ACF about zero, indicating that more than one oscillation is present. Hence, a two-factor SPP was fit, again using an approximate wavelet-based maximum likelihood, yielding the model

$$\left(1 - 1.75B + B^2\right)^{0.25} \left(1 - 0.99B + B^2\right)^{0.14} (m_t - \tilde{s}_{4,t}) = \epsilon_t,$$

where $f_1 \approx 0.081$ and $f_2 \approx 0.163$, both in cycles per year, and $\hat{\sigma}^2 = 0.00084$. This two-factor time series model captures the annual cycle again, with nearly identical Gegenbauer frequency and a slight decrease in the annual fractional difference parameter $\hat{\delta}_1 = 0.25$, but also picks out the 6-month cycle with $\hat{\delta}_2 = 0.14$. The decrease in δ_1 is reasonable since when the two oscillations are in phase, the 6-month cycle boosts the strength of the annual cycle. The log-likelihood for this particular model is -3265.68 and shows a decrease of -31.52. If one prefers

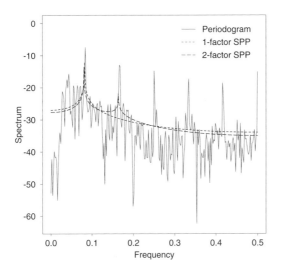

FIGURE 5.15 Estimated spectrum of the monthly percentage changes in money supply for Mexico (de-trended). The solid line is the periodogram, the short-dashed line is the model-based spectrum using a one-factor SPP, and the long-dashed line uses a two-factor SPP. Both models adequately capture their respective spectral peaks, but additional factors must be included to better resolve the high-frequency oscillations.

to use a model selection criterion,[8] such as the Akaike Information Criterion (AIC) or Bayesian Information Criterion (BIC), a better comparison may be made between the one- and two-factor SPP models. The AIC is a penalized log-likelihood defined to be

$$-2 \log L(\cdot | x) + 2p,$$

where $L(\cdot | x)$ is the likelihood function and p is the number of parameters in the model. Hence, the AIC for a one-factor SPP applied to Mexican money supply is $-3234.16 + 6 = -3228.16$, and the AIC for a two-factor model is $-3265.68 + 10 = -3255.68$. The smaller AIC for the two-factor model adds support to allowing another two parameters in order to fit an additional singularity in the spectrum. Although not presented here, we would propose to add factors to the SPP model until no improvement is seen in the AIC as one model-building strategy.

---

[8] The Akaike Information Criterion (AIC) was originally proposed by Akaike (1973, 1974) in order to apply a decision-making strategy based on the Kullback-Leibler information measure. He argued that the AIC provides a natural criterion for ordering alternate statistical models for data.

5.5.2   Japanese GNP, Seasonality, and Trends

The previous section analyzed a monthly time series of substantial length ($N = 512$). Here we approach a quarterly data set q_t (Japanese gross national product) with a maximum length of $N = 169$. These data were previously analyzed by Hecq (1998), among others, to determine what effect seasonal adjustment have on detecting significant (or spurious) correlations. We proceed to fit several SPP models to show that small sample sizes, as is common with sparsely sampled data, and oscillations that occur on the boundary between frequency partitions – that is, $f = 1/4$ – do not adversely affect the wavelet-based ML estimation.

The original series (log transformed) exhibits a clear annual cycle ($f = 1/4$) and trend; see Figure 5.16. The first wavelet detail $\widetilde{d}_1$ picks out a portion of the annual cycle and its first harmonic ($f = 1/2$) and the second wavelet detail $\widetilde{d}_2$ captures another portion of the annual cycle. This happens because the annual cycle happens to fall exactly on the boundary between two frequency intervals. The wavelet filters are approximations to ideal band-pass filters and therefore some of the variability is captured by adjacent wavelet scales. There also appears to be a low-frequency oscillation in the frequency interval $\lambda_{5,1} = (1/64, 1/32]$ associated with $\widetilde{d}_5$. The wavelet smooth $\widetilde{s}_5$ appears to capture the nonstationary trend.

Bowing to parsimony we propose a one-factor SPP model as a first step in our model fitting procedure. First, to simplify the estimation procedure only the last 128 observations are used thus keeping a dyadic sample size for the DWPT. The wavelet-based MLEs produce the following model:

$$\left(1 + 0.038B + B^2\right)^{0.32} (q_t - \widetilde{s}_{5,t}) = \epsilon_t,$$

where the Gegenbauer frequency is approximately 0.256 cycles per year and $\hat{\sigma}^2 = 0.00099$. The log-likelihood for this model is -794.06. Looking at the periodogram for Japanese GNP (Figure 5.17), there is obviously a second spectral peak around $f = 1/2$ and some activity at the other frequencies. An easy remedy to the second spectral peak is to include a second factor into our SPP model. This two-factor model has the following form:

$$\left(1 + 0.029B + B^2\right)^{0.36} \left(1 + 2B + B^2\right)^{0.09} (q_t - \widetilde{s}_{5,t}) = \epsilon_t,$$

where $f_1 \approx 0.252$ and $f_2 \approx 0.5$, both in cycles per year, and $\hat{\sigma}^2 = 0.00081$. The log-likelihood for this particular model is -817.47 and shows a decrease of -23.41. The model-based spectrum in Figure 5.17 appears to match the periodogram at both spectral peaks but fails to capture the features at lower frequencies. We suggest fitting additional short-memory (ARMA) components to better track the low-frequency events.

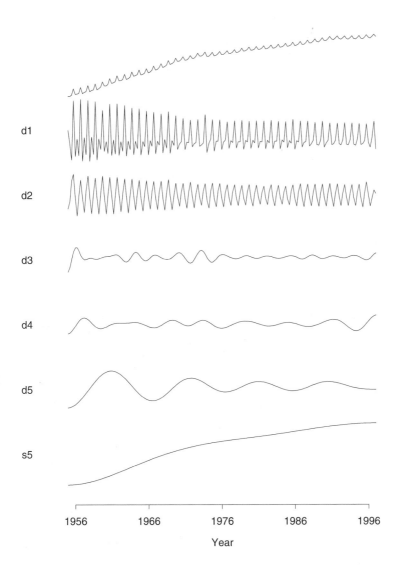

FIGURE 5.16 MB(8) MODWT multiresolution analysis of the Japanese gross domestic expenditures (1955Q1–1997Q1). The original series (log transformed) exhibits a clear annual cycle and trend. These features are captured by the first two wavelet details ($\widetilde{d}_1$ and $\widetilde{d}_2$) and wavelet smooth $\widetilde{s}_5$, respectively. All wavelet details are plotted on same vertical scale, which is different from the one used for the data and wavelet smooth.

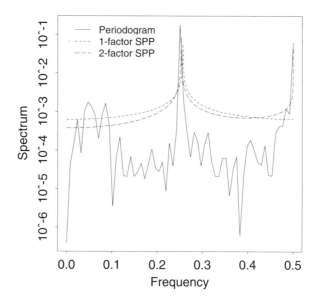

FIGURE 5.17 Estimated spectrum of the quarterly Japanese gross national product (de-trended). The solid line is the periodogram, the short-dashed line is the model-based spectrum using a one-factor SPP, and the long-dashed line uses a two-factor SPP. The one-factor model has a problem matching the spectral peak with the observed periodogram, but the two-factor model does well at both $f = 1/4$ and $f = 1/2$.

5.5.3   U.S. Unemployment, Consumer Price Index, and Tourism Revenues

In this section we analyze three time series: U.S. unemployment, the U.S. consumer price index, and U.S. tourism revenues. We denote these series as u_t, c_t and r_t, respectively. We apply the first difference operator $(1 - B)$ to each series in order to remove low-frequency content, otherwise known as trends. These first differenced series are plotted in Figure 5.18. Both unemployment and the consumer price index are monthly values, while tourism is measured quarterly. Seasonal models seem appropriate for unemployment and tourism, while the consumer price index appears to exhibit some long-range dependence better modeled by a fractional difference process.

Starting with unemployment u_t, we fit a one-factor SPP yielding

$$\left(1 - 0.49B + B^2\right)^{0.14}(1 - B)u_t = \epsilon_{u,t},$$

where the Gegenbauer frequency is approximately 0.17 cycles per year, or roughly

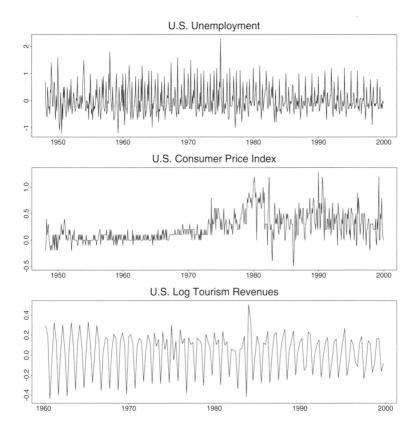

FIGURE 5.18 Time series plots of U.S. Unemployment u_t, U.S. Consumer Price Index c_t, and (log) U.S. Tourism Revenues $\log r_t$ (first differences). Both u_t and c_t are observed monthly, while r_t is observed on a quarterly basis. All three time series have been differenced in order to remove potential trends.

a 2-year oscillation, and $\hat{\sigma}_u^2 = 0.10773$. The log-likelihood for this model is -785.05. A two-factor SPP produces the following model:

$$\left(1 - 0.49B + B^2\right)^{0.30} \left(1 + 0.87B + B^2\right)^{0.17} (1 - B)u_t = \epsilon_{u,t},$$

where the frequencies are $f_1 = 0.17$ and $f_2 = 0.42$, corresponding to 2- and 5-year oscillations, and $\hat{\sigma}_u^2 = 0.09040$. The log-likelihood for this model is -870.33, producing a decrease of 85.28. The induced spectra from these two models is plotted against the periodogram for $(1 - B)u_t$ in Figure 5.19, showing how well each model captures its spectral peaks. A third factor could be included to pick up the peak at 3 years, with additional factors potentially needed to capture the 1- and 4-year peaks.

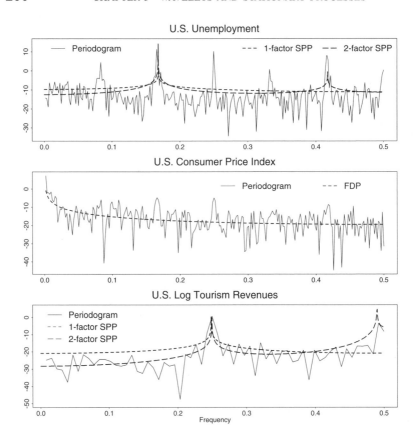

FIGURE 5.19 Estimated spectra via the periodogram (solid line) of the first differenced U.S. Unemployment, U.S. Consumer Price Index, and (log) U.S. Tourism Revenues. U.S. Unemployment and log U.S. Tourism Revenues were modeled by one-factor and two-factor SPPs (short-dashed and long-dashed lines, respectively). The seasonal time series models capture the two most dominant spectral peaks in each case. For U.S. Unemployment, more factors may need to be included in order to properly model its seasonal behavior. The U.S. Consumer Price Index was modeled by an FDP (short-dashed line). This particular time series model adequately tracks the main features of the estimated spectrum.

Moving on to the consumer price index, we fit an FDP to the first differences of c_t and come up with the following model:

$$(1 - B)^{0.42}(1 - B)c_t = \epsilon_{c,t}$$

where $\hat{\sigma}_u^2 = 0.02$ and a log-likelihood of -1642.83. If we plot the model-based spectrum against the periodogram of $(1 - B)c_t$ (Figure 5.19), there is very good agreement throughout the spectrum.

For the quarterly series of tourism revenues, we first take the log transform then first differences before modeling. A one-factor SPP produces the model:

$$\left(1 - 0.009B + B^2\right)^{0.29} (1 - B) \log r_t = \epsilon_{r,t},$$

where the Gegenbauer frequency is approximately 0.25 cycles per year, or roughly a half yearly oscillation, and $\hat{\sigma}_u^2 = 0.01227$. The log-likelihood for this model is -470.62. A two-factor SPP produces the following model

$$\left(1 - 0.001B + B^2\right)^{0.38} \left(1 + 0.998B + B^2\right)^{0.38} (1 - B) \log r_t = \epsilon_{r,t},$$

where the frequencies are $f_1 = 0.25$ and $f_2 = 0.49$, corresponding to 6-month and 1-year oscillations, and $\hat{\sigma}_u^2 = 0.00722$. The log-likelihood for this model is -526.11, producing a decrease of 55.49. The induced spectra from these two models is plotted against the periodogram for $(1 - B) \log r_t$ in Figure 5.19, showing how well each model captures its spectral peaks. The one-factor model fails to capture the second spectral peak, but also exhibits increased energy in the lower frequencies. By allowing for two peaks, the model successfully captures the two obvious peaks and adequately models the low-frequency content.

6

WAVELET DENOISING

6.1 INTRODUCTION

Observed time series are almost never simple objects. The inherent variability of any process produces complicated features that may or may not be present in the underlying signal. Hence, developing techniques to help researchers discriminate the signal from the noise has been of interest as long as measurements have been taken. One avenue of interest is to find an appropriate way to re-express the observed time series. The discrete Fourier transform is a technique with an established history. Its basic premise is that any signal may be expressed as an infinite superposition of sinusoidal functions. This seems ideal for observed processes which have underlying signals that are periodic and globally stationary (i.e., their basic structure does not vary over time). Even with noise added to the signal, it should be quite straightforward to discriminate between the Fourier coefficients that are associated with the particular sinusoids and ones that are not.

When the underlying signal is not easily represented by a particular combination of sinusoids, then the Fourier transform may not be the most effective representation. As we will argue here, the DWT provides a powerful way of summarizing the information contained in a wide variety of signals. Although

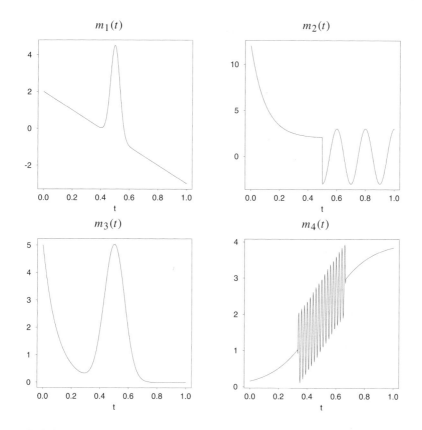

FIGURE 6.1 Example functions $m_1, \dots, m_4$ defined via Equations 6.1-6.4.

it may not outperform alternative techniques under special circumstances, its adaptiveness is very appealing.

As an illustration, consider four example functions (for now we will not bother with including additive noise) and three ways to summarize them: the time domain, the frequency domain, and the wavelet domain. The functions m are as follows (Engel, 1994, Figure 6.1):[1]

1. Linear decaying function with peak

$$m_1(t) = 2 - 5t + 5e^{-500(t-0.5)^2};$$ (6.1)

2. Exponentially decaying function followed by a cosine function

$$m_2(t) = \begin{cases} 10e^{-10t} + 2 & \text{for } t \leq 0.5 \\ 3\cos(10\pi t) & \text{for } t > 0.5; \end{cases}$$ (6.2)

_____

[1] Note, the function definitions in Engel (1994) do not match the figures in his article. The plots in Figure 6.1 do match the definitions provided in the text above.

3. Exponentially decaying function with peak

$$m_3(t) = 5e^{-100(t-0.5)^2} + 5e^{-10t};$$ (6.3)

4. Logistic function with superimposed harmonic function

$$m_4(t) = \frac{4}{1 + e^{-6.4t+3.2}} + \cos(100\pi t)I_{[1/3,2/3]}(t);$$ (6.4)

where

$$I_A(t) = \begin{cases} 1 & \text{if } t \in A \\ 0 & \text{otherwise.} \end{cases}$$

These functions are meant to exhibit the characteristics one may observe in economic or financial data (trends, seasonal behavior, peaks, etc.). Most important, they do not appear to be stationary in the sense that their behavior over time changes. The first function $m_1(t)$ only exhibits change in the middle of the series apart from the linear trend, the second function $m_2(t)$ is the concatenation of two different functions, the third function $m_3(t)$ exhibits a local peak embedded in a slow decay, and the fourth function $m_4(t)$ is a high-frequency oscillation on top of a trend. The wavelet representation should be able to capitalize on the local nature of these functions.

To measure the efficiency of the three representations, we look at the normalized cumulative sum of squares (NCSS) applied to the ordered coefficients from each transformation.[2] Here, by ordering the transformed coefficients in increasing magnitude, we wish to look at the rate of accumulation of the sum of squared coefficients through each representation. Let $x_{(n)}$ denote the nth largest coefficient (in squared magnitude) of the length N vector x; that is,

$$|x_{(0)}|^2 \geq |x_{(1)}|^2 \geq \cdots \geq |x_{(N-1)}|^2.$$

The quantity of interest is the NCSS, defined to be

$$\mathcal{E}_n = \frac{\sum_{i=0}^{n} |x_{(i)}|^2}{\sum_{i=0}^{N-1} |x_{(i)}|^2}, \quad n = 0, \ldots, N-1.$$

Note that the denominator $\sum_{i=0}^{N-1} |x_{(i)}|^2 = \|x\|^2$ since the norm is invariant to permutations. Plotting $\mathcal{E}_n$ against n indicates how sparse the given set of coefficients are (how many non-zero coefficients are present). The better the representation, the faster the curve will climb toward one.

The continuous functions $m_1, \ldots, m_4$ were sampled at $2^7 = 128$ equally spaced locations to create discrete versions of them. The Fourier and Haar

---

[2] The NCSS was applied to the raw wavelet coefficients in Section 7.3 to test for sudden changes in variability in a time series.

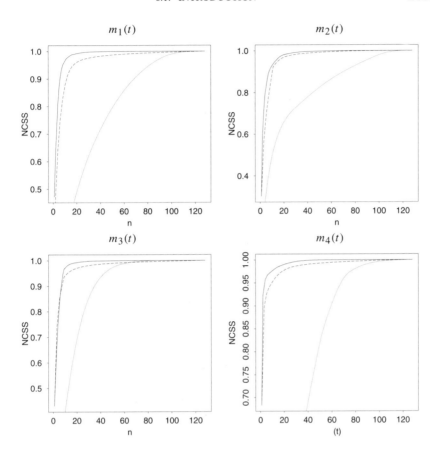

FIGURE 6.2 Normalized cumulative sum of squares (NCSS) for sampled versions ($N = 128$) of the functions $m_1, \ldots, m_4$ plotted against the index n of the largest coefficient in squared magnitude. Each plot displays the time-domain (dotted line), Fourier domain (dashed line), and Haar wavelet domain (solid line) representations. The faster a curve reaches 100%, the more efficient the representation is for that particular function. The wavelet domain representation is the most efficient representation for all functions presented here, in that it captures the most information in the least number of coefficients.

wavelet transforms were then applied to each discrete function. The Haar wavelet filter was chosen because it does not suffer from boundary affects. Figure 6.2 shows the NCSS applied to the ordered coefficients from the Fourier transform, wavelet transform, and original function. As in Section 4.1, the original function may be thought of as a basis with infinite resolution in the time domain and no resolution in the frequency domain. Among all four functions the time-domain representation is the least efficient, as indicated by the relatively slow rate of increase in the dotted curves. The frequency-domain representation, given by the Fourier transform coefficients, are more efficient when compared to the original function coefficients in terms of its NCSS. Finally, the wavelet-domain representation performs slightly better than the Fourier transform for all four functions.

Subtle differences in performance between the frequency and wavelet-domain representations may be explained as follows. The first function $m_1(t)$ is the most difficult for the Fourier transform to efficiently summarize since there are no obvious periodicities. It must use a combination of high- and low-frequency sinusoids to capture these features. The wavelet transform, on the other hand, will zoom in on the local peak with a few coefficients at each scale and capture the linear trend through a few larger-scale (lower-frequency) coefficients. The second and third functions ($m_2(t)$ and $m_3(t)$) both exhibit some oscillations, though only for a limited portion of the function. In the case of $m_3(t)$, you may interpret the decay and peak as a portion of a low-frequency oscillation. Hence, the wavelet transform does not appear exceedingly superior to the Fourier transform for these functions. The fourth function $m_4(t)$ is mostly a harmonic function and therefore should be well represented via the Fourier transform. Indeed, both the wavelet and Fourier transforms appear to well summarize $m_4(t)$ for the first seven to eight coefficients, but then the Fourier transform loses its competitiveness. This is most likely because the Fourier transform is having difficulty concisely capturing the low-frequency oscillation (trend) while resolving the dominating high-frequency oscillation.

When projecting (correlating) the function values onto wavelet basis functions, the wavelet transform possesses an advantage to the Fourier transform in its local structure. The Fourier basis functions are sinusoids that are not allowed to vary in amplitude over the entire sampling interval. This is not very appealing for the functions $m_1, \ldots, m_4$ presented here, because they are "nonstationary" in nature. Of course, if one constructed a function entirely of overlapping sinusoids then the Fourier transform would be more efficient at representing such a function and its NCSS would increase extremely rapidly.

To see what is gained, or lost, by the wavelet and Fourier representations, we propose to construct an approximation to a given function (denoted by the length N vector x) by only taking the M largest in squared magnitude coefficients. The reasoning behind this is that the coefficients associated with the beginning of its NCSS in Figure 6.2 possess the majority of variance (a proxy for the "information") in the function and therefore would make the best candidates for constructing an approximation. Figure 6.3 shows the IBM volatility previously analyzed in Sections 4.4.5 and 4.5.4. Below the original time series are three approximations using the LA(8) partial DWT ($J_p = 4$) and discrete Fourier transform. Although the length of the original series is $N = 368$, we see that 100 wavelet coefficients do a fair job at capturing the main structure of the series without the high-frequency variations. Including 100 additional wavelet coefficients visually improves the approximation by enhancing the difference between the first half and second half of the volatility series. Throughout the entire series, more of the high-frequency variation is displayed by these additional wavelet

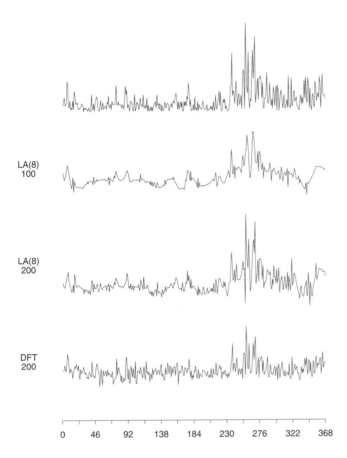

FIGURE 6.3 IBM volatility series ($N = 368$) and approximations using the 100 largest LA(8) wavelet coefficients, 200 largest LA(8) wavelet coefficients, and 200 largest discrete Fourier coefficients. All coefficients are largest in squared magnitude.

coefficients. In contrast, the approximation given by the Fourier transform using 200 coefficients is better than the wavelet approximation with 100 coefficients in that most of the high-frequency features have been captured, but it does little to capture the difference between the first half and second half of the series when compared to the wavelet approximation with 200 coefficients.

6.2 NONLINEAR DENOISING VIA THRESHOLDING

Although linear methods are available to us for use in shrinkage estimation,[3] we prefer to concentrate on nonlinear methods because of their ability to adapt

---

[3] The term "shrinkage" is commonly used in the statistics literature when trying to estimate a smooth function from noisy observations. Here we will use the term "denoising" from now on.

to rapidly changing nonstationary features in an observed process (Donoho and Johnstone, 1998).

As in Chapter 2, we consider observing a process

$$y_t = x_t + \epsilon_t, \quad t = 1, \ldots, N, \tag{6.5}$$

where x_t is a time-varying signal on equally spaced time points with $\epsilon_t \sim N(0, \sigma_\epsilon^2)$. We are interested in estimating the signal at each time point from the noisy observations. In vector notation, Equation 6.5 is

$$y = x + \epsilon,$$

where

$$y = \begin{bmatrix} y_1 \\ y_2 \\ \vdots \\ y_N \end{bmatrix} \quad x = \begin{bmatrix} x_1 \\ x_2 \\ \vdots \\ x_N \end{bmatrix} \quad \text{and} \quad \epsilon = \begin{bmatrix} \epsilon_1 \\ \epsilon_2 \\ \vdots \\ \epsilon_N \end{bmatrix}.$$

Our estimator of the signal $\hat{x}$ will be assessed through the risk (or MSE) given by

$$R(\hat{x}, x) = \frac{1}{N} E \left\| \hat{x} - x \right\|_2^2 = \frac{1}{N} \sum_{t=1}^{N} E(\hat{x}_t - x_t)^2.$$

Let $\mathcal{W}$ be an $N \times N$ orthonormal matrix defined by the wavelet transform; then applying it to Equation 6.5 yields

$$\mathcal{W}y = o = s + \epsilon' = \mathcal{W}x + \mathcal{W}\epsilon.$$

Through orthogonality of $\mathcal{W}$, the following relationship holds for the risk $R(\hat{x}, x)$ = $R(\hat{o}, o)$, and the distribution of the transformed error is given by $\epsilon'_t \sim N(0, \sigma_\epsilon^2)$. The simplest method of nonlinear wavelet denoising is via thresholding (all wavelet coefficients less than a fixed constant in magnitude are set to zero). Two thresholding rules were instrumental in the initial development of wavelet denoising, both for their simplicity and performance: *hard* and *soft* thresholding. Since Donoho and Johnstone presented their work in the early 1990s, a vast amount of research has gone into producing alternative thresholding rules that perform better than soft or hard thresholding in some way.[4] The thresholding functions presented here are relatively simple and have been firmly established in the statistical literature.

---

[4] An exhaustive list of references is not provided here, but some recent references may be found in Donoho (1997) and Donoho and Johnstone (1998).

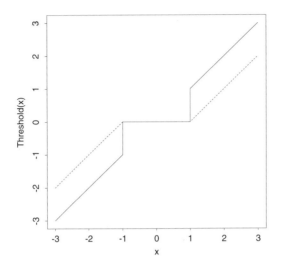

FIGURE 6.4 Hard (solid line) and soft (dashed line) thresholding rules for $\eta = 1$. To interpret this figure, a coefficient x before thresholding takes values on the horizontal axis. If applying hard thresholding, $x \leq -\eta$ or $x \geq \eta$ means x will remain unchanged (thus following the 45° solid line). For $|x| < \eta$, x will be put to zero. Soft thresholding works similarly, but all values of x are pushed toward zero by the amount η. If $|x| - \eta \leq 0$, then x is simply put to zero. Thus, the dotted line is parallel to the solid one for $x \leq -\eta$ and $x \geq \eta$, and the dotted line is the same as the solid line for $|x| < \eta$.

6.2.1 Hard Thresholding

Literally interpreting the statement of "keep or kill," hard thresholding is a straightforward technique for implementing wavelet denoising. The operation of hard thresholding (for our purposes a thresholding rule is generally denoted as $\delta_\eta(x)$ where x is the input coefficient and η is a scalar or vector of parameter values) on the wavelet coefficient o_t is given by

$$\delta_\eta^{\mathrm{H}}(o_t) = \begin{cases} o_t & \text{if } |o_t| > \eta \\ 0 & \text{otherwise.} \end{cases}$$

This operation is not a continuous mapping, as seen in Figure 6.4, and only affects input coefficients that are less than or equal to the threshold.

6.2.2 Soft Thresholding

The other standard technique for wavelet denoising is soft thresholding of the wavelet coefficient o_t via

$$\delta_\eta^{\mathrm{S}}(o_t) = \mathrm{sign}(o_t)(|o_t| - \eta)_+,$$

where

$$\text{sign}(o_t) = \begin{cases} +1 & \text{if } o_t > 0 \\ 0 & \text{if } o_t = 0 \\ -1 & \text{if } o_t < 0, \end{cases} \quad \text{and} \quad (x)_+ = \begin{cases} x & \text{if } x \geq 0 \\ 0 & \text{if } x < 0. \end{cases} \quad (6.6)$$

Note that $\text{sign}(x)$ is the same as the *signum* activation function from neural networks (Chapter 8). Instead of forcing o_t to zero or leaving it untouched, soft thresholding pushes all coefficients toward zero (Figure 6.4). If the wavelet coefficient happens to be smaller in magnitude than the threshold, then it is set to zero as in hard thresholding. Thus, the operation of soft thresholding is a continuous mapping. The choice between these two thresholding rules depends on what characteristics are desired in the resulting estimate. For instance, if large spikes are present in the observed series, then hard thresholding will preserve the magnitude of these spikes while soft thresholding, because it affects all wavelet coefficients, will suppress them. On the other hand, soft thresholding will in general produce a smoother estimate because all wavelet coefficients are being pushed toward zero. It is up to the practitioner to weigh these differences and apply the most appropriate thresholding rule.

6.2.3   Other Thresholding Rules

An interesting compromise between the soft and hard thresholding rules was introduced by Gao and Bruce (1997) under the name *firm* (or *semi-soft*) thresholding and is given by

$$\delta_{\eta_1,\eta_2}^{F}(o_t) = \begin{cases} 0 & \text{if } |o_t| \leq \eta_1 \\ \text{sign}(o_t) \frac{\eta_2(|o_t|-\eta_1)}{\eta_2-\eta_1} & \text{if } \eta_1 < |o_t| \leq \eta_2 \\ o_t & \text{if } |o_t| > \eta_2, \end{cases}$$

and shown with parameters $\eta_1 = 1$ and $\eta_2 = 2$ in Figure 6.5. Firm denoising, as the name implies, is a compromise between hard and soft thresholding rules. It is illustrative to observe that with the particular choices of the parameters η_1 and η_2, we have

$$\lim_{\eta_2 \to \infty} \delta_{\eta_1,\eta_2}^{F}(o_t) = \delta_{\eta_1}^{S}(o_t),$$

and

$$\lim_{\eta_2 \to \eta_1} \delta_{\eta_1,\eta_2}^{F}(o_t) = \delta_{\eta_1}^{H}(o_t)$$

(Vidakovic, 1999, Sec. 6.5.3). Thus, we can mimic the performance of either the hard or soft thresholding rules by selecting the pair η_1 and η_2 appropriately. The extra flexibility of having two parameters allows firm thresholding to have uniformly smaller risks than hard denoising, but not soft thresholding. Specifically, for any given η there exists a pair of thresholds $\eta_1 < \eta < \eta_2$ such that

$$R_{\eta_1,\eta_2}^{F}(\theta) < R_{\eta}^{H}(\theta) \quad \text{for all } \theta$$

(Gao and Bruce, 1997).

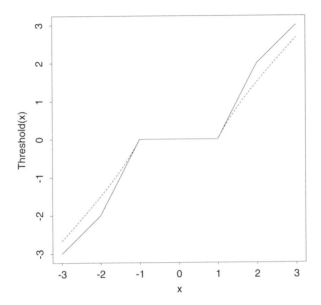

FIGURE 6.5 Firm (solid line) and *nn*-garrote (dotted line) thresholding rule. The parameters for firm denoising are $\eta_1 = 1$ and $\eta_2 = 2$ and for *nn*-garrote denoising $\eta = 1$. Both thresholding rules put x to zero in the same range as hard and soft thresholding. Firm thresholding includes an intermediate step: when $\eta_1 < |x| \le \eta_2$, a version of soft thresholding is applied; otherwise $x < -\eta_2$ or $x > \eta_2$ leaves x unchanged like hard thresholding. Thus, firm thresholding is a combination or soft and hard thresholding. Non-negative garrote thresholding mimics firm thresholding while using only one parameter.

In subsequent work, Gao (1998) produced the nonnegative garrote (*nn-garrote*)[5] thresholding rule given by

$$\delta_\eta^{\mathrm{nnG}}(o_t) = o_t \left[1 - (\eta/o_t)^2 \right]_+ = \begin{cases} 0 & \text{if } |o_t| \le \eta \\ o_t - \eta^2/o_t & \text{if } |o_t| > \eta. \end{cases}$$

Visual comparison between firm and *nn*-garrote denoising shows little difference (Figure 6.5), the latter being a smoother version of the former. The appealing quality of *nn*-garrote denoising is that it only depends on one thresholding parameter. Although the major advantage, in terms of reduced L_2 risk, of firm denoising over either hard or soft thresholding rules is precisely its extra thresholding parameter, this produces complications when implementing the rule in practice (Gao, 1998).

---

[5] Garrote type "denoising" was introduced by Strawderman and Cohen (1971) in the context of admissibility of generalized Bayes rules; see Gao (1998) for more details.

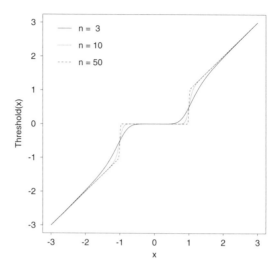

FIGURE 6.6   The n-degree garrote thresholding rule for $n \in \{3, 10, 50\}$. This thresholding rule is an "adjustable" version of hard thresholding where n allows one to soften the boundary between keeping and killing the original value x.

A further alternative, with the spirit of hard thresholding in mind, is found in the n-degree garrote thresholding rule

$$\delta_{n,\eta}^{\mathrm{nG}}(o_t) = \frac{o_t^{2n+1}}{\eta^{2n} + o_t^{2n}},$$

which was considered by Breiman (1996b) for model selection ($n = 1$). It goes to the hard thresholding rule pointwise as $n \to \infty$ except when $o_t = \pm\eta$ (Figure 6.6).

6.3   THRESHOLD SELECTION

The key parameter in all thresholding rules provided in the last section is η. Optimal thresholding occurs when the thresholding parameter is set to the noise level $\eta = \sigma_\epsilon$. Thus, the coefficients o_t to be included in the regression model satisfy the hard thresholding rule with η being set to the *known* noise level – that is, $\delta_{\sigma_\epsilon}^{\mathrm{H}}(o_t)$. Setting $\eta < \sigma_\epsilon$ will allow unwanted noise to enter the estimate while setting $\eta > \sigma_\epsilon$ will destroy information that really belongs to the underlying signal. Setting $\eta = \sigma_\epsilon$ is only possible if we possessed an "oracle" that would allow us to know σ_ϵ exactly (Donoho and Johnstone, 1994). The ideal risk of the diagonal projection associated with the oracle knowledge is given by

$$R(\text{dp}, \boldsymbol{o}) = \sum_{t=1}^{N} \min(|s_t|, \sigma_\epsilon).$$

This risk cannot be attained in practice by any estimator, linear or nonlinear. The following sections propose thresholding rules that attempt to come close to the risk $R(\text{dp}, \boldsymbol{o})$.

6.3.1 Universal Thresholding

Donoho and Johnstone (1994) suggested a *universal threshold* by setting

$$\eta^{\text{U}} = \hat{\sigma}_\epsilon \sqrt{2 \log N}. \tag{6.7}$$

When η^{U} is incorporated into the soft thresholding rule, this is known under the name *VisuShrink* since it results in a visually appealing signal estimate. The fundamental property behind the universal threshold is the following. Let $z_1, \ldots, z_N$ be a sequence of independently and identically distributed (IID) $N(0, \sigma_\epsilon^2)$ random variables, then

$$P\left[\max_t(|z_t|) \le \sigma_\epsilon \sqrt{2 \log N}\right] \to 1,$$

as $N \to \infty$. By utilizing the universal threshold we are assured, for large sample sizes, that the probability of all noisy coefficients being shrunk to zero is high. Keep in mind that this result is an asymptotic one and does not guarantee ideal performance with respect to small sample sizes.

As already mentioned, the combination of a soft thresholding rule and universal threshold is known as *VisuShrink*. It produces visually appealing function estimates as shown in Figure 6.7 for sampled versions of $m_1(t)$ and $m_2(t)$. When compared with their original functions in Figure 6.1, the universal estimators of $m_1(t)$ and $m_2(t)$ are quite smooth and appear to capture the distinguishing features of the original functions. The major drawback in the *VisuShrink* procedure is that by producing visually appealing estimators it underfits the function by setting the threshold too high.

6.3.2 Minimax Estimation

In addition to proposing the universal threshold, Donoho and Johnstone (1994, 1998) proposed the *optimal minimax threshold* η^*. When η^* is incorporated into the soft thresholding rule, it is known under the name *RiskShrink* (although using the hard thresholding rule achieves the same asymptotic performance). The threshold is optimal in terms of L^2 risk and is not available in a closed form expression. The idea is to seek an estimator $\hat{\boldsymbol{x}}$ that attains the *minimax risk*

$$\widetilde{\mathcal{R}}(\mathcal{F}) = \inf_{\hat{\boldsymbol{x}}} \sup_{\boldsymbol{x}} R(\hat{\boldsymbol{x}}, \boldsymbol{x}),$$

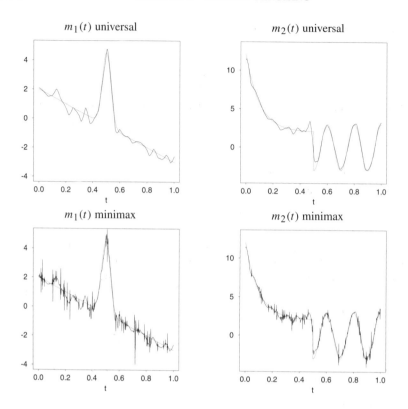

FIGURE 6.7   Universal and minimax estimators for sampled versions of the example functions $m_1(t)$ and $m_2(t)$ with $N = 1024$. The true functions (dotted lines) are drawn for comparison. The soft thresholding rule was used for all estimates.

where $\mathcal{F}$ is a certain class of smooth functions. We know that x belongs to $\mathcal{F}$, but nothing more. Minimax threshold values may be approximately numerically and are provided in Table 6.1, taken from Donoho and Johnstone (1994).

Estimators using a minimax threshold and the soft thresholding rule are given in the bottom row of Figure 6.7 for sampled versions of $m_1(t)$ and $m_2(t)$. The minimax estimators differ from their universal counterparts by not over-smoothing in order to produce a visually appealing function. This is due to the fact that the minimax threshold is concentrating on reducing the overall mean square error and should pick up abrupt changes by not oversmoothing.

6.3.3   Stein's Unbiased Risk Estimate

Donoho and Johnstone (1995) introduced a level-dependent thresholding selection scheme (i.e., for each level j of the wavelet decomposition a threshold η_j will be computed and applied to the wavelet coefficients w_j at that level). The key to this scheme is minimizing Stein's unbiased estimator of risk (Stein, 1981).

N	η^*	N	η^*
64	1.474	4096	2.594
128	1.669	8192	2.773
256	1.860	16,384	2.952
512	2.048	32,768	3.131
1024	2.232	65,536	3.310
2048	2.414		

TABLE 6.1　Minimax thresholds η^* for various dyadic sample sizes, taken from Donoho and Johnstone (1994).

Suppose $z_1, \ldots, z_k$ are IID observations distributed via $z_i \sim N(\mu_i, 1)$. Let $\hat{\mu}$ be an estimator of $\mu = (\mu_1, \ldots, \mu_k)$. If the function $g(\cdot)$ is weakly differentiable, then Stein (1981) provided an unbiased estimator of the loss function for an estimator of μ written as $\hat{\mu} = z + g(z)$ via

$$E \left\| \hat{\mu} - \mu \right\|^2 = k + E \left[\| g(z) \|^2 + 2\nabla g(z) \right], \tag{6.8}$$

where $\nabla g(z) = \sum_i \frac{\partial}{\partial_i} g_i(z)$. Applying Equation 6.8 to the soft threshold rule $\delta_\eta^S(z)$ gives

$$\text{SURE}(z, \eta) = k - 2 \cdot \#\{i : |z_i| \le \eta\} + \sum_{i=1}^{k} \min^2(|z_i|, \eta),$$

where $\#S$ denotes the cardinality (number of elements) of the set S.[6] The SURE threshold is based on the observed data z and minimizes the estimated risk; that is,

$$\eta^S = \arg \min_{\eta \ge 0} \text{SURE}(z, \eta). \tag{6.9}$$

Ogden (1996, Sec. 8.1) noted that slightly rewriting Equation 6.8 provides a clear relation between the SURE criterion and Akaike's Information Criterion (AIC). Both criteria involve a function to be minimized and a penalty term based on the number of parameters to be estimated.

Computing the SURE threshold in practice is straightforward. This has been done in Figure 6.8 for the first three levels of a Haar DWT of the function $m_1(t)$, sampled at $N = 1204$ equally spaced values. The left-hand column of plots are the ordered wavelet coefficients $|w_{j,(0)}| \le |w_{j,(1)}| \le \cdots \le |w_{j,(N-1)}|$ and the SURE threshold η_j^S (given by a dotted line). Using the soft thresholding rule, all wavelet coefficients below the dotted line will be replaced by zero and all coefficients above the dotted line will be reduced in magnitude by η_j^S.

---

[6] A more thorough treatment may be found in Percival and Walden (2000, pp. 441–444).

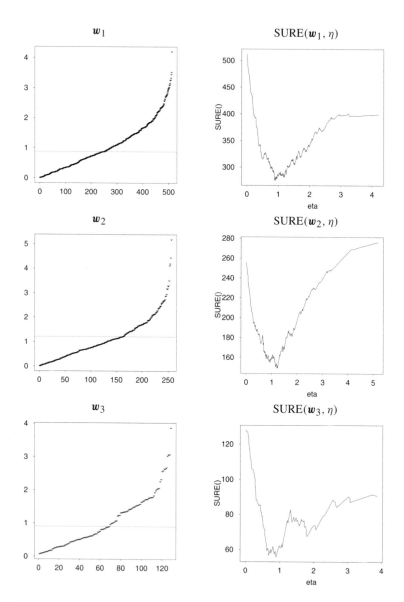

FIGURE 6.8 Wavelet coefficients and SURE functions for the first three levels of a Haar DWT applied to a sampled version of $m_1(t)$ with $N = 1024$. The dotted lines in the left-hand column of plots are $\eta_j^S = \arg\min_\eta \text{SURE}(\boldsymbol{w}_j, \eta)$ for $j = 1, 2, 3$. Selecting the minimum value of the curves plotted in the right-hand column determines the level-dependent SURE threshold plotted in the left-hand columns (dotted lines).

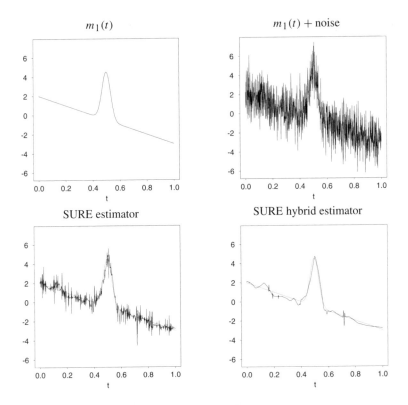

FIGURE 6.9 Example function $m_1(t)$, sampled at $N = 1024$ equally spaced points, with and without additive noise. Below them are estimators using the SURE threshold and SURE hybrid threshold in a soft thresholding rule.

A slight modification to the SURE approach is to apply the universal threshold to some levels of the DWT and apply the SURE threshold to the others. This was recommended by Donoho and Johnstone (1995) because the SURE function is sometimes quite shallow around where it achieves its minimum (although this is not the case for our example in Figure 6.9). A measure for "sparsity" in a vector of wavelet coefficients is simply the sum of squared wavelet coefficients $\text{WSS}(\lambda_j) = \sum_t W_{j,t}^2$. A level is said to be sparse if

$$\text{WSS}(\lambda_j) \leq 1 + \frac{(\log_2 N_j)^{3/2}}{\sqrt{N_j}},$$

where N_j is the number of wavelet coefficients at level j. When a level is determined to be sparse, the universal threshold is used, otherwise the SURE threshold for that level is used.

The SURE and SURE hybrid estimators for a sampled version of $m_1(t)$ are shown in Figure 6.9. Although the SURE estimator (lower left-hand corner) follows the general shape of the original function, it allows quite a bit of "noise" back into the reconstruction. The hybrid estimator does a much better job at at discriminating between signal and noise producing a much better function estimate.

6.3.4   Hypothesis Testing

The idea of using a Kolmogorov-type statistic for wavelet coefficients was proposed previously by Ogden and Parzen (1996a). They were interested in applying change-point methods to the problem of wavelet thresholding. Their result is a threshold that is determined by the data being analyzed on a scale-by-scale basis. Additional references with respect to data-dependent threshold selection include Abramovich and Benjamini (1995) and Ogden and Parzen (1996b).

Let $x_1, \ldots, x_N$ be a sequence of independent Gaussian random variables with mean $\mu_1, \ldots, \mu_N$ and common variance. The hypothesis of interest is the standard change point problem

$$H_0 \;:\; \mu_1 = \mu_2 = \cdots = \mu_N$$
$$H_1 \;:\; \mu_1 = \cdots = \mu_s \neq \mu_{s+1} = \cdots = \mu_N.$$

That is, our null hypothesis is that all N random variables have the same mean versus the alternative hypothesis that there is a sudden shift (change point) in the mean at an unknown location s. A standard nonparametric test statistic for such a problem is the cumulative sum (CUSUM) process. Various functionals may be applied to the CUSUM process in order to detect sudden changes. The Kolmogorov–Smirnov functional, maximum of the absolute values, will be focused on here. The procedure is based on a sample Brownian bridge process

$$\widehat{B}_N(u) = \left\{ \begin{array}{ll} \frac{1}{\sigma_g \sqrt{N}} \left[\sum_{i=1}^{\lfloor uN \rfloor} g(x_i) - \frac{\lfloor uN \rfloor}{N} \sum_{i=1}^{N} g(x_i) \right] & \frac{1}{N} \leq u \leq 1 \\[2ex] 0 & 0 \leq u < \frac{1}{N}, \end{array} \right.$$

$$(6.10)$$

where $g(x)$ is a nonlinear function, $\sigma_g^2 = \mathrm{Var}\{g(x_i)\}$ and $\lfloor x \rfloor$ is the greatest integer less than or equal to x. The process $\widehat{B}_N(t)$ converges in distribution to a Brownian bridge process $B(t)$, a continuous Gaussian process on $0 \leq t \leq 1$ with mean zero and covariance function $\mathrm{Cov}\{B(s), B(t)\} = \min(s, t) - st$ (Ross, 1983). The Brownian bridge process is "tied down" at its end points such that $B(0) = B(1) = 0$. Figure 6.10 shows a sample Brownian bridge process constructed from random variables with a standard normal distribution.

In practice, this so-called *data-analytic* thresholding technique is implemented on a scale-by-scale basis to sequences of wavelet coefficients as follows:

1. Form the sample Brownian bridge process in Equation 6.10 using the scale λ_j wavelet coefficients and test against the null distribution; see, for example, Table 4.2 in Stephens (1986) for appropriate critical values of boundary crossing probabilities for a Brownian bridge process.

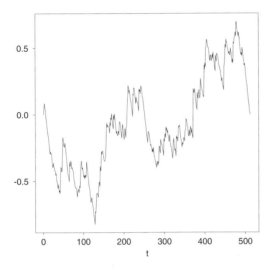

FIGURE 6.10 Sample Brownian bridge process $\widehat{B}_N(t)$.

2. If the null hypothesis is rejected, remove the wavelet coefficient with the greatest absolute value, reduce N to $N - 1$, and return to Step 1.

3. If the null hypothesis is not rejected, set the scale-dependent threshold η_j^{HT} equal to the absolute value of the largest in absolute magnitude wavelet coefficient.

Although several transformations and empirical distribution function tests are available, Ogden and Parzen (1996a) used the transformation $g(x) = x^2$ in Equation 6.10 and the Kolmogorov–Smirnov test statistic. It should be pointed out that σ_g will not be known in practice and hence must be estimated from the data via Equation 6.11. By formulating the test statistic as in Section 7.3, the σ_g term is no longer involved; it is replaced by $\sqrt{2}$, which is scale independent (Whitcher, 1998).

As with the SURE threshold, the data-analytic threshold η_j^{HT} is easily computed using the steps provided above. Figure 6.11 displays the sample Brownian bridge process for the unit scale wavelet coefficient vector w_1 and the reduced vector (as output from the procedure outlined above) from a noisy version of $m_3(t)$. The first four coefficients were deemed worthy and the remaining wavelet coefficients less than $\eta_1^{HT} = 1.2$ are considered to be noise. According to the Kolmogorov–Smirnov criterion, the sample path in Figure 6.11b is indistinguishable from a true Brownian bridge process like the one in Figure 6.10.

The data-analytic estimators for sampled versions of $m_2(t)$ and $m_3(t)$ are shown in Figure 6.12. The dotted lines are the original functions, as in Figure 6.1,

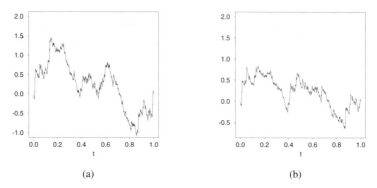

(a) (b)

FIGURE 6.11 Sample Brownian bridge processes for (a) the complete set of unit scale wavelet coefficients w_1 from a LA(8) DWT of a sampled version of the function $m_3(t)$ with $N = 1024$ and (b) the reduced set of wavelet coefficients less than the threshold $\eta_1^{\text{HT}} = 1.2$.

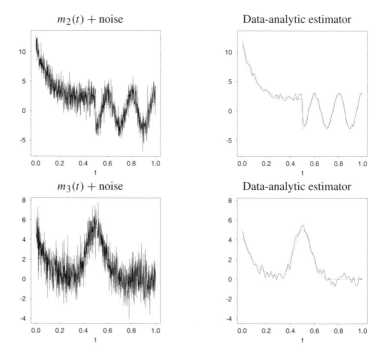

FIGURE 6.12 Example functions $m_2(t)$ and $m_3(t)$, sampled at $N = 1024$ equally spaced points, with additive noise. To the right of each noisy function are data-analytic estimators using the level-dependent threshold η_j^{HT} in a soft thresholding rule. The true functions (dotted lines) are drawn with the data-analytic estimates for comparison.

and compare favorably with the data-analytic estimates even for a relatively high amount of noise.

6.3.5 Bayesian Methodology

Bayesian methods have been employed by various authors to develop denoising rules similar to those previously discussed (see Vidakovic (1999) and references therein). We provide a simple motivating example taken from Vidakovic (1998). We begin with the usual setup from before, namely observing a vector of coefficients o, which are composed of a signal and additive noise, and apply the orthonormal matrix $\mathcal{W}$ to both sides yielding

$$o = s + \epsilon.$$

We do not differentiate between ϵ' and ϵ since they are equivalent in distribution. Instead of viewing the true function s as fixed and data as random, we turn this viewpoint around and treat s as a random variable too. Let the distribution of the observed wavelet coefficient be[7]

$$\left[o_t | s_t, \sigma_\epsilon^2 \right] \sim N(s_t, \sigma_\epsilon^2),$$

with σ_ϵ^2 unknown. Hence, we must place a prior distribution on both s and σ_ϵ^2. Let us put an exponential prior distribution on σ_ϵ^2; that is,

$$\sigma_\epsilon^2 \sim \mathcal{E}(\mu),$$

where $f(\sigma_\epsilon^2) = \mu e^{-\mu \sigma_\epsilon^2}$. Integrating out σ_ϵ^2 gives the marginal distribution (likelihood) of o_t conditioned on μ to be distributed as a double exponential

$$[o_t | s_t] \sim \mathcal{DE}\left(s_t, (2\mu)^{-1/2} \right),$$

where $f(o_t | s_t) = 2^{-1} \sqrt{2\mu} e^{-\sqrt{2\mu}|o_t - s_t|}$. Vidakovic (1998) recommended using a Student t distribution for the prior of the underlying signal with location zero, scale τ, and n degrees of freedom

$$s_t \sim t_n(0, \tau).$$

Examples of *Bayes rules* derived from this formulation are provided in Vidakovic (1999, p. 249). The Bayes rule (denoising function) may be fine-tuned by selection of the hyperparameter τ or the number of degrees of freedom associated with the t distribution. More elaborate Bayesian techniques are provided in Vidakovic (1999, Chp. 8) and Müller and Vidakovic (1999).

---

[7] The notation $[x|y]$ denotes the conditional distribution of the random variable x given y.

6.3.6 Cross-Validation

Cross-validation methods for wavelet denoising were initially explored by Weyrich and Warhola (1995) and Nason (1994, 1996). Greenblatt (1997) looked at not only selecting the threshold, but also the most appropriate orthonormal basis from a wavelet packet tree, using a cross-validation technique. Cross-validation is based on minimizing the prediction error for new observations based on selecting an appropriate smoothing parameter. When no additional observations are forthcoming, a standard method is *leave-one-out* cross-validation (a simple generalization is leave-*n*-out cross-validation). This procedure involves omitting one observation and using the remaining $N - 1$ observations to estimate the function of interest. We outline here two procedures for applying cross-validation methodology to determining a threshold for wavelet denoising: two-fold and leave-one-out cross validation.

Restricting ourselves to a dyadic number of observations $N = 2^J$, we begin our two-fold cross-validation procedure (Nason, 1996) by splitting the data into the sequence of even and odd observations, respectively,

$$
\boldsymbol{y}^{\mathrm{E}} = \begin{bmatrix} y_0^{\mathrm{E}} \\ y_1^{\mathrm{E}} \\ \vdots \\ y_{N/2}^{\mathrm{E}} \end{bmatrix} \quad \text{and} \quad \boldsymbol{y}^{\mathrm{O}} = \begin{bmatrix} y_0^{\mathrm{O}} \\ y_1^{\mathrm{O}} \\ \vdots \\ y_{N/2}^{\mathrm{O}} \end{bmatrix}.
$$

Two estimates of the underlying signal are obtained using wavelet denoising on the even and odd indexed sequences resulting in $\hat{\boldsymbol{x}}^{\mathrm{E}}(\eta)$ and $\hat{\boldsymbol{x}}^{\mathrm{O}}(\eta)$, respectively (see Section 6.4.1 for a step-by-step implementation of standard wavelet denoising). To compare the estimator based on even observations with the left-out odd data, an interpolated estimator is constructed via

$$
\bar{\boldsymbol{x}}^{\mathrm{E}}(\eta) = \frac{1}{2} \begin{bmatrix} \hat{x}_0^{\mathrm{E}} + \hat{x}_1^{\mathrm{E}} \\ \hat{x}_1^{\mathrm{E}} + \hat{x}_2^{\mathrm{E}} \\ \vdots \\ \hat{x}_{\frac{N}{2}-2}^{\mathrm{E}} + \hat{x}_{\frac{N}{2}-1}^{\mathrm{E}} \\ \hat{x}_{\frac{N}{2}-1}^{\mathrm{E}} + \hat{x}_0^{\mathrm{E}} \end{bmatrix} \quad \text{and} \quad \bar{\boldsymbol{x}}^{\mathrm{O}}(\eta) = \frac{1}{2} \begin{bmatrix} \hat{x}_{\frac{N}{2}-1}^{\mathrm{O}} + \hat{x}_0^{\mathrm{O}} \\ \hat{x}_0^{\mathrm{O}} + \hat{x}_1^{\mathrm{O}} \\ \vdots \\ \hat{x}_{\frac{N}{2}-3}^{\mathrm{O}} + \hat{x}_{\frac{N}{2}-2}^{\mathrm{O}} \\ \hat{x}_{\frac{N}{2}-2}^{\mathrm{O}} + \hat{x}_{\frac{N}{2}-1}^{\mathrm{O}} \end{bmatrix}.
$$

The cross validation approach seeks to minimize

$$
\widehat{M}_1(\eta) = \sum_{t=0}^{N/2-1} \left[\left(\bar{x}_{t+1}^{\mathrm{E}}(\eta) - y_{2t+1} \right)^2 + \left(\bar{x}_{t+1}^{\mathrm{O}}(\eta) - y_{2t} \right)^2 \right],
$$

and, hence, the cross-validation threshold is given by

$$
\eta_{\frac{N}{2}}^{\mathrm{CV}} = \arg\min_{\eta \geq 0} \widehat{M}(\eta),
$$

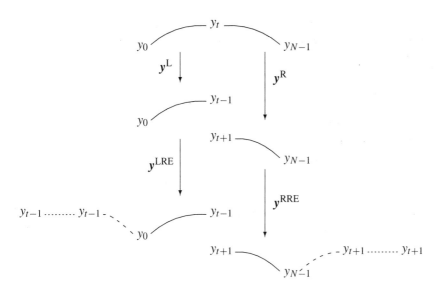

FIGURE 6.13 Reflection and extension of the "left" and "right" subvectors around the point y_t. The original vector y is first split about y_t to create two length $N/2 - 1$ subvectors y^L and y^R. Each subvector is then reflected (dashed line) and padded (dotted line) to the next dyadic length using the "last" value, thus creating y^{LRE} and y^{RRE}. This figure was adapted from Nason (1996).

based on $N/2$ observations. A correction factor is then applied in order to scale the threshold up to N observations so that

$$\eta_N^{CV} = \left(1 - \frac{\log 2}{\log N}\right)^{1/2} \eta_{\frac{N}{2}}^{CV}.$$

This adjustment is based on the relationship between the universal threshold and its sample size; i.e., $\eta^U = \hat{\sigma}_\epsilon \sqrt{2 \log N}$.

Nason (1996) went on to describe an alternative technique utilizing leave-one-out cross-validation that works for an arbitrary sample size N. First, the observed data vector y is broken into left and right subvectors (Figure 6.13) around the point y_t, $1 < t < N$ such that

$$y^L = \begin{bmatrix} y_0 \\ y_1 \\ \vdots \\ y_{t-1} \end{bmatrix} \quad \text{and} \quad y^R = \begin{bmatrix} y_{t+1} \\ y_{t+2} \\ \vdots \\ y_{N-1} \end{bmatrix}.$$

Now reflect y^L and y^R at the left and right ends, respectively, and pad each vector to the next largest power of two using the end points y_{t-1} and y_{t+1} (Figure 6.13), respectively, to obtain

$$
\begin{aligned}
y^{\text{LRE}} &= [y_{t-1}, \ldots, y_{t-1}, y_{t-2}, \ldots, y_1, y_0, y_1, \ldots, y_{t-1}]^T, \\
y^{\text{RRE}} &= [y_{t+1}, \ldots, y_{N-1}, y_{N-1}, \ldots, y_t, y_{t+1}, \ldots, y_{t+1}]^T.
\end{aligned}
$$

Now apply wavelet denoising with threshold η to compute estimates of the underlying signal in each subvector, denoted $\hat{x}_\eta^L$ and $\hat{x}_\eta^R$, and form an estimate for the missing observation y_t via

$$
\hat{y}_{\eta,t} = \left(\hat{x}_{\eta,N_L-1}^L + \hat{x}_{\eta,0}^R \right)/2.
$$

The predicted value $\hat{y}_{\eta,t}$ is simply the average between the right and left-hand end points of the estimated signal for the left and right subvectors, respectively. The resulting MSE under this procedure is

$$
\widehat{M}_2(\eta) = \sum_{t=1}^{N-2} (\hat{y}_{\eta,t} - y_t)^2,
$$

and the resulting leave-one-out cross-validation threshold minimizes $\widehat{M}_2(\eta)$. Nason (1996) extended his cross-validation procedures to more than one dimension, making it possible to also apply this methodology to images.

6.4   IMPLEMENTING WAVELET DENOISING

6.4.1   Standard Denoising

Several thresholding rules and procedures for selecting a threshold have been proposed in this chapter, we now outline how to implement wavelet denoising using the model $y = x + \epsilon$, where x is a deterministic signal and ϵ is a vector of mean zero Gaussian random variables with common variance σ_ϵ^2. If any of these assumptions are in doubt, then additional considerations and alternative techniques may be required to obtain a reasonable estimate of the underlying signal. A few common violations are mentioned at the end of this section.

The wavelet denoising procedure consists of the following steps (Figure 6.14):

1. Compute a partial DWT (level J_p)

$$
w_p = \mathcal{W}_p y
$$

to obtain the wavelet coefficient vectors $w_1, w_2, \ldots, w_{J_p}$ and the scaling coefficient vector v_{J_p}. The smooth features contained in v_{J_p} will contribute directly to the estimate of the signal.

2. Select a threshold η using one of the methods introduced in Section 6.3. The threshold may be a scalar or vector (in the case of the firm thresholding rule) and may be level dependent or independent. The standard deviation of the noise, if unknown, may be estimated using Equation 6.11.

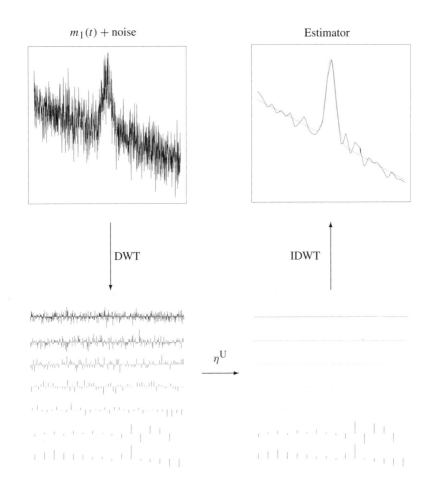

FIGURE 6.14 Flow diagram illustrating wavelet denoising applied to a noisy version of $m_1(t)$. First, a partial DWT is performed on the observed function, then soft thresholding is applied using the universal threshold η^U to eliminate "noisy" wavelet coefficients, and finally the inverse DWT (IDWT) is performed on the thresholded coefficients to give a "smooth" estimate of the original function (dotted line).

3. Put the wavelet coefficients $w_{j,t}$, $j = 1, \ldots, J_p$ and $t = 0, \ldots, N/2^j - 1$, through a thresholding rule using η to produce a collection of thresholded wavelet coefficients $\check{w}_{j,t}$. Organizing the thresholded wavelet coefficients yields the vector $\check{\boldsymbol{w}}_p$.

4. Produce an estimate of $\boldsymbol{x}$ by performing the inverse partial DWT

$$\hat{\boldsymbol{x}} = \mathcal{W}_p^T \check{\boldsymbol{w}}_p.$$

The standard deviation of the noise σ_ϵ, required by certain thresholds, will not be known in most practical situations and hence must be estimated. If we assume that noise is present in our observed signal, then the usual estimator of the standard deviation will be highly sensitive to the affected coefficients. The most commonly used estimator of σ_ϵ is the *maximum absolute deviation* (MAD) standard deviation using only the first scale of wavelet coefficients w_1, defined to be

$$\hat{\sigma}_{\text{MAD}} = \frac{\text{median}(|w_{1,0}|, |w_{1,1}|, \ldots, |w_{1,N/2-1}|)}{0.6745}. \tag{6.11}$$

The denominator is needed to rescale the numerator so that $\hat{\sigma}_{\text{MAD}}$ is tuned to estimating the standard deviation for Gaussian white noise. The median is used in order to produce a robust estimator of the noise variance, isolating it from the signal variance.

One common departure from the assumptions outlined at the beginning of this section is correlated Gaussian noise. Johnstone and Silverman (1997) tackled this problem and proposed a level-dependent threshold chosen to minimize an unbiased risk criterion based on the data. Embedded in this level-dependent procedure is the estimation of level-dependent noise $\sigma_{\epsilon,j}^2$ to compute the universal threshold η_j^{U} or, alternatively, apply SURE on a level-by-level basis. These are straightforward generalizations of Equations 6.11, 6.7, and 6.9, respectively. Wang (1996) focused attention on denoising under the assumption of noise with long-range dependence. He proposed a level-dependent universal threshold, by correcting for the correlation structure of the noise, and a level-dependent cross-validation procedure. Hall and Patil (1995) developed a theoretical framework for estimating smooth functions with wavelets and discussed the linear part of the wavelet estimator with classical kernel methods, while Hall and Patil (1996) gave the necessary and sufficient conditions on the form of the threshold for the resulting curve estimator to achieve optimal convergence rates, in the case of smooth and piecewise-smooth functions.

Percival and Walden (2000), building on the earlier work of Moulin (1994) and Gao (1993, 1997), investigated correlated Gaussian and non-Gaussian error structures in the context of nonparametric spectrum estimation. They proposed both level-dependent and level-independent thresholding of the wavelet coefficients of the log-transformed spectrum estimate and found that level-independent appeared to outperform level-dependent thresholding for their examples. Recent attention has focused on including "local" information into wavelet denoising. Vidakovic and Lozoya (1998) investigate "time-dependent" wavelet denoising and applied it to images while Kovac and Silverman (2000) looked at "robust" wavelet denoising by utilizing a running local median to eliminate outliers and performing *VisuShrink* on the remaining unequally spaced coefficients which remained. Multiple wavelets have also been used in denoising schemes. Downie and Silverman (1998) reported improved performance when applying a *multivariate universal threshold* to test functions over univariate methods like the ones proposed here. Their method is similar to earlier work on *complex Daubechies wavelets* by J. M. Lina (Lina, 1997) and coworkers (Lina and MacGibbon, 1997; Lina and Mayrand, 1995).

6.4.2 Translation-Invariant Denoising

Translation-invariant denoising was originally proposed by Coifman and Donoho (1995) by producing an estimated signal $\hat{x}_s$ that is based on a circularly shifted version of x by s units and then averaging all possible estimators to yield

$$\tilde{x}_s = \frac{1}{2^J} \sum_{s=0}^{2^j-1} C^{-s} \hat{x}_s,$$

where C is a $N \times N$ matrix that circularly shifts a length T vector by one unit. Percival and Walden (2000, Sec. 10.5) noted that this technique is more easily implemented in terms of the MODWT. That is, produce a $(J+1)N \times N$ vector of MODWT coefficients $\tilde{w}$, apply a thresholding method to each element of $\tilde{w}$, and obtain $\tilde{x}_s$ by taking the inverse MODWT.

Two things to note, the thresholding rule must be level-dependent since the MODWT coefficients are renormalized versions of the DWT; that is, the universal threshold η^U becomes the level-dependent universal threshold $\eta_j^U = \eta^U/2^{j/2}$, and the noise variance σ_ϵ^2 may be estimated by the MAD estimator applied to the finest level of MODWT coefficients via

$$\tilde{\sigma}_{\text{MAD}} = \frac{\sqrt{2}\,\text{median}(|\tilde{w}_{1,0}|, |\tilde{w}_{1,1}|, \ldots, |\tilde{w}_{1,N-1}|)}{0.6745}.$$

Translation-invariant estimators for sampled versions of $m_1(t)$ and $m_2(t)$ are shown in Figure 6.15 using a universal threshold. The dotted lines are the original functions, as in Figure 6.1, and are very similar to the translation-invariant estimates. The hard thresholding of $m_1(t)$ allows a few spurious wavelet coefficients through the procedure and does not provide a better estimate of the peak when compared to soft thresholding. Both translation-invariant estimates of $m_1(t)$ exhibit a slightly reduced peak when compared with the DWT denoising estimate in Figure 6.7. The translation-invariant estimate using hard thresholding of $m_2(t)$ is quite similar to the DWT denoising estimate using soft thresholding, while the translation-invariant estimate using soft thresholding shows slight improvement. These results mimic those found in Percival and Walden (2000, Sec. 10.5).

6.5 APPLICATIONS

6.5.1 IBM Stock Prices

Here we apply wavelet denoising to estimating the trend in the IBM stock (log) prices $\log(p_t)$. There are $N = 369$ prices, so we remove the first observation

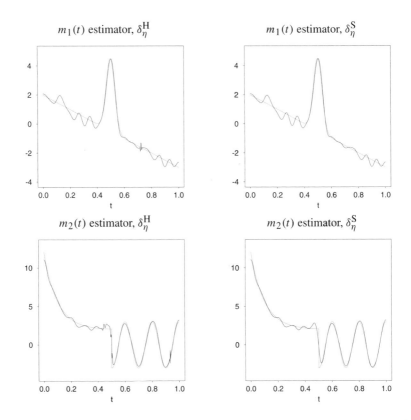

FIGURE 6.15 Translation-invariant estimators for sampled versions of the example functions $m_1(t)$ and $m_2(t)$. The left-hand column uses a hard thresholding rule, while the right-hand column uses soft thresholding. All plots use the universal threshold. The true functions (dotted lines) are drawn for comparison.

and perform a partial LA(8) DWT ($J = 4$) to the remaining 368 prices. The original series is shown in Figure 6.16, along with five estimates obtained from different thresholds. All estimates were obtained using the soft thresholding rule. The signal-to-noise ratio here is quite large and hence the differences between the observed (log) stock prices are only in the higher frequencies. The dominating trend in the stock prices is preserved, with the SURE and data-analytic methods producing the smoothest estimate. There is little difference between the universal estimator whether applying it to the DWT or MODWT, while the minimax estimator is the least smooth.

6.5.2 IBM Stock Returns

Here we apply wavelet denoising to estimating the trend in the IBM stock returns defined to be $r_t = \log(p_{t+1}) - \log(p_t)$, where p_t is the stock price at time t. There are $N = 368$ returns so we perform a partial LA(8) DWT ($J = 4$) to this

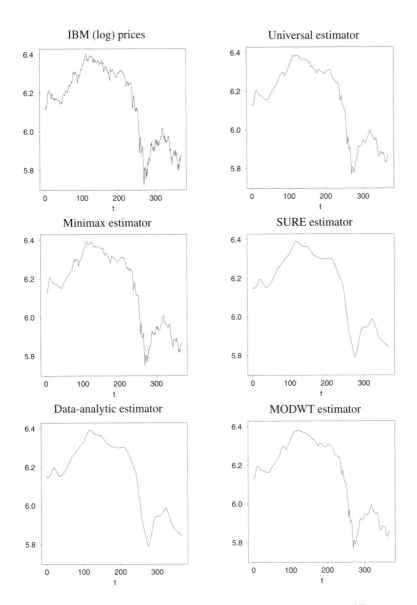

FIGURE 6.16 IBM stock (log) prices and wavelet denoising estimates. All estimators use the soft thresholding rule δ_η^S. The MODWT estimator uses the universal threshold.

series. The wavelet coefficients are provided in Figure 4.17b. By taking the first difference of the log-transformed prices, we expect any significant trend to be removed from the series. Recall, the first difference is equivalent to applying a filter with squared gain function $\mathcal{D}(f) = 4\sin^2(\pi f)$, which is proportional to the Haar wavelet filter, to the original series.

The original series is shown in Figure 6.17 along with five estimates obtained from different thresholds. All estimates were obtained using the soft thresholding rule. As we observed before with simulated data sets, the minimax estimator allows more coefficients to survive the thresholding and therefore produces a rougher estimate when compared with the universal estimate. This is reasonable, since the universal threshold is quite conservative and the minimax threshold does not in general produce a visually pleasing estimate but one that minimizes the maximum MSE. The SURE and data-analytic estimates are identical and allow no wavelet coefficients from the first four scales to contribute. Thus, the function produced in both cases is simply the wavelet smooth s_4. The fact that the sample size is only divisible by $2^4 = 16$ limits our ability to decompose this series without explicitly handling the nondyadic length of the data by, say, padding with zeros; see Section 4.6.2. With an appropriate extension to the next highest dyadic length, we would expect to produce an estimate that is zero everywhere, as one might expect for this return series.

The MODWT estimator also uses a universal threshold, and therefore appears similar with the universal estimator, but because it is not limited to any specific sample size, we have performed the decomposition down to level 7. Although the wavelet coefficients that exceeded the threshold appear to be identical regardless of using the DWT or MODWT, the MODWT has eliminated several more low-frequency coefficients and thus produces a smoother estimate where no noisy coefficients exist. Using the MODWT in combination with other thresholding rules (e.g., SURE or the data-analytic) would most likely produce an estimate that is identically zero for all time points.

6.5.3   IBM Volatility

Here we apply wavelet denoising to estimating the trend in the IBM stock volatility defined to be $v_t = |r_t|$, where r_t is the stock return at time t. There are $N = 368$ volatilities so we perform a partial LA(8) DWT ($J = 4$) to this series. The wavelet coefficients are provided in Figure 4.19a. The original series is shown in Figure 6.18, along with five estimates obtained from different thresholds. All estimates were obtained using the soft thresholding rule. As with the stock prices and returns, the SURE and data-analytic methods produce the smoothest estimate of the volatility series. The universal estimator retains the large variance in the volatility around $t = 400$, both with the DWT or MODWT, although the MODWT smooths out the bumps recovered using the DWT. The minimax estimator appears to be a noisier version of the universal estimate using the DWT.

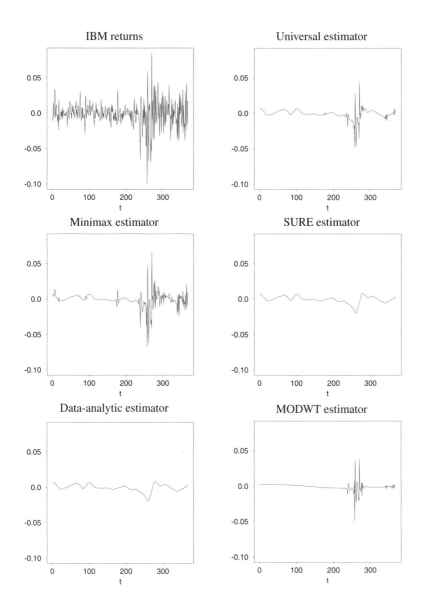

FIGURE 6.17 IBM stock returns and wavelet denoising estimates. All estimators use the soft thresholding rule δ_η^S. The MODWT estimator uses the universal threshold.

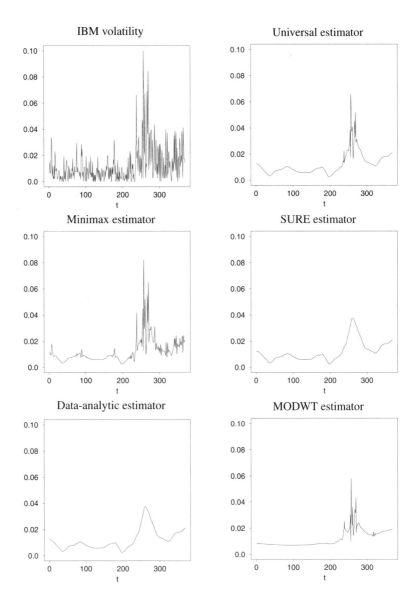

FIGURE 6.18   IBM volatility and wavelet denoising estimates. All estimators use the soft thresholding rule δ_η^S. The MODWT estimator uses the universal threshold.

6.5.4 Outlier Testing

Greenblatt (1996) proposed a novel approach to testing for outliers using the DWT. We introduce his method here and discuss under what conditions we may expect it to work in practice. Let $w_1 = (w_{1,0}, \ldots, w_{1,N/2-1})$ be the unit scale DWT coefficient vector from a length N time series x. The test-statistic

$$\mathcal{D}_2 = \frac{\max_t |w_{1,t} - \bar{w}_1|}{\hat{\sigma}_x(\lambda_1)},$$

where $\bar{w}_1$ is the sample mean of the $N/2$ wavelet coefficients and $\hat{\sigma}_x(\lambda_1)$ is the unit scale sample wavelet standard deviation, will be used to test for a single outlier in the wavelet coefficients, and therefore in the original time series. This particular test-statistic is taken from David (1981, Sec. 8.2). Since outliers are high-frequency events – that is, they only occur very few times in the entire time series – they should be captured quite well by w_1 because its coefficients are associated with frequencies $1/4 \le f \le 1/2$. We note that using $\bar{w}_1$ is in fact not necessary since the wavelet coefficients have mean zero as long as the spectrum of the underlying process does not vary in the interval $1/4 \le f \le 1/2$, and therefore the test-statistic may be computed via $\mathcal{D}_2 = \max_t |w_{1,t}|/\hat{\sigma}_x(\lambda_1)$.

A small simulation study was conducted to assess the ability of $\mathcal{D}_2$ to detect outliers in the following time series:

$$y_t = \sin(x_t) + \sin(2x_t) + \log(1 + x_t) + \epsilon_t, \tag{6.12}$$

where $x_t \in (0, 10\pi)$ and $\epsilon_t \sim N(0, 1)$. This process exhibits a trend and seasonal behavior, as is common in most economic series. To create the outlier, the observation y^* with the largest error ϵ^* is augmented via

$$y^* = y^* + \text{sign}(\epsilon^* - \hat{\mu}) \cdot \hat{\sigma} \cdot \xi,$$

where $\hat{\mu}$ is the sample mean of the error process, $\hat{\sigma}$ is the standard deviation of the error process, ξ is a positive integer, and $\text{sign}(x)$ is defined in Equation 6.6. Thus, an observation with a "large" magnitude of error is transformed into a large (positive or negative) outlier.

Figure 6.19 shows a length $N = 1024$ realization of Equation 6.12 with an induced outlier ($\xi = 3$) at $t = 432$. We generated 1000 realizations of Equation 6.12 without inducing an outlier. The test-statistic was computed for each case to create an empirical distribution for $\mathcal{D}_2$, shown in Figure 6.19c. The vertical line is the value of $\mathcal{D}_2$ for unit scale wavelet coefficients with the outlier present. It looks to be statistically significant when compared with the Monte Carlo distribution and in fact it is greater than 990 of the realizations. Hence, we can reject the null hypothesis that the wavelet coefficients are IID Gaussian random variables with this Monte Carlo distribution at a significance level of $\alpha = 0.01$.

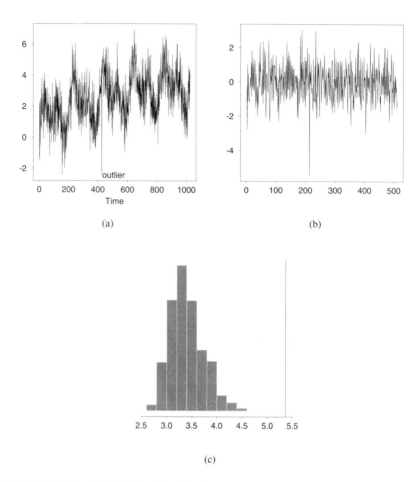

FIGURE 6.19 Wavelet-based outlier detection. (a) Simulated time series with an induced outlier at $t = 432$, (b) unit scale DWT coefficients using the Haar wavelet filter and (c) Monte Carlo distribution of $\mathcal{D}_2$ based on 1000 realizations where the vertical line is the value of $\mathcal{D}_2$ from (b).

The original formulation of $\mathcal{D}_2$ in David (1981) assumed the observations $x = (x_0, \ldots, x_{N-1})$ to be IID $N(\mu, \sigma^2)$ random variables. Clearly, the time series in Figure 6.19a does not satisfy this assumption. Since the spectrum of y_t is essentially constant at the higher frequencies, the unit scale DWT coefficients will approximately follow the assumption of IID Gaussianity. This follows the argument outlined in Section 5.2.2 for long-memory processes and is used again in Section 7.3 when testing for homogeneity of variance. In broad terms, the scale λ_j DWT coefficients may be assumed to be uncorrelated when the underlying spectrum is relatively flat across the frequency interval $(1/2^j, 1/2^{J+1})$ and allows one to apply IID test statistics to functions exhibiting correlation.

7

WAVELETS FOR
VARIANCE-COVARIANCE
ESTIMATION

7.1 INTRODUCTION

The wavelet transform has proven to be very effective in adapting to "local" features in time series when the focus was an estimation of the mean function (Chapter 6). Donoho and Johnstone (1994, 1998) introduced wavelet techniques to the statistics community using nonparametric function estimation as their vehicle. The wavelet transform performs well because it efficiently partitions the time-frequency plane, as seen in Figure 4.2, by using short basis functions for high-frequency oscillations and long basis functions for low-frequency oscillations. An important characteristic of the wavelet transform (DWT or MODWT) is its ability to decompose (analyze) the variance of a stochastic process. Let w and $\widetilde{w}$ be the DWT and MODWT coefficient vectors, respectively, of the mean zero series x, then we have the following relationship:

$$\|x\|^2 = \|w\|^2 = \|\widetilde{w}\|^2 . \tag{7.1}$$

Since $\|x\|^2 = x^T x = \sum x_t^2 \propto \mathrm{Var}(x)$, the relationship in Equation 7.1 in fact provides a decomposition of variance between the original series and either the DWT or MODWT wavelet coefficients. In the previous chapters we used wavelet transforms (DWT and MODWT) as alternative representations and decompositions for the coefficients of a time series. Here we have an alternative representation for the variability (variance, autocovariance, etc.) of a time series via its squared wavelet coefficients.

The classical method of decomposing the variance of a stationary time series x_t is through the *spectral representation theorem* (Priestley, 1981, Sec. 4.11). Without getting into the details, the spectral representation theorem allows one to express any discrete stationary process as an infinite sum of complex exponentials with random amplitudes and phases – the integrated spectrum $I(f)$. If $I(f)$ is differentiable everywhere, then its derivative $S(f)$ is defined to be the *spectrum* or *spectral density function*. If the autocovariance sequence (ACVS) of x_t is square summable ($\sum \gamma_{x,\tau}^2 < \infty$), then the spectrum of x_t may also be expressed as the Fourier transform of its ACVS via

$$S_x(f) = \sum_{\tau=-\infty}^{\infty} \gamma_{x,\tau} e^{-i2\pi f\tau} \quad \text{for} \quad |f| \leq \frac{1}{2}. \tag{7.2}$$

Thus, the spectrum exhibits large coefficients when the sinusoid associated with a particular frequency f is highly correlated with $\gamma_{x,\tau}$. One relation we will make use of later on in this chapter is for a special case of Equation 7.2 when $\tau = 0$ such that

$$\text{Var}(x_t) = \text{Cov}(x_t, x_t) = \int_{-1/2}^{1/2} S_x(f)\, df,$$

and therefore $S_x(f)$ decomposes the variance of x_t on a frequency-by-frequency basis. The duality between the spectrum and ACVS is given by the inverse DFT

$$\int_{-1/2}^{1/2} S_x(f) e^{i2\pi f\tau}\, df = \gamma_{x,\tau}, \quad \tau = 0, \pm 1, \pm 2, \dots,$$

so one may easily go back and forth between the two representations of variability in the process x_t.

Figure 7.1 displays the autocorrelation function (ACF), spectrum and wavelet variance for three different stationary time series models. The ACF is defined by $\rho_{x,\tau} = \gamma_{x,\tau}/\gamma_{x,0}$ and the wavelet variance is introduced in Section 7.2. The ACF is measuring the level of association between random variables at different distances (lag τ) from each other. The AR(1) process ($\phi = 0.9$) exhibits exponential decay in $\rho_{x,\tau}$ and there is essentially no correlation beyond lags $\tau > 40$. The fractional difference process (FDP) (Section 5.2.1) is an example of a long-memory process and has the characteristic hyperbolic decay of $\rho_{x,\tau}$. Thus, even for large lags a significant amount of correlation is observed. The seasonal persistent process (SPP) (Section 5.4.1) is a seasonal long-memory process with a persistent oscillation every 12 observations, and, therefore, we observe a slowly decaying periodic oscillation in its ACF.

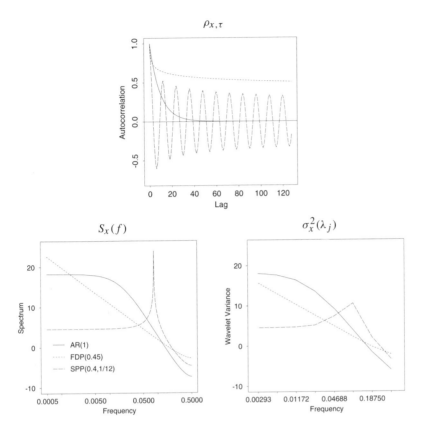

FIGURE 7.1 Alternative representations for the second-order properties of stationary time series. The autocorrelation function $\rho_{x,\tau}$, spectrum $S_x(f)$ and wavelet variance $\sigma_x^2(\lambda_j)$ for an AR(1) with $\phi = 0.9$ (solid line), FDP(0.45) (dotted line), and SPP(0.4, 1/12) (dashed line).

The spectra of the processes in Figure 7.1, plotted on log-log axes, follow from Equation 7.2. That is, they are the amount of correlation when the ACFs have sinusoids projected on them. The AR(1) process shows a large amount of spectral energy in the low frequencies that decreases as $f \to 0$ while the FDP is approximately linear and does *not* exhibit any decrease its energy as $f \to 0$. The SPP is associated with a period of 12 and hence is strongest in spectral energy at $f = 1/12$. When the wavelet variance is plotted not according to its scale λ_j but the midpoint of $[1/2^{j+1}, 1/2^j]$, it mimics the behavior of the SDF for the process. Thus, the wavelet variances for all three time series models in Figure 7.1 are very similar to the corresponding spectra. This similarity is strongest for the FDP and worst for the SPP. Of course, using the discrete wavelet packet transform (DWPT), the wavelet variance may be generalized into the wavelet packet variance in order to better adapt to features (e.g., peaks) in the spectrum of a process at arbitrary locations on the frequency axis.

The wavelet variance is not limited to simply mimicking the behavior of the Fourier spectrum. It takes advantage of time-frequency partitioning of the wavelet transform in order to better capture the low-frequency features of a time series. Thus, for processes with more spectral energy in the lower frequencies (e.g., persistent processes), the wavelet variance is a very appealing alternative to the spectrum. A second consequence of the partitioning of the time-frequency plane is the interpretation of wavelet variance as it pertains to the original process.

As mentioned earlier, the SDF is a frequency-by-frequency decomposition of a process and does well at capturing oscillations that are regular and long standing. On the other hand the wavelet variance looks at a scale-by-scale decomposition. If one believes that the process under study is composed of several simple processes that move across different time horizons, this falls naturally into the wavelet variance framework. Examples come from atmospheric science where climatological variables observed at a particular location may be composed of day-to-day weather patterns, broadband oscillations that roll through the region, annual fluctuations in weather patterns, and also long-term oscillations or financial markets where individual investors make rapid changes with only a minor impact or where large financial institutions react slowly but induce major changes. When combined, these processes on different timescales interact to produce a very complicated series to observe. The wavelet variance allows one to peel back the different time horizons, much like layers of an onion, to reveal much simpler sub-series. In Chapter 5 we found that the wavelet (packet) decomposition of an FDP (SPP) allows us to treat the wavelet (packet) coefficients within scale as uncorrelated Gaussian random variables whose variance only depends on the wavelet (packet) variance. These are two examples of a better understanding, with emphasis on modeling here and eventually forecasting, using the information gleaned from a wavelet (packet) variance decomposition.

Wavelet analysis of variance is not limited to univariate time series. The concepts of wavelet covariance and wavelet correlation may also be defined using natural extensions to time-domain time series analysis in order to address multiscale behavior between processes. The rest of this chapter is devoted to introducing and providing the necessary methodology to perform a wavelet analysis of variance-covariance.

7.2   THE WAVELET VARIANCE

When discussing the DWT in Section 4.4, we pointed out that a vector of wavelet coefficients is associated with changes at a particular scale. For example, the level j wavelet coefficients $w_{j,t}$ are associated with the scale $\lambda_j = 2^{j-1}$. This means that each wavelet coefficient was constructed using a difference of two weighted averages, each one of length λ_j. Applying the DWT to a stochastic process produces a decomposition on a scale-by-scale basis. While analyzing a signal in this way is useful for estimating the mean (as in Chapter 6), we now move onto decomposing the variance of a stochastic process.

Let x_t be a real-valued stochastic process – not necessarily zero mean or stationary. The *time-varying wavelet variance* for x_t is defined to be the variance of the scale λ_j wavelet coefficient $w_{j,t}$ via

$$\sigma^2_{x,t}(\lambda_j) = \frac{1}{2\lambda_j} \, \text{Var}(w_{j,t}).$$

If we assume that the wavelet variance is independent of t (this is true for stationary processes), then we may summarize the time-dependent wavelet variance through the *time-independent wavelet variance* or simply the *wavelet variance:*

$$\sigma^2_x(\lambda_j) = \frac{1}{2\lambda_j} \, \text{Var}(w_{j,t}). \tag{7.3}$$

Whereas the SDF decomposes the process variance on a frequency-by-frequency basis, the wavelet variance decomposes the variance of x_t on a scale-by-scale basis via

$$\sum_{j=1}^{\infty} \sigma^2_x(\lambda_j) = \text{Var}(x_t)$$

(Percival, 1995). The scale λ_j is associated with the frequency interval $[1/2^{j+1}, 1/2^j]$, and we can use this property to obtain an approximate relation between the wavelet variance and the SDF of x_t via

$$\sigma^2_{x,t}(\lambda_j) \approx 2 \int_{1/2^{j+1}}^{1/2^j} S_x(f) \, df. \tag{7.4}$$

The factor of 2 is needed because the spectrum is an even function of frequency over the interval $[-1/2, 1/2]$. One way to visualize the wavelet variance is through Equation 7.4 where the wavelet variance is a piecewise constant function with respect to frequency; see Figure 7.2. This approximation holds reasonably well for the majority of the frequency interval, showing a severe underestimation of the spectrum at $[1/128, 1/64]$. This is due to the fact that all wavelet coefficients affected by the boundary were removed, leaving a very small sample size with which to estimate the spectrum at lower frequencies.

   The ability to handle certain types of nonstationary processes, the so-called difference stationary processes where performing a finite number of differences produces a stationary process, is yet another advantage of the wavelet variance. Recent attention to nonstationary long-memory processes may be found in Velasco (1999) for estimation of the fractional difference parameter d and Craigmile *et al.* (2000) for estimating the trend. For example, a random walk process may be formed via $x_0 = 0$ and

$$x_t = \sum_{u=1}^{t} \epsilon_u, \quad t \geq 1,$$

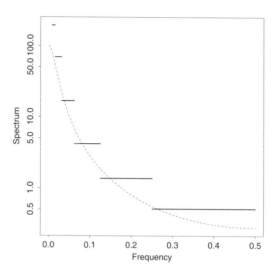

FIGURE 7.2 Piecewise constant interpretation of the wavelet variance. Instead of decomposing the variance of the stationary process, in this case an AR(1) with $\phi = 0.9$, on a frequency-by-frequency basis like the Fourier transform, the wavelet transform decomposes it on a scale by scale basis. Each scale may be interpreted as a frequency interval and thus the wavelet variance is a piecewise approximation to the spectrum.

where ϵ_t is a Gaussian white noise process. This process is nonstationary since its variance is time dependent. However, by applying the first difference operation to x_t, so that $y_t = x_t - x_{t-1}$, we have $y_t = \epsilon_t$ for $t \geq 1$ and therefore y_t is a stationary process. Recall that the Haar wavelet is nearly identical to the first difference operator, via its squared gain function $\mathcal{H}^{\text{Haar}}(f) = 2\sin^2(\pi f)$, so applying the Haar DWT to the random walk x_t will produce stationary wavelet coefficients at all levels. Therefore among processes with stationary differences and order of integration one, the Haar wavelet filter is sufficient to produce stationary wavelet coefficients. What about higher orders of integration? If we let x_t be formed by a double sum of a Gaussian white noise process, then

$$x_t = \sum_{u=1}^{t}\sum_{v=1}^{u}\epsilon_v, \quad t \geq 1,$$

with $x_0 = 0$. It is easy to see that the first difference of x_t is now a random walk and the second difference is Gaussian white noise. The D(4) wavelet filter has squared gain function $\mathcal{H}^{\text{D4}}(f) \propto 2\sin^4(\pi f)$ and is closely related to the second difference operator. Hence, applying the D(4) DWT will ensure stationary wavelet coefficients for all levels. By increasing the length of the Daubechies wavelet filter we guarantee the resulting DWT coefficients will be stationary and thus protect ourselves from problems caused by a nonstationary time series. These properties also apply to deterministic polynomial trends in the original series. A length $L > 2p$, Daubechies wavelet filter will produce mean zero stationary wavelet coefficients when the original series exhibits a polynomial trend of order p.

7.2.1 Estimating the Wavelet Variance

Consider a dyadic length $N = 2^J$ realization $x = (x_0, x_1, \ldots, x_{N-1})$ of the stochastic process x_t and apply the partial DWT of order $J_p \leq J$ to produce the length N vector of wavelet coefficients w. An unbiased estimator of the wavelet variance based on the DWT is given by

$$\hat{\sigma}_x^2(\lambda_j) = \frac{1}{2\lambda_j \widehat{N}_j} \sum_{t=L'_j}^{N/2^j - 1} w_{j,t}^2, \qquad (7.5)$$

where $L'_j = \lceil (L-2)(1-2^{-j}) \rceil$ is the number of DWT coefficients computed using the boundary and hence $\widehat{N}_j = N/2^j - L'_j$ is the number of wavelet coefficients at scale λ_j unaffected by the boundary.

Relaxing the requirement of dyadic sample size to any arbitrary length N realization, one may compute the partial MODWT of order $J_p < \log_2(N)$ to produce the length $(J_p + 1)N$ vector of wavelet coefficients $\tilde{w}$. An unbiased estimator of the wavelet variance is based on the MODWT using

$$\tilde{\sigma}_x^2(\lambda_j) = \frac{1}{\widetilde{N}_j} \sum_{t=L_j-1}^{N-1} \tilde{w}_{j,t}^2, \qquad (7.6)$$

where $L_j = (2^j - 1)(L-1) + 1$ is the length of the scale λ_j wavelet filter and $\widetilde{N}_j = N - L_j + 1$ is the number of coefficients unaffected by the boundary. The normalization by $2\lambda_j$ is not required in Equation 7.6 since the wavelet filter $\tilde{h}_l$ associated with the MODWT is a rescaled version of the DWT filter h_l (Section 4.5).

The large-sample properties of the wavelet variance follow from previous work on the Allan variance (Allan, 1966). The estimator $\tilde{\sigma}_x^2(\lambda_j)$ is asymptotically Gaussian distributed with mean $\sigma_x^2(\lambda_j)$ and variance $S_{\varpi,j}(0)/\widetilde{N}_j$, where $S_{\varpi,j}(0)$ is the SDF of the scale λ_j squared wavelet coefficients $\varpi_{j,t} = w_{j,t}^2$ evaluated at frequency zero and is given by

$$S_{\varpi,j}^G(0) = 2 \int_{-1/2}^{1/2} S_j^2(f) \, df \qquad (7.7)$$

(Percival, 1983, 1995). This result holds when $\tilde{w}_{j,t}$ is a Gaussian stationary process (implying that x_t is also a Gaussian process) and its spectrum $S_j(f)$ is greater than zero almost everywhere.

Even if x_t is a non-Gaussian process, the asymptotic distribution of its wavelet variance may be known. For a broad class of non-Gaussian or non-linear processes, $\tilde{\sigma}_x^2(\lambda_j)$ is again asymptotically Gaussian distributed with mean $\sigma_x^2(\lambda_j)$ and large sample variance given by $S_{\varpi,j}(0)/\tilde{N}_j$, where $S_{\varpi,j}(f)$ is the SDF for the scale λ_j squared wavelet coefficients but has no convenient form as in Equation 7.7 (Serroukh et al., 2000). Recently, Hong and Lee (1999) addressed the issue of estimating the SDF around a neighborhood of $f = 0$ in order to obtain heteroskedastic and autocorrelation consistent covariance matrices.

7.2.2 Confidence Intervals for the Wavelet Variance

Constructing a confidence interval (CI) is a natural step after calculating a point estimate for the parameter of interest. If we have a sequence of random variables $z_0, z_1, \ldots, z_{N-1}$ with common mean $\mu = E(z_t)$ and variance $\sigma^2 = \text{Var}(z_t)$, then the variance of the sample mean $\bar{z} = N^{-1} \sum_0^{N-1} z_t$ is equal to

$$\text{Var}(\bar{z}) = \frac{\sigma^2}{N}.$$

To describe the variability of the point estimate $\bar{z}$, we utilize large-sample results that tell us the $(1 - \alpha)$ CI for μ is given by

$$\bar{z} \pm \zeta_{\frac{\alpha}{2}} \frac{\hat{\sigma}}{\sqrt{N}} \tag{7.8}$$

if σ^2 is unknown and must be estimated. A common estimator for σ^2 is $\hat{\sigma}^2 = (N-1)^{-1} \sum_t (z_t - \bar{z})^2$ and $\zeta_{\frac{\alpha}{2}}$ is the upper $(1 - \alpha/2)$ quantile of the standard normal distribution Φ; that is,

$$P\left[-\zeta_{\frac{\alpha}{2}} \leq \Phi \leq \zeta_{\frac{\alpha}{2}}\right] = 1 - \alpha.$$

Since the wavelet variance estimators in Section 7.2.1 are essentially sample means of the squared wavelet coefficients, a $(1 - \alpha)$ CI may be constructed using Equation 7.8 and substituting appropriate quantities for $\bar{z}$, $\hat{\sigma}^2$, and N.

First, let us construct a CI for the unbiased estimator of the scale λ_j wavelet variance based on the MODWT $\tilde{\sigma}_x^2(\lambda_j)$. If x is a length N realization of a Gaussian process, then $S_{\varpi,j}(0)$ is given by Equation 7.7 and is a function of the SDF of the scale λ_j wavelet coefficients. A simple estimator of the spectrum of the scale λ_j wavelet coefficients $S_j(f)$ is the periodogram $\widehat{S}_j^p(f)$, and appealing to Parseval's relation (Equation 2.10) we have

$$\int_{-1/2}^{1/2} \left[\widehat{S}_j^p(f)\right]^2 df = \sum_{m=-(\tilde{N}_j-1)}^{\tilde{N}_j-1} \hat{\gamma}_{j,m}^2,$$

where $\hat{\gamma}_{j,m}$ is the biased estimator of the sample ACVS for $\tilde{w}_j$. So under the Gaussian assumption we may form an unbiased estimator of $S_{\varpi,j}^G(0)$ using the expression

$$\widehat{S}^{G}_{\varpi,j}(0) = \frac{\hat{\gamma}^2_{j,0}}{2} + \sum_{m=1}^{\widetilde{N}_j-1} \hat{\gamma}^2_{j,m}$$

(Percival, 1995). Substituting $\tilde{\sigma}^2_x(\lambda_j)$, $\widehat{S}^{G}_{\varpi,j}(0)$ and $\widetilde{N}_j$ into Equation 7.8 produces an approximate $(1-\alpha)$ CI for $\sigma^2_x(\lambda_j)$ given by

$$\tilde{\sigma}^2_x(\lambda_j) \pm \zeta_{\frac{\alpha}{2}} \left[\frac{\widehat{S}^{G}_{\varpi,j}(0)}{\widetilde{N}_j} \right]^{1/2}. \tag{7.9}$$

The CI provided in Equation 7.9 uses quantiles of the standard normal distribution and does not necessarily have to be positive, although we know that $\sigma^2_x(\lambda_j) > 0$. An alternative CI was provided in Percival (1995) using an *equivalent degrees of freedom* argument (Priestley, 1981, p. 466). Instead of a CI based on the Gaussian distribution for the estimated wavelet variance, we instead claim that

$$\frac{\xi \tilde{\sigma}^2_x(\lambda_j)}{\sigma^2_x(\lambda_j)} \sim \chi^2_\xi,$$

where χ^2_ξ is a chi-squared distribution with ξ degrees of freedom.[1] Using the properties of the mean and variance of the χ^2 distribution and appealing to the large-sample result in Section 7.2.1, we conclude that

$$\xi = \frac{\widetilde{N}_j \sigma^4_x(\lambda_j)}{S^{G}_{\varpi,j}(0)},$$

and therefore the equivalent degrees of freedom may be estimated via

$$\hat{\xi} = \frac{\widetilde{N}_j \tilde{\sigma}^4_x(\lambda_j)}{\widehat{S}^{G}_{\varpi,j}(0)}. \tag{7.10}$$

The CI is no longer symmetric under this equivalent degrees of freedom argument because of the χ^2 distribution. Let $q_{\xi,1-\frac{\alpha}{2}}$ and $q_{\xi,\frac{\alpha}{2}}$ be the lower and upper $\alpha/2$ quantiles of the χ^2 distribution with ξ degrees of freedom; that is,

$$P\left[\chi^2_\xi \leq q_{\xi,1-\frac{\alpha}{2}} \right] = P\left[\chi^2_\xi \geq q_{\xi,\frac{\alpha}{2}} \right] = \frac{\alpha}{2}.$$

With these quantiles so defined, we have approximately

$$P\left[q_{\xi,1-\frac{\alpha}{2}} < \frac{\xi \tilde{\sigma}^2_x(\lambda_j)}{\sigma^2_x(\lambda_j)} < q_{\xi,\frac{\alpha}{2}} \right] = 1 - \alpha,$$

---

[1] As $\xi \to \infty$, the χ^2 distribution rapidly approaches the Gaussian distribution.

and therefore we may define an approximate $(1 - \alpha)$ CI for $\sigma_x^2(\lambda_j)$ via

$$\left[\frac{\xi \tilde{\sigma}_x^2(\lambda_j)}{q_{\xi,1-\frac{\alpha}{2}}}, \frac{\xi \tilde{\sigma}_x^2(\lambda_j)}{q_{\xi,\frac{\alpha}{2}}} \right], \tag{7.11}$$

where ξ is estimated via Equation 7.10 in practice. Additional CIs are found in Percival (1995) by making stronger assumptions on the underlying SDF of the process of interest.

If we do not assume the underlying stochastic process x_t is Gaussian, then none of the arguments used previously apply. Instead, the quantity $S_{\varpi,j}(0)$ must be estimated directly. Serroukh *et al.* (2000) used multitaper spectrum estimation to produce the estimator $\widehat{S}_{\varpi,j}^{\mathrm{mt}}(0)$ of the SDF for the scale λ_j squared wavelet coefficients evaluated at zero frequency. Substituting $\tilde{\sigma}_x^2(\lambda_j)$, $\widehat{S}_{\varpi,j}^{\mathrm{mt}}(0)$ and $\widetilde{N}_j$ into Equation 7.8 yields the approximate $(1 - \alpha)$ CI

$$\tilde{\sigma}_x^2(\lambda_j) \pm \zeta_{\frac{\alpha}{2}} \left[\frac{\widehat{S}_{\varpi,j}^{\mathrm{mt}}(0)}{\widetilde{N}_j} \right]^{1/2}, \tag{7.12}$$

which is applicable for a much wider class of processes. When computing CIs for the wavelet variance under Gaussianity when it is an incorrect assumption, Equation 7.9 produces much narrower intervals that may not reflect the true variability of the point estimate.

7.2.3   Example: Simulated AR(1) Model

The wavelet variances for the AR(1) process in Equation 4.30, with approximate 95% CIs, are plotted against wavelet scale λ_j in Figure 7.3. The first set of CIs (dotted lines) were computed using Equation 7.9 assuming a Gaussian error process. The second set of CIs (dashed lines) were computed using Equation 7.12 assuming a non-Gaussian error process. If the errors were indeed non-Gaussian, we would expect the approximate CI from the non-Gaussian assumption to be much larger than the CI under the Gaussian assumption, but this is not the case. The upper bounds for both CIs are very similar across all scales. The lower bounds differ between the two methods, but this is exaggerated when plotted on the log-scale and is not that different when comparing the raw numbers.

7.2.4   Example: IBM Stock Prices

The IBM stock price series exhibits a clear increase in volatility around observation 230. The extent of this nonstationary feature was explored via an LA(8) multiresolution analysis (MRA) in Figure 4.25. The increase in volatility is confined to the first three wavelet details, which capture frequencies $f \in [1/16, 1/2]$. When looking at $\tilde{d}_4$, there is no apparent difference in volatility throughout its length. Hence, $\tilde{d}_4$ may be thought of as "stationary" for practical purposes. We may use the wavelet variance to quantify the relationship between the volatility

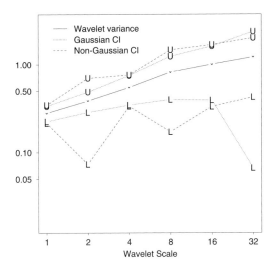

FIGURE **7.3** Wavelet variances with approximate 95% confidence intervals for an AR(1) process plotted on a logarithmic y-axis. The dotted lines represent the approximate 95% confidence interval assuming a Gaussian process and the dashed lines represent an approximate 95% confidence interval assuming a non-Gaussian process. Lines with "U" denote the upper bound for the 95% confidence interval while "L" denotes the lower bound.

in this series. Figure 7.4a displays the MODWT-based wavelet variance with a 95% approximate CI using the χ^2 distribution in Equation 7.11. There is an approximate linear relationship between the $\tilde{\sigma}^2_{\mathrm{IBM}}(\lambda_j)$ and the wavelet scale λ_j indicating the potential for long memory in the volatility series (Section 5.2.6).

Since the MODWT decomposes a series by local and scale, we may partition the wavelet variance according to where we believe a change in variance occurs. Let $\tilde{\sigma}^2_1(\lambda_j)$ denote the wavelet variance associated with scale λ_j for the first 235 observations in the IBM volatility series and $\tilde{\sigma}^2_2(\lambda_j)$ denote the wavelet variance for the remaining observations. These two quantities are plotted in Figure 7.4b with their approximate 95% CIs using Equation 7.11. For the first three wavelet scales the approximate CIs do *not* overlap. This provides a "visual" method to test the hypothesis

$$H_0 : \sigma^2_1(\lambda_j) = \sigma^2_2(\lambda_j).$$

At the fourth wavelet scale, the CIs overlap one another and therefore we cannot reject the null hypothesis H_0. Thus, the wavelet variance with its large-sample theory allows us to perform statistical hypothesis tests on the variability of a time series. We revisit these data in Section 7.3.2 where a specific test is developed to detect and locate changes in variance.

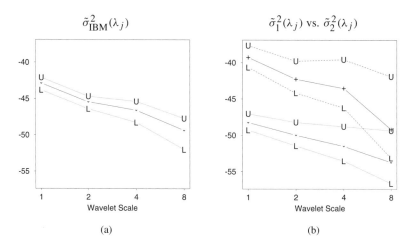

FIGURE 7.4 Wavelet variance for the IBM stock price volatility plotted on a log scale with approximate 95% confidence intervals . (a) Wavelet variance computed using all observed volatilities $N = 368$. (b) Wavelet variance $\tilde{\sigma}_1^2(\lambda_j)$ computed using the observations $t \le 235$ and the wavelet variance $\tilde{\sigma}_2^2(\lambda_j)$ using the remaining observations $t > 235$. The dashed lines with the characters "L" and "U" denote the lower and upper bounds of the approximate confidence interval, respectively.

7.3 TESTING HOMOGENEITY OF VARIANCE

Suppose we have a sequence of observations that we consider to be an example of a long-memory process. An important assumption behind any (second-order) stationary process is that its variance is independent of t. Here, we demonstrate how the DWT may be used to construct a statistical test for homogeneity of variance in an observed time series exhibiting long-range dependence. The DWT was used previously to investigate other types of nonstationary behavior, for example, detecting jumps and sharp cusps of signals embedded in Gaussian white noise (Wang, 1995) and developing a data-dependent threshold for removing noise from a signal (Section 6.3.4). Lee and Hong (2001) recently developed a method for testing serial correlation of unknown form using the wavelet transform as an alternative to kernel-based methods.

The key property of the DWT that makes it useful for studying non-stationary behavior is that it decomposes a time series into wavelet coefficients associated with changes at various scales and specific times. For long-memory processes, the wavelet coefficients from the DWT are approximately uncorrelated within scale; see Section 5.2.2. Whitcher (1998) and Whitcher *et al.* (1998) showed that this approximation is good enough to apply a test for homogeneity of variance on a scale-by-scale basis to long-memory processes. If the null hypothesis is rejected at small scales (high frequencies), this indicates that a sudden shift in the variance has occurred somewhere in the time series. Using the MODWT

(Section 4.5), we also investigate an alternative test statistic that estimates the
time at which the variance change took place.

Let $w_0, w_1, \dots, w_N$ be a sequence of scale λ_j DWT coefficients. Given that
the length of the wavelet filter L is sufficient to eliminate any possible polynomial
trends, $E(w_{j,t}) = 0$ and $\mathrm{Var}(w_{j,t}) = \sigma_t^2(\lambda_j)$. We wish to test the hypothesis

$$H_0 : \sigma_{L_j'}^2(\lambda_j) = \sigma_{L_j'+1}^2(\lambda_j) = \cdots = \sigma_{\widehat{N}-1}^2(\lambda_j). \tag{7.13}$$

As with computing the wavelet variance using the DWT, we discard all wavelet
coefficients affected by the boundary. A test statistic that can discriminate between this null hypothesis and a variety of alternative hypotheses, such as

$$H_1 : \sigma_{L_j'}^2(\lambda_j) = \cdots = \sigma_k^2(\lambda_j) \neq \sigma_{k+1}^2(\lambda_j) = \cdots = \sigma_{\widehat{N}-1}^2(\lambda_j),$$

where k is an unknown change point, is the normalized cumulative sum of squares
(NCSS) test statistic D, which has previously been investigated by, among others,
Brown *et al.* (1975), Hsu (1977), and Inclán and Tiao (1994). Let

$$\mathcal{P}_k = \frac{\sum_{j=1}^k w_j^2}{\sum_{j=1}^N w_j^2}, \quad k = 1, \dots, N-1,$$

and define $D = \max(D^+, D^-)$, where

$$D^+ = \max_k \left(\frac{k - L_j' + 1}{\widehat{N}_j - 1} - \mathcal{P}_k \right) \quad \text{and} \quad D^- = \max_k \left(\mathcal{P}_k - \frac{k - L_j'}{\widehat{N}_j - 1} \right).$$

Percentage points for the distribution of D under the null hypothesis can be
readily obtained through Monte Carlo simulations. When $N = 2$,

$$P(D \le x) = \begin{cases} 0 & x < \frac{1}{2} \\ P\left\{ 1 - x \le B\left(\frac{1}{2}, \frac{1}{2}\right) \le x \right\} & \frac{1}{2} \le x < 1, \\ 1 & x \ge 1, \end{cases}$$

where $B(\frac{1}{2}, \frac{1}{2})$ is a beta random variable with parameters $\frac{1}{2}$ and $\frac{1}{2}$ (Whitcher,
1998). In order to perform hypothesis testing here, we require knowledge of the
distribution of D under H_0. Let x_p be the $p \times 100\%$ percentage point for this
distribution; that is, $P(D \le x_p) = p$. Inclán and Tiao (1994) proved that, for
large $\widehat{N}_j$ and $x_p > 0$,

$$P(D \le x_p) \approx 1 + 2 \sum_{l=1}^{\infty} (-1)^l e^{-l^2 \widehat{N}_j x_p^2}. \tag{7.14}$$

This large sample result was shown to be effective when $\widehat{N}_j$ exceeds 128. Another method is to develop an empirical distribution for D using Monte Carlo
simulations. That is, generate $\widehat{N}_j$ random variables with the appropriate characteristics, compute D, and repeat. Simulations of size 40,000 were used to
compute x_p in Whitcher *et al.* (1998).

7.3.1   Locating a Variance Change

Once an observed time series has been tested and the null hypothesis rejected at some scale λ_j, we have succeeded in detecting a significant change in variance somewhere in the series. It may be of interest to estimate where this change occurred, but the DWT has poor time resolution – especially as j increases. The MODWT provides a useful alternative to more precisely determine the location of a variance change after it has been detected. Through its superior time resolution, where each wavelet coefficient is associated with each t regardless of scale, the location of a variance change may be associated with a specific observation in the original time series. Let

$$
\widetilde{\mathcal{P}}_k = \frac{\sum_{t=L_j-1}^{k} \widetilde{w}_{j,t}^2}{\sum_{t=L_j-1}^{N-1} \widetilde{w}_{j,t}^2}, \quad k = L_j - 1, \dots, N - 2,
$$

and define $\widetilde{D} = \max(\widetilde{D}^+, \widetilde{D}^-)$, where

$$
\widetilde{D}^+ = \max_k \left(\frac{k - L_j + 2}{N - L_j} - \widetilde{\mathcal{P}}_k \right) \quad \text{and} \quad \widetilde{D}^- = \max_k \left(\widetilde{\mathcal{P}}_k - \frac{k - L_j + 1}{N - 1} \right).
$$

The estimated location of the variance change $\hat{k}$ is the point at which $\widetilde{D}$ is achieved. Whitcher (1998) showed that $\widetilde{D}$ can accurately locate a change of variance when applied to wavelet coefficients from long-memory processes. The accuracy of this method improves as the ratio of the variances before and after $\hat{k}$ moves away from unity. When the null hypothesis is rejected over several scales, the estimated location associated with the lowest level of the wavelet transform (highest frequency interval) is recommended.

7.3.2   Example: IBM Stock Prices

Here we apply the methodology developed in this section to daily IBM stock prices from May 17, 1961, to November 2, 1962. An obvious increase in volatility $v_t = |r_t|$ is observed in the latter half of the time series, as seen in the top portion of Figure 4.25, and was confirmed using the wavelet variance in Section 7.2.4. We now want to formally test for homogeneity of variance using the test statistic D in Section 7.3. Testing through the DWT is necessary because we cannot assume the volatility v_t has mean zero and is uncorrelated. The approximate decorrelation property of the DWT allows us to apply the test statistic to each subseries of wavelet coefficients. Although the time series is not a multiple of a power of two, we can easily adapt the procedure by first padding the series with $512 - 368 = 144$ zeros and then selecting on the first $\widehat{N}_j = \lfloor 368/2^j \rfloor$ wavelet coefficients in $\mathbf{w}_j$. The values of D for the first four scales are provided in Table 7.1, along with critical values computed via Monte Carlo simulations. Since D for $\lambda_1 = 1$ day is greater than any of the tabulated critical values, we can reject the null hypothesis of homogeneity of variance at all three critical levels.

λ_j	$\widehat{N}_j$	D	Critical levels		
			10%	5%	1%
1	184	0.4668	0.1503	0.1666	0.1995
2	92	0.4522	0.2107	0.2351	0.2832
3	46	0.4517	0.2989	0.3334	0.4007
4	23	0.2765	0.4287	0.4767	0.5689

TABLE 7.1 Results of testing IBM stock volatility for homogeneity of variance using the D(4) wavelet filter critical values determined by computer simulation.

We can also make the same statement for $\lambda_2 = 2$ days and $\lambda_3 = 4$ days. For the fourth scale, we cannot reject the null hypothesis at any reasonable level of significance.

After rejecting the null hypothesis of homogeneity of variance for the first three scales of IBM stock volatility, we can now estimate the location of the variance change point using the MODWT-based procedure in Section 7.3.1. The three lower panels in Figure 7.5 display the NCSS for the first three scales of its MODWT coefficients. As per the recommendation of Whitcher et al. (1998), we use the location estimate from the lowest scale of wavelet coefficients, which corresponds to observation 237. Inclán (1993) found evidence of two change points in the variance at observations 235 and 279 using her posterior odds technique.

de Alba and Boue (2000) found a very large probability of a change in variance at observation 235 and only weak evidence of a second variance change point conditional on the first. The wavelet-based procedure illustrated here was not designed to detect multiple change points and the IBM series was selected because of its obvious single variance change point. Additional methodology for testing the hypothesis of homogeneity of variance in financial time series is provided in Loretan and Phillips (1994). They developed techniques for so-called heavy-tail time series where the fourth moment is assumed to be infinite. Although not applied to daily IBM stock returns, Patterson and Ashley (2000, Ch. 6) looked for nonlinear serial dependence in the daily S&P 500 stock index and found a tendency to reject the hypothesis of linearity before the mid-1980s more frequently than afterward.

7.3.3 Extension: Multiple Variance Changes

In practice, a given time series may exhibit more than one change in variance. A natural approach is to test the entire series first, split at a detected change point, and repeat until no change points are found. This is known as a *binary segmentation* procedure studied by Vostrikova (1981), who proved its consistency. Inclán and Tiao (1994) used the binary segmentation procedure with the test statistic D to detect and locate changes of variance in sequences of independent and identically distributed (IID) Gaussian random variables. Chen and Gupta (1997) used

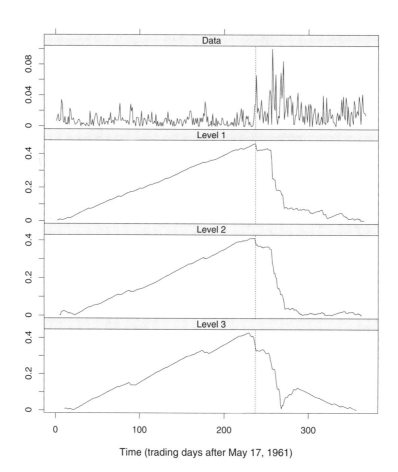

Time (trading days after May 17, 1961)

FIGURE 7.5   IBM stock price volatility (top panel) along with the normalized cumulative sum of squares for its MODWT coefficients for scales $\lambda_1 = 1$ days, $\lambda_2 = 2$ days, and $\lambda_3 = 4$ days. The dotted vertical line denotes the location of $\widetilde{D}$ for the scale λ_1 wavelet coefficients (observation 237).

a combination of this binary segmentation procedure with the Schwarz Information Criterion (SIC) to detect and locate changes of variance also in sequences of IID Gaussian random variables.

Whitcher *et al.* (2000a) used an iterated cumulative sum of squares (ICSS) procedure to test for multiple variance changes from the output of the DWT – in effect partitioning each vector of wavelet coefficients into 'stationary' segments. In order to reduce the computational time an asymptotic approximation to the distribution of D (Equation 7.14) was used. This has been shown to be adequate for sample sizes of 128 or greater (Whitcher *et al.*, 1998). For a sequence of wavelet coefficients excluding those affected by boundary conditions $w_{L'_j}, \ldots, w_{\widehat{N}_j - 1}$, the ICSS algorithm proceeds as follows (Inclán and Tiao, 1994):

1. Let $k_1 = L'_j$ and $\tilde{k}_1 = L_j - 1$.

2. Determine the test statistic D, via the equations in Section 7.3, using the wavelet coefficients $w_{k_1}, \ldots, w_{\widehat{N}_j - 1}$. If $D > x_p$ for a user-specified significance level p, define k_2 to be the location where D is achieved, then compute $\tilde{D}$ using the MODWT coefficients $\tilde{w}_{\tilde{k}_1}, \ldots, \tilde{w}_{N-1}$, record its location $\tilde{k}_2$, and proceed to the next step. If $D \leq x_p$, then stop.

3. Determine the test statistic D for the new time series $w_{k_1}, \ldots, w_{k_2 - 1}$. If $D > x_p$, then redefine k_2 to be the location where D is achieved, compute $\tilde{D}$ using the MODWT coefficients $\tilde{w}_{\tilde{k}_1}, \ldots, \tilde{w}_{\tilde{k}_2 - 1}$, redefine its location to be $\tilde{k}_2$, and begin the algorithm on the smaller sequence of wavelet coefficients. If $D \leq x_p$, then let k_0 and $\tilde{k}_0$ be the last change point.

4. Define $k_1 = k_2$ and $\tilde{k}_1 = \tilde{k}_2$. Determine the test statistic D for the new time series $w_{k_1}, \ldots, w_{\widehat{N}_j - 1}$. If $D > x_p$, then record the location where D is achieved, compute $\tilde{D}$ using the MODWT coefficients $\tilde{w}_{\tilde{k}_1 - 1}, \ldots, \tilde{w}_{N-1}$, record its location, and begin the algorithm on the smaller sequence of wavelet coefficients. If $D \leq x_p$, let k_∞ and $\tilde{k}_\infty$ be the last change point and then stop.

5. If $k_0 = k_\infty$, there is only one change point and the algorithm terminates. Otherwise there should be a sequence of change points whose estimated locations are $\tilde{k}_0, \ldots, \tilde{k}_\infty$. In increasing order go through the potential change points k_n by putting $w_{k_{n-1}}, \ldots, w_{k_{n+1}}$ through the algorithm. If a potential change point is not detected again, it is thrown out of the sequence and the process is repeated again on the reduced sequence of potential change points.

The final step prevents possible masking effects by adjacent change points and reduces an apparent overestimation of the number of change points in practice.

7.4 THE WAVELET COVARIANCE AND CROSS-COVARIANCE

Given the usefulness of the wavelet variance for univariate (one-variable) time series, this section investigates multivariate generalizations like the *wavelet covariance* and *wavelet correlation* for bivariate time series. Section 4.7.2 performed Granger causality tests between money and output in several developed countries. This section expands wavelet methodology to easily handle two observed time series. As the name of the section implies, the wavelet covariance is the covariance between the scale λ_j wavelet coefficients from a bivariate time series and the wavelet correlation is the correlation between the scale λ_j wavelet coefficients from a bivariate time series. If we introduce a lag τ between the two series, we obtain the wavelet cross-covariance and wavelet cross-correlation as natural extensions to their classical time series analogs.

Let $X_t = (x_{1,t}, x_{2,t})$ be a bivariate stochastic process with univariate spectra (also known as *autospectra*) $S_1(f)$ and $S_2(f)$, respectively, and let $W_{j,t} = (w_{1,j,t}, w_{2,j,t})$ be the scale λ_j wavelet coefficients computed from X_t. Each wavelet coefficient process is obtained from applying the wavelet transform to each process in X_t one at a time. The wavelet covariance of $(x_{1,t}, x_{2,t})$ for scale λ_j is defined to be

$$\gamma_X(\lambda_j) = \frac{1}{2\lambda_j} \operatorname{Cov}(w_{1,j,t}, w_{2,j,t}). \tag{7.15}$$

If the length of the wavelet filter is sufficient to eliminate any nonstationary features in both $x_{1,t}$ and $x_{2,t}$, then we may simply define the wavelet covariance via the expectation $\gamma_X(\lambda_j) = E(w_{1,j,t} w_{2,j,t})/(2\lambda_j)$ since we are guaranteed to have mean zero wavelet coefficients.

As with the wavelet variance for univariate processes, the wavelet covariance decomposes the covariance between two stochastic processes on a scale-by-scale basis (Whitcher, 1998). Let X_t be defined as before, then

$$\sum_{j=1}^{\infty} \gamma_X(\lambda_j) = \operatorname{Cov}(x_{1,t}, x_{2,t}); \tag{7.16}$$

that is, the wavelet covariance decomposes the covariance of a bivariate process on a scale-by-scale basis. If we define $S_X(f)$ to be the *cross spectrum* between $x_{1,t}$ and $x_{2,t}$, then this is intuitively plausible since the wavelet covariance is capturing smaller and smaller portions of the cross spectrum as λ_j increases ($f \to 0$). By introducing an integer lag τ between $w_{1,j,t}$ and $w_{2,j,t}$, we establish a definition for the *wavelet cross-covariance*

$$\gamma_{X,\tau}(\lambda_j) = \frac{1}{2\lambda_j} \operatorname{Cov}(w_{1,j,t}, w_{2,j,t+\tau}).$$

The decomposition of covariance given in Equation 7.16 is still valid provided one uses the MODWT to construct $\gamma_{\tau,X}(\lambda_j)$. The lack of translation invariance from the DWT disrupts the lag-resolution of the wavelet cross-covariance and should *not* be used to estimate $\gamma_{\tau,X}(\lambda_j)$ in practice.

7.4.1 Estimation

Suppose

$$
\begin{aligned}
X &= (X_0, X_1, \dots, X_{N-1}) \\
&= ((x_{1,0}, x_{2,0}), (x_{1,1}, x_{2,1}), \dots, (x_{1,N-1}, x_{2,N-1}))
\end{aligned}
$$

is a length N realization of the bivariate stochastic process X_t and apply a partial MODWT of order $J_p < \log_2(T)$ to each univariate process $x_{1,t}$ and $x_{2,t}$, thus producing J length N vectors of MODWT coefficients

$$\widetilde{\boldsymbol{W}}_j = \left(\widetilde{W}_{j,0}, \widetilde{W}_{j,1}, \ldots, \widetilde{W}_{j,N-1}\right)$$
$$= \left((\widetilde{w}_{1,j,0}, \widetilde{w}_{2,j,0}), (\widetilde{w}_{1,j,1}, \widetilde{w}_{2,j,1}), \ldots, (\widetilde{w}_{1,1,N/2^j-1}, \widetilde{w}_{2,1,N/2^j-1})\right),$$

and the length N vector of MODWT scaling coefficients

$$\widetilde{\boldsymbol{V}}_J = \left(\widetilde{V}_{J,0}, \widetilde{V}_{J,1}, \ldots, \widetilde{V}_{J,N-1}\right)$$
$$= \left((\widetilde{v}_{1,J,0}, \widetilde{v}_{2,J,0}), (\widetilde{v}_{1,J,1}, \widetilde{v}_{2,J,1}), \ldots, (\widetilde{v}_{1,1,N/2^J-1}, \widetilde{v}_{2,1,N/2^J-1})\right)$$

(Section 4.5). An unbiased estimator of the wavelet covariance based upon the MODWT is given by

$$\tilde{\gamma}_X(\lambda_j) = \frac{1}{\widetilde{N}_j} \sum_{l=L_j-1}^{N-1} \widetilde{w}_{1,j,l}\widetilde{w}_{2,j,l}, \qquad (7.17)$$

where $\widetilde{N}_j = N - L_j + 1$. This estimator does not include any coefficients that are affected by the boundary. A biased estimator of the wavelet covariance is constructed by simply including the MODWT wavelet coefficients affected by the boundary into Equation 7.17 and renormalizing. As alluded to in the previous section, estimation via the DWT is not discussed here. Whitcher (1998) found that the variance of the DWT-based estimator of $\gamma_X(\lambda_j)$ depends on the lag between $x_{1,t}$ and $x_{2,t}$, whereas the variance of the MODWT-based estimator is invariant with respect to the lag. Since the lag between time series in practice is generally not assumed to be known, it is therefore important to have an estimator that is invariant to circular translation.

The large-sample properties of $\tilde{\gamma}_X(\lambda_j)$ are relatively well established for a wide range of Gaussian and non-Gaussian bivariate processes. The estimator $\tilde{\gamma}_X(\lambda_j)$ is asymptotically Gaussian distributed with mean $\gamma_X(\lambda_j)$ and variance $S_{\varpi,j}(0)/\widetilde{N}_j$, where $S_{\varpi,j}(0)$ is the spectral density function (SDF) of the product of the scale λ_j wavelet coefficients $\varpi_{j,t} = w_{1,j,t}w_{2,j,t}$ evaluated at zero frequency and is given by

$$S_{\varpi,j}^{\mathrm{G}}(0) = \int_{-1/2}^{1/2} S_{1,j}(f)S_{2,j}(f)\,df + \int_{-1/2}^{1/2} S_W^2(f)\,df \qquad (7.18)$$

(Whitcher, 1998; Whitcher et al., 2000b). The autospectra $S_{1,j}(f)$ and $S_{2,j}(f)$ denote, respectively, the SDFs for $w_{1,j,t}$ and $w_{2,j,t}$, while $S_{W,j}(f)$ is the cross spectrum between $w_{1,j,t}$ and $w_{2,j,t}$. This result holds when $W_{j,t}$ is a bivariate Gaussian stationary process.

Results are still available if we relax the assumption of Gaussianity on X_t. For a broad class of non-Gaussian processes, $\tilde{\gamma}_X(\lambda_j)$ is again asymptotically Gaussian distributed with mean $\gamma_X(\lambda_j)$ and large-sample variance given by $S_{\varpi,j}(0)/\widetilde{N}_j$, where $S_{\varpi,j}(0)$ is the SDF of the product of the scale λ_j wavelet coefficients but has no convenient form as in Equation 7.18 (Serroukh and Walden, 2000).

Estimation of the wavelet cross-covariance follows directly from the biased estimator of the usual cross-covariance. For $N \geq L_j$, a biased estimator of the wavelet cross-covariance based on the MODWT is given by

$$\tilde{\gamma}_{X,\tau}(\lambda_j) = \begin{cases} \tilde{N}_j^{-1} \sum_{t=L_j-1}^{N-\tau-1} \tilde{w}_{1,j,t} \tilde{w}_{2,j,t+\tau} & \tau = 0, \ldots, \tilde{N}_j - 1 \\ \tilde{N}_j^{-1} \sum_{t=L_j-1-\tau}^{N-1} \tilde{w}_{1,j,t} \tilde{w}_{2,j,t+\tau} & \tau = -1, \ldots, -(\tilde{N}_j - 1) \\ 0 & \text{otherwise.} \end{cases}$$

(7.19)

Although the estimator is biased, no wavelet coefficients affected by the boundary are included in the calculation. Large-sample results for $\tilde{\gamma}_{X,\tau}(\lambda_j)$ follow from the arguments above, but now all quantities are a function of the lag τ since we are interested in analyzing the bivariate process $W_{j,t,\tau}$; that is, $S_{\varpi,j,\tau}(0)$ is the SDF of the product of univariate wavelet processes $\varpi_{j,t,\tau} = w_{1,j,t} w_{2,j,t+\tau}$, and so on.

7.4.2 Confidence Intervals

Confidence intervals for the wavelet covariance and cross-covariance follow from the large-sample result in the previous section. We make use of the basic form for a Gaussian CI in Section 7.2.2 and proceed by first estimating the variance of $\tilde{\gamma}_X(\lambda_j)$ using periodogram-based estimators. If X is a length N realization of a bivariate Gaussian process, then the SDF for the product of the scale λ_j wavelet coefficients $S_{\varpi,j}(0)$ is given by Equation 7.18 and is a function of the autospectra and cross spectrum of the scale λ_j wavelet coefficients. We propose to estimate these spectral quantities using the periodograms $\widehat{S}_{1,j}^{\text{p}}(f)$, $\widehat{S}_{2,j}^{\text{p}}(f)$ and cross-periodogram $\widehat{S}_{W,j}^{\text{p}}(f)$ to produce an estimator for $S_{\varpi,j}^{\text{G}}(0)$.

Parseval's relation allows us to formulate an alternative representation for $\widehat{S}_{\varpi,j}^{\text{G}}(0)$ that uses only the autocovariance and cross-covariance sequences instead of the autospectra and cross spectrum. Using Parseval's relation the first integral in Equation 7.20, substituting periodogram-based estimators for the autospectra, may be re-expressed via

$$\int_{-1/2}^{1/2} \widehat{S}_{1,j}^{\text{p}}(f) \widehat{S}_{2,j}^{\text{p}}(f) \, df = \sum_{m=-(\tilde{N}_j-1)}^{\tilde{N}_j-1} \hat{\gamma}_{1,j,m} \hat{\gamma}_{2,j,m},$$

where $\hat{\gamma}_{1,j,m}$ and $\hat{\gamma}_{2,j,m}$ are biased estimators of the ACVS for $w_{1,j,t}$ and $w_{2,j,t}$. The second integral in Equation 7.20, substituting the cross-periodogram for the cross spectrum, may be re-expressed via

$$\int_{-1/2}^{1/2} \left[\widehat{S}_{W,j}^{\text{p}}(f) \right]^2 df = \sum_{m=-(\tilde{N}_j-1)}^{\tilde{N}_j-1} \hat{\gamma}_{W,j,m}^2,$$

where $\hat{\gamma}_{W,j,m}$ is the biased sample cross-covariance sequence (CCVS) between the scale λ_j wavelet coefficients $w_{1,j,t}$ and $w_{2,j,t}$. Combining the results from Parseval's relation yields the following unbiased estimator for $S_{\varpi,j}(0)$ under the assumption of Gaussianity:

$$\widehat{S}^G_{\varpi,j}(0) = \frac{\hat{\gamma}_{1,j,0}\hat{\gamma}_{2,j,0}}{2} + \sum_{m=1}^{\tilde{N}_j-1} \hat{\gamma}_{1,j,m}\hat{\gamma}_{2,j,m} + \frac{1}{2} \sum_{m=-(\tilde{N}_j-1)}^{\tilde{N}_j-1} \hat{\gamma}^2_{W,j,m}$$

(Whitcher, 1998; Whitcher *et al.*, 2000b). Substituting $\tilde{\gamma}_X(\lambda_j)$, $\widehat{S}^G_{\varpi,j}(0)$ and $\tilde{N}_j$ into Equation 7.8 produces an approximate $(1 - \alpha)$ CI for $\gamma_X(\lambda_j)$ given by

$$\tilde{\gamma}_X(\lambda_j) \pm \zeta_{\frac{\alpha}{2}} \left[\frac{\widehat{S}^p_{\varpi,j}(0)}{\tilde{N}_j} \right]^{1/2}. \tag{7.20}$$

If we do not restrict ourselves to an underlying Gaussian bivariate stochastic process, we must forgo the previous argument and estimate $S_{\varpi,j}(0)$ directly. Serroukh and Walden (2000) used multitaper spectrum estimation to produce an estimator $\widehat{S}^{mt}_{\varpi,j}(0)$ of the SDF for the product of the scale λ_j wavelet coefficients evaluated at zero frequency. Substituting $\tilde{\gamma}_X(\lambda_j)$, $\widehat{S}^{mt}_{\varpi,j}(0)$ and $\tilde{N}_j$ into Equation 7.8 gives the approximate $(1 - \alpha)$ CI

$$\tilde{\gamma}_X(\lambda_j) \pm \zeta_{\frac{\alpha}{2}} \left[\frac{\widehat{S}^{mt}_{\varpi,j}(0)}{\tilde{N}_j} \right]^{1/2},$$

for a wider class of bivariate processes.

7.4.3 Example: Monthly Foreign Exchange Rates

We perform a wavelet variance/covariance analysis of monthly foreign exchange rates for the Deutsche Mark – U.S. Dollar (DEM-USD) and Japanese Yen – U.S. Dollar (JPY-USD). Here we investigate the returns series $r_t = \log(p_t) - \log(p_{t+1})$; see Figure 7.6. Both series appear to have similar characteristics, in terms of mean and variance, but a more thorough description is available to use through a multiscale analysis.

Figures 7.7a and 7.7b show the MODWT-based wavelet variances for the DEM-USD and JPY-USD returns series using the D(4) wavelet filter. Approximate confidence intervals were computed using Equation 7.11. There is virtually no difference between the two plots. This means the two series appear to exhibit the same variability at all six wavelet scales.

A natural question to ask is how well these two series are associated with one another. The wavelet covariance is a measure of this association when comparing the two series at the same time point. Figure 7.8 provides the MODWT-based wavelet covariance $\tilde{\gamma}_X(\lambda_j)$ with approximate confidence interval given by Equation 7.20. The wavelet covariance follows a similar pattern to the wavelet variance

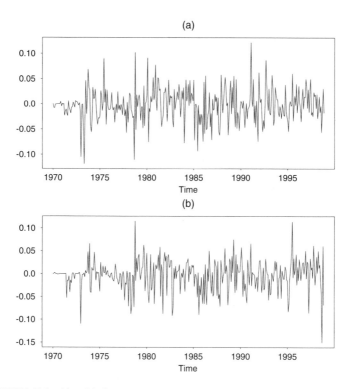

FIGURE 7.6   Monthly foreign exchange returns spanning 1970:1–1998:12 ($N = 347$) for (a) Deutsche Mark – U.S. Dollar and (b) Japanese Yen – U.S. Dollar.

given in Figure 7.7 – that is, it roughly decreases with increasing wavelet scale. The wavelet covariances are positive and appear to be significantly different from zero (at the $\alpha = 0.05$ level of significance) except for the last two wavelet scales shown. Although there appears to be positive association between the two returns series, it is difficult to compare wavelet scales because of the differing variability exhibited by them. Standardizing by the variance of each series, at each scale, would be a simple way of overcoming this influence and make it possible to compare the magnitude of the association across scales. The wavelet correlation is therefore a natural quantity to use instead of the wavelet covariance. An analysis of the wavelet cross-correlation between these two series is provided in Section 7.5.3.

7.5 THE WAVELET CORRELATION AND CROSS-CORRELATION

Although the wavelet covariance decomposes the covariance between two stochastic processes on a scale-by-scale basis, in some situations it may be beneficial

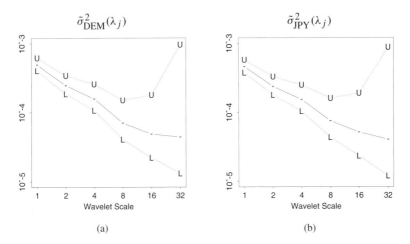

FIGURE 7.7 Wavelet variance for the (a) DEM-USD and (b) JPY-USD exchange rate returns. The dashed lines with the characters "L" and "U" denote the lower and upper bounds for the approximate 95% confidence interval , respectively. Notice there is very little difference between the two sets of estimated wavelet variances at all scales.

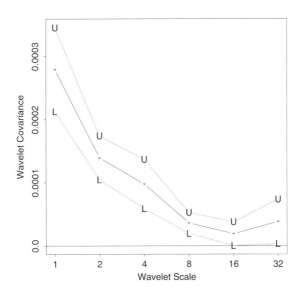

FIGURE 7.8 Wavelet covariance between the DEM-USD and JPY-USD exchange rate returns. The dashed lines with the characters "L" and "U" denote the lower and upper bounds for the approximate 95% confidence interval , respectively.

to normalize the wavelet covariance by the variability inherent in the observed wavelet coefficients. This leads to another statistical quantity, based on the wavelet covariance, the *wavelet correlation* defined to be

$$\rho_X(\lambda_j) = \frac{\gamma_X(\lambda_j)}{\sigma_1(\lambda_j)\sigma_2(\lambda_j)},$$

where $\sigma_1^2(\lambda_j)$ and $\sigma_2^2(\lambda_j)$ are, respectively, the wavelet variances for $x_{1,t}$ and $x_{2,t}$ associated with scale λ_j. As with the usual correlation coefficient between two random variables, $|\rho_X(\lambda_j)| \leq 1$. The wavelet correlation is analogous to its Fourier equivalent, the complex coherency (Section 7.7.4). Allowing the two processes to differ by an integer lag τ, we define the *wavelet cross-correlation*

$$\rho_{X,\tau}(\lambda_j) = \frac{\gamma_{X,\tau}(\lambda_j)}{\sigma_1(\lambda_j)\sigma_2(\lambda_j)}.$$

Just as the usual cross-correlation is used to determine lead/lag relationships between two processes, the wavelet cross-correlation should be able to provide a lead/lag relationship on a scale-by-scale basis.

7.5.1   Estimation

Since the wavelet correlation is simply made up of the wavelet covariance for $X_t = (x_{1,t}, x_{2,t})$ and wavelet variances for $x_{1,t}$ and $x_{2,t}$, an unbiased estimator of the wavelet correlation based on the MODWT is given by

$$\tilde{\rho}_X(\lambda_j) = \frac{\tilde{\gamma}_X(\lambda_j)}{\tilde{\sigma}_1(\lambda_j)\tilde{\sigma}_2(\lambda_j)}, \tag{7.21}$$

where $\tilde{\gamma}_X(\lambda_j)$ is defined as in Equation 7.17, and $\tilde{\sigma}_1^2(\lambda_j)$ and $\tilde{\sigma}_2^2(\lambda_j)$ are computed via Equation 7.6. To compute the biased estimator of the wavelet cross-correlation $\tilde{\rho}_{X,\tau}(\lambda_j)$, simply insert the estimated wavelet cross-covariance $\tilde{\gamma}_{X,\tau}(\lambda_j)$ (Equation 7.19) into Equation 7.21.

The large-sample theory of $\tilde{\rho}_X(\lambda_j)$ has been established for Gaussian stationary and certain nonstationary processes. The wavelet correlation is a nonlinear function of the wavelet covariance and wavelet variances, which are essentially sample means of vectors of MODWT coefficients; that is,

$$\bar{a}_j = \tilde{\sigma}_1^2(\lambda_j) = \frac{1}{\tilde{N}_j}\sum_{t=L_j-1}^{N-1} \tilde{w}_{1,j,t}^2$$

$$\bar{b}_j = \tilde{\sigma}_2^2(\lambda_j) = \frac{1}{\tilde{N}_j}\sum_{t=L_j-1}^{N-1} \tilde{w}_{2,j,t}^2$$

$$\bar{c}_j = \tilde{\gamma}_X(\lambda_j) = \frac{1}{\tilde{N}_j}\sum_{t=L_j-1}^{N-1} \varpi_{j,t}.$$

Hence, we may express the wavelet correlation via

$$\tilde{\rho}_X(\lambda_j) = g\left(\bar{a}_j, \bar{b}_j, \bar{c}_j\right) = \frac{\bar{c}_j}{\sqrt{\bar{a}_j \bar{b}_j}}.$$

Applying the Mann–Wald theorem, we know that the estimator $\tilde{\rho}_X(\lambda_j)$ is asymptotically Gaussian distributed with mean $\rho_X(\lambda_j)$ and large sample variance $R_{abc,j}(0)/\tilde{N}_j$, where

$$R_{abc,j}(0) = \nabla g_{abc,j}^T S_{abc,j}(0) \nabla g_{abc,j}, \tag{7.22}$$

with $\nabla g_{abc,j}$ being the gradient vector of $g(a_j, b_j, c_j)$ and $S_{abc,j}(0)$ being the 3×3 spectral matrix defined via

$$S_{abc,j}(0) = \begin{bmatrix} S_{a^2,j}(0) & S_{ab,j}(0) & S_{ac,j}(0) \\ S_{ab,j}(0) & S_{b^2,j}(0) & S_{bc,j}(0) \\ S_{ac,j}(0) & S_{bc,j}(0) & S_{c^2,j}(0) \end{bmatrix}$$

(Whitcher, 1998). Assuming X_t is a Gaussian bivariate process, then $R_{abc,j}(0)$ may be expressed as a linear combination of wavelet autocorrelation and cross-correlation sequences of $W_{j,t}$; see, for example, Brockwell and Davis (1991, p. 416). Large-sample results for the wavelet cross-correlation $\tilde{\rho}_{X,\tau}(\lambda_j)$ follow from the arguments above, but now all quantities are a function of the lag τ since we are interested in analyzing the bivariate process $W_{j,t,\tau}$.

7.5.2 Confidence Intervals

We now use the large-sample result provided in the previous section to construct CIs for the wavelet correlation and cross-correlation. Similar to the wavelet covariance, using asymptotic normality of $\tilde{\rho}_X(\lambda_j)$ we may start from the basic form of Equation 7.8 for the CI. The difficulty lies in estimating $R_{abc,j}(0)$. As previously discussed, we may express Equation 7.22 as a linear combination of scale λ_j wavelet autocorrelation and cross-correlation sequences assuming X_t is Gaussian (Whitcher, 1998). Substituting $\tilde{\rho}_X(\lambda_j)$, $\widehat{R}_{abc,j}^G(0)$ and $\tilde{N}_j$ into Equation 7.8 produces an approximate $(1 - \alpha)$ CI for $\rho_X(\lambda_j)$ given by

$$\tilde{\rho}_X(\lambda_j) \pm \zeta_{\frac{\alpha}{2}} \left[\frac{\widehat{R}_{abc,j}^G(0)}{\tilde{N}_j} \right]^{1/2}. \tag{7.23}$$

The CI in Equation 7.23 does *not* have to produce an interval that is bounded by ± 1, although we know that $|\rho_X(\lambda_j)| \leq 1$. It is also well known that the correlation coefficient is distinctly non-Gaussian when estimated using small sample sizes. A nonlinear transformation is sometimes required to produce reasonable CIs for the correlation coefficient – Fisher's z-transformation (Kotz et al., 1982, Volume 3), which is defined to be

$$h(\rho) = \tanh^{-1}(\rho).$$

For an estimated correlation coefficient $\hat{\rho}$, based on N independent Gaussian observations,

$$\sqrt{N-3}\left[h(\hat{\rho}) - h(\rho)\right] \sim N(0, 1). \tag{7.24}$$

The factor $\sqrt{N-3}$ leads to a better approximation of the standard normal distribution. Hence, substituting $h[\tilde{\rho}_X(\lambda_j)]$, 1 and $\widehat{N}_j$ into Equation 7.8 produces an approximate $(1 - \alpha)$ CI for $h(\rho_X(\lambda_j))$ which lives on $[-\infty, \infty]$. Applying the transformation tanh maps the CI back to $[-1, 1]$ to produce an approximate $(1 - \alpha)$ CI for $\rho_X(\lambda_j)$ given by

$$\tanh\left\{ h[\tilde{\rho}_X(\lambda_j)] \pm \zeta_{\frac{\alpha}{2}} \left(\frac{1}{\widehat{N}_j - 3} \right)^{1/2} \right\}. \tag{7.25}$$

The quantity $\widehat{N}_j$ is the number DWT coefficients associated with scale λ_j. The assumption of uncorrelated observations in order to use the distributional statement from Fisher's z-transformation (Equation 7.24) is only valid if we believe no systematic trends or nonstationary features exist in both scale λ_j wavelet processes $w_{1,j,t}$ and $w_{2,j,t}$. From Section 5.2.2 we know that the DWT approximately decorrelates a wide range of times series and thus provides a reasonable measure of the scale-dependent sample size.

7.5.3 Example: Monthly Foreign Exchange Rates

Figure 7.9 shows the wavelet cross-correlation between the DEM-USD and JPY-USD exchange rate returns previously analyzed in Section 7.4.3 using the D(4) wavelet filter. The correlation estimates are better quantities to look at since each covariance estimate has been standardized by the standard deviations of the individual series. Approximate confidence intervals were computed using Equation 7.25 and are not symmetric about zero because of the hyperbolic tangent function.

The first three scales, associated with periods of 1–2, 2–4, and 4–8 months, indicate only a small number of lags (mostly around zero) where the wavelet cross-correlation is different from zero (positive) and then a group of lags (both positive and negative) that show a slight negative wavelet correlation. These negative correlations appear to fall after one period. All three wavelet cross-correlations appear to be roughly symmetric about zero lag. The wavelet cross-correlation function on scale λ_4, associated with 8- to 16-month oscillations and therefore capturing the annual cycle, is quite asymmetric where the DEM-USD series is correlated with the JPY-USD series at lag zero and then again around one year in the past. This memory does not exist when looking at how the past DEM-USD series is related to the present JPY-USD exchange rate returns. There is no statistically significant correlation between the two series at wavelet scale λ_5 (periods of 16–32 months). There is again a slight positive correlation between DEM-USD and JPY-USD exchange rate returns when looking at longer periods (i.e., scale λ_6 which is associated with 32- to 64-month periods).

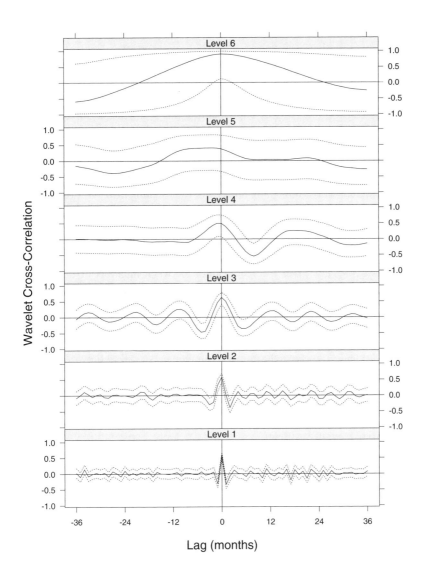

FIGURE 7.9 Wavelet cross-correlation between the DEM-USD and JPY-USD exchange rate returns. The individual cross-correlation functions correspond to – from bottom to top – wavelet scales $\lambda_1, \ldots, \lambda_6$, which are associated with changes of 1, 2, 4, 8, 16, and 32 months. The dotted lines bound the approximate 95% confidence interval for the wavelet cross-correlation. At each wavelet scale there are only a few lags, very close to zero, which do *not* include zero and therefore indicate multiscale correlations significantly different from zero.

7.6   APPLICATIONS

7.6.1   Scaling Laws in FX Markets

In this section we examine the behavior of the size of the foreign exchange (FX) returns as a function of the data frequency. There is no privileged time interval to restrain the investigation of a data-generation process and it is important to study how the different data frequencies relate to each other. Within the context of the FX markets, one way of implementing this is to analyze the dependence of the expectation of volatility on the time interval on which the returns are measured. For stochastic processes like the random walk, this dependence gives rise to very simple scaling laws. Since the study of Müller *et al.* (1990), which empirically documents the existence of scaling laws in FX rates, there has been a large volume of work confirming these empirical scaling laws; see, for example, Fisher *et al.* (1997), Weron *et al.* (1999), Andersen *et al.* (2001), and Mantegna and Stanley (2000). This evidence is confirmed with other financial instruments (Mantegna and Stanley, 1995; Ballocchi *et al.*, 1999) and examined theoretically in Barndorff-Nielsen and Prause (2001).

The scaling law gives a direct relation between intervals of time Δt and the average volatility measured as a certain power p of the absolute returns (or volatility)

$$\left\{ E[|r|^p] \right\}^{1/p} = c(p)\Delta t^{D(p)}, \tag{7.26}$$

where $c(p)$ and $D(p)$ are deterministic functions. We call D the *drift exponent*, similar to the characterization of Mandelbrot (1983). We choose this form for the left-hand-side of Equation 7.26 in order to obtain, for a Gaussian random walk, a constant drift exponent of 0.5 whatever the choice of p. A typical choice is $p = 1$, which corresponds to absolute returns or volatility. Taking the logarithm of Equation 7.26, the estimation of c and D can be carried out by an ordinary least squares (OLS) regression (Section 4.5).

In principle, a scaling law study can empirically be implemented by a measure of volatility. There are two limitations to the precision of the estimation of realized volatility. For long time intervals (a year and more) it becomes difficult to assess the statistical significance of the volatility estimation since there are not more than a handful of independent observations. This number grows and the noise shrinks when the return measurement intervals shrink, but then the measurement bias starts to grow. Until now, the only choice was a clever trade-off between the noise and the bias, which led to typical return intervals of about an hour. Tick frequency and data gaps play a major role. The goal is to define a superior realized volatility that combines the low noise of short return interval sizes with the low bias of large return intervals.

Instead of calculating realized volatilities at different data frequencies, Gençay *et al.* (2001a) proceeded with a multiresolution analysis (MRA) implemented through the MODWT (Section 4.5). The studied data sets are the 5-min Deutsche Mark – U.S. Dollar (DEM-USD) and Japanese Yen – U.S. Dollar

(JPY-USD) price series for the period from December 1, 1986, to December 1, 1996.[2] Bid and ask prices at each 5-min interval are obtained by linear interpolation. Prices are computed as the average of the logarithm of thebid and ask prices:

$$P_t = \frac{1}{2}\left[\log P_t(\text{bid}) + \log P_t(\text{ask})\right], \quad t = 1, \dots, 751, 645. \quad (7.27)$$

Olsen & Associates applied data cleaning filters to the price series (as received from Reuters) in order to correct for data errors and to remove suspected outliers. We also removed the weekend quotes from Friday 21:05 GMT to Sunday 21:00 GMT. Apart from this, we did not apply any further filtering to the data set nor did we exclude any data points. Continuously compounded 5-min returns are calculated by

$$r_{t_5} = 100 \cdot (P_t - P_{t-1}), \quad t_5 = 1, \dots, 751, 644. \quad (7.28)$$

It is often argued that price changes observed at very high frequencies can be overly biased by the buying and selling intentions of the quoting institutions (Guillaume *et al.*, 1997). We therefore decided to work with 20-minute aggregated returns[3] defined via

$$r_{t_{20}} = \sum_{i=0}^{3} r_{t_5-i}, \quad t_{20} = 1, \dots, 187, 911. \quad (7.29)$$

Therefore, our sample covers 2610 business days in 10 years with 72 observations per day.[4] The 20-min volatilities are defined to be the 20-min absolute returns $|r_{t,20}|$.

We use $|r_{t,20}|$ to obtain the MODWT decomposition of the variances of absolute return series on a scale-by-scale basis for both DEM-USD and JPY-USD series. The study covers wavelet scales from 20-min to approximately one month. This coverage is achieved with a MODWT ($J = 12$) decomposition using an LA(8) wavelet filter. It is important to note that the MODWT MRA methodology does not assume any distributional form for the returns.

Our results provide evidence that the scaling behavior breaks for returns measured at higher intervals than one day; see also Gençay *et al.* (2001a). Figure 7.10 reports the decomposition of the variance on a scale-by-scale basis through the MODWT MRA.[5] For example, the first wavelet scale λ_1 is associated with changes at 20-min, the second wavelet scale λ_2 is associated with $2 \cdot 20 = 40$-min changes, and so on. Each increasing scale captures lower frequencies from the original process. The first six scales ($\lambda_1, \dots, \lambda_6$) capture

---

[2] The data set is provided by Olsen & Associates in Zürich, Switzerland.

[3] We could have worked with the raw data set and simply ignored wavelet scales associated with higher frequencies. However, aggregation greatly reduces the computational burden.

[4] The last day in the sample is a Friday. Since we removed the weekend quotes starting from Friday 21:05, there are only 63 20-min return observations for the last day in the sample. Therefore, the sample size is $N = (72 \cdot 209) + 63 = 187, 911$.

[5] An extensive study of scaling in economics and finance is presented in Dacorogna *et al.* (2001).

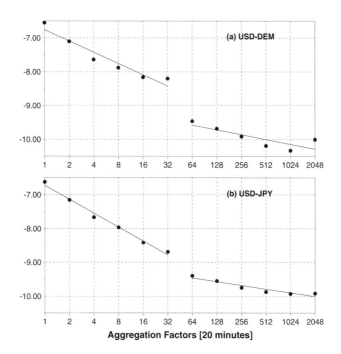

FIGURE 7.10   MODWT MRA ($J = 12$) wavelet variance for 20-min absolute returns of (a) USD-DEM and (b) USD-JPY from December 1, 1986, through December 1, 1996 on a log-log scale. The circles are the estimated variances for each wavelet scale and the straight lines are ordinary least squares (OLS) estimates. Each wavelet scale is associated with a particular time period (e.g., the first wavelet scale λ_1 is associated with 20-min changes, the second wavelet scale λ_2 with $2 \cdot 20 = 40$-min changes, the third wavelet scale λ_3 with $2^2 \cdot 20 = 160$-min changes, and so on). The seventh wavelet scale λ_7 is associated with $2^7 \cdot 20 = 1280$-min changes. Since there are 1440 minutes per day, λ_7 corresponds to approximately one day. The last wavelet scale λ_{12} is associated with changes of approximately 28 days.

frequencies $1/128 \leq f \leq 1/2$; that is, oscillations with a period of 40–2560 minutes. Since there are $72 \cdot 20 = 1440$ minutes in one day, we conclude that the first six scales are related to the intraday dynamics of the observed time series.

An apparent break in the scaling law is observed in the variance at the seventh wavelet scale λ_7 (associated with $64 \cdot 20 = 1280$-min changes) for both the DEM-USD and JPY-USD series. Since there are 1440 minutes in one day, the seventh scale corresponds to 0.89 day. Therefore, the seventh and higher scales are taken to be related to one day and higher dynamics.

7.6.2   Multiscale Beta Estimation

In Section 3.6.4, the capital-asset pricing model, the CAPM of Sharpe (1964) and Lintner (1965) was introduced. A simple time-varying beta estimation of the CAPM with the Kalman filter was also presented in the same section. In this

	Coca-Cola	GE	GM	IBM	P&G	SR
Raw data	0.75	1.18	0.88	1.07	0.87	0.93
λ_1	2.41	1.77	1.31	2.09	1.47	0.70
λ_2	1.83	1.29	1.98	1.93	0.88	2.34
λ_3	1.22	1.18	0.69	0.43	1.08	0.67
λ_4	0.81	1.20	0.91	1.23	0.57	0.97
λ_5	0.72	1.27	0.93	0.94	0.46	0.95
λ_6	0.64	1.24	0.93	0.92	0.83	0.93
λ_7	0.73	1.19	0.93	0.92	0.91	0.99

TABLE 7.2 Wavelet estimates of betas for different companies. Return series are calculated form daily observations. Wavelet analysis is based on MODWT using the LA(8) wavelet filters. The first detail λ_j captures oscillations with a period length of 2 to 4 days. The last detail λ_7 captures oscillations with a period length of 128 to 256 days. GE: General Electric, GM: General Motors, IBM: International Business Machines, P&G: Procter & Gamble, SR: Sears Roebuck. Sample period is December 31, 1993, to July 28, 2000. Source: Datastream

section, we introduce *multiscale beta estimation* with wavelets (i.e., a changing beta with changing scale).

In finance literature, there are several capital asset pricing models to describe how investors assess the risk and value of different cash flows. Among them, the CAPM is the most commonly used one by financial managers. According to the CAPM model, the risk of a project is measured by the beta of the cash flow with respect to market return. The beta of a company is defined as

$$\beta_i = \frac{\text{Cov}(r_{it}, r_{mt})}{\sigma_m^2}, \tag{7.30}$$

where $\text{Cov}(r_{it}, r_{mt})$ is the covariance between the return r_{it} on investing in project i and market return r_{mt}. The variance of the market return is denoted by σ_m^2. A low beta value for a company (or a project) would indicate a relatively low risk, while a beta greater than one would indicate a risky investment.

Wavelet cross-covariance and wavelet variance can be utilized to estimate company (or industrial) betas at different timescales. Specifically, a zero-lag wavelet cross-covariance between daily return for an asset and daily return in the market at a particular detail can be divided by the wavelet variance of the market return at that specific detail to obtain a *timescale beta* of a company. In other words, we can substitute the wavelet covariance and the wavelet variance at each scale into Equation 7.30 to obtain the beta at that particular scale.

Table 7.2 presents wavelet-based betas for six different companies: Coca-Cola, General Electric, General Motors, IBM, Procter & Gamble, and Sears

Roebuck. We obtained price series from the Datastream for the sample period of December 31, 1993, to July 28, 2000. We choose this particular sample period since there were no major business cycles during this time. Market return is taken as the daily percentage change in Standard & Poors (S&P) 500 Index.

Wavelet betas at different details reveal important information about how risky a particular asset is. For example, raw data (average of all time scales) indicates that Coca-Cola stocks have relatively small risk. However, wavelet analysis shows that the Coca-Cola shares are much riskier at the first three scales relative to higher scales. An investor operating at the first three scales would be subject to a high risk by holding a Coca-Cola share in his or her portfolio, contrary what the OLS estimate suggests about this stock. The riskiness of the Coca-Cola stock declines with increasing scales. A similar pattern is observed for IBM and General Motors and a similar argument can be put forward for these stocks as well (i.e., the riskiness of a stock is scale dependent and enough care should be taken). Sears Roebuck gives a different picture. The riskiness of this stock is also scale dependent. However, its riskiness increases with increasing scale. On the other hand, the beta for General Electric remains almost constant at all scales.

This example provides a new approach to beta estimation in financial markets. Since risk and value are timescale-dependent concepts, any attempt to measure risk, such as a beta calculation, must take this fact into account. Wavelets are natural tools for this purpose.

7.7   UNIVARIATE AND BIVARIATE SPECTRUM ANALYSIS

7.7.1   Univariate Spectrum Analysis

As with the Fourier transform, we also require concepts from the spectrum analysis of time series in order to better describe and understand wavelet methodology. The topics described here can be found, using similar notation, within Percival and Walden (1993) and, with much greater detail, within Priestley (1981).

Let us begin with the *spectral representation theorem* for a discrete parameter stationary process. There exists an orthogonal process $Z(f)$ defined on the interval $[-1/2, 1/2]$ such that

$$x_t \overset{\text{ms}}{=} \int_{-1/2}^{1/2} e^{i2\pi ft} \, dZ(f) \qquad (7.31)$$

for all integers t, where the equality is in the mean square sense. That is, the squared norm between the left-hand side and right-hand side is zero. We define $E[|dZ(f)|^2] = dI(f)$ for all $|f| \leq 1/2$, and call $I(f)$ the *integrated spectrum* of x_t. For our purposes here, we will assume the integrated spectrum is differentiable everywhere with derivative $S(f)$, so that

$$E[|dZ(f)|^2] = dI(f) = S(f)df.$$

The autocovariance sequence (ACVS) of a stationary process x_t, with zero mean, can be written as

$$\gamma_\tau = E(x_t x_{t+\tau}) = \int_{-1/2}^{1/2} S(f) e^{i2\pi f \tau} \, df.$$

Conversely, if γ_τ is square-summable, the spectrum of x_t can be defined in terms of the ACVS via

$$S(f) = \sum_{\tau=-\infty}^{\infty} \gamma_\tau e^{-i2\pi f \tau}, \tag{7.32}$$

and therefore the two quantities form a Fourier transform pair $\gamma_\tau \longleftrightarrow S(f)$.

7.7.2 Univariate Spectrum Estimation

Suppose the time series x_t, $t = 1, \ldots, N$, is a realization of a portion of a zero mean stationary process with SDF $S(f)$ and autocovariance sequence γ_τ. Let $\hat{\gamma}_\tau$ be the usual biased estimator of the autocovariance sequence (Equation 3.19); that is,

$$\hat{\gamma}_\tau = \frac{1}{N} \sum_{t=1}^{N-|\tau|} x_t x_{t+|\tau|} \quad \text{for} \quad 0 \le \tau \le N - 1,$$

and $\hat{\gamma}_\tau = 0$ for $|\tau| \ge N$. The method of moments spectrum estimator is the *periodogram*

$$\widehat{S}^{\mathrm{P}}(f) = \sum_{\tau=-(N-1)}^{N-1} \hat{\gamma}_\tau e^{-i2\pi f \tau} = \frac{1}{N} \left| \sum_{t=1}^{N} x_t e^{-i2\pi f t} \right|^2. \tag{7.33}$$

The disadvantages of the periodogram are well documented; see, for example, Percival and Walden (1993, p. 197). We will not concern ourselves with such matters, except to point out the existence of one of several alternative spectrum estimators – the *multitaper spectrum estimator* (Percival and Walden, 1993; Thomson, 1982). We introduce a set of K orthonormal data tapers[6] $h_{t,k}$ for $t = 1, \ldots, N$ and $k = 0, \ldots, K - 1$; that is,

$$\sum_{t=1}^{N} h_{t,j} h_{t,k} = \begin{cases} 1 & j = k \\ 0 & \text{otherwise.} \end{cases}$$

Sine tapers were designed to minimize the spectral window bias and can be approximated well using the following closed form expression:

$$h_{t,k}^{\mathrm{sine}} = \left(\frac{2}{N+1} \right)^{1/2} \sin\left[\frac{(k+1)\pi t}{N+1} \right].$$

---

[6] Examples of common data tapers are the *sine tapers* (Riedel and Sidorenko, 1995) and *discrete prolate spheroidal sequences* (DPSS) data tapers (Percival and Walden, 1993; Slepian, 1978; Thomson, 1982).

In contrast, the discrete prolate spheroidal sequences (DPSS)[7] data tapers minimize the spectral window sidelobes,[8] using a resolution bandwidth parameter W and must be calculated using techniques such as inverse iteration, numerical integration, or a tridiagonal formulation (Percival and Walden, 1993, Ch. 8). The role of any data taper is to protect against leakage, and all the sine tapers provide moderate leakage protection where the DPSS data tapers offer adjustable leakage protection through the parameter W. In practice there is little difference in the multitaper spectrum estimators when using either data taper.

The typical multitaper spectrum estimator is given by

$$\widehat{S}^{\text{mt}}(f) = \frac{1}{K} \sum_{k=0}^{K-1} \widehat{S}_k^{\text{mt}}(f) \quad \text{with} \quad \widehat{S}_k^{\text{mt}}(f) = \left| \sum_{t=1}^{N} h_{t,k} x_t e^{-i2\pi f t} \right|^2.$$

Thus, the multitaper spectrum estimator is the average of several direct spectrum estimators (more specifically, *eigenspectra*) using an set of orthonormal data tapers. Multitaper spectrum estimators overcome several of the inadequacies of the periodogram and possess reasonable bias, variance, and resolution properties.

7.7.3 Equivalent Degrees of Freedom for a Spectral Estimator

We want to approximate the asymptotic distribution of our spectrum estimate $\widehat{S}(f)$ using a distribution of the form $a\chi_\nu^2$ because the true distribution is difficult to determine, where the constants a and ν are found by moment matching (Priestley, 1981, pp. 466–468). Using the properties of the χ^2 distribution, we know

$$E\left[\widehat{S}(f)\right] = E\left(a\chi_\nu^2\right) = a\nu \quad \text{and} \quad \text{Var}\left[\widehat{S}(f)\right] = \text{Var}\left(a\chi_\nu^2\right) = 2a^2\nu.$$

Solving for a and ν, we obtain

$$\nu = \frac{2\left\{E\left[\widehat{S}(f)\right]\right\}^2}{\text{Var}\left[\widehat{S}(f)\right]} \quad \text{and} \quad a = \frac{E\left[\widehat{S}(f)\right]}{\nu}. \tag{7.34}$$

---

[7] The eigenfunctions $\mathcal{I}_k(N, W, f)$, $k = 0, 1, \ldots, N-1$ are known as *discrete prolate spheroidal wave functions* and are solutions to

$$\int_{-W}^{W} \frac{\sin N\pi(f - f')}{\sin \pi(f - f')} \mathcal{I}_k(N, W, f') \, df' = \iota_k(N, W) \cdot \mathcal{I}_k(N, W, f),$$

where $0 < W < 1/2$ is the bandwidth and $\iota_k(N, W)$ are the eigenvalues. The Fourier transforms of discrete prolate spheroidal wave functions are known as *discrete prolate spheroidal sequences*

$$v_t^{(k)}(N, W) = \frac{1}{\varepsilon_k \iota_k(N, W)} \int_{-W}^{W} \mathcal{I}_k(N, W, f) \exp\{-i2\pi f[t - (N-1)/2]\} \, df$$

for $k = 0, 1, \ldots, N-1$ and all t, where ε_k is 1 for k even and i for k odd (Thomson, 1982).

[8] The spectral window for data tapers share the common feature of having one large peak (main lobe) and subsequent peaks on either side (sidelobes) with decreasing magnitude (Priestley, 1981, Sec. 6.2.3).

If we express the spectral estimate as a lag window spectrum estimator (Percival and Walden, 1993, Sec. 6.7), then we can rewrite Equation 7.34 as

$$\nu = \frac{2N\Delta t}{C_h \int_{-f_{(N)}}^{f_{(N)}} W_m^2(\phi)d\phi} \quad \text{and} \quad a = \frac{S(f)}{\nu}, \quad (7.35)$$

where C_h is a constant that depends on the data taper used[9] and $W_m(f)$ is the smoothing window. Hence, the quantity ν is the *equivalent degrees of freedom* of the spectrum estimator $\widehat{S}(f)$.

7.7.4 Bivariate Spectrum Analysis

The material presented in the following sections closely follows an introduction to bivariate spectrum analysis in Percival (1994) and is a natural extension of univariate topics found in Percival and Walden (1993) using similar notation. A recent article by Walden (2000) provides a unified view of multiple taper spectrum estimation. A more thorough introduction to multivariate spectrum analysis can be found in, for example, Brillinger (1981), Koopmans (1974), and Priestley (1981).

Let x_t and y_t be zero-mean weakly stationary processes with spectral density functions (*autospectra*) $S_x(f)$ and $S_y(f)$, respectively. The *cross spectral density function* (CSDF) of (x_t, y_t) is defined to be

$$S_{xy}(f) = \sum_{\tau=-\infty}^{\infty} \gamma_{\tau,xy} e^{-i2\pi f\tau}, \quad -\frac{1}{2} \le f \le \frac{1}{2},$$

where $\gamma_{\tau,xy}$ is the *cross covariance sequence* (CCVS) given by

$$\gamma_{\tau,xy} = \text{Cov}(x_t, y_{t+\tau}) = E(x_t y_{t+\tau}).$$

The complete spectral properties of a bivariate time series at frequency f can be summarized by the spectral matrix

$$S(f) = \begin{bmatrix} S_x(f) & S_{xy}(f) \\ S_{yx}(f) & S_x(f) \end{bmatrix}. \quad (7.36)$$

Although this is not a symmetric matrix, there are numerous ways of expressing the cross-diagonal terms (Brillinger, 1981, p. 23); that is,

$$S_{xy}(f) = S_{xy}^*(-f) = S_{yx}(-f) = S_{yx}^*(f),$$

where z^* is the complex conjugate of z. Thus, the spectral matrix can be expressed in terms of three distinct quantities instead of four

$$S(f) = \begin{bmatrix} S_x(f) & S_{xy}(f) \\ S_{xy}(-f) & S_x(f) \end{bmatrix}.$$

---

[9] See Table 248 in Percival and Walden (1993) for values of C_h.

Whereas the spectrum of a real-valued process is real valued, since the ACVS is symmetric about 0, the CSDF (or *cross spectrum*) is usually complex valued. This allows us to express $S_{xy}(f)$ in Cartesian form as

$$S_{xy}(f) = R_{xy}(f) - i Q_{xy}(f),$$

where $R_{xy}(f)$ is the *cospectrum* and $Q_{xy}(f)$ is the *quadrature spectrum*. It may also be expressed in polar notation as

$$S_{xy}(f) = A_{xy}(f) e^{i\theta_{xy}(f)},$$

where $A_{xy}(f) = |S_{xy}(f)|$ is the *amplitude spectrum* and $\theta_{xy}(f)$ is the *phase spectrum*. These new functions are at least real valued and may be more easily handled than the cross spectrum. The *complex coherency*

$$\zeta_{xy}(f) = \frac{S_{xy}(f)}{\sqrt{S_X(f)S_Y(f)}} \tag{7.37}$$

depends on both the cross spectrum and the autospectra for x_t and y_t. The complex coherency is a complex valued frequency domain "correlation coefficient." It measures the correlation in the random amplitudes assigned to the complex exponentials with frequency f in the spectral representations of x_t and y_t. The quantity $|\zeta_{xy}(f)|^2$ is called the *magnitude squared coherence* (MSC) at the frequency f. Thus, we have

$$|\zeta_{xy}(f)|^2 = \frac{|S_{xy}(f)|^2}{S_x(f)S_y(f)} = \frac{A_{xy}^2(f)}{S_x(f)S_y(f)},$$

that is, the MSC is a normalized version of the square of the cross-amplitude spectrum. The MSC captures the "amplitude" part of the cross spectrum, but completely ignores its phase, so the MSC and phase spectrum can be used together to summarize the "information" in the complex-valued cross spectrum.

7.7.5   Bivariate Spectrum Estimation

Let x_t, y_t, $t = 1, \ldots, N$, be a realization of a portion of a zero mean stationary process (x_t, y_t) with cross spectrum $S_{xy}(f)$ and autospectra $S_x(f)$ and $S_y(f)$, respectively. Just as the periodogram was used in the univariate case (Section 7.7.2), the *cross periodogram*

$$\widehat{S}_{xy}^p(f) = \sum_{\tau=-(N-1)}^{N-1} \widehat{C}_{\tau,xy} e^{-i2\pi f\tau}$$

is utilized here to estimate the cross spectrum. The *sample CCVS* is defined to be

$$\widehat{C}_{\tau,xy} = \frac{1}{N} \sum_t x_t y_{t+\tau},$$

where the summation goes from $t = 1$ to $N - \tau$ for $\tau \geq 0$ and from $t = 1 - \tau$ to N for $\tau < 0$. The cross periodogram can also be written in a more computationally friendly form as

$$\widehat{S}_{xy}^{\mathrm{p}}(f) = \frac{1}{N} \left[\sum_{t=1}^{N} x_t e^{-i2\pi f t} \right]^* \left[\sum_{t=1}^{N} y_t e^{-i2\pi f t} \right], \tag{7.38}$$

where the asterisk denotes complex conjugation.

The multitaper estimator of the cross spectrum is given by

$$\widehat{S}_{xy}^{\mathrm{mt}}(f) = \frac{1}{K} \left[\sum_{t=1}^{N} h_{k,t} x_t e^{-i2\pi f t} \right]^* \left[\sum_{t=1}^{N} h_{k,t} y_t e^{-i2\pi f t} \right],$$

where $h_{k,t}$ is the kth-order data taper for a sequence of length N normalized such that $\sum_t h_{k,t}^2 = 1$, $k = 1, \ldots, K$. Thus, the multitaper estimators for the phase spectrum and magnitude squared coherence are given by

$$\widehat{\theta}_{xy}^{\mathrm{mt}}(f) = \arg\left\{ \widehat{S}_{xy}^{\mathrm{mt}}(f) \right\} \quad \text{and} \quad \left| \widehat{\xi}_{xy}^{\mathrm{mt}}(f) \right|^2 = \frac{\left| \widehat{S}_{xy}^{\mathrm{mt}}(f) \right|^2}{\widehat{S}_x^{\mathrm{mt}}(f) \widehat{S}_y^{\mathrm{mt}}(f)},$$

respectively. The phase spectrum $\widehat{\theta}_{xy}^{\mathrm{mt}}(f)$ takes on values between $-\pi$ and π and, hence, is modulo 2π. This can lead to discontinuities around $\pm\pi$. Priestley (1981, p. 709) described a method to avoid these discontinuities – by simultaneously plotting the original estimate and translated versions of it.

8

ARTIFICIAL NEURAL NETWORKS

8.1   INTRODUCTION

An artificial neural network is a parallel distributed statistical model made up of simple data processing units[1] that processes information in currently available data and makes generalizations for future events. Although it is common to use neural network models in a time series context, they can also be used with problems pertaining to cross-section environments.

The inputs and the output(s) of a neural network model can be interpreted as regressors and the regressand, respectively, as in a typical regression model. Estimation of the parameters of a neural network is often called *training*. This is similar to the parameter estimation in a regression model. The estimation of the parameters of a neural network model is carried out either with recursive or with nonrecursive nonlinear optimization algorithms. The recursive methods are useful for online, and the nonrecursive methods are for offline estimations.[2]

---

[1] Artificial neural networks are also referrred to as *neural networks*.

[2] In an offline application, many alternative models can be estimated and one would be chosen based on some model selection criterion. This preferred model, afterward, would be used for inference, testing, or prediction purposes. In an online application, one does not have the luxury of choosing a model among alternatives. Rather, a model is estimated and the corresponding results are utilized in realtime.

Most of these optimization algorithms are familiar to a typical graduate student in economics and finance. This chapter focuses on the function approximation and filtering capabilities of neural networks within the context of a regression model.

A natural question to ask would be why use a neural network model when there are plenty of other nonlinear modeling and prediction methods available such as Taylor series expansions, radial basis functions, threshold methods, spline methods, and kernel methods. All of these techniques essentially involve interpolating or approximating unknown functions from scattered data points. The idea behind the Taylor series expansion is to increase the order of the expansion to the point where a curved surface of that order can follow the curvature of the local data points closely. The trade-off with this method is that the number of terms in a multidimensional Taylor series expansion increases quite rapidly with the order. Indeed, the number of parameters needed for a Taylor series of a given order grows multiplicatively as the order of the expansion is increased, and this method involves a choice of an optimal order of expansion. Castagli (1989) pointed out that polynomials of high degree have an undesirable tendency to oscillate wildly.

The nonparametric kernel estimation is a method for estimating probability density functions from observed data. It is a generalization of histograms to continuously differentiable density estimators. The kernel density estimation involves the choice of a kernel function and a smoothing parameter. The idea behind this method is to determine the influence of each data point by placing a weight to each of the data points. The kernel function determines the shape of these weights and the window width determines their width. The approximation of an unknown function from the data can be obtained by calculating the conditional mean of the regression function. The kernel density estimator has desirable approximation capabilities in regression models with a small number of regressors. However, as the number of regressors gets larger, the rate of convergence of the nonparametric kernel density estimator slows down considerably, which leads to the deterioration of the estimator of the conditional mean in finite samples. There is further deterioration in the partial derivatives of the conditional mean estimator. The kernel type methods are studied extensively in Härdle (1990) and Pagan and Ullah (1999).

Among nonlinear methods, neural networks are one of the most recent techniques used in nonlinear modeling. This is partly due to some modeling problems encountered in the early stage of development within the neural networks field. In the earlier literature, the statistical properties of neural networks estimators and their approximation capabilities were questionable. For example, there was no guidance in terms of how to choose the number of neurons and their configurations in a given layer and how to decide the number of hidden layers in a given network. Recent developments in the neural network literature, however, have provided the theoretical foundations for the universality of feedforward networks as function approximators. The results in Cybenko (1989), Funahashi

(1989), Hornik *et al.* (1989, 1990), and Hornik (1991) indicate that feedforward networks with sufficiently many hidden units and properly adjusted parameters can approximate an arbitrary function arbitrarily well. Hornik *et al.* (1990) and Hornik (1991) further show that the feedforward networks can also approximate the derivatives of an arbitrary function.

The universal approximation property that both the unknown function and its derivatives can be uncovered from data is an important result theoretically and has immediate implications for financial and economic modeling. In options pricing, for instance, Hutchinson *et al.* (1994) and Garcia and Gençay (2000) demonstrated that feedforward networks can be used successfully to estimate a pricing formula for options, with good out-of-sample pricing and delta-hedging performance. In the option-pricing framework, it is crucial to approximate both the function and the derivatives of the function accurately as the derivatives of the option-pricing formula are the risk-management tools (e.g. delta, gamma of an option). A small function approximation error may lead to larger errors in the derivatives of the function and therefore poorly approximated risk-management tools. Garcia and Gençay (2000) and Gençay and Qi (2001) showed that feedforward networks provide great enhancements over the parametric econometric tools in terms of providing more accurate pricing and hedging performances.

There have been many applications of neural network models ranging from forecasting, testing, seasonality modeling to bankruptcy prediction. Refenes and Azema-Barac (1994) investigated neural network applications in financial asset management. Moody and Wu (1996) studied optimization of trading systems and portfolios with neural networks. Donaldson and Kamstra (1997) constructed a semiparametric nonlinear GARCH model based on feedforward networks to forecast stock return volatility. Franses and Griensven (1998) indicated that utilizing past buy-sell signals of foreign exchange rates in a feedforward network improves out-of-sample generalizations. Fernández-Rodriguez *et al.* (2000) investigated the profitability of simple technical trading rules based on artificial neural networks. Their results indicated that technical rules are superior to a buy-and-hold strategy in the absence of trading costs. Franses and Draisma (1997) proposed a method on artificial neural networks to investigate how and when seasonal patterns in macroeconomic time series change over time. Yang *et al.* (1997) used probabilistic neural networks in bankruptcy prediction. Blake and Kapetanios (2000) proposed a test for ARCH that uses artificial neural networks. Heinemann (2000) investigated how adaptive learning of rational expectations may be modeled with the help of neural networks.

For studying chaotic dynamical systems, the accurate estimation of the derivatives of an unknown function is also needed. A typical measure of a chaotic system is the existence of a positive largest Lyapunov exponent,[3] which

---

[3] Lyapunov exponents measure the average exponential divergence or convergence of nearby initial points in the phase space of a dynamical system. A positive Lyapunov exponent is a measure of the average exponential divergence of two nearby trajectories, whereas a negative Lyapunov exponent is a measure of the average exponential convergence of two nearby trajectories. If a discrete nonlinear

was introduced to economics by Brock (1986) and Brock and Sayers (1988). Empirical measures of Lyapunov exponents require the estimation of the derivatives of the true data process. A poor approximation of the derivatives implies an inaccurate measure of the Lyapunov exponents. The universal approximation capabilities of feedforward network models provide a suitable environment to estimate a chaotic system and its Lyapunov exponents. Gençay and Dechert (1992), Gençay (1994), Dechert and Gençay (1992), Dechert and Gençay (1996a), and Dechert and Gençay (1996b) all demonstrate of the Lyapunov exponent estimations with feedforward network models.

One advantage of the neural networks over some other methods is that neural network models derive their approximation capabilities from their parallel structure. The building block of a neural network model is a *neuron* or a *hidden unit*, which is used to process information. An *activation function* describes the nature of the relationship between inputs and the neurons (hidden units). One activation function by itself may have no desirable approximation capabilities. The universal approximation capabilities emerge when a number of activation functions are connected through a set of parameters. This parallel structure tackles very complicated problems by decomposing a large problem into a number of simpler problems. An activation function can be either linear or nonlinear. If the activation function is nonlinear, this nonlinearity is distributed across network through its network connection parameters. Therefore, the type of nonlinearity in a neural network is also called *distributed nonlinearity*. One other advantage is that most neural network models can be designed as *adaptive* nonlinear models.[4] The adaptivity implies that the network's generalization capabilities remain accurate and robust in an environment whose characteristics may change overtime. This is also referred to as a nonstationary environment. The neural network estimation methods deal with nonstationary time series environments by assuming that the data are *pseudo-stationary* (or locally-stationary) in a short time window such as 10 minutes, 1 hour, or a few days. This pseudo-stationary property of the underlying data dynamics allows the reestimation of the network to absorb the changes in the underlying data structure.

One further advantage of network models over other methods mentioned above is that feedforward network models use only *linearly many* parameters, whereas traditional polynomial, spline, and trigonometric expansions use

---

system is dissipative, a positive Lyapunov exponent is an indication that the system is chaotic. An extensive treatment of Lyapunov exponents can be found in Gençay and Dechert (1992).

[4] There is distinct literature based on artificial agents. Bullard and Duffy (1997) studied adaptive learning and emulation with adaptive agents in an overlapping generations model. LeBaron *et al.* (1999) designed an experimental computer simulated stock market where market artificial intelligence algorithms take the role of traders. Arifovic and Gençay (2000) studied the time-series properties of exchange rates where agents update their savings and portfolio decisions using genetic algorithms in an overlapping generations model. Duffy (2001) designed an artificial agent-based model for the search model of money. Skouras (2001) studied trading rules which are selected by artificially intelligent agents who learn from experience in the form of an artificial technical analyst.

exponentially many parameters to achieve the same approximation rate (Barron, 1994). A comprehensive survey on artificial neural networks can be found in Kuan and White (1994), while White (1992) presents a collection of papers on the mathematical analysis of the approximation and learning capabilities of neural network models. Bishop (1995), and Haykin (1999) have excellent and in-depth coverage of neural network methods and literature.

In this chapter we will study two types of neural network models: feedforward and recurrent neural network models. In feedforward networks, signals flow in only one direction, without feedback. Applications in forecasting, filtering, and control require explicit treatment of dynamics. Feedforward networks can accommodate dynamics by including lagged dependent variables in an augmented set of inputs. A much richer dynamic representation results from also allowing for internal network feedbacks. These types of network models are called recurrent network models. In some recurrent networks, the recurrence may be through past values of the network output feeding back as a regressor. This type of a recurrent network is called an output-recurrent network and is shown in Figure 8.14. In some other recurrent network models, the recurrence originates from the past values of the hidden units feeding back into themselves. These networks are called the hidden-recurrent networks, as shown in Figure 8.15.

Our interest in this chapter is confined to the function approximation and filtering capabilities of these neural network models. We start with the elements of a typical neural network model and progress through feedforward and recurrent neural network models.

8.2 ACTIVATION FUNCTIONS

A neural network is a parallel distributed model made up of simple data processing units. These simple data processing units are called *artificial neurons* or *activation functions*, which are a particular class of flexible functions. An activation function can be a linear or a nonlinear function. A neural network model consisting of nonlinear activation functions would distribute this nonlinearity in its parallel structure.

8.2.1 Deterministic Activation Functions

An activation function, denoted by $g(x)$, determines the output of a neuron in relation to the input variable x. There are a number of different activation functions, such as the *threshold function, piecewise linear function*, and *sigmoidal function*. Each activation may be suited for a particular type of problem at hand. The threshold activation function (Figure 8.1) is

$$g(x) = \begin{cases} 1 & \text{if } x \geq 0 \\ 0 & \text{if } x < 0. \end{cases} \tag{8.1}$$

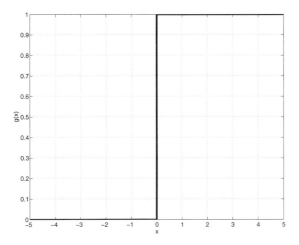

FIGURE 8.1 The threshold activation function.

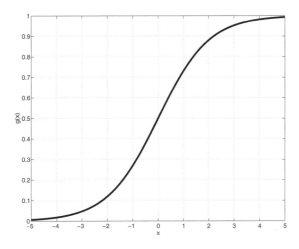

FIGURE 8.2 The sigmoidal (logistic) activation function.

The piecewise linear activation function (Figure 8.3) is

$$g(x) = \begin{cases} 1 & \text{if } x \geq a \\ x & \text{if } a > x > b \\ 0 & \text{if } x \leq b, \end{cases} \tag{8.2}$$

where a and b are threshold parameters. The sigmoidal activation function (also called the squashing function) (Figure 8.2) is

$$g(x) = \frac{1}{1 + e^{-ax-b}}, \tag{8.3}$$

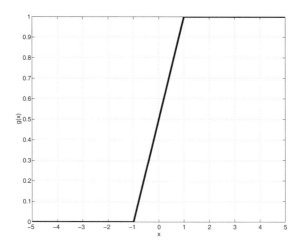

FIGURE 8.3 An example of a piecewise linear activation function with $a = 1, b = -1$, and $g(x) = 0.5 + 0.5x$.

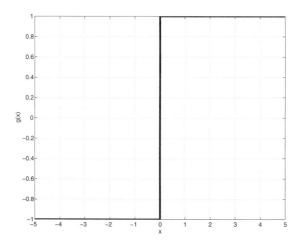

FIGURE 8.4 The signum activation function.

where a and b are slope and location parameters, respectively. As the slope parameter approaches infinity, the sigmoidal function becomes a threshold function. The sigmoidal function above is also called a *logistic* function.

For certain applications, it is desirable to have an activation function that ranges from -1 to $+1$. This activation function is called a *signum function* (Figure 8.4) and it is defined by

$$g(x) = \begin{cases} 1 & \text{if } x > 0 \\ 0 & \text{if } x = 0 \\ -1 & \text{if } x < 0. \end{cases} \tag{8.4}$$

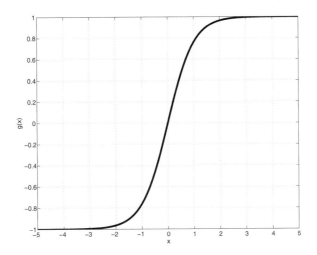

FIGURE 8.5 The hyperbolic tangent activation function.

The continuous version of the signum function is defined by the *hyperbolic tangent function* (Figure 8.5), which is

$$g(x) = \tanh(x). \tag{8.5}$$

8.3 FEEDFORWARD NETWORKS

In a feedforward network model, the neurons (activation functions) are organized in layers. The layer that contains the inputs is called the input layer. Similarly, the layer where the outputs of the network are located is called the output layer. There can be a number of layers between the input and the output layers. These layers, because they are kept between the input and the output layers, are called the hidden layers. Depending on the network complexity or the nature of the studied problem, there can be a number of hidden layers in a neural network model. A single layer feedforward network has only one hidden layer whereas a multilayer feedforward network would have several hidden layers.

An example of a single-layer feedforward network is presented in Figure 8.6. This figure demonstrates a two-input single-layer feedforward network:

$$f(\boldsymbol{x}_t, \theta) = \beta_0 + \beta_1 g(\alpha_{10} + \alpha_{11}x_{1t} + \alpha_{12}x_{2t})$$
$$+ \beta_1 g(\alpha_{20} + \alpha_{21}x_{1t} + \alpha_{22}x_{2t}), \tag{8.6}$$

where $\boldsymbol{x}_t = (x_{1t}, x_{2t})$ are the inputs at time t, α_{10}, α_{11}, and α_{12} are the parameters of the first activation function, α_{20}, α_{21}, and α_{22} are the parameters of the second activation function, and β_0, β_1, and β_2 are the intercept and the slope parameters.

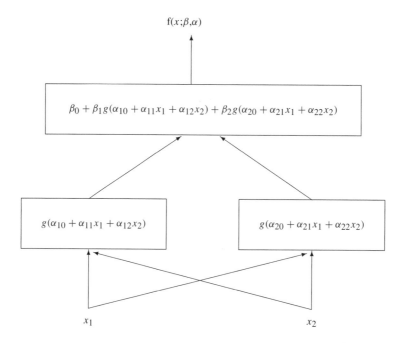

FIGURE 8.6 A two input and two hidden unit single-layer feedforward network. This network is presented in Equation 8.6.

The underlying functional form $f(x_t, \theta)$ is the network output, which depends on the inputs and the network parameters. The x_t here represents a vector of all inputs at time t and the symbol θ represents the vector of parameters, α's and β's. Often, f is termed to be the network output function. This example demonstrates that a simple feedforward network model can easily be seen as a nonlinear flexible regression model, which can be estimated with the standard optimization tools used in econometrics.

A further variation of this example would be to restrict the output to a binary response. This can be achieved by assigning a threshold or signum type activation functions between the hidden and the output layers. If the output must be restricted to a certain interval and can take any value within this interval, the piecewise linear, sigmoidal, or hyperbolic tangent activation functions can be used in an output layer.

The architecture of a neural network model determines the exact nature of the function f. Different types of network architectures would lead to different types of functions. An example of a single-layer feedforward network with four inputs and four hidden units is presented in Figure 8.7. An example of a two-layer feedforward network with six inputs, four hidden units in the first hidden layer, and two hidden units in the second layer is presented in Figure 8.8. In both figures, there is a single output unit in the output layer.

As pointed out in Section 8.1, even a *single*-layer feedforward network with sufficiently many hidden units and properly adjusted parameters can theoretically approximate an arbitrary function arbitrarily well. Although these are important theoretical results, which establish the universal approximation capabilities of feedforward networks, they may have limited practical implications. One element of the theoretical universal approximation results is the requirement of sufficiently many activation functions in a single hidden layer. In practice, the number of activation functions (or hidden units) used in a network is constrained by the available degrees of freedom,[5] which is controlled by the data length and the total number of parameters of the network. Therefore, a sufficiently *large* number of hidden units in a single layer may not be feasible in certain problems such as macroeconomic data where there may be only two or three decades of annual observations available.

For complex problems with finite data, the alternative methodology is to abandon a single-layer feedforward network and work with two or higher level feedforward networks. Single-layer feedforward network models are, in general, *global* networks due to the fact that any change in one of the parameters of the network would influence the entire network performance. The limitation of this interaction is that it makes it difficult to improve the network's generalization properties both at high and low-frequency components of the underlying data.[6] An improvement of a high-frequency feature may worsen a low-frequency feature of the underlying data dynamics. As pointed out in Funahashi (1989), a two-layer feedforward network can accomodate both high and low-frequency data features with minimal trade-off. Some of the first hidden layer activation functions are used to partition the input space into regions, and the remaining first-layer activation functions are used to approximate the high-frequency features of these regions. The activation functions in the second layer process the low-frequency features of the data with the high-frequency features provided from the first layer. The advantage of a two or higher layer network is that it is possible to localize the influence of certain features of the data and therefore control high and low-frequency data features simultaneously.

Let x_t and y_t be the input (regressors) and the target (regressand) vectors with dimensions $1 \times n$ and $1 \times w$ with t indicating the time index.[7] The observations for a sample size N are denoted by $x_1, x_2, \ldots, x_N$ and $y_1, y_2, \ldots, y_N$. Given inputs $x_t = (x_{1,t}, \ldots, x_{n,t})$, a single-layer feedforward network regression model with

---

[5] The "degrees of freedom" refers to the number of independent unrestricted random variables constituting a statistic.

[6] In principle, data features can be classified as high and low-frequency.

[7] For simplicity, we will assume that $w = 1$ here.

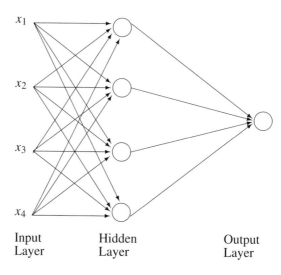

Input
Layer

Hidden
Layer

Output
Layer

FIGURE 8.7   A single-layer feedforward network with four inputs, four hidden units, and a single output unit.

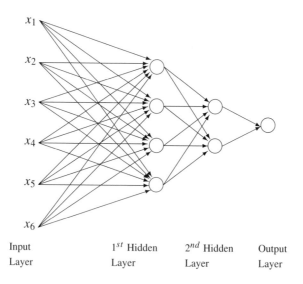

Input
Layer

1st Hidden
Layer

2nd Hidden
Layer

Output
Layer

FIGURE 8.8   A two-layer feedforward network with six inputs, six hidden units with a single output unit.

q hidden units is written as

$$y_t = s\left(\beta_0 + \sum_{i=1}^{q} \beta_i h_{i,t}\right) + \epsilon_t$$

$$h_{i,t} = g\left(\alpha_{i0} + \sum_{j=1}^{n} \alpha_{ij} x_{j,t}\right), \tag{8.7}$$

for $i = 1, \ldots, q$ or

$$y_t = s\left[\beta_0 + \sum_{i=1}^{q} \beta_i g\left(\alpha_{i0} + \sum_{j=1}^{n} \alpha_{ij} x_{j,t}\right)\right] + \epsilon_t$$

$$= f(\boldsymbol{x}_t, \theta) + \epsilon_t, \tag{8.8}$$

where s and g are known activation functions, ϵ_t is an error term distributed with zero mean and variance σ_t^2, and the parameters to be estimated are $\theta = (\beta_0, \ldots, \beta_q, \alpha_1, \ldots, \alpha_q)'$ and $\alpha_j = (\alpha_{j,0}, \ldots, \alpha_{j,n})$. The range of the output values of the feedforward network model is controlled by s such that if the output takes discrete values, then s can be chosen to be a threshold function, piecewise linear function, or a signum function. If the range of the output function is not restricted to a particular interval, then it can simply be set to an identity function, where $s(x) = x$. In a typical neural network model, s is normally an identity function.

Given the network structure in Equation 8.8 and the chosen functional forms for s and g, a major empirical issue in the neural networks is to estimate the unknown parameters θ with a sample of data values. A recursive estimation methodology, which is called *backpropagation*, is such a method to estimate the underlying parameter vector θ from data.[8] In backpropagation, the starting point is a random weight θ vector that is updated[9] according to

$$\hat{\theta}_{t+1} = \hat{\theta}_t + \eta \nabla f(\boldsymbol{x}_t, \hat{\theta}_t)\left[y_t - f(\boldsymbol{x}_t, \hat{\theta}_t)\right], \tag{8.9}$$

where $\nabla f(\boldsymbol{x}_t, \hat{\theta})$ is the (column) gradient vector of f with respect to $\hat{\theta}$, and η is the parameter that controls the learning rate. This estimation procedure is characterized by the recursive updating of estimated parameters. The parameter updates are carried out in response to the size of the error, which is measured by $y_t - f(\boldsymbol{x}_t, \hat{\theta})$. By imposing appropriate conditions on the learning rate and functional forms of s and g, White (1989) derived the statistical properties for this estimator. He showed that the backpropagation estimator asymptotically converges to an estimator, which locally minimizes the expected squared error loss.

---

[8] A more detailed discussion of backpropagation can be found in Haykin (1999) and White (1992).

[9] The hat symbol denotes the estimated parameter from data.

Backpropagation and nonlinear regression can be seen as alternative statistical methods to solve the least squares problem. Compared to nonlinear least squares, backpropagation fails to make efficient use of the information in the underlying data. As demonstrated in White (1989), certain modifications of the backpropagation methods can overcome these limitations. A modified version of the backpropagation is the inclusion of the Newton direction in recursively updating $\hat{\theta}_t$ (Kuan and White, 1994). The form of this recursive Newton algorithm is

$$
\begin{aligned}
\hat{\theta}_{t+1} &= \hat{\theta}_t + \eta_t \, \widehat{G}_t^{-1} \, \nabla f(x_t, \hat{\theta}_t) \left[y_t - f(x_t, \hat{\theta}_t) \right] \\
\widehat{G}_{t+1} &= \widehat{G}_t + \eta_t \left[\nabla f(x_t, \hat{\theta}_t) \nabla f(x_t, \hat{\theta}_t)^T - \widehat{G}_t \right],
\end{aligned}
\qquad (8.10)
$$

where $\widehat{G}_t$ is an estimated, approximate Newton direction matrix and η_t is a sequence of learning rates of order $1/t$. The inclusion of a Newton direction induces the recursive updating of $\widehat{G}_t$, which is obtained by considering the outer product of $\nabla f(x_t, \hat{\theta}_t)$. In practice, an algebraically equivalent form of this algorithm can be employed to avoid matrix inversion.

These recursive estimation techniques are important for large samples and real-time applications since they allow for adaptive estimation. However, recursive estimation techniques do not fully utilize the information in the data sample. White (1989) further showed that the recursive estimator is not as efficient as the nonlinear least squares (NLS) estimator. One important aspect of the backpropogation methods is the choice of the learning rate η. The inefficiency of the backpropagation originates from keeping the learning rate constant in an environment where the influence of random movements in x_t are not accounted for in y_t. This would lead the parameter vector $\hat{\theta}$ to fluctuate indefinitely. A minimum requirement is to gradually drive the learning rate zero to achieve convergence. In fact, White (1989) demonstrated that η_t has to be chosen not as a vanishing scalar but as a gradually vanishing matrix of a very specific form. These arguments on learning rates are only valid if the environment is not changing over time (stationary). If the environment is evolving (nonstationary), a gradually vanishing learning rate may fail and a constant learning rate may be more suitable (see White, 1989).

The NLS estimator is obtained by minimizing

$$
\min_\theta L(\theta) = \sum_{t=1}^{N} [y_t - f(x_t, \theta)]^2.
\qquad (8.11)
$$

Here, the goal is to choose the parameter vector θ such that the sum of squared errors is minimized as much as possible. Since the function f is nonlinear (a neural network model) and it is a nonlinear function of θ, this procedure is named as nonlinear least squares or nonlinear regression. This is a straightforward multivariate minimization problem. Conjugant gradient routines studied in Gençay and Dechert (1992) work very well for this problem. Gallant and White (1992) showed that the least squares method can consistently estimate a function and its derivatives from a feedforward network model, provided that the number of hidden units increases with the size of the data set. This would mean that a larger number of data points would require a larger number of hidden units to avoid overfitting in noisy environments.

8.3.1 Example: IBM Stock Price and Volatility Prediction

Here we apply the feedforward network regression to daily IBM stock prices from May, 1961, to November, 1962, a total of $t = 1, 2, \ldots, 369$ observations. This is the classic data studied in Box and Jenkins (1976). This series has been analyzed for changes in variance in Inclán (1993) and de Alba and Boue (2000).

The logarithmic price series and their volatilities are plotted in Figure 8.9. A return series was computed via the first difference of the log-transformed prices—that is, $r_t = \log(p_t) - \log(p_{t-1})$. The volatility is measured by the absolute return $v_t = |r_t|$. The series exhibits low volatility behavior up to observation 226 and a higher volatility state afterward. We choose two training sets to model the price series with feedforward networks. These training sets are with observations, $t = 1, 2, \ldots, 220$ and $t = 1, 2, \ldots, 268$. The first training set contains only the observations from the low-volatility state, whereas the second training set contains information from both low and high-volatility states. In each training set, the remaining observations are used for prediction purposes. The feedworward network model has 10 inputs and 10 hidden units in each case. The feedforward network for the price model is

$$\log(p_t) = f\left(\log(p_{t-1}), \log(p_{t-2}), \ldots, \log(p_{t-10}), \theta\right) + \epsilon_t, \qquad (8.12)$$

where ϵ_t is distributed with zero mean and variance σ_t^2.

The price predictions are presented in Figure 8.10. For both training sets, the estimated parameters are strictly obtained from the training sample. Hence, there is no updating of the network parameters and they are fixed from the training sample. The predictions are one-step-ahead predictions. The estimation of the feedforward network regression is carried out by nonlinear least squares as pointed out in Equation 8.11. In both cases, the feedforward network model succesfully captures the movements in the out-of-sample and the differences between two training sample performances are similar. The mean squared prediction errors (MSPEs) are 5.64e-008 and 4.73e-008 for Figure 8.10a and Figure 8.10b, respectively.

The feedforward network for the volatility model is

$$\log(v_t) = f\left(\log(v_{t-1}), \log(v_{t-2}), \ldots, \log(v_{t-10}), \theta\right) + \epsilon_t, \qquad (8.13)$$

where ϵ_t is distributed with zero mean and variance σ_t^2. The results are presented in Figure 8.11. The in-sample performance of the second training sample

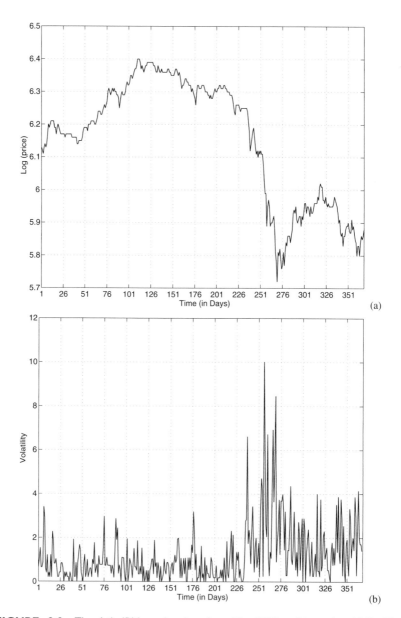

FIGURE 8.9   The daily IBM stock prices from May 1961 to November 1962. This is the classic data set studied in Box and Jenkins (1976). (a) Log prices. (b) Volatility measured by the absolute returns.

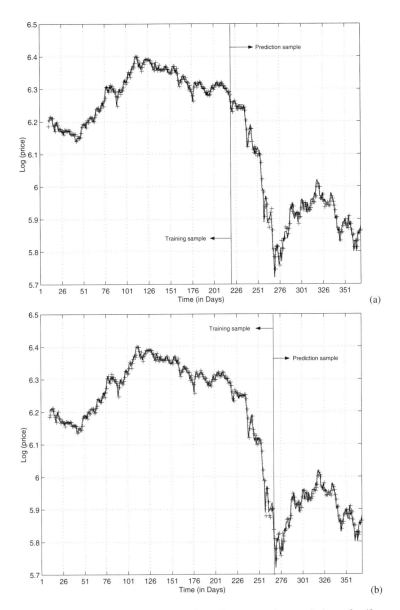

FIGURE 8.10 The daily IBM log(price) predictions with a single-layer feedforward network model. The feedforward network model (Equation 8.12) has 10 hidden units and 10 past log(price)'s. Actual data is in solid line. Estimated and predicted points are represented with a + sign. (a) Training set with $t = 1, 2, \ldots, 220$. (b) Training set with $t = 1, 2, \ldots, 268$.

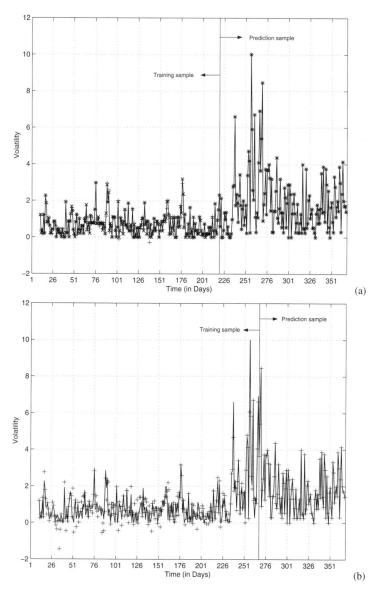

FIGURE 8.11   The daily IBM volatility predictions with a single-layer feedforward network model. The feedforward network model (Equation 8.13) with 10 hidden units and 10 past volatilities. Actual data is in the solid line. Estimated and predicted points are represented with a + sign. (a) Training set with $t = 1, 2, \ldots, 220$. (b) Training set with $t = 1, 2, \ldots, 268$.

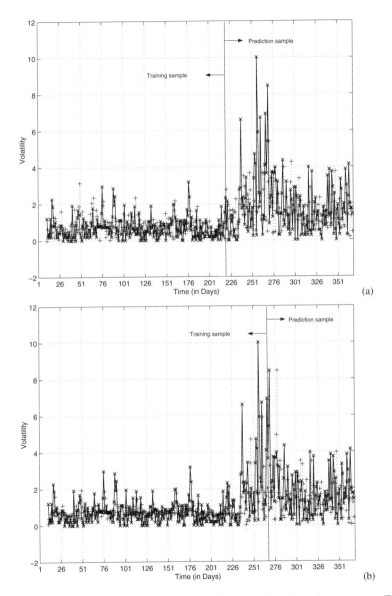

FIGURE 8.12 The daily IBM volatility predictions with a kernel regression. The kernel model has 10 past volatilities as inputs. Actual data is in solid line. Estimated and predicted points are represented with a + sign. (a) Training set with $t = 1, 2, \ldots, 220$. (b) Training set with $t = 1, 2, \ldots, 268$.

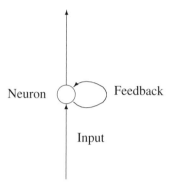

FIGURE 8.13   A typical feedback in a recurrent network.

(Figure 8.11b) is worse than that of the first training sample. There are a number of negative volatility estimates in the second training sample relative to the first sample. The one-step-ahead volatility predictions, for both samples, are equally successful. The MSPEs are $5.93e\text{-}013$ and $1.10e\text{-}016$ for Figure 8.11a and Figure 8.11b, respectively.

For comparison purposes, kernel regression volatility estimators and forecasts are also presented in Figure 8.12. The MSPEs from the kernel regression are 3.56 and 2.84, respectively. These values are much larger than the MSPE performance of the feedforward network regression. The poor performance of the kernel regression is also observed in Figure 8.12 where the kernel regression forecasts miss large volatility movements.

8.4   RECURRENT NETWORKS

The majority of the function approximation related neural network literature has been dominated by the feedforward network models. A recurrent neural network distinguishes itself from a feedforward network with the presence of at least one *feedback* connection. A typical feedback connection is presented in Figure 8.13, where a delayed (lagged) value of the processed information feeds back into the neuron.

In general, feedforward networks do not have the intrinsic capability of processing temporal information and can be exploited by a feature known as *feedback*. Recurrent networks, with the consideration of feedbacks, are more general models than the feedforward networks and embed feedforward networks as special cases. There are two important considerations as to why recurrent networks are attractive tools for modeling: inference and prediction in noisy environments. In a typical recurrent network architecture, the hidden unit activation functions are fed back at every time step to provide an *additional input* as shown in Figure 8.13.

In a recurrent network, the feedback of hidden units enables the filtered data of the previous period to be used as an additional input in the current period. In other words, each time period network is subject to not only the new noisy data but the past history of all noisy inputs as well as their filtered counterparts. This additional information of filtered input history acts as additional guidance to evaluate the current noisy input and its signal component. In contrast, filtered history never enters into a feedforward network. This is where recurrent networks differ from a feedforward network. Secondly, because recurrent networks have the ability to keep past history of the filtered inputs as additional information in the memory, a recurrent network would have the ability to filter noise even when the noise distribution is allowed to vary over time. In a feedforward network, however, complete new training has to be performed with a new set of examples containing the new type of noise structure.

Recurrent networks may also be viewed as nonlinear autoregressive (NAR) or nonlinear autoregressive moving average (NARMA) models (Haykin, 1999, Ch. 15). The NAR models with exogenous inputs are also referred to as NARX models. The NARX models are studied in Chen *et al.* (1990), Narendra and Parthasarathy (1990), Lin *et al.* (1990), and in Siegelmann *et al.* (1990) within the context of recurrent networks.

In this section, we will study three types of recurrent networks with global feedbacks. These recurrent network models are the output-recurrent model, the hidden-recurrent model, and the output-hidden recurrent model.

8.4.1 Output-Recurrent Model

The output recurrent neural network model is represented by

$$y_t = s \left(\beta_0 + \sum_{i=1}^{q} \beta_i h_{i,t} \right) + \epsilon_t \tag{8.14}$$

and

$$h_{i,t} = g \left(\alpha_{i0} + \sum_{j=1}^{n} \alpha_{ij} x_{j,t} + \sum_{p=1}^{k} \delta_{ip} s_{t-p} \right), \tag{8.15}$$

where s_{t-p} is the output of the network at time $t - p$. The temporal memory of the output-recurrent recurrent models can also be expressed by

$$y_t = f(x_{1,t}, x_{2,t}, \ldots, x_{n,t}, s_{t-1}, s_{t-2}, \ldots, s_1, \theta) + \epsilon_t, \tag{8.16}$$

where the lagged output values of the network, s_{t-p}'s, are fed back into the network *nonlinearly* as additional inputs. This recurrence provides the network nonlinear temporal dependence through its past output history. This type of network architecture is studied in Jordan (1986) in modeling serial order.[10]

---

[10] The examination of human behavior reveals different types of serially ordered action sequences. Our limb movements, our speech, and even our internal train of thought appear to involve sequences

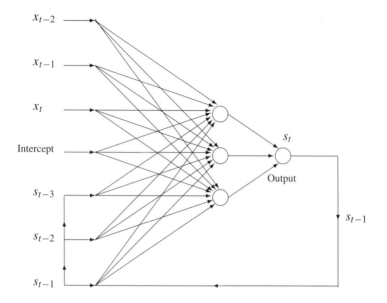

FIGURE 8.14   An output-recurrent network with three inputs and three hidden units.

An example of an output-recurrent network is presented in Figure 8.14. The recurrence of the past output values (fitted values) enables the filtered information of the previous period to be used as an additional input in the current period. In other words, the network at time t is subject not only to the new information (possibly contaminated with noise) but filtered historical information as well. This additional filtered input history acts as additional guidance to evaluate the current noisy input and its signal component.

8.4.2   Hidden-Recurrent Model

The hidden-recurrent network is represented as

$$y_t = s\left(\beta_0 + \sum_{i=1}^{q} \beta_i h_{i,t}\right) + \epsilon_t \tag{8.17}$$

$$h_{i,t} = g\left(\alpha_{i0} + \sum_{j=1}^{n} \alpha_{ij} x_{j,t} + \sum_{\ell=1}^{q} \delta_{i\ell} h_{\ell,t-1}\right), \tag{8.18}$$

of events that follow one another in time. Furthermore, humans are capable of performing a large number of sequences in a variety of contexts and orderings. The theory of "serial order" studies such complex nonlinear temporal behavior. More information about serial order and related literature can be found in Jordan (1986).

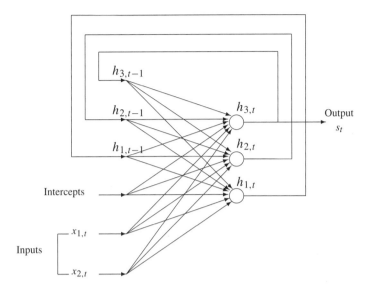

FIGURE 8.15   A hidden-recurrent network with two inputs and three hidden units.

where the hidden unit activation functions are fed back at every time step to provide an *additional input*. This type of network is also called an *Elman* network (Elman, 1990), where lagged (time delayed) outputs of the hidden units are fed back into the hidden units themselves. The hidden units therefore have some record of their prior performance, which enables the network to possess internal memory. An example of a hidden-recurrent network with two inputs and three hidden units in a single layer is presented in Figure 8.15.

The temporal memory of a hidden-recurrent network can be represented by

$$
\begin{aligned}
y_t \;=\; & f\left(x_{1,t}, x_{2,t}, \ldots, x_{n,t}, h_{1,t-1}, h_{1,t-2}, \ldots,\right. \\
& \left. h_{1,1}, \ldots, h_{q,t-1}, h_{q,t-2}, \ldots, h_{q,1}, \ldots, \theta\right) + \epsilon_t, \quad (8.19)
\end{aligned}
$$

where exactly how this internal memory is represented is not determined in advance. Instead, the network must discover the underlying temporal dynamics and learn to approximate the structure internally. This type of network is used in foreign exchange forecasting by Kuan and Liu (1995) and in Gençay and Liu (1997).

8.4.3 Output-Hidden Recurrent Model

The output-hidden recurrent neural network model is represented as

$$
y_t = s\left(\beta_0 + \sum_{i=1}^{q} \beta_i h_{i,t}\right) + \epsilon_t
$$

$$
h_{i,t} = g\left(\alpha_{i0} + \sum_{j=1}^{n} \alpha_{ij} x_{j,t} + \sum_{\ell=1}^{q} \delta_{i\ell} h_{\ell,t-1} + \sum_{p=1}^{k} \delta_{ip} s_{t-p}\right), \quad (8.20)
$$

where both lagged output values and the lagged hidden units are fed back into the current hidden units. The output-hidden recurrent network in Equation 8.20 is a single-layer network, although the multilayer generalizations are available in Puskorius and Feldkamp (1994). The temporal dynamics of a output-hidden recurrent network can also be represented by

$$
y_t = f\left(x_{1,t}, x_{2,t}, \ldots, x_{n,t}, h_{1,t-1}, h_{1,t-2}, \ldots, h_{1,1}, \ldots, h_{q,t-1}, \right.
$$
$$
\left. h_{q,t-2}, \ldots, h_{q,1}, \ldots, s_{t-1}, s_{t-2}, \ldots, s_1, \theta\right) + \epsilon_t. \quad (8.21)
$$

An example of an output-hidden recurrent network is presented in Figure 8.16 with three inputs. The output layer has three units so that the network has a multivariate nature. As Figure 8.16 demonstrates, the feedbacks both originate from the output layer as well as within/across the hidden units themselves.

8.5 NETWORK SELECTION

8.5.1 Information Theoretic Criteria

The specification of a neural network model requires the choice of the type of inputs, the number of hidden units, the number of hidden layers, and the connection structure between the inputs and the output layers. The common choice for this specification design is to adopt the model-selection approach. Information based criteria such as the Schwarz Information Criterion (SIC) and the Akaike Information Criterion (AIC) are used widely. The SIC is computed by (Schwarz, 1978),

$$
\text{SIC} = \log\left[\frac{1}{N}\sum_{t=1}^{N}(y_t - \hat{y}_t)^2\right] + \frac{w}{N}\log(N), \quad (8.22)
$$

where w is the number of parameters in the model and N is the number of observations. The model with the smallest SIC is the preferred model. The first term in the SIC criterion is the mean squared error (MSE),

$$
\text{MSE} = \frac{1}{N}\sum_{t=1}^{N}(y_t - \hat{y}_t)^2, \quad (8.23)
$$

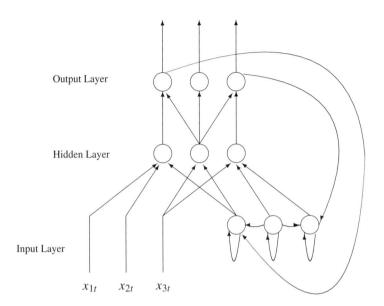

Output Layer

Hidden Layer

Input Layer

x_{1t} x_{2t} x_{3t}

FIGURE 8.16 An output-hidden-recurrent network with three inputs. The output layer has three units so that the network is in multivariate nature. The feedbacks both originate from the output layer as well as within/across the hidden units themselves. This network is studied in Jordan (1986). Not all connections are shown.

where y_t is the target variable at time t and $\hat{y}_t$ is the estimated network output at time t. The second term in the SIC indicates that the simple estimation model with fewer parameters is better if both models give the same MSEs. When two models have the same number of parameters, the comparison of SIC is the same as the comparison of the mean squared errors.

The AIC is computed by (Akaike, 1973, 1974)

$$\text{AIC} = \log\left[\frac{1}{N}\sum_{t=1}^{N}(y_t - \hat{y}_t)^2\right] + \frac{2}{w}N, \qquad (8.24)$$

where w is the number of parameters and N is the number of observations.

Swanson and White (1995) reported that the SIC fails to select sufficiently parsimonious models in terms of being a reliable guide to the out-of-sample performance. Since the SIC imposes a more severe penalty than the AIC, the AIC would give even worse results for the out-of-sample prediction. Kuan and Liu (1995) noted that the SIC is computationally demanding because nonlinear least squares estimation is required for estimating every possible network. They instead propose the Predictive Stochastic Complexity (PSC) criterion of

Rissanen (1986a; 1986b). The PSC is calculated by

$$\text{PSC} = \frac{1}{N-k} \sum_{t=k+1}^{N} \left[y_t - f(x_t, \hat{\theta}_t) \right]^2, \tag{8.25}$$

where $\hat{\theta}_t$ is the parameter estimate obtained from data up to time $t - 1$. In the calculation of the prediction error $y_t - f(x_t, \hat{\theta}_t)$, no information at time t or beyond is used to calculate $\hat{\theta}_t$. A model is selected if it has the smallest PSC within a class of models. If two models have the same PSC, the simpler one is selected. The PSC criterion is based on forward validation, which is desirable for forecasting purposes.

8.5.2 Cross-Validation

As pointed out in Section 8.5.1, an important property of network training is to estimate the network parameters such that the network can generalize outside of the training data. Within this context, a network complexity with a given number of hidden layers, the number of activation functions in each layer, and the values of the parameters in each activation function need to be determined. The cross-validation method offers such a platform for network selection. Although the cross-validation methodology has been known at least as early as 1930s, its refinement took place in 1970s as the result of work by Stone (1974) and Geisser (1975) in two independent studies. It was in Stone (1974) that it was named the "cross-validating" methodology.

In the implementation of the cross-validation, the data set is split into three parts, namely, training, validation, and prediction (or test) samples. A given network is estimated in the training sample and it is evaluated in the validation sample. The reason to evaluate the network in the validation sample is to minimize any overfitting that might occur with the training sample. Once an optimal network complexity is chosen, its generalization properties would be measured with the prediction sample.

There are different variations of cross-validation. In some variants, the data set is split into n equal (approximate) subsets. The network is trained in all subsets except one, and the validation of the network is performed on the left-out data subset. This process is repeated n times by leaving out a different data subset as a validation sample each time. The overall performance of the network is measured by averaging the performance criterion of n runs.[11] This form of cross-validation is also referred to as *multifold* cross-validation. If the total data set is not large, there may not be sufficient observations to split the data set into subsets. In that case, one observation may be left-out and the estimation is carried out with $n - 1$ observations. The validation is performed on the observation excluded in the estimation sample. This process is repeated n times by leaving out a different

---

[11] A typical performance criterion is the squared errors or absolute errors between the true observation and its estimate.

observation each time for validation. The overall performance is measured by averaging the performance criterion from the n distinct runs. This type is called the *leave-one-out* cross-validation method. The cross-validation methodology is studied extensively within the context of neural network models in Haykin (1999).

8.5.3 Bayesian Regularization

To design a network that generalizes outside of the training data, MacKay (1992) proposed a method to constrain the size of the network parameters through the so-called regularization. With regularization, the objective function becomes

$$F = \gamma E_D + (1 - \gamma)E_\theta, \tag{8.26}$$

where E_D is the sum of the squared errors, E_θ is the sum of squares of the network parameters, and γ is the performance ratio, the magnitude of which dictates the emphasis of the training. If γ is very large, then the training algorithm will drive the errors to be small. But if γ is very small, then training will emphasize parameter size reduction at the expense of network errors, thus producing a smoother network response.

The optimal regularization parameter γ can be determined by the Bayesian techniques.[12] In the Bayesian framework, the weights of the network are considered random variables. Let $D = (y, x)$ represent the data set, θ represent the vector of network parameters, and M represent the particular neural network model used. With the data set D, the density function for the weights can be updated according to the Bayes rule

$$P(\theta|D, \gamma, M) = \frac{P(D|\theta, \gamma, M)P(\theta|\gamma, M)}{P(D|\gamma, M)}, \tag{8.27}$$

where $P(\theta|\gamma, M)$ is the prior density, which represents our knowledge of the weights before any data are collected, and $P(D|\theta, \gamma, M)$ is the likelihood function, which is the probability of the data occurring given the weights θ. $P(D|\gamma, M)$ is a normalization factor, which guarantees that the total probability is 1. If we assume that the noise and the prior distribution for the weights are both Gaussian, the probability densities can be written as

$$P(D|\theta, \gamma, M) = (\pi/\gamma)^{-N/2}e^{-\gamma E_D} \tag{8.28}$$

and

$$P(\theta|\gamma, M) = [\pi/(1 - \gamma)]^{-L/2}e^{-(1-\gamma)E_\theta}, \tag{8.29}$$

where L is the total number of parameters in the neural network model. Substituting Equation 8.29 into Equation 8.27, we obtain

$$P(\theta|D, \gamma, M) = Z_F(\gamma)e^{-F(\theta)}. \tag{8.30}$$

---

[12] MacKay (1992) and Foresee and Hagan (1997) have provided detailed studies on this issue.

In the Bayesian framework, the optimal weights should maximize the posterior probability $P(\theta|D, \gamma, M)$, which is equivalent to minimizing the regularized objective function given in Equation 8.26.

The performance ratio can also be optimized by applying the Bayes rule,

$$P(\gamma|D, M) = \frac{P(D|\gamma, M)P(\gamma|M)}{P(D|M)}. \qquad (8.31)$$

Assuming a uniform prior density $P(\gamma|M)$ for the regularization parameter γ, the maximizing the posterior is achieved by maximizing the likelihood function $P(D|\gamma, M)$. Since all probabilities have a Gaussian form, the normalization factor can be expressed as

$$P(D|\gamma, M) = (\pi/\gamma)^{-N/2}[\pi/(1-\gamma)]^{-L/2}Z_F(\gamma). \qquad (8.32)$$

Assuming that the objective function has a quadratic shape in a small area surrounding a minimum point, we can expand $F(\theta)$ around the minimum point of the posterior density θ^*, where the gradient is zero. Solving for the normalizing constant yields

$$Z_F \approx (2\pi)^{L/2}\{\det[(H^*)^{-1}]\}^{1/2}e^{-F(\theta^*)}, \qquad (8.33)$$

where $H = \gamma \nabla^2 E_D + (1-\gamma) \nabla^2 E_\theta$ is the Hessian matrix of the objective function. Substituting Equation 8.33 into Equation 8.32, we can solve for the optimal value of γ at the minimum point. This is done by taking the derivative with respect to the log of Equation 8.32 and setting it equal to zero.

The Bayesian optimization of the regularization parameters requires the computation of the Hessian matrix of $F(\theta)$ at the minimum point θ^*. Foresee and Hagan (1997) proposed using the Gauss-Newton approximation to the Hessian matrix, which is readily available if the Levenberg-Marquardt optimization algorithm is used to locate the minimum point. The additional computation required of the regularization is thus minimal.

8.5.4   Early Stopping

With a goal of obtaining a model with desirable generalization properties, it is difficult to decide when it is best to stop training by just looking at the learning curve for training by itself. It is possible to overfit the training data if the training session is not stopped at the right point.

The onset of overfitting can be detected through cross-validation in which the available data are divided into training, validation, and testing subsets. The training subset is used for computing the gradient and updating the network weights. The error on the validation set is monitored during the training session. The validation error will normally decrease during the initial phase of training (see Figure 8.17), as does the error on the training set. However, when the network begins to overfit the data, the error on the validation set will typically

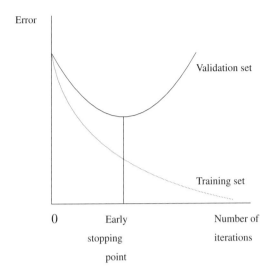

FIGURE 8.17 Early stopping method. The validation error will normally decrease during the initial phase of training, as does the error on the training set. However, when the network begins to overfit the data, the error on the validation set will typically begin to rise. In the method of early stopping, when the validation error increases for a specified number of iterations, the training is stopped, and the weights at the minimum of the validation error are returned.

begin to rise. In the method of early stopping, when the validation error starts to increase after a number of iterations, the training is stopped, and the weights at the minimum of the validation error are returned for the optimum network complexity.

8.5.5 Bagging

In bagging (or bootstrap aggregating), multiple versions of a predictor are generated and they are used to get an aggregated predictor, see Breiman (1996a; 1996b). The multiple versions are formed by making bootstrap replicates of the training set and using these as new training sets. When predicting a numerical outcome, the aggregation takes the average over the multiple versions that are generated from bootstrapping. According to Breiman (1996a; 1996b), both theoretical and empirical evidence suggest that bagging can greatly improve the forecasting performance of a good but unstable model, whereas a small change in the training data can result in large changes in model, but can slightly degrade the performance of stable models.

Let L represent the training set that consists of data $\{(y_t, \boldsymbol{x}_t) : t = 1, ..., N_L\}$, where N_L is the number of observations in the training set. A neural network model is fitted to the training set and this generates a predictor $f(\boldsymbol{x}_t, L)$—that is, if the input is $\boldsymbol{x}_t$, y_t is predicted by $f(\boldsymbol{x}_t, L)$. Now, suppose we have a sequence of training sets $\{L_k : k = 1, ..., K\}$ each consisting of N_L independent observations from the same underlying distribution as L. We can use the $\{L_k\}$ to get a better predictor than the single learning set predictor $f(x_t, L)$ by working with the sequence of predictors $\{f(x_t, L_k)\}$. An obvious procedure is to replace $f(x_t, L)$ by the average of $f(x_t, L_k)$ over k—that is, by $f_A(x_t) = \sum_{k=1}^{K} f(x_t, L_k)$. However, usually there is only a single training set L without the luxury of replicates of L. In this case, repeated bootstrap[13] samples $L^{(b)} = \{(y_t^{(b)}, x_t^{(b)}) : t = 1, ..., N_L\}$ can be drawn from $L = \{(y_t, x_t) : t = 1, ..., N_L\}$. Each $\{(y_t^{(b)}, x_t^{(b)})\}$ is a random pick from the original training set $\{(y_t, x_t), t = 1, ..., N_L\}$ with replacement. The bootstrap samples $L^{(b)}$ are used to form predictors $\{f(x_t, L^{(b)})\}$. The bagging predictor f_B can thus be calculated as

$$f_B(x_t) = \sum_{b=1}^{B} f(x_t, L^{(b)}), \qquad (8.34)$$

where B represents the total number of bootstrap replicates of the training set.

Gençay and Qi (2001) and Gençay and Salih (2001) investigated the effectiveness of cross-validation, Bayesian regularization, early stopping, and bagging to mitigate overfitting and improving generalizations for pricing and hedging derivative securities with daily S&P 500 index daily call options from January 1988 to December 1993. Their results indicate that Bayesian regularization can generate significantly smaller pricing and delta-hedging errors than the baseline neural network model (based on SIC) and the Black-Scholes (BS) model for some years. While early stopping does not affect the pricing errors, it significantly reduces the hedging error in 4 of the 6 years they investigate. Although computationally most demanding, bagging seems to provide the most accurate pricing and delta-hedging. Furthermore, the standard deviation of the mean squared prediction error of bagging is far less than that of the baseline model in all 6 years, and the standard deviation of the average hedging error of bagging is far less than that of the baseline model in 5 out of 6 years. Since Gençay and Qi (2001) found in general that these regularization methods work as effectively as a homogeneity hint (see Section 8.8.1 for hints on option pricing), they suggested that they be used at least in cases when no appropriate hints are available.[14]

---

[13] Different bootstrap procedures can be implemented according to the nature of the data.

[14] A method with hints describes a situation where, in addition to the set of input-output pairs of an unknown function, there is additional prior information about the properties of the unknown function which is provided to the learning algorithm. In general, hints provide auxiliary information about the unknown function which can be used to guide the learning process. The idea of using auxiliary information about the target function to help the learning process is clearly a basic one, and has been used in the literature under different names such as hints, prior knowledge and explicit rules. Because hints impose additional constraints on the set of allowable solutions to which the learning process may converge, the hints may tend to worsen the in-sample performance by excluding some solutions that might otherwise fit the data better. This clearly helps to avoid overfitting in the learning algorithms. The main purpose of using hints is to improve the out-of-sample performance of the learning algorithms. See Section 8.8 for the literature on models with hints.

Gençay and Qi (2001) slightly modified the bagging procedure of Breiman (1996a) to integrate it with the cross-validation method. First, the available data are divided into the training, validation, and testing samples. Second, a bootstrap sample is selected from the training set. The bootstrap sample is then used to train the neural network with 1 to 10 hidden layer units. The validation set is used to select the best neural network that has the optimal number of hidden layer units, and the best model is used to generate one set of predictions on the testing set. This is repeated 25 times giving 25 sets of predictions ($B = 25$). Third, the bagging prediction is the average across the 25 sets of predictions, and the prediction error is computed as the difference between the actual and the bagging prediction values.

8.6 ADAPTIVITY

When the underlying data dynamics are stationary, the estimated network parameters do not change over time. If, on the other hand, the underlying data dynamics are nonstationary such that parameters of the underlying process vary over time, the estimated network parameters would not be able to respond to these changes and the estimated network may lose its generalization properties. Recursive filtering is one way to overcome this difficulty. In a recursive setting, the network parameters are allowed to be updated in response to the newly received data in a real-time setting. The recursive setting implies that the network's generalization capabilities remain accurate and robust to changes in a nonstationary environment. The neural network estimation methods deal with nonstationarity by assuming that the data is *pseudo-stationary* (or locally-stationary) in a short time window. This time window may vary from minutes to a few days depending on the nature of the studied problem. Under this pseudo-stationary property, the network parameters are reestimated to absorb the changes in the underlying data structure. A typical dynamic approach to adaptive filtering is to use the moving sample approach in a specified time window. In this approach, the network parameters are estimated with the data allowed by this chosen time window. As new observations become available, the window is moved forward by adding the new observation to the data set and dropping the last observation from it. With this updated data set, the network parameters are reestimated. This process repeats itself as new observations become available. It is this recursive filtering approach that gives a neural network model its adaptive features.

8.7 ESTIMATION OF RECURRENT NETWORKS

Recurrent networks, with the consideration of the internal feedback, are more general models than the feedforward networks.   The salient property of the recurrent network architecture is that the hidden unit activation functions (internal states) are fed back at every time step to provide an additional input. This recurrence gives the network dynamical properties, which make it possible for the network to possess internal memory, but also make the estimation of these networks difficult. In this section, we briefly review the available estimation methodologies for recurrent networks.

8.7.1   Extended Kalman Filter for Recurrent Networks

Extensive usage of recurrent networks has been limited due to a number of estimation difficulties. One of these difficulties is the calculation of the total partial derivatives of a recurrent network model's output(s) with respect to its parameters. In a real-time updating algorithm, the calculation of these derivatives can be computationally expensive. Another difficulty is that the estimation of recurrent networks with gradient descent methods often tends to be trapped in a local optima due to highly correlated hidden unit outputs at successive time steps. Puskorius and Feldkamp (1994) have argued that estimation methods based on the extended Kalman filter (EKF) require significantly fewer iterations than the pure gradient descent methods and are computationally economical. Puskorius and Feldkamp (1994) extended the dynamic backpropagation framework developed by Narendra and Parthasarathy (1990, 1991) to recurrent networks as an EKF where gradients are calculated by dynamic backpropogation.

Atiya and Parlos (2000) proposed an algorithm for recurrent network training which is based on approximating the error gradient, has lower computational complexity in computing the weight update, and reaches the optimum with smaller number of iterations relative to existing backpropogation algorithms.[15] Parlos et al. (2000) studied multi-step-ahead prediction in complex system using dynamic recurrent neural networks. Parlos et al. (2001) investigated nonlinear state filtering in complex systems using recurrent neural networks.

8.7.2   Multistream Training for Recurrent Networks

Recurrent networks are often regarded as difficult network architectures to train when the underlying data dynamics are heteroskedastic. This is when a certain portion of the data exhibits small variations which are followed by small variations, and when large variations are followed by large variations in various portions of the data. In addition to the danger of being trapped in a local optima, this type of heteroskedasticy causes what is called the *recency effect*. When the recency effect occurs, the network forgets the information content of the earlier learning from the past data as it processes new information. Feldkamp and Puskorius (1998) propose a method called *multistream* learning to tackle the recency effect. Multistream learning is based on the principle that parameter updates should simultaneously satisfy the demands of multiple input-output pairs. The estimation framework is such that the data set is split into multiple subsets (streams) and the parameter updates are carried out in each stream independently. The coordination between these independent parameter updates is not carried out by simple averaging but through a weight matrix that takes into account the de-

---

[15] Atiya and El-Shoura (1999) compared neural network forecasting techniques for river flow forecasting.

mands from various data streams. Feldkamp and Puskorius (1998) demostrated that multistream learning improves the generalization properties of the recurrent network models and this improvement is an increasing function of the number of independent streams used in the estimation environment.

8.7.3 An Example: IBM Volatility Prediction

In this section, we model the IBM data log(price) series used in Section 8.3.1 to estimate a hidden-recurrent network. The model has 10 inputs (10 lagged values of the log(price)'s) and 10 hidden units where each hidden unit has a feedback. The results are presented in Figure 8.18. The MSPEs are 6.71e-008 and 5.59e-008. These results are slighly worse than those obtained with the feedforward network model in Section 8.3.1. This is due to the fact that it is more difficult to estimate recurrent networks numerically and achieve an optimal convergence. This is why the multistream training type methods mentioned in Section 8.7.2 are useful tools in recurrent network estimation.

8.8 APPLICATIONS OF NEURAL NETWORK MODELS

8.8.1 Option Pricing

The Black and Scholes (1973) pricing formula's appeal to practitioners often originates from its analytical simplicity to determine the price of a European option on a non-dividend paying asset by

$$C_t = S_t N(d_1) - K e^{-r\tau} N(d_2) \tag{8.35}$$

with

$$d_1 = [\ln(S_t/K) + (r + 0.5\sigma^2)\tau]/(\sigma\sqrt{\tau})$$
$$d_2 = d_1 - \sigma\sqrt{\tau},$$

where N is the cumulative normal distribution, S_t is the price of the underlying security, K is the exercise price, r is the prevailing risk-free interest rate, τ is the time-to-maturity and σ is the volatility of the underlying asset. Equation 8.35 contains neither preferences of individuals nor the preferences of the aggregate market.

The Black-Scholes derivation has been mostly criticized for its distributional assumptions of the underlying security. Empiricial studies of stock price find too many outliers for a simple constant variance log-normal distribution (Merton, 1976). Alternative explanations have been suggested by many researchers. Oldfield et al. (1977) and Ball and Torous (1985) fitted mixtures of continuous and jump processes to the stock price data. Attempts to accomodate stochastic volatility and stochastic interest rates within the framework of Black-Scholes analysis have been complicated by the complexity of the estimation of the market price of risk. Bakshi et al. (1997) provided closed form solutions for valuing options under stochastic volatility and stochastic interest rates using the Fourier inversion method of Heston (1993) to calculate volatility and interest rate market

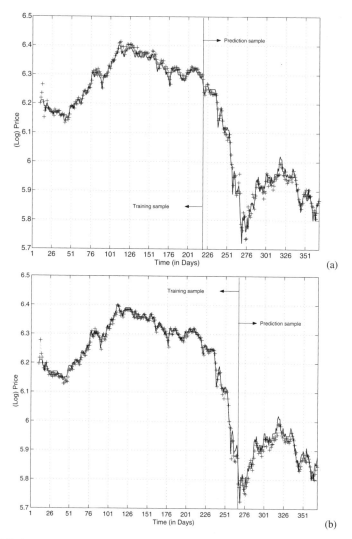

FIGURE 8.18   The daily IBM log(price) predictions with a hidden-recurrent network model. The model has 10 inputs (10 lagged values of the log(price)'s) and 10 hidden units where each hidden unit has a feedback. Actual data are in solid line. Estimated and predicted points are represented with a + sign. (a) Training set with $t = 1, 2, \ldots, 220$. (b) Training set with $t = 1, 2, \ldots, 268$.

risk premiums. Their results documented that stochastic volatility and stochastic interest rate models are structurally misspecified. However adding the stochastic volatility feature to the Black-Scholes model improves out-of-sample pricing and hedging performance of the model. In a later paper Sarwar and Krehbiel (2000) reported that the Black-Scholes model calculated with daily revised implied volatilities performs as well as the stochastic volatility model for European currency call options. Derman and Kani (1994), Dupire (1994) and Rubinstein (1994) developed a deterministic volatility function (DVF) option valuation model in an attempt to exactly explain the observed cross-section of option prices. However, Dumas *et al.* (1998) reported that the DVF option valuation model's fit is no better than an ad hoc procedure that merely smooths Black-Scholes implied volatilities across exercise prices and time-to-maturity.

Nonparametric valuation models are a natural extension as it is easier to relax the distributional assumptions. A natural nonparametric function for pricing a European call option on a nondividend paying asset relates the price of the option to the set of variables that characterize the option, namely, the price of the underlying asset S_t, the strike price K, and the time to maturity τ. Therefore, the option pricing function can be written as

$$C_t = f(S_t, K, \tau). \tag{8.36}$$

This approach is followed by Hutchinson *et al.* (1994). The function will also be valid to learn prices generated by a Black-Scholes model as the interest rate and volatility parameters present in the formula are constant and cannot be identified by a nonparametric estimator of the function f. It is generally more difficult to estimate nonparametrically such a function when the number of input variables is large. To reduce the number of inputs, Hutchinson *et al.* (1994) divided the function and its arguments by K and wrote the pricing function as follows:

$$\frac{C_t}{K} = f\left(\frac{S_t}{K}, 1, \tau\right). \tag{8.37}$$

This form assumes the homogeneity of degree one[16] in the asset price and the strike price of the pricing function f.

Garcia and Renault (1995) proposed an equilibrium model that ensures the homogeneity property which keeps the Black-Scholes functional shape. Garcia and Gençay (2000) used a generalized Black-Scholes formula suggested in Garcia and Renault (1995),

$$\frac{C_t}{K} = \frac{S_t}{K} f_1\left(\frac{S_t}{K}, \tau\right) - b(\tau) f_2\left(\frac{S_t}{K}, \tau\right), \tag{8.38}$$

---

[16] The crucial challenge is to determine to what extent this homogeneity property is restrictive for the nonparametric learning of the option pricing function. From Merton (1995), we know that the call pricing function is homogeneous of degree one in the asset price and the strike price when the unconditional distribution of returns is independent of the level of the asset price. In Garcia and Renault (1995), Proposition 2 establishes that a necessary and sufficient condition for homogeneity is the conditional independence (under the pricing probability measure) between future returns and the current price, given the currently available information other than the history of the underlying asset price.

where theoretical restrictions stemming from the absence of arbitrage or from equilibrium constrain the functions f_1 and f_2 to approximate the same function (for example, the normal distribution function in the Black-Scholes formula), with possibly different arguments. These theoretical restrictions are accounted for by constraining the neural network structure to be the same for f_1 and f_2, where $b(\tau)$ is a function of the maturity of the option.

The benchmark option pricing function in Equation 8.37 and the generalized form in Equation 8.38 are estimated with the following feedforward regressions:

$$f^{nh}\left(\frac{S_t}{K}, \tau; \theta\right) = \beta_0 + \sum_{j=1}^{d} \frac{\beta_j}{1 + \exp\left[-\gamma_{j0} - \gamma_{j1}\left(\frac{S_t}{K}\right) - \gamma_{j2}\tau\right]} \tag{8.39}$$

$$f^{wh}\left(\frac{S_t}{K}, \tau; \theta\right) = \beta_0 + \frac{S_t}{K}\left(\sum_{j=1}^{d} \frac{\beta_j^1}{1 + \exp\left[-\gamma_{j0}^1 - \gamma_{j1}^1\left(\frac{S_t}{K}\right) - \gamma_{j2}^1\tau\right]}\right) \tag{8.40}$$

$$- e^{-\alpha\tau}\left(\sum_{j=1}^{d} \frac{\beta_j^2}{1 + \exp\left[-\gamma_{j0}^2 - \gamma_{j1}^2\left(\frac{S_t}{K}\right) - \gamma_{j2}^2\tau\right]}\right),$$

where f^{wh} and f^{nh} refer to models with hint and with no hint, respectively.

A method with hints describes a situation where, in addition to the set of input-output pairs of an unknown function, there is additional prior information about the properties of the unknown function which is provided to the learning algorithm. In general, hints provide auxiliary information about the unknown function which can be used to guide the learning process. The idea of using auxiliary information about the target function to help the learning process is clearly a basic one, and has been used in the literature under different names such as hints, prior knowledge and explicit rules. Because hints impose additional constraints on the set of allowable solutions to which the learning process may converge, the hints may tend to worsen the in-sample performance by excluding some solutions that might otherwise fit the data better. This clearly helps to avoid overfitting in the learning algorithms. The main purpose of using hints is to improve the out-of-sample performance of the learning algorithms.

There are different types of hints common to different applications. Invariance hints of Hu (1962), Duda and Hart (1973), Hinton (1987), and Minsky and Papert (1988) are the most common types of hints in pattern recognition applications. An invariance hint asserts that the target function is invariant under certain transformations of the input. Monotonicity hints, as in Abu-Mostafa (1993), are common in applications such as medical diagnosis and credit-rating where the target function is assumed to be monotonic in certain variables. Symmetry hints are commonly used in foreign exchange predictions by technical analysts. Abu-Mostafa (1994, 1995) indicated that appropriately placed restrictions would lead to improved out-of-sample generalizations. Abu-Mostafa (2001) augmented the loss function with consistency hint error functions based on the Kullback-Leibler distance for financial model calibration.

The data are daily S&P 500 Index European options from the Chicago Board Options Exchange for the period 1990 to 1993. The S&P 500 index options market is extremely liquid and it is one of the most active options markets in the United States. This market is the closest to the theoretical setting of the Black-Scholes model. In constructing the data used in the estimation, options with zero volume are not used. For each year, the sample is split into three parts: first half of the year (training period), third quarter (validation period), and fourth quarter (prediction period). The complexity of the networks is based on their performance in an out-of-sample validation period. Equations 8.39 and 8.40 show that the networks for the model with hint will always have about twice as many parameters as the networks without the hint for a given number of hidden units. For a fair performance comparison of the two networks, a three-step strategy is adopted. First, f^{nh} is estimated with 1 to 10 hidden units, and f^{wh} is estimated with 1 to 5 hidden units over half of the data points for a particular sample, the training period. Next, the network in each family that gives the best MSPE in the validation period is selected. Finally, the prediction performance (MSPE) is evaluated for the data in the prediction sample.

Results are presented in Table 8.1. For each year, the average MSPE obtained over the five experiments for each family of networks and the average number of hidden units selected are reported. Not surprisingly, the linear model provides the poorest performance in terms of MSPE. The MSPE performance of the Black-Scholes model is significantly better than the linear model but worse than the feedforward network models. Between the feedforward network models, the average MSPE for the models with the homogeneity hint is always smaller than the MSPE of the models with no hint. The average MSPE ratios of the models with and without hint for 1990 to 1993 are 92, 93, 92, and 72%, respectively. Furthermore, the ratio of the MSPE standard deviations across the five experiments substantially favors the model with the homogeneity hint. In most years, this ratio is lower than 50%. The values of the Diebold and Mariano (1995) (D&M) statistic are all large and positive, which means that we strongly reject the equality of the forecast errors in favor of the feedforward neural networks with hint.

To investigate for which options the two types of networks differ in their out-of-sample pricing performance, Table 8.2 reports the out-of-sample MSPEs for various categories of options based on maturity and moneyness for 1993. The ratios of the means and standard deviations of the feedforward networks with and without the homogeneity hint are lowest for the two ends of the spectrum, the short-term out-of-the money options and the long-term in-the-money options. The networks predict with the least difference for the medium-term near-the-money options. Garcia and Gençay (2000) presented evidence that this breakdown of predictions by maturity and moneyness emphasizes that the homogeneity hint appears most useful to generalize out of sample when there are

Statistics	MSPE With Hint	MSPE No Hint	Ratio	MSPE Linear/BS
(1990, Total: 3605, Validation: 2075, Prediction: 2166)				
$\bar{x}$	0.6761 (3)	0.7253 (6)	0.92	8.15/2.62
σ	0.0763	0.1222	0.62	
D&M	5.04			
(1991, Total: 4481, Validation: 1922, Prediction: 2061)				
$\bar{x}$	0.3498 (4)	0.3775 (8)	0.93	3.45/1.73
σ	0.0148	0.0336	0.44	
D&M	11.57			
(1992, Total: 4374, Validation: 1922, Prediction: 1848)				
$\bar{x}$	0.1511 (4)	0.1649 (7)	0.92	2.39/1.36
σ	0.0115	0.0126	0.91	
D&M	14.97			
(1993, Total: 4214, Validation: 1973, Prediction: 2030)				
$\bar{x}$	0.1054 (4)	0.1453 (6)	0.72	2.28/0.74
σ	0.0222	0.0498	0.44	
D&M	11.24			

TABLE 8.1   Out-of-sample mean square prediction errors of the S&P-500 call options. This table presents the out-of-sample mean square prediction error (MSPE) performance of a neural network with and without a hint, and of a linear model for call option prices from the S&P-500 call options. The table reports the average ($\bar{x}$) of the five MSPEs corresponding to five networks estimated from different seeds. The average number of hidden units of the five runs are reported between parentheses next to the average MSPEs. σ is the standard deviation of the five MSPEs of the estimated networks. The "Ratio" is the ratio between the corresponding statistics of the feedforward network model with hint and without hint. D&M refers to the Diebold and Mariano (1995) test for a mean loss differential (Mizrach, 1995, has a similar test for a mean loss differential). This test statistic is distributed standard normal for large samples. All D&M test statistics are calculated from the loss differential of the MSPEs between the feedforward network models with and without the homogeneity hint. MSPE figures reported have been multiplied by 10^4.

fewer observations in the learning sample. The results reported for 1993 are representative of those obtained for the other years.

The pricing performance of the competing feedforward network models indicates that the networks with hint predict better than the networks without hint. This section demostrates that pricing accuracy gains can be made by exploiting

MSPE $\times 10^4$	No of Options	Mean No Hint	Mean Hint	Ratio	St. Dev No Hint	St. Dev Hint	Ratio
Short Term							
Out	128	0.0720	0.0492	0.68	0.0271	0.0149	0.55
Near	473	0.1168	0.0910	0.78	0.0155	0.0149	0.96
In	143	0.2160	0.2323	1.08	0.0834	0.0385	0.46
Medium Term							
Out	198	0.0292	0.0216	0.74	0.0068	0.0064	0.94
Near	409	0.0511	0.0503	0.91	0.0067	0.0060	0.92
In	72	0.1962	0.1907	0.97	0.0140	0.0176	1.25
Long Term							
Out	186	0.0672	0.0512	0.76	0.0131	0.0193	1.47
At	337	0.0526	0.0439	0.84	0.0118	0.0016	0.14
In	84	1.5109	0.8149	0.54	1.0780	0.3484	0.32

TABLE 8.2 Out-of-sample mean square prediction errors per maturity and moneyness. This table presents a comparison between the out-of-sample mean square prediction error (MSPE) performance of a neural network with a homogeneity hint (WH) and of a regular feedforward network (NN) for the S&P 500 European call options of different maturity and moneyness. The means and standard deviations are computed over five MSPEs obtained from five estimated networks starting from five different seeds. The maturity cutoff points are less than 0.1 (short term), between 0.1 and 0.2 (medium term), and above 0.2 (long term). The moneyness cutoff points are less than 0.97 (out of the money), between 0.97 and 1.05 (near the money), and above 1.05 (in the money).

the implications of the homogeneity property of the options prices in a neural network framework. Instead of setting up a learning network mapping the ratio S_t/K and the time to maturity (τ) directly into the derivative price, Garcia and Gençay (2000) broke down the pricing function into two parts, one controlled by the ratio S_t/K, the other one by a function of time to maturity. The results indicate that the homogeneity hint always reduces the out-of-sample mean squared prediction error compared with a feedforward neural network with no hint.

8.8.2 Filtering, Adaptation, and Predictability in Foreign Exchange Markets

In Section 2.4.4, we studied simple moving averages as linear filters. This section investigates the linear and nonlinear predictability of spot foreign exchange rate returns from past buy-sell signals of the simple technical trading rules[17] by using

---

[17] In the earlier technical trading rules literature, Cornell and Dietrich (1978) showed that the filter type rules generate profits in excess of the buy-and-hold strategy. Later, Sweeney (1986) documented

the feedforward network regressions. Let p_t, $t = 1, 2, \ldots, N$ be the daily spot exchange rate series. The return series are calculated by $r_t = \log(p_t) - \log(p_{t-1})$. Let m_t^n denote the time t value of a moving average rule of length n. Consequently, m_t^n is calculated by

$$m_t^n = \frac{1}{n} \sum_{i=0}^{n-1} p_{t-i}. \tag{8.41}$$

The buy and sell signals are calculated by

$$s_t^{n1,n2} = m_t^{n1} - m_t^{n2}, \tag{8.42}$$

where $n1$ and $n2$ are the short and the long moving averages, respectively. The rules used here are $(n1, n2) = [(1, 50), (1, 200)]$, where $n1$ and $n2$ are in days.

The single-layer feedforward network regression model with past buy and sell signals and with q hidden units is written as

$$r_t = \alpha_0 + \sum_{i=1}^{q} \beta_i g \left(\alpha_{i0} + \sum_{i=1}^{p} \alpha_{ij} s_{t-i}^{n1,n2} \right) + \epsilon_t, \quad \epsilon_t \sim (0, \sigma_t^2), \tag{8.43}$$

where g is the logistic activation function. Feedforward network regression models require a choice for the number of hidden units in a network, which is determined by a cross-validation method. The number of hidden units is set to be $1, 2, \ldots, 15$ and the number of lags is set to $p = 9$ to capture the potential persistence in the series.

The data set is divided into two parts, namely the in-sample and out-of-sample data sets. For the implementation of the cross-validation, the 250 most recent observations (approximately one year of trading data) in the in-sample data are used first to calculate the optimal number of hidden units corresponding to the smallest cross-validated mean square error (MSE) among all possible hidden units. Afterward, one observation from the further past is added to the set of 250 observations, which brings the total number of observations to 251. The cross-validation takes place in order to calculate the optimal number of hidden units corresponding to the smallest cross-validated MSE among all possible hidden units.

This process of adding observations further from the past is carried out until all in-sample observations are utilized. This process gives us a sequence of

---

the profitability of filter rules with the Deutsche Mark. Taylor and Allen (1992) and Taylor (1992) found similar evidence for even more extensive sets of rules and data series. Neftci (1991) designed formal algorithms to represent various forms of technical analysis in order to determine whether these rules are well defined. He concluded that trading rules provide forecast power only when the underlying process under study is nonlinear. LeBaron (1999) investigated the technical trading rule profitability and foreign exchange intervention; Levich and Thomas (1993) followed the methodology of Brock *et al.* (1992) and used bootstrap simulations to demonstrate the statistical significance of the technical trading rules against well-known parametric null models of exchange rates. Franses and Griensven (1998) investigated the ability to forecast exchange rates using neural networks and technical trading rules.

optimal hidden units corresponding to each in-sample data length. From this sequence, the number of hidden units corresponding to the smallest MSE is determined. This choice of the number of hidden units also corresponds to a certain in-sample data length. These choices for the number of hidden units and the in-sample data length are used to predict the *first* available *forecast observation* and to calculate the *corresponding forecast error*.

In the next step, the sample is rolled one observation forward and the second observation in the forecast sample is studied in the same manner as described for the first forecast observation. This procedure is repeated until all observations are covered in the forecast sample. In the final step, sign predictions and the D&M tests are calculated based on the MSPEs of the test and the random walk models.

This adaptive dynamic updating is clearly an expensive one. It does, however, have the following advantages:

- The number of hidden units and the number of observations needed for the in-sample estimation are determined optimally, which prevents *overfitting* in noisy environments. This procedure may utilize only a certain number of in-sample observations rather than the entire in-sample if a certain subset of the in-sample observations provides smaller MSE relative to the MSE of the entire in-sample set. In other words, the data are filtered in an adaptive fashion such that the generalization properties of the network are preserved as much as possible.

- It is a *fair* procedure as it only relies on *in-sample* performance. The parameter estimates used for forecasting purposes are obtained from the in-sample estimation and the observations in the forecast sample (out-of-sample observations) are *not* utilized at any stage of the model specification or estimation. Finally, this model selection methodology is completely data driven.

For each exchange rate, the out-of-sample predictive performance of the random walk process, GARCH(1,1) process (Bollerslev, 1986; Engle, 1982), and the feedforward networks are examined. The data set consists of daily spot rates for the British Pound (BP), Deutsche Mark (DM), French Franc (FF), Japanese Yen (JY) and Swiss Franc (SF). The data set is from the period of January 2, 1973, to July 7, 1992, for a total of 4894 observations. The summary statistics of the daily returns are presented in Table 8.3. The daily returns are calculated as the log differences of the levels. All five series exhibit slight skewness and high kurtosis, which is common in high-frequency financial time series data. The first 10 autocorrelations ($\rho_1, \ldots, \rho_{10}$) and the Bartlett standard errors from these series are also reported in Table 8.3.[18] All series show evidence of autocorrelation. The

---

[18] Bartlett standard error is defined to be $1/\sqrt{N}$ where N is the sample size.

Description	FF	DM	JY	SF	BP
Sample size	4893				
Mean*100	0.000	0.016	0.018	0.021	-0.004
Std.*100	0.663	0.679	0.622	0.771	0.634
Skewness	-0.107	0.061	0.946	-0.063	-0.083
Kurtosis	10.499	8.385	19.754	6.724	7.085
Max	0.060	0.062	0.095	0.044	0.046
Min	-0.059	-0.059	-0.063	-0.058	-0.038
ρ_1	0.035	0.042	0.050	0.038	0.067
ρ_2	-0.012	-0.016	0.012	-0.003	-0.008
ρ_3	0.020	0.025	0.037	0.009	-0.011
ρ_4	0.000	-0.011	-0.004	-0.013	-0.007
ρ_5	0.023	0.029	0.030	0.015	0.045
ρ_6	-0.009	0.016	0.008	0.018	-0.010
ρ_7	0.023	0.005	0.015	-0.004	-0.012
ρ_8	0.028	0.038	0.010	0.025	0.011
ρ_9	0.043	0.039	0.037	0.034	0.036
ρ_{10}	0.011	0.014	0.039	0.017	-0.022
Bartlett std. errors	0.014				
LBP	27.6	33.0	38.3	20.3	44.0
$\chi^2_{0.05}(10)$	18.307				

TABLE 8.3 Summary statistics for the daily exchange rates: Log First Difference, January 2, 1973 to July 7, 1992. FF, DM, JY, SF and BP refer to French Franc, Deutsche Mark, Japanese Yen, Swiss Franc and British Pound, respectively. $\rho_1, \ldots, \rho_{10}$ are the first 10 autocorrelations of each series. LBP refers to the Ljung-Box-Pierce statistic and it is distributed $\chi^2(10)$ under the null hypothesis of identical and independent distribution.

Ljung-Box-Pierce[19] statistics are shown in the last row. These are calculated for the first 10 lags and are distributed $\chi^2(10)$ under the null hypothesis of identical and independently distributed observations. All five series reject the null hypothesis of identical and independent observations.

The out-of-sample forecasts are calculated from the last one-third of the data set. In total, there are 4684 observations for estimation so that the last 1561 observations are kept for the out-of-sample predictions. As a measure of performance, the out-of-sample MSPE and sign predictions are used. To assess the statistical significance of the out-of-sample predictions, the D&M test is calculated for all currencies. This is a test of the null hypothesis of no difference in the accuracy for the two competing forecasts and it is used to evaluate

---

[19] In the time series literature, numerous tests for residual autocorrelation have been proposed. The widely used tests are proposed by Ljung and Box (1978) and Pierce (1977). The book by Davidson and MacKinnon (1993) has more discussion on testing for serial correlation.

the statistical significance of the MSPEs of the GARCH(1,1) and feedforward network regression models relative to that of the random walk model. In addition to the D&M test, the percentage correct sign predictions of the out-of-sample forecasts are reported. Out-of-sample forecasts are completely *ex ante*, using only information actually available. The out-of-sample forecasts with the buy-sell signals as the conditioning set are computed recursively by estimating the conditional mean $E(r_t|s_{t-1}^{n1,n2}, \ldots, s_{t-p}^{n1,n2})$, and then $E(r_{t+1}|s_t^{n1,n2}, \ldots, s_{t-p+1}^{n1,n2})$ and so forth, in real time. The out-of-sample forecasts with past returns as the conditioning set are computed in a similar fashion.

In Table 8.4, the predictability of the current returns with the past buy-sell signals of the moving average rules is investigated with the (1,50) and (1,200) rules. With rule (1,50) for BP, DM, FF, JY, and SF, the feedforward network provides 10.7, 11.0, 10.5, 12.0, and 11.3% forecast improvement over the random walk model and an average of 58% correct sign predictions for the five currencies. Overall, the feedforward network regression forecasts outperform the GARCH(1,1) and the random walk model forecasts. The comparison of the (1,50) rule with (1,200) also indicates that the (1,50) rule provides more accurate forecasts over the (1,200) rule. This may be due to the fact that the (1,200) rule oversmooths the data.

This section demonstrates that although the adaptive methods for model selection and data updating are computationally expensive, they have the advantage that the model complexity, and the number of observations needed for the in-sample estimation are determined optimally, which prevents overfitting in noisy environments. In other words, this procedure may utilize only a certain number of in-sample observations rather than the entire in-sample if a certain subset of the in-sample observations provides a smaller mean square error relative to the mean square error of the entire in-sample set. It is a fair procedure as it only relies on in-sample performance. In other words, observations in the forecast sample (out-of-sample observations) are *not* utilized at any stage of the model specification.

Models	Statistics	BP	DM	FF	JY	SF
		MA=[1,50]				
GARCH (1,1)						
	MSPE Ratio	0.993	0.992	0.994	0.995	0.994
	D&M	0.145	0.143	0.156	0.152	0.138
	Sign	0.51	0.50	0.49	0.49	0.51
Feedforward Networks						
	MSPE Ratio	0.893	0.890	0.895	0.880	0.887
	D&M	0.007	0.006	0.011	0.007	0.008
	Sign	0.59	0.57	0.58	0.57	0.59
	Hidden Units	9	6	8	7	8
		MA=[1,200]				
GARCH (1,1)						
	MSPE Ratio	0.987	0.991	0.992	0.993	0.991
	D&M	0.134	0.146	0.154	0.149	0.142
	Sign	0.52	0.51	0.50	0.49	0.51
Feedforward Networks						
	MSPE Ratio	0.897	0.891	0.893	0.883	0.886
	D&M	0.006	0.006	0.009	0.008	0.007
	Sign	0.58	0.57	0.57	0.57	0.58
	Hidden Units	8	7	8	9	10

TABLE 8.4 Out-of-sample prediction results with rule MA=[1,50] and with MA=[1,200]. The data set consists of daily spot rates for the British pound (BP), Deutsche mark (DM), French franc (FF), Japanese yen (JY) and Swiss franc (SF). The data set is from the period of January 2, 1973, to July 7, 1992, for a total of 4894 observations. The MSPE ratio is the ratio of the MSPE of the corresponding model to that of the random walk model. D&M refers to the Diebold and Mariano (1995) test for a mean loss differential. This test statistic is distributed standard normal in large samples. All D&M test statistics are calculated from the loss differential of the mean square prediction errors of the corresponding model to that of the random walk model. In the table above, the p-values of the D&M statistics are reported and underlined if less than 5%. Sign refers to the percentage of the correct signs in the out-of-sample period. For the hidden units and feedforward regressions, the average number of hidden units and the number of hidden units from the in-sample estimation are reported in last rows of the corresponding panels for each method.

NOTATIONS

Non-Greek conventions

$\mathcal{A}$	system matrix (state-space representation)
$B(a, b)$	beta distribution with parameters a and b
$\mathcal{B}$	orthonormal basis (DWPT), coefficient matrix of the control vector (state-space representation)
B_j	jth level bandpass variance
$\mathcal{C}$	observation matrix (state-space representation)
d_j	jth level wavelet detail
D	homogeneity of variance test statistic (DWT)
$\widetilde{D}$	homogeneity of variance test statistic (MODWT)
e	base e
e_N	estimation error (residual)
f	frequency index
f_G	Gegenbauer frequency
$f()$	generic function
$g()$	generic function
g_l	DWT scaling filter

$\tilde{g}_l$	MODWT scaling filter
$G()$	frequency response (transfer, gain) function
$\mathcal{G}()$	squared gain function
h_l	DWT wavelet filter, hidden unit (neural net)
$\tilde{h}_l$	MODWT wavelet filter
$H()$	frequency response (transfer, gain) function
$\mathcal{H}()$	squared gain function
i	$\sqrt{-1}$, index for filter
I	information set
j	level (scale) in wavelet decomposition
k	wavelet shift index, length of a vector (neural net)
k_N	Kalman gain (scalar case)
$\mathcal{K}_N$	Kalman gain (state-space representation)
l	index for filter
L	length of a (unit scale) wavelet filter
L_j	length of the jth level wavelet filter
m	number of hidden units (neural net)
M	number of lags in a filter sequence
n	number of hidden units (neural net)
N	sample size, number of leads in a filter sequence
$N(\mu, \sigma^2)$	Gaussian random variable with mean μ and variance σ^2
p_t	price series
P	prediction (Kalman filter)
$\mathcal{P}_N^e$	variance-covariance matrix of estimation error (Kalman filter)
$\mathcal{P}_N^p$	variance-covariance matrix of prediction error (Kalman filter)
q	degrees of freedom, length of a vector (neural net)
$\mathcal{Q}_t$	system noise variance-covariance matrix (Kalman filter)
r	number of recurrence in a recurrent network (neural net)
r_t	return series
$\boldsymbol{r}_j$	jth level wavelet rough

$R(,)$	risk (mean square error)
$\mathcal{R}_N$	observation noise variance-covariance matrix (Kalman filter)
s	average, function (neural net)
s_j	jth level wavelet smooth
$S()$	spectral density function (SDF)
$\mathcal{S}_N$	error variance-covariance matrix (Kalman filter)
t	time index
$\mathcal{T}$	wavelet packet tree
$u_{n,l}$	wavelet packet filter
$U()$	frequency response (transfer, gain) function
U_t	control vector (state-space representation)
$\mathcal{U}()$	squared gain function
v_t	volatility series
w_t	filter length
w	finite length vector of DWT coefficients
w_j	jth level finite length vector of DWT coefficients
$\tilde{w}$	finite length vector of MODWT coefficients
$\tilde{w}_j$	jth level finite length vector of MODWT coefficients
$W(,)$	continuous wavelet transform
$\mathcal{W}$	orthonormal matrix defining the DWT
$\mathcal{W}_\mathcal{B}$	orthonormal matrix defining the DWPT with basis $\mathcal{B}$
$\tilde{\mathcal{W}}$	matrix defining the MODWT
x_t	discrete signal
$x()$	continuous signal
x	vector of coefficients
$X()$	Fourier transform of x_t
X_k	discrete Fourier transform of x_t
X_t	vector of unobserved signal (Kalman filter)
y_t	observed process
y	vector of observations
Y_t	vector of observations (Kalman filter)

Greek conventions

β_N	Kalman gain in estimation
χ_n^2	chi-square random variable with n degrees of freedom
δ	thresholding rule
Δ	difference operator
ϵ_t	noise, measurement error, shock
η	threshold
γ_t	autocovariance sequence
Γ	covariance matrix
$\Gamma()$	gamma function
λ	decay factor (EWMA), smoothing coefficient (HP filter)
λ_j	jth level wavelet scale
μ	population mean
ν_t	noise, measurement error, shock
ω	frequency index (in radians)
Ω	diagonal variance-covariance matrix
Φ	Fourier transform of ϕ, activation function (neural net)
$\psi()$	mother wavelet
Ψ	Fourier transform of ψ, activation function (neural net)
ρ_t	autocorrelation sequence
σ	population standard deviation
Σ_x	variance-covariance matrix for x
τ	lag index
θ	angle (in radians)
ξ_j	integer shifts for the jth level wavelet/scaling coefficients

Operators

B	backward difference operator
$Cov()$	covariance
$E()$	expectation
$f * g_t$	convolution of sequences f_t and g_t

$k \bmod N$	remainder of the integer division of k modulo N
$\mathrm{Var}()$	variance
$\nabla f(\boldsymbol{x}_t, \theta)$	(column) gradient vector of f with respect to θ

Abbreviations

ACF	autocorrelation function
ACVS	autocovariance sequence
ARIMA	autoregressive integrated moving average
ARMA	autoregressive moving average
ADF	augmented Dickey–Fuller
AIC	Akaike Information Criterion
AR	autoregression
BK	Baxter–King
BP	British Pound
BS	Black and Scholes
BVAR	Bayesian vector autoregression
CAPM	capital-asset pricing model
CCVS	cross-covariance sequence
CI	confidence interval
CPI	consumer price index
CSDF	cross spectral density function
CWT	continuous wavelet transform
dB	decibel
DEM	Deutsche Mark
DFT	discrete Fourier transform
DWPT	discrete wavelet packet transform
DWT	discrete wavelet transform
EKF	extended Kalman filter
EWMA	exponentially weighted moving average
FDP	fractional difference process

FF	French Franc
FFF	flexible Fourier form
FIR	finite impulse response
GARCH	generalized autoregressive conditional heteroskedasticity
GDE	gross domestic expenditure
GDP	gross domestic product
GMT	Greenwich Mean Time
GNP	gross national product
GPH	Geweke and Porter-Hudak
HP	Hodrick–Prescott
ICSS	iterated cumulative sum of squares
IDWT	inverse discrete wavelet transform
IID	independent and identically distributed
IIR	infinite impulse response
IPI	industrial production index
JPY	Japanese Yen
LA	least asymmetric
LBP	Ljung-Box-Pierce statistic
MA	moving average
MB	minimum bandwidth
MBDT	minimum-bandwidth discrete-time
ML	maximum likelihood
MLE	maximum likelihood estimate
MODWPT	maximal overlap discrete wavelet packet transform
MODWT	maximal overlap discrete wavelet transform
MRA	multiresolution analysis
MSE	mean square error
MSPE	mean square prediction error
NAR	nonlinear autoregressive
NARMA	nonlinear autoregressive moving average
NARX	nonlinear autoregressive model with exogenous inputs

NBER	National Bureau of Economic Research
NCSS	normalized cumulative sum of squares
NLS	nonlinear least squares
OLG	overlapping generations
OLS	ordinary least squares
OTC	over-the-counter
PDF	probability density function
PSC	predictive stochastic complexity
SDF	spectral density function
SF	Swiss Franc
SIC	Schwarz information criterion
SNR	signal-to-noise ratio
SPP	seasonal persistent process
STFT	short-time Fourier transform
SURE	Stein's unbiased risk estimate
USD	U.S. Dollar
VAR	vector autoregression
VaR	Value-at-Risk
WLS	weighted least squares

BIBLIOGRAPHY

Abramovich, F. and Benjamini, Y. (1995). Thresholding of wavelet coefficients as multiple hypotheses testing procedure. In Antoniadis and Oppenheim (1995), 5–14.

Abry, P. and Veitch, D. (1998). Wavelet analysis of long-range-dependent traffic. *IEEE Transactions on Information Theory*, 44, 2–15.

Abry, P., Gonçalvès, P., and Flandrin, P. (1995). Wavelets, spectrum analysis and $1/f$ processes. In Antoniadis and Oppenheim (1995), 15–29.

Abu-Mostafa, Y. (1993). A method for learning from hints. In S. H. et al., editor, *Advances in Neural Information Processing Systems*, 5, 73–80. Morgan Kaufmann, San Mateo, CA.

Abu-Mostafa, Y. (1994). Learning from hints. *Journal of Complexity*, 10, 165–178.

Abu-Mostafa, Y. (1995). Financial market applications of learning from hints. In A. Refenes, editor, *Neural Networks in the Capital Markets*, 221–232. Wiley, London, U.K.

Abu-Mostafa, Y. (2001). Financial model calibration using consistency hints. *IEEE Transactions on Neural Networks*, 12.

Acar, E. and Satchell, S. (1997). *Advanced Trading Rules*. Butterworth-Heinemann.

Akaike, H. (1973). Information theory and an extension of the maximum likelihood principle. In B. N. Petrov and E. Csaki, editors, *Proceedings of the 2nd*

International Symposium on Information Theory, Akademia Kiado, Budapest, 267–281.

Akaike, H. (1974). A new look at the statistical model identification. *IEEE Transactions on Automatic Control*, 19, 716–723.

Allan, D. W. (1966). Statistics of atomic frequency standards. *Proceedings of the IEEE*, 31, 221–230.

Almon, S. (1965). The distributed lag between capital appropriations and expenditures. *Journal of American Statistical Association*, 33, 178–196.

Anděl, J. (1986). Long memory time series models. *Kybernetika*, 22, 105–123.

Andersen, T. G. and Bollerslev, T. (1997). Heterogeneous information arrivals and return volatility dynamics: Uncovering the long-run in high frequency returns. *Journal of Finance*, 52, 975–1005.

Andersen, T. G. and Bollerslev, T. (1998). DM-Dollar volatility: Intraday activity patterns, macroeconomic announcements and longer-run dependencies. *Journal of Finance*, 53, 219–265.

Andersen, T. G., Bollerslev, T., Diebold, F. X., and Labys, P. (2001). The distribution of realized exchange rate volatility. *Journal of the American Statistical Association*, 96, 42–55.

Andersen, T. G., Bollerslev, T., Diebold, F. X., and Labys, P. (2001). Exchange rate returns standardized by realized volatility are (nearly) Gaussian. *Multinational Finance Journal*, forthcoming.

Anderson, B. D. O. and Moore, J. B. (1979). *Optimal Filtering*. Prentice-Hall, Englewood Cliffs, New Jersey.

Anderson, T. W. (1971). *The Statistical Analysis of Time Series*. John Wiley and Sons, Inc., New York.

Antoniadis, A. and Oppenheim, G., editors (1995). *Wavelets and Statistics*, Volume 103 of *Lecture Notes in Statistics*. Springer-Verlag, New York.

Aoki, M. (1987). *State Space Modeling of Time Series, Third Edition*. Springer-Verlag, New York.

Arifovic, J. and Gençay, R. (2000). Statistical properties of genetic learning in a model of exchange rate. *Journal of Economic Dynamics and Control*, 24, 981–1005.

Arteche, J. and Robinson, P. M. (2000). Semiparametric inference in seasonal and cyclical long memory processes. *Journal of Time Series Analysis*, 21, 1–25.

Atiya, A. F. and El-Shoura, S. M. (1999). A comparison between neural network forecasting techniques—Case study: River flow forecasting. *IEEE Transactions on Neural Networks*, 10, 402–409.

Atiya, A. F. and Parlos, A. G. (2000). New results on recurrent network training: Unifying the algorithms and accelerating convergence. *IEEE Transactions on Neural Networks*, 11, 697–709.

Bakshi, G., Cao, C., and Chen, Z. (1997). Empirical performance of alternative option pricing models. *Journal of Finance*, 52, 2003–2049.

Ball, A. C. and Torous, W. (1985). On jumps in common stock prices and their impact on call option pricing. *Journal of Finance*, 40, 155–174.

Ballocchi, G., Dacorogna, M. M., Gençay, R., and Piccinato, B. (1999). Intraday statistical properties of Eurofutures. *Derivatives Quarterly*, 6, 28–44.

Barndorff-Nielsen, O. E. and Prause, K. (2001). Apparent scaling. *Financial Stochastics*, 5, forthcoming.

Barnett, W. A., editor (1989). *Bubbles, and Nonlinearity (International Symposia in Economic Theory and Econometrics)*. Cambridge University Press, Cambridge.

Barnett, W. A., Salmon, M., and Kirman, A., editors (1996). *Nonlinear Dynamics and Economics : Proceedings of the Tenth International Symposium in Economic Theory and Econometrics*. Cambridge University Press, Cambridge.

Barnett, W. A., Hendry, D. F., Hylleberg, S., and Würtz, A., editors (2000). *Nonlinear Econometric Modeling in Time Series Analysis : Proceedings of the Eleventh International Symposium in Economic Theory*. Cambridge University Press, Cambridge.

Barro, R. J. (1993). *Macroeconomics, Fourth Edition*. Wiley, New York.

Barron, A. (1994). Approximation and estimation bounds for artificial neural networks. *Machine Learning*, 14, 115–133.

Baxter, M. and King, R. G. (1999). Measuring business cycles: Approximate band-pass filters for economic time series. *The Review of Economics and Statistics*, 81, 573–593.

Benhabib, J., editor (1992). *Cycles and Chaos in Economic Equilibrium*. Princeton University Press, Princeton.

Beran, J. (1994). *Statistics for Long-Memory Processes*, Volume 61 of *Monographs on Statistics and Applied Probability*. Chapman & Hall, New York.

Beveridge, S. and Nelson, C. R. (1981). A new approach to decomposition of economic time series into permanent and transitory components with particular attention to measurement of the business cycle. *Journal of Monetary Economics*, 7, 151–174.

Bierens, H. J. and Gallant, A. R., editors (1997). *Nonlinear Models (International Library of Critical Writings in Econometrics Series)*. Edward Elgar Publishers, Cheltenham.

Bishop, C. M. (1995). *Neural Networks for Pattern Recognition*. Clarendon Press, Oxford, New York.

Black, A., Fraser, P., and Power, D. (1992). UK unit trust performance 1980-1989: A passive time varying approach. *Journal of Banking and Finance*, 16, 1015–1033.

Black, F. (1972). Capital market equilibrium with restricted borrowing. *Journal of Business*, 45, 444–455.

Black, F. and Scholes, M. (1973). The pricing of options and corporate liabilities. *Journal of Political Economy*, 81, 637–654.

Black, F., Jensen, M., and Scholes, M. (1972). The capital asset pricing model: Some empirical tests. In *Studies in the Theory of Capital Markets,* edited by Michael Jensen. Prager Publishers, New York.

Blackman, R. B. and Tukey, J. W. (1958). *The Measurement of Power Spectra.* Dover Publications, Inc., New York.

Blake, A. P. and Kapetanios, G. (2000). A radial basis function artificial neural network test for ARCH. *Economics Letters*, 69, 15–23.

Blanchard, O. J. and Fischer, S. (1989). *Lectures on Macroeconomics.* The MIT Press, Cambridge.

Bloomfield, P. (2000). *Fourier Analysis of Time Series : An Introduction, Second Edition.* John Wiley & Sons, New York.

Bollerslev, T. (1986). Generalized autoregressive conditional heteroskedasticity. *Journal of Econometrics*, 31, 307–327.

Bomhoff, E. J. (1994). *Financial Forecasting for Business and Economics.* Academic Press, London.

Bos, T. and Newbold, P. (1984). An empirical investigation of the possibility of systematic stochastic risk in the market model. *Journal of Business*, 57, 35–41.

Box, G. E. P. and Jenkins, G. M. (1976). *Time Series Analysis: Forecasting and Control, Second Edition.* Time Series Analysis and Digital Processing. Holden Day, San Francisco.

Braun, P., Nelson, D., and Sunier, A. (1995). Good news, bad news, volatility and betas. *Journal of Finance*, 50, 1575–1603.

Breiman, L. (1996a). Bagging predictors. *Machine Learning*, 24, 123–140.

Breiman, L. (1996b). Heuristics of instability and stabilization in model selection. *Annals of Statistics*, 24, 2350–2383.

Briggs, W. L. and Henson, V. E. (1995). *The DFT: An Owner's Manual for the Discrete Fourier Transform.* Society for Industrial and Applied Mathematics, Philadelphia.

Brillinger, D. R. (1981). *Time Series: Data Analysis and Theory.* Holden-Day Series in Time Series Analysis. Holden-Day, San Francisco. Expanded edition.

Brock, W. A. (1986). Distinguishing random and deterministic systems: Abridged version. *Journal of Economic Theory*, 40, 168–195.

Brock, W. A. (2000). Whither nonlinear? *Journal of Economic Dynamics and Control*, 24, 663–678.

Brock, W. A. and Kleidon, A. W. (1992). Periodic market closure and trading volume: A model of intraday bids and asks. *Journal of Economic Dynamics and Control*, 16, 451–489.

Brock, W. A. and Sayers, C. (1988). Is the business cycle characterized by deterministic chaos? *Journal of Monetary Economics*, 22, 71–90.

Brock, W. A., Hsieh, D., and LeBaron, B. (1991). *Nonlinear Dynamics, Chaos and Instability*. MIT Press, Cambridge.

Brock, W. A., Lakonishok, J., and LeBaron, B. (1992). Simple technical trading rules and the stochastic properties of stock returns. *Journal of Finance*, 47, 1731–1764.

Brockwell, P. J. and Davis, R. A. (1991). *Time Series: Theory and Methods, Second Edition*. Springer-Verlag, New York.

Brockwell, P. J. and Davis, R. A. (1996). *Introduction to Time Series and Forecasting*. Springer-Verlag, New York.

Brooks, R. D., Faff, R. W., and McKenzie, M. D. (1998). Time varying beta risk of Australian industry portfolios: A comparison of modeling technics. *Australian Journal of Management*, 23, 1–22.

Brown, R. G. and Hwang, P. Y. C. (1996). *Introduction to Random Signals and Applied Kalman Filtering with Matlab Exercises and Solutions, Third Edition*. John Wiley & Sons, Inc., New York.

Brown, R. L., Durbin, J., and Evans, J. M. (1975). Techniques for testing the constancy of regression relationships over time. *Journal of the Royal Statistical Society B*, 37, 149–163.

Bruce, A. and Gao, H.-Y. (1996). *Applied Wavelet Analysis with S-PLUS*. Springer, New York.

Bryan, M. F. and Cechetti, S. G. (1993). The consumer price index as a measure of inflation. *Economic Review of the Federal Reserve Bank of Cleveland*, 29, 15–24.

Bucland, R. and Fraser, P. (2001). Political and regulatory risk: Beta sensitivity in UK electricity distribution. *Journal of Regulatory Economics*, 19, 5–25.

Bullard, J. and Duffy, J. (1997). A model of learning and emulation with artificial adaptive agents. *Journal of Economic Dynamics and Control*, 22, 179–207.

Burns, A. and Mitchell, W. C. (1946). *Measuring Business Cycles*. National Bureau of Economic Research, New York.

Burnside, C. (1998). Detrending and business cycle facts: A comment. *Journal of Monetary Economics*, 41, 513–532.

Burrus, C. S., Gopinath, R. A., and Guo, H. (1998). *Introduction to Wavelets and Wavelet Transforms: A Primer*. Prentice Hall, New Jersey.

Campbell, J. Y., Lo, A. W., and MacKinlay, A. C. (1997). *The Econometrics of Financial Markets*. Princeton University Press, Princeton, New Jersey.

Canova, F. (1998a). Detrending and business cycle facts. *Journal of Monetary Economics*, 41, 475–512.

Canova, F. (1998b). Detrending and business cycle facts: A user's guide. *Journal of Monetary Economics*, 41, 533–540.

Carmona, R. A., Hwang, W. L., and Torrésani, B. (1998). *Practical Time-Frequency Analysis: Gabor and Wavelet Transforms with an Implementation in S*, Volume 9 of *Wavelet Analysis and Its Applications*. Academic Press, San Diego.

Castagli, M. (1989). Nonlinear prediction of chaotic time series. *Physica D*, 35, 335–356.

Chatfield, C. (1984). *The Analysis of Time Series: An Introduction, Third Edition*. Chapman and Hall, New York.

Chatfield, C. and Yar, M. (1991). Prediction intervals for multiplicative Holt-Winters. *International Journal of Forecasting*, 7, 31–37.

Chen, J. and Gupta, A. K. (1997). Testing and locating variance changepoints with application to stock prices. *Journal of the American Statistical Association*, 92, 739–747.

Chen, S., Billings, S., and Grant, P. (1990). Nonlinear system identification using neural networks. *International Journal of Control*, 51, 1191–1214.

Cheng, J. W. (1997). A switching regression approach to the stationarity of systematic and nonsystematic risks: The Hong Kong experience. *Applied Financial Economics*, 7, 45–58.

Chiang, A. (1984). *Fundamental Methods of Mathematical Economics, Third Edition*. McGraw Hill, New York.

Chui, C. K. (1992). *An Introduction to Wavelets, Wavelet Analysis and Its Applications*, Volume 1. Academic Press, San Diego.

Chui, C. K. (1997). *Wavelets: A Mathematical Tool for Signal Analysis*. SIAM Monographs on Mathematical Modeling and Computation. Society for Industrial and Applied Mathematics, Philadelphia.

Clark, W. C. (1985). Scales of climate impacts. *Climatic Change*, 7, 5–27.

Clements, M. P. and Hendry, D. F. (1999). *Forecasting Non-Stationary Economic Time Series (Zeuthen Lecture Series)*. The MIT Press, Cambridge.

Cochrane, J. (1989). The return of the liquidity effect : A study of the short-run relation between money growth and interest rates. *Journal of Business and Economic Statistics*, 7, 75–83.

Cogley, T. and Nason, J. M. (1995). Effects of the Hodrick-Prescott filter on trend and difference stationary time series: Implications for business cycle research. *Journal of Economic Dynamics and Control*, 19, 253–278.

Cogley, T. (2001). Alternative definitions of the business cycle and their implications for business cycle models: A reply to Torben Mark Pederson. *Journal of Economic Dynamics and Control*, 25, 1103–1107.

Cohen, A., Daubechies, I., and Vial, P. (1993). Wavelets on the interval and fast wavelet transforms. *Applied and Computational Harmonic Analysis*, 1, 54–81.

Coifman, R. R. and Donoho, D. (1995). Time-invariant wavelet de-noising. In Antoniadis and Oppenheim (1995), 125–150.

Coifman, R. R. and Wickerhauser, M. V. (1992). Entropy-based algorithms for best basis selection. *IEEE Transactions on Information Theory*, 38, 713–718.

Cooley, T. F. and LeRoy, S. F. (1985). Atheoretical macroeconometrics: A critique. *Journal of Monetary Economics*, 16, 283–308.

Cornell, W. B. and Dietrich, J. K. (1978). The efficiency of market for foreign exchange under floating exchange rates. *Review of Economics and Statistics*, 60, 111–120.

Craigmile, P. F., Percival, D. B., and Guttorp, P. (2000). Wavelet-based parameter estimation for trend contaminated fractionally differenced processes. Technical Report 47, National Research Center for Statistics and the Environment.

Cybenko, G. (1989). Approximation by superposition of a sigmoidal function. *Mathematics of Control, Signals and Systems*, 2, 303–314.

Dacorogna, M. M., Müller, U. A., Nagler, R. J., Olsen, R. B., and Pictet, O. V. (1993). A geographical model for the daily and weekly seasonal volatility in the foreign exchange markets. *Journal of International Money and Finance*, 12, 413–438.

Dacorogna, M. M., Gençay, R., Müller, U. A., Olsen, R. B., and Pictet, O. V. (2001). *An Introduction to High Frequency Finance*. Academic Press, San Diego.

Daubechies, I. (1992). *Ten Lectures on Wavelets*, Volume 61 of *CBMS-NSF Regional Conference Series in Applied Mathematics*. Society for Industrial and Applied Mathematics, Philadelphia.

David, H. A. (1981). *Order Statistics*. Wiley, New York.

Davidson, R. and MacKinnon, J. (1993). *Estimation and Inference in Econometrics*. Oxford University Press, Oxford.

Davies, R. B. and Harte, D. S. (1987). Tests for Hurst effect. *Biometrika*, 74, 95–101.

de Alba, E. and Boue, M. (2000). A Bayesian algorithm for detecting multiple changes of variance in a time series. ITAM and The University of Waterloo.

Dechert, W. D., editor (1996). *Chaos Theory in Economics: Methods, Models and Evidence*. Edward Elgar Publishing Company, Cheltenham.

Dechert, W. D. and Gençay, R. (1992). Lyapunov exponents as a nonparametric diagnostic for stability analysis. *Journal of Applied Econometrics*, 7, 41–60.

Dechert, W. D. and Gençay, R. (1996a). The identification of spurious Lyapunov exponents in Jacobian algorithms. *Studies in Nonlinear Dynamics and Econometrics*, 1, 145–154.

Dechert, W. D. and Gençay, R. (1996b). The topological invariance of Lyapunov exponents in embedded dynamics. *Physica D*, 90, 40–55.

Derman, E. and Kani, I. (1994). Riding on the simile. *Risk*, 7, 32–39.

Devaney, R. L. (1986). *An Introduction to Chaotic Dynamical Systems*. Benjamin/Cummings, Menlo Park, California.

Dhrymes, P. (1998). *Time Series, Unit Roots, and Cointegration*. Academic Press, San Diego.

Dickey, D. A. and Fuller, W. A. (1979). Distributions of the estimators for autoregressive time series with a unit root. *Journal of American Statistical Association*, 74, 427–431.

Dickey, D. A. and Fuller, W. A. (1981). Likelihood ratio statistics for autoregressive time series with a unit root. *Econometrica*, 49, 1057–1072.

Diebold, F. X. and Mariano, R. S. (1995). Comparing forecasting accuracy. *Journal of Business and Economic Statistics*, 13, 253–263.

Diebold, F. X. and Rudebusch, G. D. (1999). *Business Cycles : Durations, Dynamics, and Forecasting*. Princeton University Press, Princeton, New Jersey.

Doan, T., Litterman, R., and Sims, C. A. (1984). Forecasting and conditional projections using realistic prior distributions. *Economic Reviews*, 3, 1–100.

Donaldson, R. G. and Kamstra, M. (1997). An artificial neural network-garch model for international stock return volatility. *Journal of Empirical Finance*, 4, 17–46.

Donoho, D. L. (1997). CART and best-ortho-basis: A connection. *Annals of Statistics*, 25, 1870–1911.

Donoho, D. L. and Johnstone, I. M. (1994). Ideal spatial adaptation by wavelet shrinkage. *Biometrika*, 81, 425–455.

Donoho, D. L. and Johnstone, I. M. (1995). Adapting to unknown smoothness by wavelet shrinkage. *Journal of the American Statistical Association*, 90, 1200–1224.

Donoho, D. L. and Johnstone, I. M. (1998). Minimax estimation via wavelet shrinkage. *Annals of Statistics*, 26, 879–921.

Downie, T. R. and Silverman, B. W. (1998). The discrete multiple wavelet transform and thresholding methods. *IEEE Transactions on Signal Processing*, 46, 2558–2562.

Duda, R. and Hart, P. (1973). *Pattern Classification and Scene Analysis*. John Wiley, New York.

Duffy, J. (2001). Learning to speculate: Experiments with artificial and real agents. *Journal of Economic Dynamics and Control*, 25, 295–319.

Dumas, B., Fleming, J., and Whaley, R. E. (1998). Implied volatility functions: Empirical tests. *Journal of Finance*, 53, 2059–2106.

Dupire, B. (1994). Pricing with a smile. *Risk*, 7, 18–20.

Durbin, J. and Koopman, S. J. (2001). *Time Series Analysis by State Space Models*. Oxford University Press, Oxford.

Edwards, R. D. and Magee, J. F. (1997). *Technical Analysis of Stock Trends, Seventh Edition*. Amacom.

Elman, J. L. (1990). Finding structure in time. *Cognitive Science*, 14, 179–211.

Enders, W. (1998). *Applied Econometric Time Series*. John Wiley & Sons, New York.

Engel, J. (1994). A simple wavelet approach to nonparametric regression from recursive partitioning schemes. *Journal of Multivariate Analysis*, 49, 242–254.

Engle, R. (1982). Autoregressive conditional hereoskedasticity with estimates of the variance of UK inflation. *Econometrica*, 50, 987–1008.

Engle, R. F. and Granger, C. W. J. (1987). Co-integration and error correction: representation, estimation and testing. *Econometrica*, 55, 251–276.

Engle, R. F. and Watson, M. (1987). The Kalman filter: Applications to forecasting and rational expectations models. *Advances in Econometrics, Fifth World Congress*, 1, 245–283.

Fabozzi, F. and Francis, J. (1978). Beta as a random coefficient. *Journal of Financial and Quantitative Analysis*, 13, 101–115.

Fama, E. F. and French, K. (1992). The cross-section of expected stock returns. *Journal of Finance*, 47, 427–466.

Fama, E. F. and MacBeth, J. (1973). Risk, return and equilibrium: Empirical tests. *Journal of Political Economy*, 81, 607–636.

Fan, Y. (2000). An asymptotically efficient wavelet estimator of the partial linear model. University of Windsor, Windsor, Ontario.

Feldkamp, L. A. and Puskorius, G. V. (1998). A signal processing framework based on dynamic neural networks with application to problems in adaptation, filtering and classification. *Proceedings of The IEEE*, 86, 2259–2277.

Fernández-Rodriguez, F., González-Martel, C., and Sosvilla-Rivero, S. (2000). On the profitability of technical trading rules based on artificial neural networks. *Economics Letters*, 69, 89–94.

Fischer, I. (1937). Note on a short-cut method for calculating distributed lags. *Bulletin de L'Institut International de Statistique*, 29, 323–328.

Fisher, A. J., Calvet, L. E., and Mandelbrot, B. B. (1997). Multifractality of Deutschemark US-Dollar exchange rates. *Cowles Foundation Discussion Paper*, 1166.

Foresee, F. D. and Hagan, M. T. (1997). Gauss-Newton approximation to Bayesian learning. *Proceedings of IEEE International Conference on Neural Networks*, 3, 1930–1935.

Fox, R. and Taqqu, M. S. (1986). Large-sample properties of parameter estimates for strongly dependent stationary Gaussian time series. *Annals of Statistics*, 14, 517–532.

Franses, P. H. (1998). *Time Series Models for Business and Economic Forecasting*. Cambridge University Press, Cambridge.

Franses, P. H. and Dijk, D. V. (2000). *Non-Linear Time Series Models in Empirical Finance*. Cambridge University Press, Cambridge.

Franses, P. H. and Draisma, G. (1997). Recognizing changing seasonal patterns using artificial neural networks. *Journal of Econometrics*, 81, 273–280.

Franses, P. H. and Griensven, K. (1998). Forecasting exchange rates using neural networks for technical trading rules. *Studies in Nonlinear Dynamics and Econometrics*, 2, 109–114.

Friedman, M. (1956). *A Theory of the Consumption Function*. Princeton University Press, Princeton, New Jersey.

Friedman, M. (1984). Lessons form the 1979–1982 monetary policy experiment. *American Economic Review*, 74, 397–400.

Friedman, M. (1992). *Money Mischief: Episodes in Monetary History*. Harcourt Brace Jovanovich, New York.

Fuller, W. A. (1976). *Introduction to Statistical Time Series*. John Wiley & Sons, New York.

Funahashi, K. (1989). On the approximate realization of continuous mappings by neural networks. *Neural Networks*, 2, 183–192.

Gabor, D. (1946). Theory of communication. *Journal of the IEE*, 93, 429–457.

Gallant, A. R. (1987). *Nonlinear Statistical Models*. John Wiley & Sons, New York.

Gallant, A. R. and White, H. (1992). On learning the derivatives of an unknown mapping with multilayer feedforward networks. *Neural Networks*, 5, 129–138.

Gao, H.-Y. (1993). *Wavelet Estimation of Spectral Densities in Time Series Analysis*. Ph.D. thesis, University of California, Berkeley.

Gao, H.-Y. (1997). Choice of thresholds for wavelet shrinkage estimate of the spectrum. *Journal of Time Series Analysis*, 18, 231–251.

Gao, H.-Y. (1998). Wavelet shrinkage denoising using non-negative garrote. *Journal of Computational and Graphical Statistics*, 7, 469–488.

Gao, H.-Y. and Bruce, A. (1997). WaveShrink with firm shrinkage. *Statistica Sinica*, 7, 855–874.

Garcia, R. and Gençay, R. (2000). Pricing and hedging derivative securities with neural networks and a homogeneity hint. *Journal of Econometrics*, 94, 93–115.

Garcia, R. and Renault, R. (1995). Risk aversion, intertemporal substitution and option pricing. Université de Montréal, Montréal, Quebec.

Geisser, S. (1975). The predictive sample reuse method with applications. *Journal of the American Statistical Association*, 70, 320–328.

Gençay, R. (1994). Nonlinear prediction of noisy time series with feedforward networks. *Physica Letters A*, 187, 397–403.

Jensen, M. J. and Whitcher, B. (2000). Time-varying long-memory in volatility: Detection and estimation with wavelets. Technical report, University of Missouri at Columbia and EURANDOM.

Johnstone, I. M. and Silverman, B. W. (1997). Wavelet threshold estimators for data with correlated noise. *Journal of the Royal Statistical Society B*, 59, 319–351.

Jordan, M. I. (1986). Serial order: A parallel distributed processing approach. University of California, San Diego, Unpublished doctoral dissertation.

Kadiyala, K. R. and Karlsson, S. (1993). Forecasting with generalized Bayesian vector autoregressions. *Journal of Forecasting*, 12, 365–378.

Kadiyala, K. R. and Karlsson, S. (1997). Numerical methods for estimation and inference in Bayesian VAR models. *Journal of Applied Econometrics*, 12, 99–132.

Kaiser, R. and Maraval, A. (2000). *Measuring Business Cycles in Economic Time Series*. Springer-Verlag, New York.

Kalman, R. E. (1960). A new approach to linear filtering and prediction. *Transactions of the ASME-Journal of Basic Engineering*, 82, 35–45.

Kalman, R. E. and Bucy, R. (1961). New results in linear filtering and prediction. *Transactions of the ASME-Journal of Basic Engineering*, 83, 95–108.

Kashyap, R. L. and Eom, K. B. (1988). Estimation in long-memory time series model. *Journal of Time Series Analysis*, 9, 35–41.

Kim, C. J. and Nelson, C. (1999). *State-Space Models With Regime Switching : Classical and Gibbs-Sampling Approaches with Applications*. The MIT Press, Cambridge.

King, R. G. and Rebelo, S. T. (1993). Low frequency filtering and real business cycles. *Journal of Economic Dynamics and Control*, 17, 207–231.

Koopmans, L. H. (1974). *The Spectral Analysis of Time Series*. New York. Academic Press.

Kotz, S., Johnson, N. L., and Read, C. B., editors (1982). *Encyclopedia of Statistical Sciences*. Wiley, New York.

Kovac, A. and Silverman, B. W. (2000). Extending the scope of wavelet regression methods by coefficient-dependent thresholding. *Journal of the American Statistical Association*, 95, 172–183.

Kuan, C. M. and Liu, T. (1995). Forecasting exchange rates using feedforward networks and recurrent neural networks. *Journal of Applied Econometrics*, 10, 347–364.

Kuan, C. M. and White, H. (1994). Artificial neural networks: An econometric perspective. *Econometric Reviews*, 13, 1–91.

LeBaron, B. (1999). Technical trading rule profitability and foreign exchange intervention. *Journal of International Economics*, 49, 125–143.

LeBaron, B., Arthur, W. B., and Palmer, R. (1999). Time series properties of an artificial stock market. *Journal of Economic Dynamics and Control*, 23, 1487–1516.

Lee, J. and Hong, Y. (2001). Testing for serial correlation of unknown form using wavelet methods. *Econometric Theory*, 17, 386–423.

LeSage, J. P. and Magura, M. (1991). Using inter-industry input-output relations as a Bayesian prior in employment forecasting models. *International Journal of Forecasting*, 7, 231–238.

Levich, R. M. and Thomas, L. R. (1993). The significance of technical trading-rule profits in the foreign exchange market: A bootstrap approach. *Journal of International Money and Finance*, 12, 451–474.

Liang, J. and Parks, T. W. (1996). A translation-invariant wavelet representation algorithm with applications. *IEEE Transactions on Signal Processing*, 44, 225–232.

Lin, T., Horne, B. G., Tino, P., and Giles, C. L. (1990). Learning long-term dependencies in NARX recurrent neural networks. *IEEE Transactions on Neural Networks*, 7, 1329–1338.

Lina, J.-M. (1997). Image processing with complex Daubechies wavelets. *Journal of Mathematical Imaging and Vision*, 7, 211–223.

Lina, J.-M. and MacGibbon, B. (1997). Nonlinear shrinkage estimation with complex Daubechies wavelets. In A. Aldroubi, A. F. Laine, and M. A. Unser, editors, *Wavelet Applications in Signal and Image Processing V*, Volume 3169 of *Proceedings of SPIE*, 67–79.

Lina, J.-M. and Mayrand, M. (1995). Complex Daubechies wavelets. *Applied and Computational Harmonic Analysis*, 2, 219–229.

Lintner, J. (1965). The valuation of risk assets and the selection of risky investments in stock portfolio and capital budgets. *Review of Economics and Statistics*, 47, 13–37.

Litterman, R. B. (1979). Techniques of forecasting using vector autoregressions. Ph.D. dissertation, University of Minnesota, Minnesota.

Litterman, R. B. (1986). Forecasting with Bayesian vector autoregressions: Five years of experience. *Journal of Business and Economic Statistics*, 4, 25–38.

Ljung, G. M. and Box, G. E. P. (1978). On the measure of lack of fit in time series models. *Biometrika*, 66, 297–303.

Lobato, I. N. and Savin, N. E. (1998). Real and spurious long-memory properties of stock-market data. *Journal of Business and Economic Statistics*, 16, 261–283.

Loretan, M. and Phillips, P. C. B. (1994). Testing the covariance stationarity of heavy-tailed time series: An overview of the theory with applications to several financial datasets. *Journal of Empirical Finance*, 1, 211–248.

Lucas, R. and Sargent, T. J. (1979). After Keynesian macroeconometrics. *Federal Reserve Bank of Minneapolis Quarterly Review*, 3, 1–16.

Lucas, R. E. (1980). Two illustrations of the quantity theory of money. *American Economic Review*, 70, 1005–1014.

Lutkepohl, H. (1993). *Introduction to Multiple Time Series Analysis, Second Edition*. Springer Verlag.

MacKay, D. J. C. (1992). Bayesian interpolation. *Neural Computation*, 4, 415–447.

MacKinnon, J. G. (1991). Critical values for cointegration test. In R. F. Engle and C. W. F. Granger, editors, *Long-Run Economic Relationships*. Oxford University Press, Oxford.

Mallat, S. (1989). A theory for multiresolution signal decomposition: The wavelet representation. *IEEE Transactions on Pattern Analysis and Machine Intelligence*, 11, 674–693.

Mallat, S. (1998). *A Wavelet Tour of Signal Processing*. Academic Press, San Diego.

Mandelbrot, B. B. (1983). *The Fractal Geometry of Nature*. W.H. Freeman and Company, New York.

Mandelbrot, B. B. and van Ness, J. W. (1968). Fractional Brownian motions, fractional noises and applications. *SIAM Review*, 10, 422–437.

Mandelbrot, B. B. and Wallis, J. R. (1969). Some long-run properties of geophysical records. *Water Resources Research*, 5, 321–340.

Mantegna, R. N. and Stanley, H. E. (1995). Scaling behavior in the dynamics of an economic index. *Nature*, 376, 46–49.

Mantegna, R. N. and Stanley, H. E. (2000). *An Introduction to Econophysics—Correlations and Complexity in Finance*. Cambridge University Press, Cambridge.

Markowitz, H. (1959). *Portfolio Selection: Efficient Diversification of Investments*. Wiley, New York.

McCallum, B. T. (2000). Alternative monetary policy rules: A comparison with historical settings for the United States, the United Kingdom, and Japan. *Economic Quarterly of the Federal Reserve Bank of Richmond*, 86, 49–79.

McCandless, G. T. and Wallace, N. (1991). *Introduction to Dynamic Macroeconomic Theory, An Overlapping Generations Approach*. Harvard University Press, Cambridge.

McCoy, E. J. and Walden, A. T. (1996). Wavelet analysis and synthesis of stationary long-memory processes. *Journal of Computational and Graphical Statistics*, 5, 26–56.

McCoy, E. J., Percival, D. B., and Walden, A. T. (1995). On the phase of least-asymmetric scaling and wavelet filters. Technical Report TR-95-15, Dept. of Mathematics, Imperial College of Science, Technology and Medicine.

McNelis, P. D. (2001). *Neural Networks and Genetic Algorithms in Finance.* Academic Press, San Diego, forthcoming.

Merton, R. C. (1976). Option pricing when underlying stock returns are discontinuous. *Journal of Financial Economics*, 3, 125–144.

Merton, R. C. (1995). Rational theory of option pricing. *Bell Journal of Economics and Management Science*, 4, 141–183.

Mills, T. C. (1999). *The Econometric Modelling of Financial Time Series.* Cambridge University Press, Cambridge.

Minsky, M. and Papert, S. (1988). *Perceptrons.* MIT Press, Cambridge, MA.

Mizrach, B. (1995). Forecast comparisons L2. *Rutgers University Discussion Paper*, 24.

Moody, J. and Wu, L. (1996). Optimization of trading systems and portfolios. in*Proceedings of Neural Networks in Capital Markets*, Pasadena, CA, November, 1996.

Morgan, J. P. (1996). *RiskMetrics-Technical Manual, Fourth Edition.* Morgan Guaranty Trust Company.

Morris, J. M. and Peravali, R. (1999). Minimum-bandwidth discrete-time wavelets. *Signal Processing*, 76, 181–193.

Moulin, P. (1994). Wavelet thresholding techniques for power spectrum estimation. *IEEE Transactions on Signal Processing*, 42, 3126–3136.

Müller, P. and Vidakovic, B., editors (1999). *Bayesian Inference in Wavelet-based Models*, Volume 141 of *Lecture Notes in Statistics.* Springer Verlag, New York.

Müller, U. A., Dacorogna, M. M., Olsen, R. B., Pictet, O. V., Schwarz, M., and Morgenegg, C. (1990). Statistical study of foreign exchange rates, empirical evidence of a price change scaling law and intraday analysis. *Journal of Banking and Finance*, 14, 1189–1208.

Murphy, J. J. (1999). *Technical Analysis of the Financial Markets : A Comprehensive Guide to Trading Methods and Applications.* Prentice Hall Press, Paramus, New Jersey.

Murray, C. J. (2001). Cyclical properties of Baxter-King filtered time series. University of Houston, Houston, Texas.

Muth, J. F. (1960). Optimal properties of exponentially weighted forecasts. *Journal of American Statistical Association*, 55, 299–306.

Narendra, K. S. and Parthasarathy, K. (1990). Identification and control of dynamical systems using neural networks. *IEEE Transactions on Neural Networks*, 1, 4–27.

Narendra, K. S. and Parthasarathy, K. (1991). Gradient methods for the optimization of dynamical systems containing neural networks. *IEEE Transactions on Neural Networks*, 2, 252–262.

Nason, G. P. (1994). Wavelet regression by cross-validation. Technical report, Department of Mathematics, University of Bristol.

Nason, G. P. (1996). Wavelet shrinkage by cross-validation. *Journal of the Royal Statistical Society B*, 58, 463–479.

Nason, G. P. and Silverman, B. W. (1995). The stationary wavelet transform and some statistical applications. In Antoniadis and Oppenheim (1995), 281–300.

Neftci, S. N. (1991). Naive trading rules in financial markets and Wiener-Kolmogorov prediction theory: A study of technical analysis. *Journal of Business*, 64, 549–571.

Neftci, S. N. (2000). *An Introduction to the Mathematics of Financial Derivatives, Second Edition*. Academic Press, San Diego.

Nielsen, M. (2001). On the construction and frequency localization of finite orthogonal quadrature filters. *Journal of Approximation Theory*, 108, 36–52.

Niemira, M. P. and Klein, P. A. (1994). *Forecasting Financial and Economic Cycles*. John Wiley & Sons, New York.

Oh, H. S., Naveau, P., and Lee, G. (2001). Polynomial boundary treatment for wavelet regression. *Biometrika*, 88, 291–298.

Ogden, R. T. (1996). *Essential Wavelets for Statistical Applications and Data Analysis*. Birkhauser, Boston.

Ogden, R. T. (1997). On preconditioning the data for the wavelet transform when the sample size is not a power of two. *Communications in Statistics B*, 26, 267–285.

Ogden, R. T. and Parzen, E. (1996a). Change-point approach to data analytic wavelet thresholding. *Statistics and Computing*, 6, 93–99.

Ogden, R. T. and Parzen, E. (1996b). Data dependent wavelet thresholding in nonparametric regression with change-point applications. *Computational Statistics & Data Analysis*, 22, 53–70.

Oldfield, G. S., Rogalski, R. J., and Jarrow, R. A. (1977). An autoregressive jump process for common stock returns. *Journal of Financial Economics*, 5, 389–418.

Oppenheim, A. V. and Schafer, R. W. (1989). *Discrete-Time Signal Processing*. Prentice–Hall, Englewood Cliffs, New Jersey.

Pagan, A. and Ullah, A. (1999). *Nonparametric Econometrics*. Cambridge University Press, New York.

Parke, W. R. (1999). What is fractional integration? *Review of Economics and Statistics*, 81, 632–638.

Parlos, A., Rais, O., and Atiya, A. F. (2000). Multi-ste-ahead prediction in complex systems using dynamic recurrent neural networks. *Neural Networks*, 13, 765–786.

Parlos, A., Menon, S., and Atiya, A. F. (2001). Nonlinear state filtering in complex systems using recurrent neural networks. *IEEE Transactions on Neural Networks*, 12.

Patterson, D. M. and Ashley, R. A. (2000). *A Nonliner Time Series Workshop: A Toolkit for Detecting and Identifying Nonlinear Serial Dependence*. Kluwer Academic Publishers, Boston.

Pedersen, T. M. (2001). The Hodrick-Prescott filter, the Slutzky effect, and the distortionary effect of filters. *Journal of Economic Dynamics and Control*, 25, 1081–1101.

Percival, D. B. (1983). *The Statistics of Long Memory Processes*. Ph.D. thesis, Department of Statistics, University of Washington.

Percival, D. B. (1992). Simulating Gaussian random processes with specified spectra. *Computing Science and Statistics*, 24, 534–538.

Percival, D. B. (1993). Three curious properties of the sample variance and autocovariance for stationary processes with unknown mean. *The American Statistician*, 47, 274–276.

Percival, D. B. (1994). Spectral analysis of univariate and bivariate time series. In J. L. Stanford and S. B. Vardeman, editors, *Statistical Methods for Physical Science*, Volume 28 of *Methods of Experimental Physics*, 313–348. Academic Press, Inc., Boston.

Percival, D. B. (1995). On estimation of the wavelet variance. *Biometrika*, 82, 619–631.

Percival, D. B. and Guttorp, P. (1994). Long-memory processes, the Allan variance and wavelets. In E. Foufoula-Georgiou and P. Kumar, editors, *Wavelets in Geophysics*, Volume 4 of *Wavelet Analysis and Its Applications*, 325–344. Academic Press, Inc, San Diego.

Percival, D. B. and Mofjeld, H. O. (1997). Analysis of subtidal coastal sea level fluctuations using wavelets. *Journal of the American Statistical Association*, 92, 868–880.

Percival, D. B. and Walden, A. T. (1993). *Spectral Analysis for Physical Applications: Multitaper and Conventional Univariate Techniques*. Cambridge University Press, Cambridge, England.

Percival, D. B. and Walden, A. T. (2000). *Wavelet Methods for Time Series Analysis*. Cambridge University Press, Cambridge, England.

Percival, D. B., Sardy, S., and Davision, A. (2001). Wavestrapping time series: Adaptive wavelet-based bootstrapping. In B. J. Fitzgerald, R. L. Smith, A. T. Walden, and P. C. Young, editors, *Nonlinear and Nonstationary Signal Processing*, 442–471. Cambridge University Press, Cambridge, England.

Pesquet, J.-C., Krim, H., and Carfantan, H. (1996). Time-invariant orthonormal wavelet representations. *IEEE Transactions on Signal Processing*, 44, 1964–1970.

Pierce, D. A. (1977). Relationships and the lack of thereof between economic time series with reference to money and interest rates. *Journal of the American Statistical Association*, 72, 11–22.

Piessons, R., de Doncker-Kapenga, E., Überhuber, C. W., and Kahaner, D. K. (1983). *QUADPACK: A Subroutine Package for Automatic Integration*, Volume 1 of *Springer Series in Computational Mathematics*. Springer-Verlag, Heidelberg.

Pollock, D. (1999). *A Handbook of Time-Series Analysis, Signal Processing and Dynamics*. Academic Press, London.

Pollock, D. S. G. (2000). Trend estimation and de-trending via rational square-wave filters. *Journal of Econometrics*, 99, 317–334.

Priestley, M. B. (1981). *Spectral Analysis and Time Series*. Academic Press, Inc., London.

Prisman, E. Z. (2000). *Pricing Derivative Securities*. Academic Press, San Diego.

Puskorius, G. V. and Feldkamp, L. A. (1994). Neurocontrol of nonlinear dynamical systems with Kalman filter trained recurrent networks. *IEEE Transactions on Neural Networks*, 5, 279–297.

Rainville, E. D. (1960). *Special Functions*. The Macmillan Company, New York.

Ramanathan, R. (1993). *Statistical Methods in Econometrics*. Academic Press, San Diego.

Ramsey, J. B. (1998). Regression over time scale decompositions: A sampling analysis of distributional properties. *Economic Systems Research*, 11, 163–183.

Ramsey, J. B. (1999). The contribution of wavelets to the analysis of economic and financial data. *Philosophical Transactions of the Royal Society of London A*, 357, 2593–2606.

Ramsey, J. B. and Lampart, C. (1998a). The decomposition of economic relationships by time scale using wavelets: Expenditure and income. *Studies in Nonlinear Dynamics and Economics*, 3, 23–42.

Ramsey, J. B. and Lampart, C. (1998b). Decomposition of economic relationships by timescale using wavelets: Money and income. *Macroeconomic Dynamics*, 2, 49–71.

Ramsey, J. B. and Zhang, Z. (1997). The analysis of foreign exchange data using waveform dictionaries. *Journal of Empirical Finance*, 4, 341–372.

Ramsey, J. B. and Zhang, Z. F. (1996). The application of wave form dictionaries to stock market index data. In Y. A. Kravstov and J. B. Kadtke, editors, *Predictability of Dynamical Systems*, Volume 69, 189–205. Springer Verlag, New York.

Ramsey, J. B., Uskinov, D., and Zaslavsky, G. M. (1995). An analysis of U.S. stock price behavior using wavelets. *Fractals*, 3, 377–389.

Refenes, A. and Azema-Barac, M. (1994). Neural network applications in financial asset management. *Neural Computation Applications*, 2, 13–39.

Riedel, K. S. and Sidorenko, A. (1995). Minimum bias multiple taper spectral estimation. *IEEE Transactions on Signal Processing*, 43, 188–195.

Rissanen, J. (1986a). A predictive least-squares principle. *IMA Journal of Mathematical Control and Information*, 3, 211–222.

Rissanen, J. (1986b). Stochastic complexity and modelling. *Annals of Statistics*, 14, 1080–1100.

Robertson, J. C. and Tallman, E. W. (1999). Vector autoregressions: Forecasting and reality. *Federal Reserve Bank of Atlanta Economic Review*, 1, 4–18.

Robinson, P. M. (1995). Log-periodogram regression of time series with long range dependence. *Annals of Statistics*, 23, 1048–1072.

Rolnick, A. J. and Weber, W. E. (1997). Money, inflation, and output under fiat and commodity standards. *Journal of Political Economy*, 105, 1308–1321.

Ross, S. (1983). *Stochastic Processes*. Wiley, New York.

Ross, S. (2000). *Introduction to Probability Models*. Academic Press, San Diego.

Ross, S. A., Westerfield, R. W., and Jaffe, J. (1999). *Corporate Finance, Fifth Edition*. Irwin/McGraw-Hill, Boston.

Rubinstein, M. (1994). Implied binomial trees. *Journal of Finance*, 49, 771–818.

Sargent, T. J. (1987). *Macroeconomic Theory, Second Edition*. Academic Press, California.

Sarwar, G. and Krehbiel, T. (2000). Empirical performance of alternative pricing models of currency options. *Journal of Futures Markets*, 20, 265–291.

Schwarz, G. (1978). Estimating the dimension of a model. *Annals of Statistics*, 6, 461–464.

Selçuk, F. (1992). Forecasting with Bayesian vector autoregressions: An application to post-liberalization Turkey: 1980–1991. Ph.D. dissertation, City University of New York, New York.

Serroukh, A. and Walden, A. T. (2000). Wavelet scale analysis of bivariate time series II: Statistical properties for linear processes. *Journal of Nonparametric Statistics*, 13, 37–56.

Serroukh, A., Walden, A. T., and Percival, D. B. (2000). Statistical properties of the wavelet variance estimator for non-Gaussian/non-linear time series. *Journal of the American Statistical Association*, 95, 184–196.

Shann, W. C. and Yen, C. C. (1999). On the exact values of orthonormal scaling coefficients of lengths 8 and 10. *Applied and Computational Harmonic Analysis*, 6, 109–112.

Sharpe, W. F. (1964). Capital asset prices: A theory of market equilibrium under conditions of risk. *Journal of Finance*, 19, 425–442.

Siegelmann, H. T., Horne, B. G., and Giles, C. L. (1990). Computational capabilities of recurrent NARX neural networks. *Systems, Management and Cybernetics, Part B: Cybernetics*, 27, 208–215.

Sims, C. A. (1972). Money, income and causality. *American Economic Review*, 62, 540–552.

Sims, C. A. (1980). Macroeconomics and reality. *Econometrica*, 48, 1–48.

Sims, C. A. (1992). A nine variable probabilistic macroeconomic forecasting model. In *Business Cycles, Indicators, and Forecasting*, edited by J. H. Stock and M .W. Watson. University of Chicago Press, Chicago.

Sims, C. A. and Zha, T. A. (1998). Bayesian methods for dynamic multivariate models. *International Economic Review*, 39, 949–968.

Skouras, S. (2001). Financial returns and efficiency as seen by an artificial technical analyst. *Journal of Economic Dynamics and Control*, 25, 213–244.

Slepian, D. (1978). Prolate spheroidal wave functions, Fourier analysis, and uncertainty – V: The discrete case. *Bell System Technical Journal*, 57, 1371–1430.

Stein, C. M. (1981). Estimation of the mean of a multivariate normal distribution. *Annals of Statistics*, 9, 1135–1151.

Stengos, T. and Sun, Y. (2001). Consistent model specification test for a regression function based on nonparametric wavelet estimation. *Econometric Reviews*, forthcoming.

Stephens, M. A. (1986). Tests based on EDF statistics. In R. B. D'Agostino and M. A. Stephens, editors, *Goodness-of-Fit Techniques*, Volume 68 of *STATISTICS: Textbooks and Monographs*, 97–193. Marcel Dekker, New York.

Stone, M. (1974). Cross-validatory choice and assessment of statistical predictions. *Journal of the Royal Statistical Society, B*, 36, 111–133.

Strang, G. and Nguyen, T. (1996). *Wavelets and Filter Banks*. Wellesley-Cambridge Press, Wellesley, Massachusetts.

Strawderman, W. E. and Cohen, A. (1971). Admissibility of estimators of the mean vector of a multivariate normal distribution with quadratic loss. *The Annals of Mathematical Statistics*, 42, 270–296.

Swanson, N. and White, H. (1995). A model-selection approach to assessing the information in the term structure using linear models and artificial neural networks. *Journal of Business and Economic Statistics*, 13, 265–275.

Sweeney, R. J. (1986). Beating the foreign exchange market. *Journal of Finance*, 41, 160–182.

Taswell, C. (1996). Satisficing search algorithms for selecting near-best bases in adaptive tree-structured wavelet transforms. *IEEE Transactions on Signal Processing*, 44, 2423–2438.

Taylor, M. P. and Allen, H. (1992). The use of technical analysis in the foreign exchange market. *Journal of International Money and Finance*, 11, 304–314.

Taylor, S. (1986). *Modelling Financial Time Series*. John Wiley & Sons, Chichester.

Taylor, S. J. (1992). Rewards available to currency futures speculators: Compensation for risk or evidence of inefficient pricing? *Economic Record*, 68, 105–116.

Tewfik, A. H. and Kim, M. (1992). Correlation structure of the discrete wavelet coefficients of fractional Brownian motion. *IEEE Transactions on Information Theory*, 38, 904–909.

Thoma, M. (1994). The effects of money growth on inflation and interest rates across spectral frequency bands. *Journal of Money, Credit and Banking*, 26, 218–231.

Thomson, D. J. (1982). Spectrum estimation and harmonic analysis. *IEEE Proceedings*, 70, 1055–1096.

Tkacz, G. (2000). Estimating the fractional order of integration of interest rates using a wavelet OLS estimator. Technical Report 2000-5, Department of Monetary and Financial Analysis, Bank of Canada.

Urbach, R. M. A. (2000). *Footprints of Chaos in the Markets: Analyzing Nonlinear Time Series in Financial Markets and Other Real Systems*. Prentice Hall Publishing, Englewood Cliffs, New Jersey.

Veitch, D. and Abry, P. (1999). A statistical test for the time constancy of scaling exponents. Manuscript, EMULab, University of Melbourne.

Velasco, C. (1999). Non-stationary log-periodogram regression. *Journal of Econometrics*, 91, 325–371.

Vetterli, M. and Kovačević, J. (1995). *Wavelets and Subband Coding*. Prentice Hall PTR, Englewood Cliffs, New Jersey.

Vidakovic, B. (1998). Nonlinear wavelet shrinkage with Bayes rules and Bayes factors. *Journal of the American Statistical Association*, 93, 173–179.

Vidakovic, B. (1999). *Statistical Modeling by Wavelets*. John Wiley & Sons, New York.

Vidakovic, B. and Lozoya, C. B. (1998). On time-dependent wavelet denoising. *IEEE Transactions on Signal Processing*, 46, 2549–2554.

Vostrikova, L. J. (1981). Detecting 'disorder' in multidimensional random processes. *Soviet Mathematics Doklady*, 24, 55–59.

Walden, A. T. (2000). A unified view of multitaper multivariate spectral estimation. *Biometrika*, 87, 767–788.

Wang, Y. (1995). Jump and sharp cusp detection by wavelets. *Biometrika*, 82, 385–397.

Wang, Y. (1996). Function estimation via wavelet shrinkage for long-memory data. *Annals of Statistics*, 24, 466–484.

Weigend, A. and Gerschenfeld, N. (1994). *Time Series Prediction: Forecasting the Future and Understanding the Past*. Addison-Wesley, Reading: MA.

Wells, C. (1996). *The Kalman Filter in Finance*. Kluwer Academic Publishers, Dordrecht.

Weron, R., Weron, K., and Weron, A. (1999). A conditionally exponential decay approach to scaling in finance. *Physica A*, 264, 551–561.

Weyrich, N. and Warhola, G. T. (1995). De-noising using wavelets and cross validation. In S. P. Singh, editor, *Recent Developments in Approximation Theory, Wavelets and Applications*, 523–532. Kluwar, Boston.

Whitcher, B. (1998). *Assessing Nonstationary Time Series Using Wavelets*. Ph.D. thesis, University of Washington.

Whitcher, B. (2000). Wavelet-based estimation for seasonal long-memory processes. Technical Report 00-14, EURANDOM, The Netherlands.

Whitcher, B. (2001). Simulating Gaussian stationary processes with unbounded spectra. *Journal of Computational and Graphical Statistics*, 10, 112–134.

Whitcher, B. and Jensen, M. J. (2000). Wavelet estimation of a local long memory parameter. *Exploration Geophysics*, 31, 89–98.

Whitcher, B., Byers, S. D., Guttorp, P., and Percival, D. B. (1998). Testing for homogeneity of variance in time series: Long memory, wavelets and the Nile River. Technical Report 9, National Research Center for Statistics and the Environment.

Whitcher, B., Guttorp, P., and Percival, D. B. (2000a). Multiscale detection and location of multiple variance changes in the presence of long memory. *Journal of Statistical Computation and Simulation*, 68, 65–88.

Whitcher, B., Guttorp, P., and Percival, D. B. (2000b). Wavelet analysis of covariance with application to atmospheric time series. *Journal of Geophysical Research – Atmospheres*, 105, 14,941–14,962.

White, H. (1989). Some asymptotic results for learning in single hidden-layer feedforward network models. *Journal of the American Statistical Association*, 94, 1003–1013.

White, H. (1992). *Artificial Neural Networks: Approximation and Learning*. Blackwell, Cambridge.

Wickerhauser, M. V. (1994). *Adapted Wavelet Analysis from Theory to Software*. A K Peters, Wellesley, Massachusetts.

Wiener, N. (1949). *Extrapolation, Interpolation, and Smoothing of Stationary Time Series*. Wiley, New York.

Winters, P. R. (1960). Forecasting sales by exponentially weighted moving averages. *Management Science*, 6, 324–343.

Wood, A. T. A. and Chan, G. (1994). Simulation of stationary Gaussian processes in $[0, 1]^d$. *Journal of Computational and Graphical Statistics*, 3, 409–432.

Woodward, W. A., Cheng, Q. C., and Gray, H. L. (1998). A k-factor GARMA long-memory model. *Journal of Time Series Analysis*, 19, 485–504.

Wornell, G. W. (1996). *Signal Processing with Fractals: A Wavelet Based Approach*. Prentice Hall, Englewood Cliffs, New Jersey.

Wynne, M. A. (1999). Core inflation: A review of some conceptual issues. Federal Reserve Bank of Dallas, Working Paper, 99-03.

Yaffe, R. A. (2000). *An Introduction to Time Series Analysis and Forecasting with Applications of SAS and SPSS*. With Monie McGee (contributor). Academic Press, San Diego.

Yang, Z. R., Platt, M. B., and Platt, H. D. (1997). Probabilistic neural networks in bankruptcy prediction. *Journal of Business Research*, 44, 67–74.

Zaman, A. (1996). *Statistical Foundations for Econometric Techniques*. Academic Press, San Diego.

INDEX